MW01231437

One day
AT A
time

One day AT A time

William MacDonald

GOSPEL FOLIO PRESS
P. O. Box 2041, Grand Rapids MI 49501-2041
Available in the UK from JOHN RITCHIE LTD.,
40 Beansburn, Kilmarnock, Scotland

Previously published by Everyday Publications
This edition published by Gospel Folio Press
P. O. Box 2041, Grand Rapids, MI 49501-2041

ISBN 1-882701-49-6

Cover design by John Nicholson III and J. B. Nicholson, Jr.

Printed in the United States of America

Publisher's Foreword

A common housefly is given about twenty-one days to live. In only three weeks, it's life cycle is complete. It is born, grows, reproduces, fulfills its purpose in the grand scheme of God, and dies. Some of God's creatures live only twenty-four hours from birth to death.

The Lord has blessed the human race with a longer average lifespan than that. Yet in the eternal perspective, our days on earth are still like a vapor, a passing wind, a dayflower, a tale already told.

We have no time to lose. We must buy up each golden minute and invest it in the First Bank of Eternity. We need to be *"Redeeming the time, because the days are evil"* (Eph. 5:16). Every day holds 86,400 seconds; by themselves they do not seem like much. But like snowflakes or raindrops, together they have a cumulative effect that can erode a life or bring refreshment and vigor to ourselves and others. We need to live life to the full, *One Day at a Time.*

One way to ensure that my days on earth count for God is to fill my mind and heart with the "engrafted Word" that I might grow by it. For this reason we take pleasure in reintroducing a book of invigorating meditations on the Scriptures from the crisp, Christ-exalting writings of our esteemed brother, William MacDonald. These devotionals are not intended to replace the reading of the Word itself, but to stimulate your thinking in Scripture, and, by God's grace, to help you apply the truth to your daily walk by the empowering ministry of the Holy Spirit.

An unknown author writes:

> *Begin the day with God,* kneel down to Him in prayer;
> Lift up your heart to His abode, and seek His love to share.
>
> *Open the Book of God,* and read a portion there;
> That it may hallow all your thoughts and sweeten all your care.
>
> *Go through the day with God,* whatever you may do;
> Where'er you are—at home, abroad—He still is near to you.
>
> *Converse in mind with God,* your spirit heavenward raise;
> Acknowledge every good bestowed, and offer grateful praise.
>
> *Conclude your day with God,* your sins to Him confess;
> Trust in the Lord's atoning blood and plead His righteousness.
>
> *Lie down at night with God,* who gives His servants sleep;
> And when you tread the vale of death, He will your vigil keep.

J. B. NICHOLSON, JR.
Grand Rapids, Michigan

January 1

This month shall be unto you the beginning of months:
it shall be the first month of the year to you.
EXODUS 12:2

N ew Year's resolutions are good but fragile, that is, easily broken. New Year's prayers are better; they ascend to the throne of God and set answering wheels in motion. As we come to the beginning of another year, we would do well to make the following prayer requests our own:

Lord Jesus, I rededicate myself afresh to You today. I want You to take my life this coming year and use it for Your glory. "Take my life and let it be consecrated, Lord, to Thee."

I pray that You will keep me from sin, from anything that will bring dishonor to Your Name.

Keep me teachable by the Holy Spirit. I want to move forward for You. Don't let me settle in a rut.

May my motto this year be, "He must increase; I must decrease." The glory must all be Yours. Help me not to touch it.

Teach me to make every decision a matter of prayer. I dread the thought of leaning on my own understanding. "O Lord, I know the way of man is not in himself; it is not in man who walks to direct his own steps" (Jer. 10:23).

May I die to the world and even to the approval or blame of loved ones or friends. Give me a single, pure desire to do the things that please Your heart.

Keep me from gossip and criticism of others. Rather, help me to speak what is edifying and profitable.

Lead me to needy souls. May I become a friend of sinners, as You are. Give me tears of compassion for the perishing.

> *"Let me look on the crowd as my Savior did,*
> *Till my eyes with tears grow dim.*
> *Let me view with pity the wandering sheep,*
> *And love them for love of Him."*

Lord Jesus, keep me from becoming cold, bitter, or cynical in spite of anything that may happen to me in the Christian life.

Guide me in my stewardship of money. Help me to be a good steward of everything You have entrusted to me.

Help me to remember moment by moment that my body is a temple of the Holy Spirit. May this tremendous truth influence all my behavior.

And, Lord Jesus, I pray that this may be the year of Your return. I long to see Your face and to fall at Your feet in worship. During the coming year, may the blessed hope stay fresh in my heart, disengaging me from anything that would hold me here and keeping me on the tiptoes of expectancy. "Even so, come, Lord Jesus!"

January 2

In lowliness of mind let each esteem other better than themselves.
PHILIPPIANS 2:3B

T o esteem others better than self is unnatural; fallen human nature rebels at such a blow to its ego. It is humanly impossible; we do not have the power in ourselves to live such an otherworldly life. But it is divinely feasible; the indwelling Holy Spirit empowers us to efface self in order that others might be honored.

Gideon illustrates our text. After his three hundred men had defeated the Midianites, he called for the men of Ephraim to add the final blow. They cut off the escape route and captured two Midianite princes. But they complained that they had not been called earlier. Gideon replied that the gleaning of the grapes of Ephraim was better than the vintage of Abiezer (Jud. 8:2); that is, the mopping-up operation conducted by the men of Ephraim was more illustrious than the whole campaign waged by Gideon. This spirit of selflessness appeased the Ephraimites.

Joab showed great unselfishness when he captured Rabbah and then called for David to come and administer the coup de grace (2 Sam. 12:26-28). Joab was quite content that David should get credit for the victory. It was one of the nobler moments in Joab's life.

The Apostle Paul esteemed the Philippians better than himself. He said that what they were doing was the significant sacrifice to God, whereas he was nothing more than a drink offering, poured out over the sacrifice and service of their faith (Phil. 2:17).

In more recent times, a beloved servant of Christ was waiting in an anteroom with other distinguished preachers, ready to file out onto the platform. When he finally appeared at the door and a thunderous ovation took place, he quickly stepped aside so that those who were following him would receive the applause.

The supreme example of self-abnegation is the Lord Jesus. He humbled Himself that we might be exalted. He became poor that we might become rich. He died that we might live.

"Let this mind be in you, which was also in Christ Jesus."

January 3

Do not judge according to appearance, but judge with righteous judgment.
JOHN 7:24

O ne of the most deep-seated frailties of fallen humanity is the persistent tendency to judge according to appearance. We judge a person according to his looks. We judge a used car by its body. We judge a book by its cover. No matter how often we are disappointed and disillusioned, we stubbornly refuse to learn that "all is not gold that glitters."

In his book, *Hide or Seek,* Dr. James Dobson says that physical beauty is the most highly valued personal attribute in our culture. We have made it what he calls "the gold coin of human worth." Thus a beautiful child is more favored by adults than a plain one. Teachers tend to give better grades to attractive children. Pretty children get less discipline than others. Homely children are more subject to blame for misdemeanors.

Samuel would have chosen the tall, good-looking Eliab to be king (1 Sam. 16:7), but the Lord corrected him, "Do not look at his appearance or at the height of his stature, because I have refused him. For the Lord does not see as man sees; for man looks at the outward appearance, but the Lord looks at the heart."

The greatest case of misjudgment in history occurred when the Lord Jesus visited our planet. Apparently He was not prepossessing as far as physical appearance was concerned. "He has no form or comeliness; and when we see Him, there is no beauty that we should desire Him" (Isa. 53:2). They could see no beauty in the only truly beautiful Person who ever lived!

Yet He Himself never fell into this terrible trap of judging according to looks, for before His advent, it was prophesied of Him, "He shall not judge by the sight of His eyes, nor decide by the hearing of His ears" (Isa. 11:3). To Him it was not the face but the character that counted. Not the cover but the contents. Not the physical but the spiritual.

January 4

Not by might nor by power, but by My spirit, saith the Lord.
ZECHARIAH 4:6

This verse enshrines the important truth that the work of the Lord is not carried over by human ingenuity and strength but by the Holy Spirit.

We see it in the capture of Jericho. It was not the armed might of Israel that caused the walls to fall down. The Lord was the One who delivered the city into their hands when the priests blew the trumpets seven times.

If it had depended on a huge army, Gideon would never have defeated the Midianites because his army had been thinned down to three hundred men. And their unconventional weaponry consisted of earthenware pitchers with torches inside. It could only have been the Lord who gave them the victory.

Elijah purposely eliminated any possibility that human might or power might ignite the altar by pouring twelve barrels of water over it. When the fire fell, there could be no question as to its divine source.

Left to human ingenuity, the disciples could fish all night but catch nothing. That provided the opportunity for the Lord to show them that they must look to Him for true effectiveness in service.

It's easy for us to think that money is the greatest need in Christian service. Actually, it never was and never will be. Hudson Taylor was right when he said that what we need to fear is not too little money but too much unconsecrated money.

Or we resort to behind-the-scenes politicking, or to high-powered promotional programs, or to the psychological manipulation of people, or to clever oratory. We engage in vast construction programs and in organizational empire building, vainly thinking that these are the keys to success.

But it is not by might, or by power, or by any of these things that the work of God is forwarded. It is by the Spirit of the Lord.

Much so-called Christian work today would still continue if there were no Holy Spirit. But genuine Christian work is that which makes Him indispensable by waging the spiritual warfare, not with carnal weapons but with prayer, faith, and the Word of God.

January 5

The people who are with you are too many for Me...
JUDGES 7:2

Everyone of us has a subtle desire for numbers and a tendency to judge success by statistics. There is a measure of reproach connected with small groups, whereas large crowds command attention and respect. What should our attitude be in this area?

Large numbers should not be despised if they are the fruit of the Holy Spirit's work. This was the case at Pentecost when about 3,000 souls were swept into the kingdom of God.

We should rejoice in large numbers when they mean glory for God and blessing for mankind. It is only proper for us to long to see multitudes lifting their hearts and voices in praise to God, and reaching out to the world with the message of redemption.

On the other hand, large numbers are bad if they lead to pride. God had to reduce Gideon's army lest Israel should say, "My own hand has saved me" (Jud. 7:2). E. Stanley Jones once said he loathed our contemporary "scramble for numbers, leading, as it does, to collective egotism."

Large numbers are bad if they lead to dependence on human power rather then on the Lord. This was probably the trouble with David's census (2 Sam. 24:2-4). Joab sensed that the king's motives were not pure and he protested—but in vain.

Large numbers are undesirable if, in order to achieve them, we lower standards, compromise scriptural principles, water down the message, or fail to exercise godly discipline. There is always the temptation to do this if our minds are set on crowds rather than on the Lord.

Large numbers are less than ideal if they result in a loss of close fellowship. When individuals get lost in the crowd, when they can be absent and not be missed, when nobody shares their joys and sorrows, then the whole concept of body life is abandoned.

Large numbers are bad if they stifle the development of gift in the body. It is not without significance that Jesus chose twelve disciples. A huge crowd would have been unwieldy.

God's general rule has been to work through a remnant testimony. He is not attracted by large crowds or repelled by small ones. We should not boast in large numbers, but neither should we be content with small numbers if they are the result of our own sloth and indifference.

January 6

For I know that in me (that is, in my flesh) nothing good dwells...
ROMANS 7:18

1 f a young believer learns this lesson early in his Christian life, he will save himself from a world of trouble later on. The Bible teaches that there is NO GOOD THING in our old, evil, unregenerate nature. The flesh is absolutely no good. It is not improved one iota at the time of conversion. It is not improved by a lifetime of consistent Christian living. In fact, God is not trying to improve it. He has condemned it to death at the Cross and wants us to keep it in the place of death.

If I really believe this, it will deliver me from a futile search. I will not look for anything good where God has already said it can't be found.

It will deliver me from disappointment. I am never disappointed when I don't find any good in myself. I knew it wasn't there in the first place.

It will deliver me from introspection. I start with the premise that there is no victory in self. In fact, self-occupation spells defeat.

It will guard me from psychological and psychiatric counseling which turns the searchlight on self. Such therapy only compounds the problem instead of solving it.

It teaches me to be occupied with the Lord Jesus. Robert Murray McCheyne said, "For every look you take at self, take ten looks at Christ." That is a good balance! Someone else said that even a sanctified self is a poor substitute for a glorified Christ. And the hymnwriter wrote, "How sweet away from self to flee, and shelter in our Savior."

Much modern preaching and many new Christian books send people on an introspective binge, occupying them with their temperament, their self-image, their hang-ups and inhibitions. The whole movement is a tragedy of overbalance and it leaves a trail of human wreckage.

"I am too bad to be worth thinking about; what I want is to forget myself and to look to God, who is indeed worthy of all my thoughts."

January 7

For we walk by faith, not by sight.
2 CORINTHIANS 5:7

id you ever stop to wonder why a baseball game is more exciting to most people than a prayer meeting? Yet comparative attendance records prove that it is so.

Or we might ask, "Why is the Presidency of the United States more appealing than overseership in an assembly?" Parents don't say to their sons, "Eat your food and some day you may be an elder." No, they say, "Clean your plate and some day you may grow up to be President."

Why is a successful career in business more attractive than the life of a missionary? Christians often discourage their children from going to the mission field, content to see them rise to be "titled officials in secular enterprises."

Why is a television documentary more absorbing than the study of God's Word? Think of the hours spent before the TV set and the hurried moments before the open Bible!

Why are people willing to do for dollars what they wouldn't do for love to Jesus? Many who are tireless in their work for a corporation are lethargic and unresponsive when the Savior calls.

Finally, why does our nation loom larger and more important than the Church? National politics are colorful and engrossing. The Church often seems to lumber on without dynamic.

The reason for all these things is that we walk by sight and not by faith. Our vision is distorted. We don't see things as they actually are. We value the temporal above the eternal. We value the soulish above the spiritual. We value man's judgment above God's.

When we walk by faith, all is changed. We have 20/20 spiritual vision. We see things as God sees them. We value prayer as the unspeakable privilege of having direct audience with the Sovereign of the universe. We see that an elder in an assembly means more to God than the ruler of a nation. We see, with Spurgeon, that "if God calls a man to be a missionary, it would be a tragedy to see him drivel down into a king." We see television as a never-never land of unreality, whereas the Bible holds the key to a life of fulfillment. We are willing to spend and be spent for Jesus in a way we would never be willing for an unworthy impersonal corporation. And we reckon that our local church is more important to God and to His people than the greatest empire in the world.

Walking by faith makes all the difference!

January 8

Cursed be he that doeth the work of Jehovah negligently.
JEREMIAH 48:10, ASV

The work of the Lord is so important, pressing, sublime, and awe begetting that a curse rests on anyone who does it negligently. The God who wants and deserves the best cannot bear with sloth, delays, halfheartedness, or slipshod methods. When we think of the tremendous issues involved, we are not surprised.

During the latter part of 1968, a young Christian in Prague, Czechoslovakia, witnessed to another young Czech named Jan Palach. There seemed to be a genuine interest on Jan's part, and so the Christian promised to deliver a New Testament to him. He was filled with good intentions but he let weeks pass before he even obtained the New Testament. Then he kept delaying its actual delivery.

On January 16, 1969, Jan Palach stood in St. Wencelas Square, poured gasoline over his body and set himself afire. He never lived to see the New Testament that had been promised to him.

Good intentions are not enough. It has been said that the streets of hell are paved with good intentions. But they don't get the work done. They must be translated into action. And there are a few ways to do it.

First, never refuse when the Lord directs you to do some act of service for Him. If He is Lord, then it is ours to obey without question.

Second, don't procrastinate. Delays are deadly. They rob others of needed help and blessing, and fill us with guilt and remorse.

Third, do it diligently. "Whatever your hand finds to do, do it with your might" (Eccl. 9:10). If it's worth doing at all, it's worth doing well.

Finally, do it for God's glory. "Therefore, whether you eat or drink, or whatever you do, do all to the glory of God." (1 Cor. 10:31).

We should all have the spirit of Amy Carmichael, who wrote, "The vows of God are upon me. I may not stay to play with shadows or pluck earthly flowers till I my work have done and rendered up an account."

January 9

Show piety at home.
1 TIMOTHY 5:4

ou've heard the expression, "A devil at home, a saint abroad." It describes the horrible tendency to be gracious and outgoing to those in the outside world, and yet be harsh and unkind at home.

This is a failing that is not confined to any particular class of people. Young people have to guard against it. It's so easy to be a TV personality with one's peers, yet be a terror to one's parents. Husbands may maintain a charming front with their business associates, then when they come home, they turn off the charm and are their normal, irritable selves. Preachers may have a scintillating style in the pulpit and a rotten disposition in the family room.

It is one of the perverse streaks of our fallen state that we are sometimes meanest to those who are closest to us, who do the most for us, and who, in our saner moments, we love the best. Thus Ella Wheeler Wilcox wrote:

> *One great truth in life I've found,*
> *While journeying to the West;*
> *The only folks we really wound*
> *Are those we love the best.*
> *We flatter those we scarcely know,*
> *We please the fleeting guest,*
> *And deal full many a thoughtless blow*
> *To those we love the best.*

Another poet echoed these sentiments as follows: "We have greetings for the stranger and smiles for the guest, but oft for our own the bitter tone, though we love our own the best."

"It is very easy to have a church religion, or a prayer meeting religion, or a Christian-work religion; but it is altogether a different thing to have an everyday religion. To 'show piety at home' is one of the most vital parts of Christianity, but it is also one far too rare; and it is not at all an uncommon thing to find Christians who 'do their righteousness' before outsiders 'to be seen of men,' but who fail lamentably in showing their piety at home. I knew a father of a family who was so powerful in prayer at the weekly prayer meeting, and so impressive in exhortation that the whole church was edified by his piety; but who, when he went home after the meetings, was so cross and ugly that his wife and family were afraid to say a word in his presence" (H. W. SMITH).

Samuel Johnson said, "Every animal revenges his pains upon those who happen to be near." Man should avoid this natural tendency.

What we are at home is a truer index of our Christian character than what we are in public.

January 10

...and let us run with endurance the race that is set before us.
HEBREWS 12:1, NASB

Many people have a view of the Christian life that is excessively idealistic. They think it should be one uninterrupted series of mountaintop experiences. They read Christian books and magazines and hear personal testimonies of dramatic events and conclude that this is all of life. In their dream-world, there are no problems, heartaches, trials, or perplexities. There is no hard work, no daily routine, no monotony. All is Cloud 9. When they don't find their life fitting this pattern, they feel discouraged, disillusioned, and deprived.

The true facts are these. Most of the Christian life is what G. Campbell Morgan calls "the way of plodding perseverance in the doing of apparently small things." This is the way I have found it. There has been a full share of menial tasks, of long hours of disciplined study, of service without apparent results. At times the question has arisen, "Is anything really being accomplished?" Just then the Lord would drop some token of encouragement, some wonderful answer to prayer, some clear word of guidance. And I would be strengthened to go on for a while longer.

The Christian life is a long-distance race, not a 50-yard dash, and we need endurance to run it. It is important to start well, but what really counts is the endurance that enables us to finish in a blaze of glory.

Enoch will always have an honored place in the annals of endurance. He walked with God—think of it—for 300 years (Gen. 5:22). But we need not think that those were years of undiluted glamour or uninterrupted thrill. In a world like ours, it was inevitable that he should have his share of trials, perplexities, and even persecutions. But he did not grow weary in well doing. He endured to the end.

If you are ever tempted to quit, remember the words of Hebrews 10:36, NEB, "You need endurance if you are to do God's will and win what He has promised."

A noble life is not a blaze
Of sudden glory won,
But just an adding up of days
In which God's will is done.

...that by the mouth of two or three witnesses every word may be established.
MATTHEW 18:16

s far as the Bible is concerned, there must be the testimony of two or three witnesses in order to form a valid judgment. If we would only observe this principle, we would save ourselves oceans of trouble.

The natural tendency for us is to hear one person's side of a case and to immediately decide in his favor. He sounds convincing and our sympathies go out to him. Then later we learn that his was only one side of the story. When we hear the other side, we realize that the first man had distorted the facts or at least colored them in his own favor. Thus, "the first to plead his case seems just, until another comes and examines him" (Prov. 18:17, NASB). When we make a decision before trying to ascertain the full facts, we act less righteously than the world's judicial system, and place ourselves under the censure of Proverbs 18:13, NASB, "He who gives an answer before he hears, it is folly and shame to him."

When Ziba reported to David that Mephibosheth hoped to gain the throne, David accepted the slander without investigation and gave all of Mephibosheth's property to Ziba (2 Sam. 16:1-4). Later Mephibosheth had a chance to tell the king the true facts. David then realized that he had made a decision without having sufficient evidence.

The Lord Jesus recognized this principle. He said that His testimony concerning Himself was not sufficient (Jn. 5:31). So He presented the testimony of four witnesses: John the Baptist (vv. 32-35); His works (v. 36); God, the Father (vv. 37, 38); and the Scriptures (vv. 39-40).

By failing to obtain the competent testimony of two or three witnesses, we can cause broken hearts, ruined reputations, divided churches, and severed friendships. If we follow God's Word, we will avoid tons of injustice and human hurt.

January 12

What do you have that you did not receive?
1 CORINTHIANS 4:7

This is a good question because it reduces us all to size. We do not have anything that we did not receive. We received our physical and mental equipment through birth. What we look like and how brainy we are is something too far beyond our control to justify pride. It is an accident of birth.

All that we know is a result of our education. Others have poured information into our minds. Often when we think we have had an original thought, we find it in a book we first read twenty years ago. Emerson said, "All my best thoughts were stolen by the ancients."

What about our talents? Some talents definitely run in the family. They are developed by training and by practice. But the point is that they did not originate with us. They were given to us.

Pilate was inflated by the authority he wielded, but the Lord Jesus reminded him, "You would have no authority over Me unless it had been given you from above" (Jn. 19:11, NASB).

In short, every breath man draws is a gift from God. That is why Paul goes on to ask in 1 Corinthians 4:7 (PHILLIPS), "If anything has been given to you, why boast of it as if it were something you had achieved yourself?"

And that is why, for instance, Harriet Beecher Stowe refused to take any credit for writing *Uncle Tom's Cabin:* "I, the author of *Uncle Tom's Cabin*? No, indeed, I could not control the story; it wrote itself. The Lord wrote it, and I was but the humblest instrument in His hand. It all came to me in visions, one after another, and I put them down in words. To Him alone be the praise!"

The constant realization that we have nothing that we did not receive delivers us from boasting and self-congratulation, and leads us to give God the glory for anything good that we are or have done.

So, "Let not the wise man glory in his wisdom, let not the mighty man glory in his might, nor let the rich man glory in his riches; but let him who glories glory in this, that he understands and knows Me, that I am the Lord, exercising lovingkindness, judgment, and righteousness in the earth. For in these I delight" (Jer. 9:23-24).

January 13

I can do all things through Christ who strengthens me.
PHILIPPIANS 4:13

I t is easy to misunderstand a verse like this. We read it and immediately think of hundreds of things that we cannot do. In the physical realm, for instance, we think of some ridiculous stunt requiring superhuman power. Or we think of some great mental achievement that lies far beyond us. So the words become a torture to us instead of a comfort.

What the verse actually means, of course, is that the Lord will give us power to do anything He wants us to do. Within the circle of His will there are no impossibilities.

Peter knew this secret. He knew that, left to himself, he couldn't walk on water. But He also knew that if the Lord told him to do it, then he could do it. As soon as Jesus said, "Come," Peter got out of the boat and strode across the water to Him.

Ordinarily a mountain will not slide into the sea at my command. But if that mountain stands between me and the accomplishment of God's will, then I can say "Be removed," and it will.

What it boils down to is that "His commands are His enablements." Therefore He will provide strength to bear any trial. He will enable me to resist every temptation and conquer every habit. He will strengthen me to have a clean thought life, to have pure motives, and to always do the thing that pleases His heart.

If I am not getting the strength to accomplish something, if I am threatened with physical, mental, or emotional collapse, then I may well question if I have missed His will and am seeking my own desires. It is possible to do work *for* God that may not be the work *of* God. Such work does not carry the promise of His power.

So it is important to know that we are moving forward in the current of His plans. Then we can have the joyous confidence that His grace will sustain and empower us.

January 14

All things are yours.
1 CORINTHIANS 3:21-23

The unsaintly saints in Corinth had been squabbling over human leaders in the church. To some, Paul was the ideal. Others made Apollos their favorite. And still others felt that Cephas was superlative. Paul is telling them that it is ridiculous to limit their choice to one when all these men belong to them. Instead of saying, "Apollos is mine," they ought to say, "Paul, Apollos, and Cephas are all mine."

It is a word for us today. We err when we become exclusive followers of Luther, Wesley, Booth, Darby, Billy Graham, or any other great gift to the Church. All these men are ours and we can rejoice in the measure of light that each of them gives to us. We shouldn't become followers of any one man.

But it is not only servants of the Lord who are ours. The world is ours. We are heirs of God and joint-heirs with Christ. One day we are going to come back and reign over the world with the Lord Jesus. In the meantime, unconverted men are running things as if the world belonged to them. But it doesn't. They are simply caretakers, managing it for us until the day when we take possession.

Life is ours. This does not mean simply that we have life; all men have that. It means that we have the more abundant life, eternal life, the very life of Christ. Our life is not vanity and vexation of spirit. It is meaningful, purposeful and rewarding.

And death is ours. We are no longer subject to slavery all our lives through fear of death. Now death is the messenger of God that brings our souls to heaven. Therefore, to die is gain. In addition to all this, we belong to Christ, and Christ belongs to God. When I think of this, I am reminded of Guy King's whimsical remark, "What fortunate beggars we are!"

January 15

*For you, brethren, have been called to liberty; only do not use liberty as an
opportunity for the flesh, but through love serve one another.*
GALATIANS 5:13

he liberty of the child of God is one of his priceless possessions. Made
free by the Son, he is free indeed. But he is called to responsible freedom, not to license.

Children want to be free from the restraints of home. Young people want to be
free from the discipline of study. Adults want to be free from their marriage vows.
Still others rebel against being boxed in by regular employment. But these are not
the freedoms to which we are called.

The stars are not free to leave their orbits and wander throughout space. A train
is not free to leave the tracks and meander over the countryside. A plane is not free
to leave its assigned course; its safety depends on the pilot's obeying the
regulations.

Jowett comments, "There is no realm where the lawless are the free. In whatever way we wish to go we must accept bondage if we would discover liberty. A
musician must reverence the laws of harmony if he would exult in his lovely
world. A builder must put himself in bondage to the law of gravity, or it is not a
house that emerges, but a rubbish-heap. What sort of liberty does a man enjoy
who consistently defies the laws of health? In all these realms to trespass is to be
maimed; to pay homage is to be free."

It is true that the believer is free from the law (Rom. 7:3) but that does not mean
that he is lawless. He is now enlawed to Christ, bound by the cords of love, and
committed to obey the numerous commandments that are found in the New
Testament.

The believer is free from sin as master (Rom. 6:7, 18, 22) but only to become
a servant to God and to righteousness.

The believer is free from all men (1 Cor. 9:19) in order to become a servant to
all, that he might win the more.

But he is not free to use his liberty as a pretext for evil (1 Pet. 2:16, RSV). He
is not free to indulge the flesh (Gal. 5:13). He is not free to stumble or offend
another person (1 Cor. 8:9). He is not free to bring dishonor on the Name of the
Lord Jesus (Rom. 2:23-24). He is not free to love the world (1 Jn. 2:15-17). He is
not free to grieve the indwelling Holy Spirit (1 Cor. 6:19).

Man does not find fulfillment or rest in doing his own thing. He finds it only
in taking Christ's yoke and learning of Him. "His service is perfect freedom."

January 16

Now the word of the Lord came to Jonah the second time.
JONAH 3:1

H ere is a message that glows with hope and promise. Just because a man has failed does not mean that God has put him on the shelf.

David's failures are recorded with stark realism. As we read them, we sit in the dust with him and burn with shame. But David knew how to break before the Lord, how to repent with blood-earnestness. And God was not through with him. God forgave him and restored him to a life of fruitfulness.

Jonah failed to answer God's missionary call and wound up in the belly of a great fish. In that animate submarine, he learned to obey. When God called him the second time, he went to Nineveh, preached imminent judgment, and saw the whole city plunged into deepest repentance.

John Mark made a brilliant start with Paul and Barnabas, but then he copped out and went home. God did not abandon him, however. Mark returned to the battle, regained the confidence of Paul, and was commissioned to write the Gospel of the Unfailing Servant.

Peter failed the Lord in spite of his protestations of undying loyalty. Men would write him off by saying that the bird with the broken wing could never fly as high again. But God did not write him off and Peter flew higher than ever. He opened the doors of the kingdom to 3,000 at Pentecost. He labored tirelessly and suffered repeatedly at the hands of persecutors. He wrote the two epistles which bear his name, then crowned a glorious life of service with a martyr's death.

So when it comes to service, God is the God of the second chance. He is not through with a man just because that man has failed. Whenever He finds a broken and a contrite heart, he bows to lift up the head of his fallen soldier.

This must not be taken to condone sin or failure, however. The bitterness and remorse of having failed the Lord should serve as sufficient deterrent.

Neither does it mean that God gives the unrepentant sinner a second chance after this life. There is a terrible finality about death. For the man who dies in his sins, the awful sentence is, "Wherever the tree falls, there it lies" (Eccl. 11:3, NASB).

January 17

With goodwill doing service, as to the Lord, and not to men.
EPHESIANS 6:7

Paul's instructions to slaves (Eph. 6:5-8) are freighted with meaning for all who profess to be servants of Jesus Christ.

They show, first of all, that any honorable work, no matter how menial it is, can be done to the glory of God. The slaves to whom Paul wrote may have mopped floors, cooked meals, washed dishes, tended animals, or cultivated crops. Yet the Apostle said that these chores could be done "as to Christ" (v. 5); that in performing them, the slaves were "bondservants of Christ, doing the will of God" (v. 6); that they were "doing service, as to the Lord" (v. 7); and that they would be rewarded by the Lord for doing a good job (v. 8).

It is easy in our thinking to make a dichotomy between the secular and the sacred. We think of our week-day work as being secular whereas our preaching, witnessing, and Bible teaching are sacred. But this passage teaches that for the Christian there need be no such distinction. Realizing this, the wife of a well-known preacher put a motto over her kitchen sink, "Divine services conducted here three times daily."

> *A servant with this clause*
> *Makes drudgery divine;*
> *Who sweeps a room as for Thy laws*
> *Makes that and th' action fine.*
> —GEORGE HERBERT

There is another choice lesson here, namely, that no matter how low a person may be on the social ladder, he is not shut out from the choicest blessings and rewards of Christianity. He may never exchange his work clothes for a business suit, but if his work is of such good quality as to bring glory to Christ, he will receive a full reward. "Knowing that whatever good anyone does, he will receive the same from the Lord, whether he is a slave or free" (v. 8).

Believing this, we should pray, in the lines of George Herbert:

> *Teach me, my God and King,*
> *In all things Thee to see,*
> *And what I do in anything*
> *To do it as for Thee.*

January 18

My kingdom is not of this world. If My kingdom were of this world,
My servants would fight.
JOHN 18:36

T he fact that Christ's Kingdom is not of this world is enough to keep me out of the world's politics. If I participate in politics, then I am casting a vote of confidence in the system's ability to solve the world's problems. But frankly, I have no such confidence because I know that "the whole world lies under the sway of the wicked one" (1 Jn. 5:19).

Politics has proved singularly ineffective in solving the problems of society. Political remedies are nothing but a Band-Aid on a festering sore; they do not get at the source of the infection. We know that sin is the basic trouble in our sick society. Anything that fails to deal with sin cannot be taken seriously as a cure.

It becomes a matter of priorities, then. Should I spend time in political involvement or should I devote that same time to the spread of the gospel? Jesus answered the question when He said, "Let the dead bury their own dead, but you go and preach the kingdom of God" (Lk. 9:60). Our top priority must be to make Christ known because He is the answer to this world's problems.

"For the weapons of our warfare are not carnal, but mighty in God for pulling down strongholds" (2 Cor. 10:4). This being so, we come to the daring realization that we can shape national and international history through prayer, fasting, and the Word of God more than we could ever do through the ballot.

A public figure once said that politics is by its very nature corrupt. He added this word of warning: "The church should not forget its true function by trying to participate in an area of human affairs where it must be a poor competitor…It will lose its purity of purpose by participating."

God's program for this age is to call out of the nations a people for His name (see Acts 15:14). Rather than making people comfortable in a corrupt world, He is committed to saving people out of it. I should be committed to working with God in this glorious emancipation.

When the people asked Jesus how to work the works of God, He answered that the work of God is to believe on Him whom God had sent (see Jn. 6:28-29). This then is our mission—to lead men to belief, not to the ballot-box.

January 19

*If we confess our sins, He is faithful and just to forgive us our sins
and to cleanse us from all unrighteousness.*
1 JOHN 1:9

Without the assurance of this verse, it would be practically impossible to go on in the Christian life. As we grow in grace, we have a deepening awareness of our utter sinfulness. We must have some provision for instant cleansing for sins, otherwise we are doomed to perpetual guilt and defeat.

John tells us that, for believers, provision is made through confession. The unbeliever receives judicial forgiveness from the penalty of sins through faith in the Lord Jesus. The believer receives parental forgiveness from the defilement of sins through confession.

Sin breaks fellowship in the life of the child of God, and that fellowship remains broken till the sin is confessed and forsaken. When we confess, God is faithful to His Word; He has promised to forgive. He is just in forgiving because the work of Christ at the Cross has provided a righteous basis on which He may do so.

What this verse means, then, is that when we confess our sins, we can know that the record is clear, that we have been completely cleansed, that the happy family spirit has been restored. As soon as we are conscious of sin in our lives, we can go into the presence of God, call that sin by its name, repudiate it, and know with certainty that it has been put away.

But how do we know for certain? Do we feel forgiven? It is not at all a question of feelings. We know that we have been forgiven because God says so in His Word. Feelings are undependable at best. God's Word is sure.

But suppose someone says, "I know that God has forgiven me but I can't forgive myself"? This might sound very pious, but it is actually dishonoring to God. If God has forgiven me, then He wants me to appropriate that forgiveness by faith, to rejoice in it, and to go out and serve Him as a cleansed vessel.

January 20

Their sins and their lawless deeds I will remember no more.
HEBREWS 10:17

G od's ability to forget sins that have been covered by the blood of Christ is one of the most soul-satisfying truths in Scripture.

It is a great wonder when we read, "As far as the east is from the west, so far has He removed our transgressions from us" (Ps. 103:12). It is a marvel that we can say with Hezekiah, "You have cast all my sins behind Your back" (Isa. 38:17). It boggles the mind when we hear the Lord saying, "I have blotted out, like a thick cloud, your transgressions, and like a cloud, your sins" (Isa. 44:22). But it is even more wonderful when we read, "I will forgive their iniquity, and their sin I will remember no more" (Jer. 31:34).

When we confess our sins, He not only forgives, He forgets instantly. We are not stretching the truth when we say that He immediately buries our sins in the sea of His forgetfulness. This is illustrated by the experience of a believer who was having a ding-dong struggle with a besetting sin. In a moment of weakness, he gave in to the temptation. Rushing into the presence of the Lord, he blurted out, "Lord, I've done it again." Then he thought he heard the Lord saying, "What have you done again?" The point, of course, is that in that split second following confession, God had already forgotten.

This is a delightful paradox—that the omniscient God can forget. On the one hand He knows everything. He counts the stars and names each one. He numbers our tossings and keeps count of our tears. He marks the sparrow's fall. He numbers the hairs of our head. And yet He forgets those sins that have been confessed and forsaken.

There is one final point: It has been well said that when God forgives and forgets, He puts up a sign reading "No fishing." It is forbidden for me to fish up my own past sins or the sins of others that God has forgotten. In this respect we must have a poor memory and a good forgettery.

January 21

But the Spirit of the Lord departed from Saul,
and a distressing spirit from the Lord troubled him.
1 SAMUEL 16:14

There are verses in the Bible that seem to assign evil actions to God. For example, when Abimelech had reigned three years over Israel, "God sent a spirit of ill will between Abimelech and the men of Shechem" (Jud. 9:23). In the days of Ahab, Micaiah said to the wicked king, "The Lord has put a lying spirit in the mouth of all these prophets of yours" (1 Ki. 22:23). Job attributed his losses to the Lord when he said, "Shall we indeed accept good from God, and shall we not accept adversity?" (Job 2:10). Then again the Lord Himself says in Isaiah 45:7, "I make peace and create calamity."

Yet we know that because God is holy, He can neither originate evil nor condone it. No sin, sickness, suffering or death come from the Lord. He is light, and in Him is no darkness at all (1 Jn. 1:5). It is unthinkable that He should be the cause of anything that is contrary to His own moral perfection.

It is clear from other scriptures that Satan is the author of disease, suffering, tragedy, and destruction. Job's losses and intense pain were caused by the Devil. Jesus said that the woman who was bent double had been bound by Satan for eighteen long years (Lk. 13:16). Paul spoke of his thorn in the flesh as "the messenger of Satan" (2 Cor. 12:7). Satan is the culprit behind all the troubles of mankind.

But how then do we reconcile this with the verses that picture God as creating evil? The explanation is simply this: in the Bible God is often said to do what He permits to be done. It is the difference between His directive will and His permissive will. He often allows His people to go through experiences that He never would have chosen for them in the first place. He allowed Israel to wander forty years in the wilderness whereas His directive will, if it had been accepted, would have brought them into the Promised Land by a shorter route.

Even in permitting the evil of demons and of man, God always has the last word. He overrules it for His own glory and for the blessing of those who are exercised by it.

January 22

He has not observed iniquity in Jacob, nor has He seen wickedness in Israel.
NUMBERS 23:21

The hireling prophet, Balaam, spoke a remarkable truth when he said that the all-seeing God could not see sin in His people, Israel. What was true of Israel then is wonderfully true of the believer today. As God looks upon him, He cannot find a single sin for which to punish him with eternal death. The believer is "in Christ." That means that he stands before God in all the perfection and worthiness of Christ. God accepts him in all the acceptability of His own beloved Son. It is a position of favor that cannot be improved on and that will never end. Search as He may, God cannot find any charge against the one who is in Christ.

This is illustrated by an incident involving an Englishman and his Rolls Royce. He was touring France on his vacation when the rear axle broke. The local garage could not replace the axle, so they phoned to England. The company sent not only a rear axle, but two mechanics to see that it was properly installed. The Englishman continued on his trip, then returned to England, expecting to receive the bill. When months passed and no bill arrived, he wrote to the company, described the entire incident, and asked for the bill. Shortly afterwards, he received a letter from the company, saying, "We have searched our records carefully and can find no record of a Rolls Royce ever having had a broken rear axle."

God can search His records carefully and can find no record of any sin on a believer's account that would condemn him to hell. The believer is accepted in the Beloved One. He is complete in Christ. He is clothed in all the righteousness of God. He has an absolutely perfect standing before God. He can say with triumph and confidence:

> *Reach my blest Savior first;*
> *Take Him from God's esteem;*
> *Prove Jesus bears one spot of sin,*
> *Then tell me I'm unclean.*

January 23

Do you seek great things for yourself? Do not seek them.
JEREMIAH 45:5

There is a subtle temptation, even in Christian service, to become great, to see one's name in the magazines or hear it over the radio. But it is a great snare. It robs Christ of glory. It robs ourselves of peace and joy. And it makes us prime targets for the Devil's bullets.

It robs Christ of glory. As C. H. Mackintosh said, "There is always the utmost danger when a man or his work becomes remarkable. He may be sure Satan is gaining his objective when attention is drawn to aught or anyone but the Lord Jesus Himself. A work may be commenced in the greatest possible simplicity, but through lack of holy watchfulness and spirituality on the part of the workman, he himself or the results of his work may attract general attention, and he may fall into the snare of the devil. Satan's grand and ceaseless object is to dishonor the Lord Jesus. And if he can do this by what seems to be Christian service, he has achieved all the greater victory for the time." Denney also said it well, "No man can at one and the same time prove that he is great and that Christ is wonderful."

We rob ourselves in the process. Someone said, "I never knew real peace and joy in service until I ceased trying to be great."

And the desire to be great makes us sitting ducks for Satanic attack. The fall of a well-known personality brings greater reproach on the cause of Christ.

John the Baptist assiduously renounced any claims to greatness. His motto was, "He must increase; I must decrease."

We, too, should sit down in the lowest place until the Lord calls us to go up higher. A good prayer for each of us is, "Keep me little and unknown, loved and prized by Christ alone."

Nazareth was a little place
And so was Galilee.

January 24

Don't worry over anything whatever.
PHILIPPIANS 4:6, PHILLIPS

Thoughts here is so much that a person could worry about—the possibility of cancer, heart trouble, or a multitude of other diseases; foods that are supposedly harmful, accidental death, a communist takeover, nuclear war, runaway inflation, an uncertain future, the grim outlook for children growing up in a world like this. The possibilities are numberless.

And yet we are told in God's Word, "Don't worry over anything whatever." God wants us to have lives that are free of care. And for good reasons!

Worry is unnecessary. The Lord is looking out for us. He holds us in the palms of His hands. Nothing can happen to us apart from His permissive will. We are not the victims of blind chance, accidents, or fate. Our lives are planned, ordered, directed.

Worry is futile. It never solves a problem or avoids a crisis. As someone has said, "Anxiety never robs tomorrow of its sorrow; it only saps today of its strength."

Worry is harmful. Doctors are agreed that many of their patients' ailments are caused by worry, tension, nerves. Ulcers rate high on the list of worry-related maladies.

Worry is sin. "It doubts the wisdom of God; it implies He doesn't know what He is doing. It doubts the love of God; it says He doesn't care. It doubts the power of God; it says He is not able to overcome the circumstances that cause me to worry."

Too often we are proud of our worrying. When a husband reproached his wife for her incessant worrying, she replied, "If I didn't worry, there'd be precious little of it done around here." We will never get deliverance from it until we confess it as sin and utterly renounce it. Then we can say with confidence:

> *I have nothing to do with tomorrow,*
> *My Savior will make that His care;*
> *Should He fill it with trouble and sorrow,*
> *He will help me to suffer and bear.*
> *I have nothing to do with tomorrow;*
> *Its burdens, then, why should I share?*
> *Its grace and its strength I can't borrow;*
> *Then why should I borrow its care?*

January 25

God is love.
1 JOHN 4:8

The coming of Christ brought a new word for love into the Greek language—*agape*. There was already a word for friendship *(phileo)* and one for passionate love *(eros)*, but there was none to express the kind of love which God showed in giving His only begotten Son and which He calls on His people to show to one another.

This is another-worldly love, a love with new dimensions. The love of God had no beginning and it can have no end. It is a love that has no limit, that can never be measured. It is absolutely pure, free from all taint of lust. It is sacrificial, never counting the cost. Love manifests itself in giving, for we read, "God so loved the world that He gave..." and "Christ also has loved us and given Himself for us..." (Eph. 5:2). Love ceaselessly seeks the welfare of others. It goes out to the unlovely as well as to the lovely. It goes out to its enemies as well as to its friends.

It is not drawn out by any worthiness or virtue in its objects but only by the goodness of the donor. It is utterly unselfish, never looking for anything in return and never exploiting others for personal advantages. It does not keep a count of wrongs, but throws a kindly veil over a multitude of slights and insults. Love repays every discourtesy with a kindness, and prays for its would-be murderers. Love always thinks of others, esteeming them better than self.

But love can be firm. God chastens those whom He loves. Love cannot countenance sin because sin is harmful and destructive, and love desires to protect its objects from harm and destruction. The greatest manifestation of God's love was the giving of His beloved Son to die for us on the Cross of Calvary.

> *Who Thy love, O God, can measure,*
> *Love that crushed for us its Treasure,*
> *Him in whom was all Thy pleasure,*
> *Christ, Thy Son of love?*
>
> —ALLABEN

January 26

Beloved, if God so loved us, we also ought to love one another.
1 JOHN 4:11

W e must not think of love as an uncontrollable, unpredictable emotion. We are commanded to love, and this would be quite impossible if love were some elusive, sporadic sensation, coming as unaccountably as a common cold. Love does involve the emotions but it is more a matter of the will than of the emotions.

We must also guard against the notion that love is confined to a world of dream castles with little relation to the nitty-gritty of everyday life. For every hour of moonlight and roses, there are weeks of mops and dirty dishes.

In other words, love is intensely practical. For instance, when a plate of bananas is passed at the table and one has black spots, love takes that one. Love cleans the washbasin and bathtub after using them. Love replaces paper towels when the supply is gone so that the next person will not be inconvenienced. Love puts out the lights when they are not in use. It picks up the crumpled Kleenex instead of walking over it. It replaces the gas and oil after using a borrowed car. Love empties the garbage without being asked. It doesn't keep people waiting. It serves others before self. It takes a squalling baby out so as not to disturb the meeting. Love speaks loudly so that the deaf can hear. And love works in order to have the means to share with others.

Love has a hem to its garment
That reaches right down to the dust
It can reach the stains of the streets and lanes,
And because it can, it must.
It dare not rest on the mountain;
It must go down to the vale;
For it cannot find its fullness of mind
Till it kindles the lives that fail.

January 27

I n a day when men of the world are becoming increasingly allergic to work, Christians must make the most of every passing moment. It is a sin to waste time.

Voices from every age testify to the importance of diligent labor. The Savior Himself said, "I must work the works of Him who sent Me while it is day; the night is coming when no one can work" (John 9:4).

Thomas a Kempis wrote, "Never be idle or vacant; be always reading or writing or praying or meditating or employed in some useful labor for the common good."

When asked the secret of his success as an interpreter of the Word, G. Campbell Morgan said, "Work—hard work—and again, work!"

We should never forget that when the Lord Jesus came into the world, He served as a carpenter. The greater part of His life was spent in the shop in Nazareth.

Paul was a tentmaker. He considered it an important part of his ministry.

It is a mistake to think that work is a result of the entrance of sin. Before sin entered, Adam was placed in the garden to dress it and to keep it (Gen. 2:15). The curse involved the toil and sweat that accompany work (Gen. 3:19). Even in heaven there will be work, for "His servants shall serve Him" (Rev. 22:3).

Work is a blessing. Through it we find fulfillment of our need for creativity. The mind and body function best when we work diligently. When we are usefully occupied, we enjoy greater protection from sin, because "Satan finds some mischief still for idle hands to do" (I. Watts). Thomas Watson said, "Idleness tempts the devil to tempt." Honest, diligent, faithful work is a vital part of our Christian testimony. And the results of our labor may outlive us. As someone has said, "Everyone owes it to himself to provide himself with some useful occupation while his body is lying in the grave." And William James said, "The great use of a life is to spend it for something that will outlast it."

January 28

Whoever believes will not act hastily.
ISAIAH 28:16

1 n an age of supersonic travel and high speed communications, in a culture where hurry is the watchword, it brings us up short to learn that haste is seldom used of God in a good sense in the Bible. Seldom, I say, because there is the instance where the father runs to meet the returning prodigal, suggesting that God hastens to forgive. But generally speaking, God is not in a hurry.

When David said, "the king's business required haste" (1 Sam. 21:8), he was guilty of subterfuge, and we should not use his words to justify our frenetic rushing back and forth.

The plain truth is, as our text states, if we are really trusting the Lord, we don't have to be in a hurry. The urgency of our task can be better served by a quiet walk in the Spirit than by a frenzy of carnal activity.

Here is a young man who is in a hurry to get married. He reasons that if he doesn't act quickly, someone else might get the girl. The truth is that if God wants that girl for him, no one else can get her. If she is not God's choice, then he will have to learn the hard way, "Marry in haste; repent at leisure."

Another is in a hurry to go into so-called full-time work. He argues that the world is perishing and that he cannot wait. Jesus did not argue that way during the years in Nazareth. He waited till God called Him forth to public ministry.

Too often we are in a hurry in our personal evangelism. We are so anxious to rack up professions that we pick the fruit before it is ripe. We fail to allow the Holy Spirit to thoroughly convict the person of sin. The result of such a method is a trail of false professions and of human wreckage. We should "let patience have its perfect work" (Jas. 1:4).

The true effectiveness of our lives lies not in rushing madly about on self-appointed missions, but in Spirit-directed activity that is ascertained by patiently waiting on the Lord.

January 29

Even so, Father, for so it seemed good in Thy sight.
MATTHEW 11:26

I n almost everyone's life there are things which he never would have chosen, which he would like to be rid of, but which can never be changed. There is the matter of physical impairments or abnormalities. Or it may be a chronic, low-grade illness that will not leave us alone. Again it may be a nervous or emotional disorder that lingers as a most unwelcome guest.

So many live defeated lives, dreaming of what might have been, if only... If only they were taller. If only they were better looking. If only they had been born in a different family, race, or even sex. If only they were built to excel in athletics. If only they could know perfect health.

The lesson that these people should learn is that there is peace in accepting what cannot be changed. What we are, we are by the grace of God. He has planned our lives with infinite love and infinite wisdom. If we could see as well as He, we would have arranged things exactly as He has done. Therefore we should be able to say, "Even so, Father, for so it seemed good in Thy sight."

But there is a step further. We don't have to accept these things in a spirit of meek resignation. Knowing that they were permitted by a God of love, we can make them the cause of praise and rejoice. Paul prayed three times that his thorn in the flesh might be removed. When the Lord promised grace to bear the thorn, the Apostle exclaimed, "Therefore most gladly I will rather boast in my infirmities, that the power of Christ may rest upon me" (2 Cor. 12:9).

It is one of the signs of spiritual maturity when we can rejoice in the seemingly adverse circumstances in life and use them as means of glorifying God. Fanny Crosby learned the lesson early in life. When she was only eight, the blind poetess wrote:

> Oh, what a happy child I am!
> Although I cannot see,
> I am resolved that in this world
> Contented I will be.
> How many blessings I enjoy
> That other people don't;
> So weep or sigh because I'm blind
> I cannot, and I won't!

January 30

Freely you have received, freely give.
MATTHEW 10:8

Fritz Kreisler, one of the world's greatest violinists, said, "I was born with music in my system. I knew musical scores instinctively before I knew my ABC's. It was a gift of Providence. I did not acquire it. So I do not even deserve thanks for the music...Music is too sacred to be sold. And the outrageous prices the musical celebrities charge today are truly a crime against society."

These are words that everyone in Christian work might take to heart. The Christian ministry is a ministry of giving, not of getting. The question is not, "What is there in it for me?" but rather "How can I best share the message with the greatest number?" In the service of Christ, it is far better that things should cost rather than that they should pay.

It is true that "the laborer is worthy of his wages" (Lk. 10:7) and that "those who preach the gospel should live from the gospel" (1 Cor. 9:14). But this does not justify a man's setting a price on his gift. It does not justify charging exorbitant royalties for the use of hymns. It does not justify unconscionable fees for speaking or singing engagements.

Simon the Sorcerer wanted to buy the power of conferring the Holy Spirit on others (Acts 8:19). No doubt he saw this as a way of making money for himself. By his action, he gave his name to our language (simony) to describe the buying or selling of religious privileges. It is no overstatement to say that the religious world today is shot through with simony.

If the dollar could somehow be removed from so-called Christian work, a great deal of it would stop immediately. But there would still be faithful servants of the Lord who would press on till their last ounce of strength was expended.

We have received freely; we ought to give freely. The more we give, the wider the blessing, and the greater the reward—good measure, pressed down, shaken together and running over (Lk. 6:38).

January 31

Judge not, that you be not judged.
MATTHEW 7:1

People who know little else about the Bible often know this verse and use it in a most bizarre way. Even when a person is criticized for unspeakable wickedness, they piously gurgle, "Judge not, that you be not judged." In other words, they use the verse to forbid any condemnation of evil.

The plain fact of the matter is that, while there are areas where we must not judge, there are other areas where judgment is commanded.

Here are some instances where judging is out. We must not judge people's motives; not being omniscient, we cannot know why they do what they do. We mustn't sit in judgment on the service of another believer; to his own Master he stands or falls. We mustn't condemn those who have conscientious scruples about things that are morally neutral; it would be wrong for them to violate their conscience. We mustn't judge by outward appearances or show respect of persons; it's what is in the heart that counts. And certainly we should avoid a harsh, critical censorious spirit; a habitual fault-finder is a poor advertisement for the Christian faith.

But there are other areas where we are commanded to judge. We must judge all teaching to see whether it agrees with the Scriptures. In order to avoid unequal yokes, we must judge whether others are true believers. Christians should judge disputes between believers rather than allow them to go to civil courts. The local church must judge in cases of extreme forms of sin and disfellowship the guilty offender. Those in the church must judge which men have the qualifications of elders and of deacons.

God does not expect us to throw away our critical faculty or abandon all moral and spiritual standards. All He asks is that we refrain from judging where it is forbidden and that we judge righteously where it is commanded.

February 1

...the gospel of the glory of Christ.
2 CORINTHIANS 4:4

W e should never forget that the gospel is the good news of the glory of Christ. True, it concerns the One who was crucified and who was buried. But He is no longer on the cross, no longer in the tomb. He has risen, has ascended to heaven, and is the glorified Man at God's right hand.

We do not present Him as the humble Carpenter of Nazareth, the Suffering Servant or the Stranger of Galilee. Neither do we present Him as the effeminate do-gooder of modern religious art.

We preach the Lord of life and glory. He is the One whom God has highly exalted and given a Name which is above every name. At His Name every knee shall bow, and every tongue confess Him as Lord to the glory of God the Father. He is crowned with glory and honor, a Prince and a Savior.

Too often we dishonor Him by the message we preach. We exalt man with his talents and create the impression that God would be lucky to have such a man to serve Him. We make it sound as if man were doing a colossal favor to the Lord by trusting Him. That isn't the gospel which the Apostles preached. They said, in effect, "You are the guilty murderers of the Lord Jesus Christ. You took Him and with wicked hands nailed Him to the tree. But God raised Him from the dead and glorified Him at His own right hand in heaven. He is there today, in a glorified body of flesh and bones. His nail-scarred hand holds the scepter of universal dominion. He is coming back again to judge the world in righteousness. And you'd better *repent* and turn to Him in *faith*. There is no other way of salvation. 'There is no other name under heaven, given among men, whereby we must be saved.'"

O, for a fresh vision of the Man in the glory! And for a tongue to tell forth the myriad glories that crown His brow! Surely then, as at Pentecost, sinners would tremble before Him and cry out, "Men and brethren, what shall we do?"

February 2

...the God who spoke that out of darkness light should shine...
has shone in our hearts for the shining forth of the knowledge
of the glory of God in the face of Jesus Christ.
2 CORINTHIANS 4:6, DARBY

"**G**od has shone in...for the shining forth."* Here we learn that we are not meant to be the terminals of God's blessings but only the channels. The expression, "God has shone in," refers to our conversion. Whereas in the original creation He commanded light to shine, in the new creation He Himself has shone in our hearts.

But He did not do it in order that we might selfishly hoard the floodtide of His blessings. Rather He did it so that the knowledge of His glory in the face of Jesus Christ might be made known through us to others.

In similar vein, Paul spoke of how God had revealed "His Son in me, that I might preach Him among the Gentiles" (Gal. 1:16). God reveals His Son in us that we might reveal Him to others. When the truth of this came home to me years ago, I wrote on the flyleaf of my Bible:

> *If of Jesus Christ their only view*
> *May be what they see of Him in you,*
> *MacDonald, what do they see?*

No wonder that Ian MacPherson said, "Preaching is something august, sublime, awe-begetting—a supernatural act, the transmission of a Person through a person to a company of persons, the Person so conveyed being the everlasting Jesus." He illustrated it by an incident that happened when King George V was speaking on the radio and his words were being relayed to America. A vital cable broke in the New York station, plunging the staff into panic. "Then Harold Vivien, a junior mechanic, saw in a moment what to do. Seizing the ends of the broken wire, he held them, grimly and gallantly, as the current conveying the royal message was transmitted. Electrical charges of some 250 volts shook his body, convulsing him from head to foot and causing him considerable pain. But he did not relax his grasp. Resolutely, desperately, he clung to the cable till the people heard the king."

> *Channels only, blessed Master,*
> *But with all Thy wondrous pow'r*
> *Flowing thro' us, Thou canst use us*
> *Ev'ry day and ev'ry hour.*

February 3

Then another angel, having a golden censer, came and stood at the altar.
He was given much incense, that he should offer it with the prayers of all the
saints upon the golden altar which was before the throne.

REVELATION 8:3

 e believe that the angel in this passage is none other than the Lord
Jesus Himself. And His ministry here is full of comfort and encouragement for us. What is He doing? He takes the prayers of all saints,
adds His precious incense to them and presents them to God the Father.

We know only too well that our prayers and praises are very imperfect. We
don't know how to pray as we should. Everything we do is stained with sin, with
false motives, with selfishness.

> *The holiest hours we spend in prayer upon our knees,*
> *The times when most we deem our songs of praise will please,*
> *Thou Searcher of all hearts, forgiveness pour on these.*

But before our worship and intercession ever get to God the Father, they pass
through the Lord Jesus. He removes every trace of imperfection so that when they
finally reach the Father they are flawless. And something else that is very wonderful happens. He offers the incense with the prayers of the saints. The incense
speaks of the fragrant perfection of His Person and work. It is this that gives effi-
cacy to our prayers.

What an encouragement this should be to us. We are all too aware of how we
bungle in prayer. We slaughter the rules of grammar, express ourselves inelegant-
ly, and say things that are doctrinal absurdities. But this need not discourage us
from praying. We have a Great High Priest who edits and purifies all our communications with the Father.

Mary Bowley captured the truth in poetic form when she wrote:

> *Much incense is ascending*
> *Before th' eternal throne;*
> *God graciously is bending*
> *To hear each feeble groan;*
> *To all our prayers and praises*
> *Christ adds His sweet perfume,*
> *And love the censer raises*
> *These odors to consume.*

February 4

If I had said, I will speak thus, Behold, I would have been untrue
to the generation of Your children.
PSALM 73:15

T he psalmist had been going through a rough patch. He saw the wicked prospering in the world, whereas his own life was a nightmare of trouble and suffering. He began to have doubts about the justice of God, the love of God, and the wisdom of God. It seemed as if the Lord rewarded wickedness and punished uprightness.

But Asaph made a noble resolve. He determined not to parade his doubts lest he should stumble any of God's children.

Probably most of us have doubts and questions at times. Especially when we are almost at the end of endurance, when everything seems ready to cave in on top of us, it is easy to question the providence of God. What should we do?

We are certainly permitted to share our doubts with someone who is spiritually qualified to counsel us. Sometimes we are too distracted to see the light at the end of the tunnel, whereas it is quite clear to others and they can lead us to it.

As a general rule, we should "never doubt in the darkness what has been revealed to us in the light." We should not interpret God's Word by circumstances, no matter how bleak. Rather we should interpret our circumstances by the Scriptures and realize that nothing can ever thwart God's purposes or nullify His promises.

But above all, we should not go around needlessly parading our doubts. There is the terrible danger of stumbling Christ's little ones, concerning whom He said, "But whoever causes one of these little ones who believe in Me to sin, it would be better for him if a millstone were hung around his neck, and he were drowned in the depth of the sea" (Mt. 18:6).

Our certitudes are numberless; our doubts, if any, are few. Let us share our certitudes. As Goethe said, "Give me the benefit of your convictions, if you have any, but keep your doubts to yourself, for I have enough of my own."

February 5

N o purpose of God can be thwarted. Man may have his wickedness, but God has His way. Man may have a lot to say, but God will have the last word. Solomon reminds us that "There is no wisdom or understanding or counsel against the Lord" (Prov. 21:30). And Jeremiah adds his testimony that "every purpose of the Lord shall be performed" (Jer. 51:29).

Joseph's brothers decided to get rid of him by selling him to a band of Midianites. But all they succeeded in doing was accomplishing the will of God. The Midianites provided free transportation for Joseph to Egypt where he rose to be Prime Minister and the savior of his people.

When the man who was born blind received his sight and trusted the Savior, the Jews excommunicated him from the synagogue. Was it a great victory for them? No, Jesus would have led him out anyway because the Good Shepherd "calls His own sheep by name, and leads them out" (Jn. 10:3, NASB). So they merely saved Jesus the effort of doing it.

Men's wickedness reached its Everest when they took the Lord Jesus and, nailing Him to a cross, put Him to death. But Peter reminded them that He was delivered up by "the determined purpose and foreknowledge of God" (Acts 2:23). God overruled man's gargantuan crime by raising Christ up to be Lord and Savior.

Donald Gray Barnhouse told the story of a wealthy landowner who had beautiful trees on his estate. But he had a bitter enemy who said, "I will cut down one of his trees; that will hurt him." In the dark of the night the enemy slipped over the fence and went to the most beautiful of the trees, and with saws and axes he began to work. In the first light of morning he saw in the distance two men coming over the hill on horseback, and recognized one of them as the owner of the estate. Hurriedly, he pushed the wedges out and let the tree fall; but one of the branches caught him and pinned him to the ground, injuring him so badly that he died. Before he died, he screeched out, "Well, I have cut down your beautiful tree," and the estate owner looked at him with pity and said, "This is the architect I have brought with me. We had planned to build a house, and it was necessary to cut down one tree to make room for the house; and it is the one you have been working at all night."

February 6

But be doers of the word, and not hearers only, deceiving yourselves.
JAMES 1:22

There is a subtle deception that attending meetings, conferences, and seminars is doing the work of God. We listen to messages and talk about what we know we should be doing, and the delusion creeps over us that we are accomplishing His will. What we are actually doing is increasing our responsibility and deceiving ourselves. We deceive ourselves that we are spiritual when actually we might be quite carnal. We deceive ourselves that we are growing, when the truth is that we are stagnant. We deceive ourselves that we are wise when we are pathetically foolish.

Jesus said that the wise man is the one who hears His words and does them. The foolish man also hears His words but does nothing about them.

It is not enough to listen to a sermon and walk away, saying, "What a marvelous message." The true test is when we go away, saying, "I will do something about what I heard." Someone has said that a good sermon not only stretches the mind, warms the heart, and tans the hide, but it also provokes the will to action.

In the middle of his message, a preacher once asked his audience the name of the first hymn they had sung. No one knew. He asked the text of Scripture that had been read. No one knew. He asked what announcements had been made. No one could remember. The people were playing church.

Before every meeting, we might well ask ourselves the following questions. Why did I come? Am I willing to have God speak to me personally? Will I obey Him if He does?

The Dead Sea justly earned its name by constant input without corresponding outflow. In our lives, information without application leads to stagnation. The Savior's persistent question comes home to us, "Why do you call Me Lord, Lord, and do not do the things which I say?"

February 7

I have been crucified with Christ.
GALATIANS 2:20, NASB

W hen the Lord Jesus died on the Cross, He died not only as my Substitute; He died also as my Representative. He died not only *for* me but *as* me. When He died, there is a real sense in which I died. All that I was as a child of Adam, all my old, evil, unregenerate self was nailed to the Cross. In God's reckoning, my history as a man in the flesh came to an end.

That is not all! When the Savior was buried, I too was buried. I am identified with Christ in His burial. This pictures the removal of the old "I" from God's sight forever.

And when the Lord Jesus arose from the dead, I arose, too. But the picture changes here. It is not the one who was buried who arose, not the old self. No, it is the new man—Christ living in me. I arose with Christ to walk in newness of life.

God sees all this as having taken place positionally. Now He wants it to be true practically in my life. He wants me to reckon myself to have gone through this cycle of death, burial, and resurrection. But how do I do this?

When temptation comes to me, I should reply to it exactly as a corpse reacts to any solicitation to evil. No response! I should say, in effect, "I have died to sin. You are no longer my master. I am dead as far as you are concerned."

Day by day I should reckon my old, corrupt self to have been buried in the grave of Jesus. This means I will not be introspectively occupied with it. I will not look for anything worthwhile in it or be disappointed at its utter corruption.

Finally, I will live each moment as one who has risen with Christ to newness of life—new ambitions, new desires, new motives, new freedom, and new power.

George Müller told how this truth of identification with Christ first came home to him: "There was a day when I died. Died to George Müller, his opinions, preferences, tastes and will; died to the world, its approval or censure, to the approval or blame even of my brothers or friends, and since then, I have studied only to show myself 'approved unto God.'"

February 8

He who is not with Me is against Me,
and he who does not gather with Me scatters abroad.
MATTHEW 12:30

T he Lord Jesus spoke these words concerning the Pharisees. They had just committed the unpardonable sin, attributing His miracles to Beelzebub, the prince of the demons, when actually they were done in the power of the Holy Spirit. It was now evident that they would not accept Him as the Messiah of Israel and the Savior of the world. Because they did not take a decided stand for Christ, they were necessarily against Him. Because they didn't serve on His side they worked against Him.

When it comes to the Person and work of Christ, there can be no neutrality. There is no way of straddling this fence. A man is either for Christ or he is against Him. Anyone who says he cannot decide has already decided.

When it comes to the truth concerning Christ, there can be no compromise. In biblical Christianity there are some areas where there can be a reasonable difference of opinion but this is not one of them. As A.W. Tozer has reminded us, "Some things are not negotiable." We must adhere steadfastly to the absolute deity of the Lord Jesus, His virgin birth, His true humanity, His sinless nature, His substitutionary death for sinners, His bodily resurrection, His ascension to God's right hand and His coming again. When men start to hedge on these cardinal doctrines they are left with a demi-Savior, who is no Savior at all.

The poet laid it on the line when he wrote:

"What think ye of Christ?" is the test
To try both your state and your scheme;
You cannot be right in the rest
Unless you think rightly of Him:
As Jesus appears to your view,
As He is beloved or not,
So God is disposéd to you,
And mercy or wrath is your lot.

February 9

He who is not against us is on our side.
LUKE 9:50

A t first this seems to flatly contradict our previous verse, but there is no contradiction. There the Savior was speaking to the unbelieving Pharisees and saying, "If you aren't for Me, you're against Me." But here it is a different matter. The disciples had just restrained a man who was casting out demons in Jesus' Name. They had no better reason than that he didn't associate with them. Jesus said, "Do not forbid him, for he who is not against us is on our side."

When it comes to salvation, those who are not for Christ are against Him. But when it comes to service, those who are not against Him are for Him.

We are not called to oppose others who are serving the Lord. It is a big, wide world, and there is plenty of room for all of us to get on with our work without stepping on one another's toes. We should take to heart the Savior's words, "Forbid him not."

At the same time we should notice that Jesus did not tell John and the others to go and join this man. Some use methods that are unacceptable to others. Some have different emphases in the message they preach. Some have greater light than others. And some have liberty to do things about which others have a bad conscience. We cannot expect to pour every believer into exactly the same mold as ourselves. But we can rejoice in every triumph of the gospel, as Paul did. He said, "Some indeed preach Christ even from envy and strife, and some also from good will: the former preach Christ from selfish ambition, not sincerely, supposing to add affliction to my chains; but the latter out of love, knowing that I am appointed for the defense of the gospel. What then? Only that in every way, whether in pretense or in truth, Christ is preached; and in this I rejoice, yes, and will rejoice" (Phil. 1:15-18).

Sam Shoemaker asked the perceptive question, "When shall we learn that in the great warfare of light against darkness in our time, we are going to need the support of allies who may not be to our personal taste, and learn that it is going to take all Christians working and pulling together to make headway against the storm of anti-Christ?"

February 10

I say then: Walk in the Spirit.
GALATIANS 5:16

Exactly what is involved in walking in the Spirit? Actually it is not as complicated and impractical as some tend to think. Here is what a day's walk in the Spirit would be like:

First, you start the day in prayer. You confess all known sin in your life; this makes you a clean vessel and therefore usable by God. You spend time in praise and worship; this gets your soul in tune. You turn over control of your life to Him; this makes you available for the Lord to live His life through you. In this act of rededication, you "cease from needless scheming and leave the ruling of your life to Him."

Next, you spend time feeding on the Word of God. Here you get a general outline of God's will for your life. And you may also receive some specific indication of His will for you in your present circumstances.

After your quiet time, you do the things that your hands find to do. Ordinarily they will be the prosaic, routine, mundane duties of life. This is where a lot of people have wrong ideas. They think that walking in the Spirit is foreign to the world of aprons and overalls. Actually, it is mostly composed of faithfulness and diligence in one's daily work.

Throughout the day you confess and forsake sin as soon as you are aware of it. You praise the Lord as His blessings come to mind. You obey every impulse to do good, and refuse every temptation to evil.

Then you take what comes to you during the day as being His will for you. Interruptions become opportunities to minister. Disappointments become His appointments. Phone calls, letters, visitors are seen as part of His plan.

Harold Wildish quoted the following summary in one of his books:

"As you leave the whole burden of your sin, and rest upon the finished work of Christ, so leave the whole burden of your life and service, and rest upon the present in-working of the Holy Spirit.

"Give yourself up, morning by morning, to be led by the Holy Spirit and go forth praising and at rest, leaving Him to manage you and your day. Cultivate the habit all through the day, of joyfully depending upon and obeying Him, expecting Him to guide, to enlighten, to reprove, to teach, to use, and to do in and with you what He wills. Count upon His working as a fact, altogether apart from sight or feeling. Only let us believe in and obey the Holy Spirit as the Ruler of our lives, and cease from the burden of trying to manage ourselves; then shall the fruit of the Spirit appear in us, as He wills, to the glory of God."

February 11

...the division of soul and spirit.
HEBREWS 4:12, NASB

When the Bible speaks of man in his tripartite being, the order is always spirit, soul, and body. When men use these terms together, the order almost invariably is body, soul, and spirit. Sin has turned God's order upside down. Now man puts the body first, then the soul, and the spirit last of all.

The two non-material parts of man's being are his spirit and his soul. The spirit enables him to have fellowship with God. The soul has to do with his emotions and passions. Although it is not possible for us to distinguish the spirit and soul in minute detail, we can and should learn to distinguish between what is spiritual and what is soulish.

What then is spiritual? Preaching that exalts Christ is. Prayer to God through Jesus Christ in the power of the Spirit is. Service that is motivated by love to the Lord and empowered by the Spirit is. Worship that is in spirit and truth is.

And what is soulish? Preaching that draws attention to man, to his oratory, commanding presence or wit. Mechanical prayers with no real heart involvement but designed to make an impression on others. Service that is self-appointed, carried on for monetary reward, or employing carnal methods. Worship that revolves around visible, material aids rather than the unseen spiritual realities.

What does the Church of God have to do with consecrated buildings, stained glass windows, ecclesiastical vestments, honorable titles, candles, incense and all such trappings? Or, coming closer to home, what does the Church have to do with Madison Avenue promotional efforts, with fund raising for hire, with evangelistic gimmickry, with personality cults, with musical extravaganzas?

The advertising in the average Christian magazine is enough to show how soulish we have become.

Paul draws a distinction between service that is gold, silver, precious stones and that which is wood, hay, and stubble (1 Cor. 3:12). Everything that is spiritual will resist the fire of God's discerning judgment. All that is soulish will go up in flames.

February 12

...neither on this mountain, nor in Jerusalem.
JOHN 4:21

For the Samaritans, the center of worship was on Mt. Gerizim. For the Jews, Jerusalem was the place on earth where God had placed His Name. But Jesus announced a new order to the woman of Samaria: "...The hour is coming, and now is, when the true worshippers will worship the Father in spirit and truth; for the Father is seeking such to worship Him" (Jn. 4:23).

There is no longer a single place on earth which is designated for worship. In our dispensation, a Holy Person has taken the place of a holy site. The Lord Jesus Christ is now the gathering center of His people. Jacob's words have found their fulfillment, "to Him shall be the obedience of the people" (Gen. 49:10).

We gather to Him. We are not drawn together by a consecrated building with stained glass windows and organ music. We do not gather to a man, no matter how gifted or eloquent. The Lord Jesus is the divine magnet.

The place on earth is not important; we may meet in a chapel, a home, a field, or a cave. In true worship, we enter by faith into the heavenly sanctuary. God the Father is there. The Lord Jesus is there. The angels are there in festal array. The saints of the Old Testament period are there. And the saints of the Church age who have died are there. And in such august company we are privileged to pour out our hearts in worship to God through the Lord Jesus in the power of the Holy Spirit. So while our bodies are still on earth, in spirit we pass "far, far above the restless world that wars below."

Does this contradict the Savior's words, "Where two or three are gathered together in My name, I am there in the midst of them" (Mt. 18:20)? No, this is also true. He is present in a special way when His people meet together in His Name. He takes our prayers and praises and presents them to the Father. What a privilege to have the Lord Jesus in our midst.

February 13

Owe no one anything except to love one another.
ROMANS 13:8

W e need not take this verse as a prohibition against any and every kind of debt. In our society we cannot escape telephone bills, gas and light bills, and water bills. Also under certain circumstances, it may be better discipleship to buy a house on a mortgage, thus building up equity, than to pay out the same monthly amount in rent. And it is impossible to run a business today without contracting some debts.

But the verse certainly does forbid other practices. It forbids going into debt when there is slim chance to repay. It forbids borrowing to purchase a product that depreciates in value. It forbids getting into arrears. It forbids going into debt for non-essentials. It forbids plunging into debt over our heads, the temptation to overspend on impulse because we have credit cards. It forbids wasting the Lord's money by paying exorbitant interest charges on the unpaid balance.

The verse is designed to save us from dunning creditors, from marital problems caused by overspending, and from bankruptcy court, all of which are devastating to the Christian testimony.

In general, we should practice financial responsibility by living modestly and within our means, always remembering that the borrower is slave to the lender (see Prov. 22:7).

The one debt that is always in order for the Christian is the obligation to love one another. We are obligated to love the unconverted and to share the gospel with them (Rom. 1:14). We are obligated to love the brethren and to lay down our lives for them (1 Jn. 3:16). This kind of indebtedness will never get us in trouble with the law. Rather, as Paul says, it is the fulfilling of the law.

February 14

Now, Lord, look on their threats, and grant to Your servants
that with all boldness they may speak Your Word.
ACTS 4:29

When the early Christians were undergoing persecution, they did not wait for their circumstances to change. Instead they glorified God in the circumstances.

Too often we fail to follow their example. We postpone action until conditions are more favorable. We see roadblocks as hindrances rather than as stepping-stones. We excuse our copping-out on the ground that our circumstances are not ideal.

The student remains uninvolved in Christian service until he graduates. Then he is preoccupied with romance and marriage. After that, the pressures of employment and family life keep him from throwing himself into the work. He decides to wait for retirement; then he will be free to give the rest of his life to the Lord. By the time he retires, his energy and vision are gone and he succumbs to a life of leisure.

Or it may be that we find ourselves having to work with people who rub us the wrong way. Perhaps these people have positions of leadership in the local church. Though they are faithful and hardworking, we find them objectionable. So what do we do? We sulk on the sidelines, waiting for a few first-class funerals. But it doesn't work. People like that always have surprising longevity. Waiting for funerals is unproductive.

Joseph didn't wait to get out of prison to make his life count; he had a ministry for God in prison. Daniel became a power for God during the Babylonian captivity. If he had waited till the exile was over, it would have been too late. It was during Paul's imprisonment that he wrote Ephesians, Philippians, Colossians, and Philemon. He didn't wait for his circumstances to improve.

The simple fact is that circumstances are never ideal in this life. And for the Christian, there is no promise that they are going to improve. So in service, as in salvation, now is the accepted time.

Luther said, "He who desires to wait until the occasion seems completely favorable for his work will never find it." And Solomon warned that "he who watches the wind will not sow, and he who looks at the clouds will not reap" (Eccl. 11:4, NASB).

February 15

Cast your bread upon the waters, for you will find it after many days.
ECCLESIASTES 11:1

Bread here is probably used, figuratively, for the grain from which it is made. In Egypt, seed was sown on flooded areas. As the waters receded, the crop came forth. But it did not happen immediately. The harvest came "after many days."

Today we live in an "instant" society, and we want instant results. We have instant mashed potatoes, instant tea, coffee and cocoa, instant soup and instant oatmeal. Also, we have instant credit at the bank and instant replays on TV.

But it is not like that in Christian life and service. Our kindnesses are not rewarded immediately. Our prayers are not always answered right away. And our service does not usually produce immediate results.

The Bible repeatedly uses the agricultural cycle to illustrate spiritual service. "a sower went out to sow…" "I planted, Apollos watered; but God gave the increase." "First the blade, then the head, after that the full grain in the head." It is a gradual process, over an extended period of time. The squash grows more quickly than an oak tree, but it still takes time.

Therefore, to expect instant results from our uncalculating deeds of kindness is unrealistic. To expect immediate answers to prayer is immature. To press for a decision the first time a person hears the gospel is unwise. Certainly the normal experience is to give, pray, and serve untiringly over a protracted period of time. You do so with the confidence that your labor is not in vain in the Lord. After a while, you see results—not enough to inflate you with pride, but enough to encourage you to press on. The full results will not be known till we reach heaven—which is—after all, the best and safest place to see the fruit of our labors.

February 16

Even in laughter the heart may sorrow.
PROVERBS 14:13

othing is perfect in this life. All laughter is mingled with sorrow. Every diamond has a flaw. Each person has some character defect. In all of life, there's a worm in the apple.

It is good to be idealistic; God has set within us a longing for perfection. But it is also good to be realistic; we never will find absolute perfection under the sun.

It is easy for young people to think that their family is the only one that has quarrels. Or that their parents are the only ones who don't have scintillating TV personalities.

It is easy to be disappointed with our local church fellowship, all the time supposing that everything is rosy in the church across the street.

Or it is easy to go through life forever looking for friends who are absolutely ideal. We expect perfection in others even though we can't produce it ourselves.

We should face the fact squarely that everyone has personality flaws, some more glaring than others. Often the more outstanding a person is, the more obvious his faults are. Instead of being disappointed with the flaws, we would do well to emphasize the good qualities in other believers. Everyone has some of these too. But only one Person has all of them combined, that is, the Lord Jesus.

I often think that the Lord has purposely left us with an unsatisfied desire for perfection down here so that we will look off to Him in whom there is neither spot nor blemish. He represents the sum of all moral beauties. There is no disappointment in Him.

February 17

In pressure Thou hast enlarged me.
PSALM 4:1, DARBY

I t is true that "calm seas never made a sailor." It is through tribulation that we develop patience. It is through pressure that we are enlarged.

Even men of the world have realized that difficulties have educative and broadening values. Charles Kettering once said, "Problems are the price of progress. Don't bring me anything but problems. Good news weakens me."

But especially from the Christian world come testimonies to the profit derived from trials. We read, for instance, "To suffer passes, but to have suffered endures for eternity."

The poet adds this confirmation:

> And many a rapturous minstrel among those sons of light
> Will say of his sweetest music, "I learnt it in the night;"
> And many a rolling anthem that fills the Father's home
> Sobbed out its first rehearsal in the shade of a darkened room.

Spurgeon wrote, in his inimitable way: "I am afraid that all the grace I have got out of my comfortable and easy times and happy hours might almost lie on a penny. But the good I have received from my sorrows and pains and griefs is altogether incalculable. What do I not owe to the hammer and the file? Affliction is the best bit of furniture in my house."

And yet why should we be surprised? Does not the unnamed writer to the Hebrews tell us, "Now obviously no chastening seems pleasant at the time: it is in fact most unpleasant. Yet when it is all over we can see that it has quietly produced the fruit of real goodness in the character of those who have accepted it" (Heb. 12:11, PHILLIPS).

February 18

Shall not the Judge of all the earth do right?
GENESIS 18:25

 hen there are mysteries in life too deep for us to fathom, we can relax in the confidence that the Judge of all the earth is the God of absolute and infinite righteousness.

There is the question of the status of children who die before reaching the age of accountability. For many of us, it is enough to know that "of such is the kingdom of God." We believe that they are safe through the blood of Jesus. But for others who are still not satisfied, the words of our verse should be sufficient. God can be counted on to do what is right.

There is the perennial problem of election and predestination. Does God choose some to salvation without at the same time choosing some to be damned? After the Calvinists and Armenians have all had their say, we can have full confidence that there is no unrighteousness with God.

Again there is the seeming injustice that the wicked often prosper while the righteous are passing through deep tribulation. There is the recurring question as to the fate of the heathen who have never heard the gospel. Men puzzle over why God ever allowed sin to enter. We often stand dumb in the face of tragedies, of poverty and hunger, of horrible physical and mental impairments. Doubt continually murmurs, "If God is in control, why does He permit it all?"

Faith replies, "Wait till the last chapter is written. God hasn't made His first mistake. When we are able to see things from a clearer perspective, we will realize that the Judge of all the earth has done right."

> *God writes in characters too grand*
> *For our short sight to understand;*
> *We catch but broken strokes, and try*
> *To fathom all the mystery*
> *Of withered hopes, of death, of life,*
> *The endless war, the useless strife,*
> *But there, with larger, clearer sight,*
> *We shall see this—His way was right.*
> —JOHN OXENHAM

February 19

When a man's folly brings his way to ruin, his heart rages against the Lord.
PROVERBS 19:3, RSV

T here is no book on psychology like the Bible. It gives insights on human behavior that you cannot find in any other place. Here, for instance, it describes a man whose own waywardness wrecks his life, yet rather than shoulder the blame himself, he turns around and vents his spleen on the Lord.

How true to life! We have known people who made a profession of being Christians but who then became involved in vile forms of sexual immorality. This brought them to shame, disgrace, and financial ruin. But would they repent? No, they turned against Christ, renounced the faith, and became militant atheists.

More often than we probably realize, apostasy has its roots in moral failure. A. J. Pollock told of meeting a young man who began to spew out all kinds of doubts and denials concerning the Scriptures. When Pollock asked him, "What sin have you been indulging in?" the young man broke down and poured out a lurid story of sin and indecency.

The gross injustice lies in man's perverse way of raging against the Lord for the consequences of his own sins. W. F. Adeney said, "It is monstrous to charge the providence of God with the consequences of actions which He has forbidden."

How true it is that "everyone practicing evil hates the light and does not come to the light, lest his deeds should be exposed" (Jn. 3:20). The Apostle Peter reminds us that scoffers "walking after their own lusts" are "willingly ignorant." Pollock comments, "This brings out a most important truth that the inability and reluctance to receive the truth of God is very largely because of what is moral. Often a man wants to go on with his sin, or the flesh has a natural dislike to God. Maybe the searching character of the light, and the restraining influence of the Bible are resented. It is not the head that is so much at fault as the heart."

February 20

I will not eat until I have told about my errand.
GENESIS 24:33

J

ust as Abraham's servant had a sense of urgency in connection with his mission, so should we. This does not mean we must race around in all directions at once. It does not mean that we must do everything in nervous haste. But it does mean that we should give ourselves to the task before us as a matter of top priority. We should adopt the attitude expressed in Robert Frost's lines:

The woods are lovely, dark and deep,
But I have promises to keep
And miles to go before I sleep.

Amy Carmichael wrote:

Only twelve short hours—O never
Let the sense of urgency
Die in us, Good Shepherd, ever
Let us search the hills with Thee.

And did not our blessed Savior live with a sense of urgency? He said, "I have a baptism to be baptized with, and how distressed I am till it is accomplished!" (Lk. 12:50). The Lord's disciples saw the intensity of His passion when He drove out the money changers, and recalled a prophetic quotation from Psalm 69:9 about the Messiah: "And His disciples remembered that it was written, The zeal of Thine house hath eaten Me up" (John 2:17).

Hear the urgency in the words of the intrepid Apostle Paul: "One thing I do...I press toward the goal for the prize of the upward call of God in Christ Jesus" (Phil. 3:13-14).

There is no excuse for Christians to rest on their oars.

February 21

I dwell among my own people.
2 KINGS 4:13

 prominent woman in Shunem showed hospitality to Elisha whenever he passed that way. Eventually she suggested to her husband that they build an extra bedroom so that the prophet would have his own room. Desiring to reward this gracious hostess, Elisha asked what he could do for her—perhaps an introduction to the king or to the commander-in-chief. Her simple reply was, "I dwell among my own people." In other words, "I am happy with my lot in life. I love the common people among whom I live. I don't particularly desire to move among the upper crust. Hobnobbing with famous people holds no special attraction for me."

She was a wise woman! Those who are never content unless they're socializing with the famous, the wealthy, the aristocratic often have to learn that most of earth's choicest people never make the front page—or the society page, for that matter.

I have had some contact with big names in the evangelical world, but I have to confess that, for the most part, the experience has been disappointing. And the more I have seen of what is ballyhooed in the Christian press, the more disillusioned I have become. If I have to make a choice, give me those humble, godly, solid citizens who are unknown in this world but well-known in heaven.

A.W. Tozer mirrored my sentiments well when he wrote, "I believe in saints. I've met the comics; I've met the promoters; I've met the founder who puts his name on the front of the building so people will know he founded it. I've met converted cowboys not too well converted. I have met all kinds of weird Christians throughout the United States and Canada, but my heart is looking for saints. I want to meet the people who are like the Lord Jesus Christ...Actually, what we want and ought to have is the beauty of the Lord our God in human breasts. A winsome, magnetic saint is worth 500 promoters and gadgeteers and religious engineers."

Charles Simeon voiced similar sentiments. "From the first day I set off to the present hour...my intercourse has been with the excellent of the earth, and every one of them striving to the utmost of his power to show me kindness for the Lord's sake."

So—orchids to the woman of Shunem for the spiritual insight in her words, "I dwell among mine own people."

February 22

...For the equipping of the saints for the work of ministry.
EPHESIANS 4:12, NASB

A revolutionary insight! The gifts in Ephesians 4 are given to perfect the saints for the work of the ministry. As soon as the saints can carry on, the gift can move on.

This means that success in Christian work is working one's self out of a job in the shortest possible time, then looking for new worlds to conquer.

This is what Paul did. He went to Thessalonica, for instance, preached to the Jews for three Sabbaths, and left behind a functioning assembly. No doubt that was an exception as far as speed in the establishing of a work was concerned. The longest Paul ever stayed in one place at a time was two years. That was at Ephesus.

God never intended that His saints should be perpetually dependent on any of the gifts mentioned. The gifts are expendable. If the saints remain professional sermon-tasters, never becoming involved in the work of service, they never develop spiritually the way they should and the world will never be evangelized the way God intended.

William Dillon said that a successful foreign missionary never has a foreign successor. That should be equally true of workers in the homeland—when the worker's task is completed, the saints themselves should take over, not start looking for another pulpiteer.

Too often we preachers look at our position as a lifetime appointment. We reason that others couldn't do the work as well. We excuse our permanence by the fact that the attendance would drop if we left. We complain that others can't do things right and that they're not dependable. But the fact is that they have to learn. And in order to learn they have to be given opportunities. There must be training, delegation of responsibilities, and evaluation of progress.

When the saints reach the point where they feel they can carry on without a particular preacher or teacher, that's no reason for him to sulk or nurse wounded feelings. It's cause for celebration. The worker is released to go where he's more needed.

It's a bad scene when the work of God is permanently built around a man, no matter how gifted he is. His great aim should be to multiply his effectiveness by building up the saints to the point where they are no longer dependent on him. In a world like ours, he never needs to be without work in other places.

February 23

A wise man will hear.
PROVERBS 1:5

The essential difference between the wise man and the fool in the book of Proverbs is that the wise man will hear and the fool won't.

It isn't a question of the fool's mental capacity. Actually, he may have unusual intellectual ability. But he just cannot be told anything. He labors under the fatal delusion that his knowledge is infinite and his judgments are infallible. If his friends try to counsel him, they receive scorn for their efforts. They watch him trying to escape the inevitable results of sinful and stupid actions, but they are helpless to avert the crash. And so he goes on from one crisis to another. Now his finances are a disaster. Now his personal life is in shambles. Now his business totters on the edge of chaos. But he rationalizes that life is giving him a bad deal. It never occurs to him that he is his own worst enemy. He is generous in dispensing advice to others, oblivious of his inability to run his own life. A compulsive talker, he holds forth with the aplomb of an oracle.

The wise man is made of better stuff. He realizes that everyone's mental wires have been somewhat crossed by the Fall. He knows that others can sometimes see aspects of a problem that he has overlooked. He is willing to acknowledge that his memory may be faulty at times. He is teachable, welcoming any input that will help him make the right decisions. Actually he solicits the advice of others because he knows that "in the multitude of counselors there is safety" (Prov. 11:14). Like everyone else, he sometimes makes mistakes. But he has this saving virtue that he learns from his mistakes and makes every failure a springboard to success. He is grateful for a deserved rebuke and is willing to say, "I was wrong. I am sorry." Wise children submit to parental discipline; fools rebel. Wise young people obey the scriptural precepts concerning moral purity; fools do their own thing. Wise adults judge everything by whether it is well-pleasing to the Lord; fools act according to what pleases themselves.

And so it is that the wise grow wiser, and the fools are stuck fast in the rut of their own folly.

February 24

Adam...begot a son in his own likeness, after his image.
GENESIS 5:3

It is a basic fact of physical life that we beget children in our own likeness, after our image. Adam begat a son in his own likeness, and called his name Seth. When people saw Seth they probably said what people have been saying ever since: "Like father, like son."

It is also a sobering fact of spiritual life that we beget children in our own image. When we are used to introduce others to the Lord Jesus, they insensibly take on characteristics similar to our own. Here it is not a matter of heredity but of imitation. They look up to us as the ideal of what Christians should be and unconsciously pattern their behavior after ours. Soon they manifest the family likeness.

This means that the place I give to the Bible in my life will set the standard for my children in the faith. It means that my emphasis on prayer will become theirs also. If I am a worshipper, this characteristic will probably rub off on them, too.

If I adhere to the stern demands of discipleship, they will figure that this is the norm for all believers. On the other hand, if I water down the Savior's words and live for wealth, fame, and pleasure, I can expect them to follow my lead.

Zealous soul winners tend to beget on-fire personal workers. Those who find pleasure and profit in Scripture memory pass on the vision to their spiritual children.

If you are irregular about attendance at the meetings of the assembly, you can hardly expect your protegée to be any different. If you are usually late, they will probably be late, too. If you sit in the back row, don't be surprised if that influences them to do likewise.

On the other hand, if you are disciplined, dependable, punctual, and vitally involved, your Timothys will follow your faith.

So the question for each of us is, "Am I content to beget children in my own image?" The Apostle Paul could say, "I urge you, imitate me" (1 Cor. 4:16). Can we say that?

February 25

According to your faith let it be to you.
MATTHEW 9:29

hen Jesus asked two blind men if they believed that He was able to give them sight, they replied that they did. As He touched their eyes, He said, "According to your faith let it be to you," and their eyes were opened.

It would be easy to conclude from this that if we just have enough faith, we can get anything we want, whether wealth, healing, or whatever. But that is not the case. Faith must be based upon some word of the Lord, some promise of God, some command of Scripture. Otherwise it is nothing more than wishful credulity.

What we learn from our text is that the extent to which we appropriate the promises of God depends on the measure of our faith. After promising King Joash that he would have victory over the Syrians, Elisha told him to smite the ground with his arrows. Joash smote three times, then stopped. Elisha angrily announced that the king would have only three victories over Syria whereas he could have had five or six (2 Ki. 13:14-19). The measure of his victory depended on his faith.

It is that way in the life of discipleship. We are called to walk by faith, to forsake all. We are forbidden to lay up treasures on earth. How far do we dare to go in obeying these commands? Should we do away with life insurance, health insurance, savings accounts, stocks and bonds? The answer is, "According to your faith be it unto you." If you have faith to say, "I will work hard for my current needs and the needs of my family, put everything above that in the work of the Lord, and trust God for the future," then you can be absolutely certain that the Lord will take care of your future. He has said that He would and His Word cannot fail. If, on the other hand, we feel we should exercise "human prudence" by providing for a rainy day, God will still love us and will still use us according to the measure of our faith.

The life of faith is like the waters that flow from the Temple in Ezekiel 47. You can go in to your ankles, to your knees, to your loins—or, better still, you can swim in them.

God's choicest blessings, of course, are for those who trust Him most fully. Once we have proved His faithfulness and sufficiency, we want to put away the crutches, props, and pillows of "common sense." Or, as someone has said, "Once you walk on the water, you never want to ride in a boat again."

February 26

How can you believe, who receive honor from one another,
and do not seek the honor that comes from the only God?
JOHN 5:44

By these words our Lord indicates that we cannot at the same time seek man's approbation and the approval of God. He also affirms that once we embark on a quest for human accreditation, we have dealt a body-blow to the life of faith.

In similar vein the Apostle Paul expresses the moral inconsistency between coveting man's praise and God's: "...For if I still pleased men, I would not be a bondservant of Christ" (Gal. 1:10b).

Let me illustrate. Here is a young believer who wants an advanced degree in some area of theology. But he wants the degree from an accredited university. It must be from an accredited institution. Unfortunately, the only accredited universities offering that degree are ones that deny the great fundamental truths of the faith. To list that degree after his name means so much to him that he is willing to take it from men who, though known as scholars, are enemies of the Cross of Christ. Almost inevitably he becomes defiled in the process. He never again speaks with the same conviction.

The desire to be known in the world as a scholar or a scientist has built-in hazards. There is the subtle danger to compromise, to sacrifice biblical principles for a more liberal stance, to become more critical of fundamentalists than of modernists.

Christian schools face an agonizing choice—whether or not to seek accreditation from a recognized agency in the educational world. The lust to be "accredited" often results in a watering down of their Bible emphasis and the adoption of carnal principles laid down by men who do not have the Spirit.

The thing to be greatly desired is to be "approved unto God." The alternative is too costly, for "on the coin for which we sell the truth, there is at all times, faint as it may be, the image of Anti-christ" (F. W. Grant).

February 27

God has chosen the weak things of the world
to put to shame the things which are mighty.
1 CORINTHIANS 1:27

1 f a carpenter can take waste, scrap lumber and make a splendid piece of furniture out of it, it brings more credit to him than if he uses only the finest of materials. So when God uses things that are foolish, worthless, and weak to accomplish glorious results, it magnifies His skill and power. People cannot attribute the success to the raw materials; they are forced to confess that it can only be the Lord who deserves the credit.

The book of Judges provides repeated illustrations of God using the weak things of the world to confound the things which are mighty. Ehud, for example, was a left-handed Benjamite. The left hand in Scripture speaks of weakness. Yet Ehud brought down Eglon, king of Moab, and won rest for Israel for eighty years (Jud. 3:12-30).

Shamgar went into battle wielding an ox-goad, and yet with this unlikely weapon he slew 600 Philistines and delivered Israel (3:31). Deborah was a member of the "weaker sex," yet by the power of God she won a smashing victory over the Canaanites (4:4; 5:31). Barak's 10,000 foot soldiers were a poor match, humanly speaking, against Sisera's 900 chariots of iron, yet Barak swept the field (4:10, 13). Jael, another member of the "weaker sex," killed Sisera with such a non-weapon as a tent pin (4:21). According to the Septuagint, she held the pin with her left hand. Gideon marched against the Midianites with an army that the Lord had reduced from 32,000 to 300 (7:1-7). His army is pictured under the figure of a cake of barley bread. Since barley bread was the food of the poor, the picture is one of poverty and feebleness (7:13). The unconventional weapons of Gideon's army were earthenware pitchers, torches, and trumpets (7:16). And as if that were not enough to insure defeat, the pitchers had to be broken (7:19). Abimelech was felled by a woman's hand hurling a piece of millstone (9:53). The name Tola means a worm, an inauspicious title for a military deliverer (10:1). When we first meet Samson's mother, she is a nameless, barren woman (13:2). Finally, Samson killed 1,000 Philistines with nothing more lethal than the jawbone of an ass (15:15).

February 28

He will destroy them...so that you may drive them out and destroy them.
DEUTERONOMY 9:3 NASB

I n all of God's dealings with mankind, there is a curious merging of the divine and the human.

Take the Bible, for example. There is the divine Author, and there are human authors, who wrote as they were moved by the Holy Spirit.

As far as salvation is concerned, it is of the Lord from start to finish. There is nothing a man can do to earn or deserve it. And yet he must receive it by faith. God clearly elects individuals, but they must enter in at the strait gate. And so Paul writes to Titus of "the faith of God's elect" (Titus 1:1).

From the divine standpoint, we are "kept by the power of God." Yet there is also the human side—"through faith." "Kept by the power of God through faith" (1 Pet. 1:5).

Only God can make me holy. Yet He will not make me holy without my co-operation. I must add to my faith virtue, knowledge, temperance, patience, godliness, brotherly kindness, and love (2 Pet. 1:5-7). I must put on the whole armor of God (Eph. 6:13-18). I must put off the old man and put on the new man (Eph. 4:22-24). I must walk in the Spirit (Gal. 5:16).

You find the merging of the divine and the human in the whole area of Christian ministry. Paul plants, Apollos waters, but God gives the increase (1 Cor. 3:6).

When we come to leadership in the local church, we learn that only God can make a man an elder. Paul reminded the Ephesian elders that it was the Holy Spirit who had made them overseers (Acts 20:28). Yet a man's own will is involved. He must desire to exercise oversight (1 Tim. 3:1, JND).

Finally, in the text with which we began, we see that it is God who destroys our enemies, but we must drive them out and destroy them (Deut. 9:3, NASB).

In order to be balanced Christians, we must recognize this merging of the divine and human. We must pray as if everything depended on God but work as if everything depended on us. Or to borrow the wartime exhortation, "Praise the Lord and pass the ammunition." As someone suggested, we must pray for a good harvest but keep on hoeing.

February 29

Jesus Christ—He is Lord of all.
ACTS 10:36

ne of the great themes of the New Testament is the Lordship of Jesus Christ. Over and over we are reminded that He is Lord and that we should give Him that place in our lives.

To crown Jesus as Lord means to surrender our lives to Him. It means to have no will of our own, but to want His will supremely. It means the willingness to go anywhere, do anything, and say whatever He desires. When Joshua asked the captain of the Lord's army, "Are you for us or against us?" the captain replied, in effect, "I didn't come either to assist or hinder you. I came to take over" (see Josh. 5:14). So the Lord doesn't come as sort of a glorified assistant; He comes to take supreme command of our lives.

The importance of Lordship can be seen in the fact that whereas the word "Savior, occurs only 24 times in the New Testament, the word "Lord" occurs 522 times. It is also significant that whereas men invariably say, "Savior and Lord," in that order, the Scriptures always say, "Lord and Savior."

To make Jesus our Lord is the most reasonable, logical thing we can do. He died for us; the least we can do is live for Him. He bought us; we are no longer our own. "Love so amazing, so divine, demands our souls, our lives, our all."

If we can trust Him for our eternal salvation, can we not trust Him for the management of our lives? "There is a lack of sincerity about committing the eternal soul to God and holding back the mortal life—professing to give Him the greater and withholding the lesser" (R. A. LAIDLAW).

How then, do we crown Jesus as Lord? There must be a crisis experience when for the first time we turn over the controls to Him, when every area of our life is placed under His sovereign sway. It is a total commitment with "no reserve, no retreat, no regrets."

From then on it becomes a matter of moment by moment yielding to His guidance, presenting our bodies to Him so that He can live His life through us. The crisis becomes a process.

It makes good sense! With His wisdom, love, and power, He can do a far better job of running our lives than we can.

March 1

Are there not twelve hours in the day?
JOHN 11:9

W hen Jesus suggested going back to Judea, the disciples were terrified. The Jews had tried to stone Him there only recently, and now He was talking about a return visit. In answer to the disciples' apprehension, Jesus said, "Are there not twelve hours in the day?" At first glance, the question seems to be completely disconnected from the conversation. But what the Savior was saying was this—the working day is made up of twelve hours. When a person is yielded to God, every day has its appointed program. Nothing can thwart the accomplishing of that program. So even if Jesus went back to Jerusalem, and even if the Jews tried to kill Him again, they could not succeed. His work was not finished. His hour had not yet come.

For every child of God, it is true that he is "immortal till his work is done." This should impart great peace and poise to our lives. If we are living in the will of God, and if we follow reasonable rules of health and safety, we will never die a moment ahead of time. Nothing can come to us apart from His permissive will.

Many Christians worry themselves sick over the food they eat, the water they drink, the air they breathe. In our pollution-conscious society there is always something to suggest that death is knocking at the door. But this anxiety is unnecessary. "Are there not twelve hours in the day?" Hasn't God placed a hedge around the believer (Job 1:10) which the devil is powerless to penetrate?

If we believe this, it will save us from a lot of second guessing. We will not say, "If the ambulance had only arrived sooner" or "If the doctor had only detected the growth four weeks earlier" or "If my husband had only taken a different airline." Our lives are planned by infinite wisdom and in infinite power. He has a perfect timetable for each of us, and His trains run on perfect schedule.

March 2

The fruit of the Spirit is love....
GALATIANS 5:22

T he phrase "the fruit of the Spirit" teaches us at the outset that the virtues that follow can be produced only by the Holy Spirit. An unconverted man is incapable of manifesting any of these graces. Even a true believer is powerless to reproduce them by his own strength. So when we think of these graces, we must remember that they are supernatural and other-worldly.

The love spoken of here, for instance, is not the *eros* passion, or the *phileo* of friendship, or the *storge* of affection. It is *agape* love—the kind of love which God has shown to us and which He wants us to show to others.

Let me illustrate. Dr. T. E. McCully was the father of Ed McCully, one of the five young missionaries martyred by the Auca Indians in Ecuador. One night when Dr. McCully and I were on our knees together in Oak Park, Illinois, his thoughts went back to Ecuador and to the Curaray River that holds the secret of the whereabouts of Ed's body. He prayed, "Lord, let me live long enough to see those fellows saved who killed our boys, that I may throw my arms around them and tell them I love them because they love my Christ." When we arose I saw rivulets of tears zig-zagging down his cheeks.

God answered that prayer of love. Some of those Auca Indians later professed faith in Christ. Dr. McCully went to Ecuador, met these men who murdered his son, threw his arms around them, and told them he loved them because they loved his Christ.

That is agape love. It is impartial, seeking the highest good of all—the homely as well as the handsome, foes as well as friends. It is unconditional, asking for nothing in return for its constant giving. It is sacrificial, never minding the cost. It is unselfish, more concerned with the needs of others than its own. It is pure, free from any trace of impatience, envy, pride, vindictiveness or spite.

Love is the greatest virtue of the Christian life. Without it our noblest endeavors are worthless.

March 3

The fruit of the spirit is...joy....
GALATIANS 5:22

Man never finds real joy till he finds the Lord. Then he enters into what Peter calls "joy inexpressible and full of glory" (1 Pet. 1:8).

Anyone can rejoice when circumstances are favorable, but the joy which is the fruit of the Spirit is not the result of earthly circumstances. It springs from our relationship with the Lord and from the precious promises He has given to us. Christ would have to be dethroned before the Church could be finally robbed of its joy.

Christian joy can coexist with suffering. Paul weds the two when he speaks of "all patience and longsuffering with joy" (Col. 1:11). The Thessalonian saints had received the word "in much affliction, with joy of the Holy Spirit" (1 Thess. 1:6). Suffering saints down through the centuries have testified how the Lord has given them songs in the night.

Joy can coexist with sorrow (2 Cor. 6:10). The believer can stand by the grave of a loved one, shed tears of sorrow at the loss, yet rejoice at the knowledge that the loved one is in the presence of the Lord.

But joy cannot coexist with sin. Whenever a Christian sins, he loses his song. Not until he confesses and forsakes that sin is the joy of his salvation restored.

The Lord Jesus told His disciples to rejoice when they were reviled, persecuted, and falsely accused (Mt. 5:11-12). And they did! Not many years later we read of them leaving the courtroom, "rejoicing that they were counted worthy to suffer shame for His name" (Acts 5:41).

Our joy increases as we grow in the knowledge of the Lord. At first, perhaps, we can rejoice in minor irritations, chronic ailments and trivial inconveniences. But the Spirit of God wishes to bring us to the point where we can see God when circumstances are at their worst and rejoice in the knowledge that His way is perfect. We are spiritually mature when we can say with Habakkuk, "Though the fig tree may not blossom, nor fruit be on the vines; though the labor of the olive may fail, and the fields yield no food; though the flock may be cut off from the fold, and there be no herd in the stalls—yet I will rejoice in the Lord, I will joy in the God of my salvation" (Hab. 3:17-18).

March 4

The fruit of the Spirit is...peace....
GALATIANS 5:22

 s soon as we are justified by faith, we have peace with God through our Lord Jesus Christ (Rom. 5:1). That means that the hostility between ourselves and God has ceased since Christ has effectively dealt with the cause of that hostility—our sins.

We also have peace of conscience knowing that the work is finished, Christ has paid the penalty of our sins, and God has forgotten them.

But then the Holy Spirit also wants us to enjoy the peace of God in our hearts. This is the serenity and tranquility that comes from knowing that our times are in the hands of God and that nothing can happen to us apart from His permissive will.

So we can remain calm when we have a tire blowout on the busy freeway. We don't have to lose our composure when heavy traffic causes us to miss the plane. Peace means remaining cool in a car crash. Or when grease ignites on the kitchen stove.

This fruit of the Spirit enables a Peter to sleep soundly in jail, a Stephen to pray for his murderous assailants, a Paul to comfort others in a shipwreck.

When a plane flies into clear air turbulence and is thrown around like a feather in the gale, when the wing tips flex thirteen feet, when most of the passengers are screaming as the plane lurches, falls, rises, and dips, peace enables a believer to bow his head, commit his soul to God, and praise God for whatever may be the outcome.

Or to change the illustration, the Spirit of God can give peace to us when we sit in the doctor's office and hear him say, "I'm sorry to tell you, but it's malignant." He can enable us to reply, "I'm ready to go, Doctor. I'm saved by the grace of God, and for me it will be 'absent from the body, at home with the Lord.'"

And so in the words of Bickersteth's lovely hymn, we can have "Peace, perfect peace, in this dark world of sin...by thronging duties pressed...with sorrows surging round...with loved ones far away...our future all unknown" because "Jesus we know, and He is on the throne."

March 5

The fruit of the Spirit is...longsuffering....
GALATIANS 5:22

L ongsuffering is the virtue that bears up patiently and even triumphantly under the aggravations of life. While it may refer to a patient response to adverse circumstances, it usually refers to a merciful endurance of the provocations of people.

God is longsuffering with man. Think for a moment of the gross sinfulness of the human race at the present time—the legalization of prostitution, the popularization of homosexuality, the laws permitting abortions, the breakdown of marriage and the home, the wholesale rejection of moral standards, and, of course, man's crowning sin—the utter rejection of God's Son as only Lord and Savior. One could scarcely blame God if He were to wipe out mankind with a stroke. But He doesn't do it. His goodness is designed to lead men to repentance. He is not willing that any should perish.

And His will is that this longsuffering should be reproduced in the lives of His people as they yield to the Holy Spirit. This means that we should not be quick-tempered. We should not fly off the handle easily. We should not try to get even with people when they have wronged us. Instead we should display what someone has called "a kind of conquering patience."

When Corrie and Betsie ten Boom were enduring indescribable sufferings in the concentration camp, Betsie would often say that they must help these people after they were released. They simply had to find a way to help them. Corrie thought, of course, that her sister was planning some program to rehabilitate the victims of the Nazis. It wasn't till later that Corrie realized that Betsie meant her persecutors. She wanted to find some way to teach them to love. Corrie commented, "And I wondered, not for the first time, what sort of a person she was, this sister of mine...what kind of road she followed while I trudged beside her on the all-too-solid earth" (*The Hiding Place,* p. 175).

The road Betsie followed was the road of longsuffering. And Corrie walked it too, in spite of her humble disclaimer.

March 6

The fruit of the Spirit is...kindness...
GALATIANS 5:22

 he King James Version has the word "gentleness" here but almost all modern versions read "kindness." "The fruit of the Spirit is...kindness."

Kindness describes the gentle, gracious, generous disposition that results in the doing of favors, the showing of mercies, and the bestowing of benefits on others. The kind person is gracious, not harsh; sympathetic, not indifferent; and helpful, not uninvolved. He is considerate, compassionate, and charitable.

There is a natural kindness which even the people of the world show to one another. But the kindness which is produced by the Spirit is supernatural. It goes above and beyond anything that man is capable of doing by himself. It enables a believer to lend, hoping for nothing in return. It enables him to show hospitality to those who cannot repay him. It enables him to reward every insult with a courtesy. A Christian university student displayed this supernatural kindness toward another student who was an alcoholic. The latter had become so disgusting that he had been rejected by his classmates and finally was evicted from his quarters. The Christian had an extra bed in his room and so invited the drunk to live with him. Many nights the believer had to clean up his roommate's vomit, take his clothes off, bathe him and put him to bed. It was a magnificent display of Christian kindness.

And—to complete the story—it paid off. Once, during a sober period, the dissolute fellow asked with irritation, "Say, look here, why are you doing all this for me? What are you after?" The Christian replied, "I'm after your soul"—and he got it.

When Dr. Ironside was cleaning out the cellar one day, he called a Jewish junk dealer to cart away the papers, magazines, rags and scrap metal. Dr. Ironside pretended to bargain seriously for a good price for the junk, but the junk man won, of course. When he was taking the last load out to his truck, kindly H. A. I. called him back, saying, "Oh, I forgot something. I want to give you this in the Name of the Lord Jesus." And handed him fifty cents, a substantial amount in those days.

The junk dealer went away, saying, "No one ever gave me anything in the Name of Jesus before."

"The fruit of the Spirit is...kindness...."

March 7

The fruit of the Spirit is...goodness....
GALATIANS 5:22

Goodness means excellence of character. Someone has defined it as "virtue equipped at every point," which simply means that the person possessing it is kind, virtuous, and righteous in every area of life.

Goodness is the opposite of badness. A bad man may be deceitful, immoral, treacherous, unjust, cruel, selfish, hateful, covetous, and/or intemperate. The good man, though not perfect, exemplifies truth, justice, purity, and other similarly desirable traits.

The Apostle Paul distinguishes between a righteous man and a good man in Romans 5:7. The righteous man is just, honest, and straightforward in his dealings, but he may be icily detached from others. The good man, on the other hand, is affectionate and lovable. One would scarcely die for a righteous man, but one might die for a good man.

And yet we must remember that goodness can be firm. It would not be good to condone or overlook sin. And so goodness can rebuke, correct, and discipline. We see this when the Lord Jesus, who is goodness Incarnate, cleansed the Temple.

A unique feature of goodness is that it can overcome evil. Paul wrote to the Roman believers, "Do not be overcome by evil, but overcome evil with good" (Rom. 12:21). When we allow someone else's hatred to ruin our disposition, we have been overcome by his evil. But when we rise above it and show grace, mercy, and love, we have overcome evil with good.

Murdoch Campbell tells of a godly Highland minister whose wife tried to make life miserable for him. One day as he was reading his Bible, she snatched it from his hands and threw it in the fire! He looked up into her face and said quietly, "I don't think I've ever sat by a warmer fire." His goodness overcame her evil. She became a lovely, gracious wife. As Campbell comments, "His Jezebel became a Lydia. His thorn became a lily." Goodness had conquered!

March 8

The fruit of the Spirit is...faithfulness....
GALATIANS 5:22

T his is not the faith that saves, or the trust we exercise in God day by day (although it may include that). Rather it is our fidelity and dependability in our dealings with the Lord and with one another. Someone has defined it as being "true to oneself, to one's nature, to any promise given, to any trust committed."

When we say that a man's word is his bond, we mean that in dealing with him, no written contract is necessary. If he has agreed to do something, he can be depended on to do it.

The faithful man keeps appointments on time, pays his bills on schedule, attends the meetings of the local fellowship regularly, performs tasks assigned to him without having to be constantly reminded. He is unswervingly true to his marriage vows and unfailing in the discharge of his family responsibilities. He is conscientious in setting money aside for the work of the Lord and careful also in his stewardship of time and talents.

Faithfulness means being true to one's word, even at great personal cost. The faithful man "swears to his own hurt, and does not change" (Ps. 15:4c, NASB). In other words, he does not cancel one supper engagement when he receives another that promises a better menu or more congenial company. He does not renege on a work assignment to go on a recreational trip (unless he first arranges for a satisfactory substitute). He sells his house at the agreed price even if someone later offers him $10,000 more.

The ultimate in faithfulness is being willing to die rather than renounce one's loyalty to Christ. When the king demanded that a faithful Christian retract his confession of Christ, the man replied, "The heart thought it; the mouth spoke it; the hand subscribed it; and if need be, by God's grace the blood shall seal it." When Polycarp was offered life in exchange for a denial of the Lord, he chose rather to be burned at the stake, saying, "These eighty-six years have I served my Lord. He never did me any harm, and I cannot deny my Lord and Master now."

The martyrs were faithful unto death, and will receive crown of life (Rev. 2:10).

March 9

The fruit of the Spirit is...meekness....
GALATIANS 5:23, KJV

W hen we think of meekness, we are apt to think of Caspar Milquetoast, the comic strip character who was the embodiment of timidity and weakness. But this fruit of the Spirit is something very different. It comes from supernatural power, not from weakness.

It refers first of all to a believer's loving submission to all God's dealings in his life. The meek man bows to the will of God without rebellion, questioning, or complaint. He reckons that "God is too wise to err and too loving to be unkind." Realizing that there is no chance or accident, he believes that God is working everything together for good in his life.

Meekness also includes the believer's relationship with others. Here he is self-effacing, not self-assertive and humble, not haughty. The meek man is one who practices brokenness. When he has said or done something wrong, he conquers pride by saying, "I am sorry. Please forgive me!" He would rather lose face than self-respect. When he suffers for doing what is right, he endures it patiently without any thought of fighting back. When he is falsely accused, he refrains from defending himself. As Trench says, the meek man accepts the injuries and insults of others as permitted by God for his chastening and purifying.

Someone has defined a meek man as "one who accepts the will of God without resentment, who can afford to be gentle and mild because of inward strength, and who is under the perfect control of God." When a parishioner told Dr. Alexander Whyte that a fellow minister was being castigated as an unbeliever, Dr. Whyte blazed with indignation. When the parishioner added that the critic said that Dr. Whyte himself was not a true believer, he said, "Please leave the office so that I can be alone and examine my heart before the Lord." That is meekness.

We are all called to take the yoke of Him who is "meek and lowly in heart." As we do so, we find rest for our souls and will ultimately inherit the earth.

March 10

The fruit of the Spirit is...self-control.
GALATIANS 5:23

 emperance has become associated particularly with restraint in the use of intoxicating drinks. Self-control carries the thought of moderation or abstinence in every area of life.

By the power of the Holy Spirit, the believer is enabled to exercise self-control over his thought life, his appetite for food and drink, his speech, his sex life, his temper, and every other power that God has given him. He need not be enslaved by any passion or desire.

Paul reminded the Corinthians that an athlete practices self-control in all things (1 Cor. 9:25). He himself was determined that he would not be enslaved by anything (1 Cor. 6:12) and so he pommeled his body and subdued it, lest after preaching to others, he himself should be disqualified (see 1 Cor. 9:27, RSV).

The disciplined Christian avoids overeating. If coffee, tea or Coke have a grip on him, he kicks the habit. He refuses to be mastered by tobacco in any form. He carefully avoids the use of tranquilizers, sleeping pills or other pharmaceuticals, except where medically prescribed. He controls the time given to sleeping. If he is plagued by the problem of lust, he learns to expel impure thoughts, concentrate on a clean thought life, and keep busy with constructive activity. To him every addiction or besetting sin is a Goliath to be conquered.

We often hear Christians complain that they can't break a certain habit. Such defeatism guarantees failure. It means that the Holy Spirit is not able to give the needed victory. The fact is that unconverted people, who do not have the Spirit, are often able to quit smoking or drinking or gambling or swearing. How much more easily should Christians be able to do it through the indwelling Spirit!

Self-control, like the other eight fruits of the Spirit, is supernatural. It enables believers to exercise discipline over themselves in ways that others cannot match.

March 11

Make friends quickly with your opponent at law while you are with him on the way; in order that your opponent may not deliver you to one judge, and the judge to the officer, and you be thrown into prison.

Matthew 5:25, NASB

One of the surface lessons we learn from this passage is that Christians should not be prone to engage in lawsuits. It is a natural reaction to rush to court to seek redress for grievances and damages. But the believer is guided by higher principles than natural reactions. The will of God often cuts across the grain of nature.

Our law courts today are glutted with accident claims, malpractice suits, divorce cases, and inheritance claims. In many cases, people rush to the lawyer in the hope of getting rich quick. But the Christian must settle things by the power of love and not by the processes of law. As someone has said, "If you go in for legal processes, then legal processes will get you, and you will pay the last penny."

The only one who is sure to win is the lawyer; his fee is assured. A cartoon pictured the process this way: A plaintiff was pulling the head of a cow, the defendant was pulling the tail—and the lawyer was milking the cow. In 1 Corinthians 6 Christians are positively forbidden to go to law against other Christians. For one thing, they should take their disputes to some wise man in the church. But even beyond that, they should be willing to be wronged and cheated rather than go to law before the judges of this world's system. This, incidentally, would rule out all cases of divorce involving believing partners.

But what about cases between a believer and an unbeliever? Doesn't the Christian have to stand up for his rights? The answer is that it is far better to forego his rights in order to demonstrate that Christ makes a difference in a person's life. It does not require divine life to institute a suit against someone who has wronged him. But it does take divine life to commit his cause to God and use the case as an opportunity to witness to the saving, transforming power of Christ. As much as possible, he should live at peace with all men (Rom. 12:18).

"A man started to build a fence between himself and his neighbor. The neighbor came and said; 'When you bought that lot you bought a court case along with it. That fence is going to be five feet in my land.' The man replied, 'I knew I would always have a nice neighbor next to me. I'll tell you what I suggest: You put up the fence where you think it should go, send me the bill and I'll pay for it.' The fence was never put up. No need!" (E. STANLEY JONES).

79

March 12

Inasmuch as you did it to one of the least of these My brethren, you did it to Me.
MATTHEW 25:40

 ere is both a rewarding encouragement and a warning that should bring us up short. Whatever we do to Christ's brethren is reckoned as being done unto Himself.

We can show kindness to the Lord Jesus any day by showing kindness to a fellow-believer. When we show hospitality to God's people, it is the same as if we entertain Him in our homes. If we give them the master bedroom, we are giving it to Him...

Almost anyone would be quick to do everything possible for the Savior if He came as King of kings and Lord of lords. But He commonly comes to our door in very humble guise, and it is this that puts us to the test. The way we treat the least of His brethren is the way we treat Him.

A godly old preacher visited an assembly in hopes of being able to share with the saints from the Word. He did not have personal charisma and may not have had a dynamic pulpit style. But he was a servant of God and did have a message from the Lord. The elders told him that they could not ask him to stay for meetings and suggested that he go to a meeting in the black ghetto. He did, and was warmly received by the brethren there. During his week of meetings, he took a heart attack and died. It was as if the Lord was saying to the brothers in the fashionable assembly, "You may not have wanted him but I did. In refusing him you refused Me."

In his poem, "How the Great Guest Came," Edwin Markham tells of an old cobbler who made elaborate preparations for a dreamed-of visit from the Lord. The Lord never came. But when a beggar came, the cobbler put shoes on his feet. When an old lady came, the cobbler helped her with her load and gave her food. When a lost child came, the cobbler took her back to her mother.

> *Then soft in the silence a voice he heard:*
> *Lift up your heart, for I kept My word.*
> *Three times I came to your friendly door;*
> *Three times my shadow was on your floor.*
> *I was the beggar with bruised feet,*
> *I was the woman you gave to eat,*
> *I was the child in the homeless street.*

March 13

Take heed what you hear.
MARK 4:24

he Lord Jesus cautions us to be careful what we hear. We are responsible to control what enters through the eargate, and equally responsible to put what we do hear to proper use.

We should not listen to what is blatantly false. The cults are spewing out their propaganda in unprecedented volume. They are always looking for someone who is willing to listen. John says we should not receive cultists into our house or even greet them. They are against Christ.

We should not listen to what is deceitfully subversive. Young people in colleges, universities, and seminaries are often subjected to a daily barrage of doubts and denials concerning the Word of God. They hear the miracles explained away, the Lord Jesus condemned with faint praise and the plain meaning of Scripture watered down. It is impossible to sit under subversive teaching and not be affected by it. Even if the student's faith is not destroyed, his mind is defiled. "Can a man take fire in his bosom, and his clothes not be burned? Or can a man walk on hot coals, and his feet not be scorched?" (Prov. 6:27-28, NASB). The obvious answer is "No."

We should not listen to what is impure or suggestive. The worst form of pollution in today's society is mind pollution. The one word that describes most newspapers, magazines, books, radio and TV programs, movies, and human conversations is filth. Through constant exposure to this, the Christian is in danger of losing his sense of the exceeding sinfulness of sin. And that is not the only danger! When we receive vile and suggestive stories in our minds, they have a way of coming back to haunt us during our most holy moments.

We should not fill our minds with things that are worthless or trifling. Life is too short and the task too urgent for that. "All must be earnest in a world like ours."

Positively, we should be careful to hear the Word of God. The more we saturate our minds with the Word of God and obey its sacred precepts, the more we will think God's thoughts after Him, the more we will be transformed into the image of Christ, and the more we will be separated from the moral pollution of our environment.

March 14

Therefore take heed how you hear.
LUKE 8:18

In the Christian life it is a question not only of what we hear but also of how we hear.

It is possible to hear the Word of God with an attitude of indifference. We can read the Bible as we would read any other book, seemingly unconcerned that the Almighty God is speaking to us in it.

We can hear with a critical attitude. Here we put human intellect above the Scriptures. We sit in judgment on the Bible instead of letting the Bible judge us.

We can hear with a rebellious attitude. When we come to portions that deal with the stern demands of discipleship or with women's subjection and headcovering, we become enraged and utterly refuse to obey.

We can be forgetful hearers, like the man in the Book of James "who looks at his natural face in a mirror; for once he has looked at himself and gone away, he has immediately forgotten what kind of person he was" (1:23-24, NASB).

Perhaps the most common class is the callous hearers. These people have heard the Word so much that they have become insensitive. They listen to a sermon mechanically. It has become a ho-hum routine. Their ears are jaded. Their attitude is, "What can you tell me that I haven't already heard?"

The more we hear the Word of God without obeying what we hear, the more we become judicially deafened. If we refuse to hear, we lose the capacity to hear.

The best way to hear is to hear reverently, obediently, and seriously. We should approach the Bible with the determination to do what it says, even if no one else is doing it. The wise man is the one who not only hears but does. God is looking for men who tremble at His Word (Isa. 66:2).

Paul commended the Thessalonians because when they heard the Word of God, they did not receive it "as the word of men, but as it is in truth" (1 Thess. 2:13). In the same manner, we should be careful how we hear.

March 15

For whoever desires to save his life will lose it,
but whoever loses his life for My sake will save it.
LUKE 9:24

Basically there are two attitudes we believers can take toward our life. We can try to save it or we can purposefully lose it for Christ's sake.

The natural thing is to try to save it. We can live a self-centered life, trying to protect ourselves from effort and inconvenience. We can make careful plans to cushion ourselves from shocks, to guard against loss, to avoid any form of discomfort. Our house becomes like a private estate posted with "No Trespassing" signs. It is for the family only—with minimal hospitality shown to others. Our decisions are made on the basis of how things will affect us. If they disrupt our plans or involve a lot of work or require expenditure of funds to help others, we turn thumbs down. We tend to devote inordinate attention to our personal health, refusing any service that might call for sleepless nights, for contact with sickness, or death, or any physical risks. We also give a higher priority to personal appearance than to the needs of those around us. In short, we live to cater to the body, which, in a few short years, will be eaten by worms if the Lord doesn't come.

In trying to save our life, we lose it. We suffer all the miseries of a selfish existence and miss out on all the blessings of living for others.

The alternative is to lose our life for Christ's sake. This is a life of service and of sacrifice. While we do not take needless risks or court martyrdom, we do not turn away from duty with the plea that we have to live at all cost. There is a sense in which we "fling our soul and body down for God to plow them under." We count it our greatest joy to spend and be spent for Him. Our home is open, our possessions are expendable, our time is available to those in need.

In thus pouring out our lives for Christ and for others, we find life that is life indeed. In losing our lives, we actually save them.

March 16

For I say to you, that to everyone who has will be given; and from him who does not have, even what he has will be taken away from him.
Luke 19:26

T he word "has" at the beginning of this verse means more than mere possession. It includes the idea of obeying what we have been taught and of using what we have been given. In other words, it is not just what we have but rather what we do with what we have.

Here is a great principle for us, then, in the study of the Bible. As we follow the light which we receive, God gives us more light. The man who makes the best progress in the Christian life is the one who is determined to do what the Bible says, even if he doesn't see anyone else around him doing it. In other words, it isn't a matter of one's intelligence quotient. What really counts is his obedience quotient. The Scriptures open up their treasures most readily to the obedient heart. Hosea said it well: "Let us know, let us pursue the knowledge of the Lord" (6:3). The more we practice what we have been taught, the more the Lord will reveal to us. Information plus application leads to multiplication. Information without application leads to stagnation.

The principle applies also to the use of our gifts and talents. The man whose pound increased to ten pounds was given authority over ten cities, and the man whose talent gained five pounds was given rule over five cities (Mk. 25:16-19).

This shows that the proper discharge of our responsibilities is rewarded with greater privileges and responsibilities. The man who did nothing with his pound lost it. So those who refuse to use what they have for the Lord eventually lose the ability to do so. "If you don't use it, you lose it."

We know that when we fail to use any part of the body, it atrophies or wastes away. It is through constant use that normal development takes place. So it is in spiritual life. If we bury our gift, either through timidity or laziness, we will soon find that God has put us on the shelf and is using others in our place.

Therefore it is of utmost importance that we obey the precepts of Scripture, claim the promises and use whatever abilities God has given us.

March 17

Do not be like the horse or like the mule.
PSALM 32:9

It seems to me that the horse and the mule picture two wrong attitudes we might have when we are seeking the Lord's guidance. The horse wants to charge ahead; the mule wants to lag behind. The horse tends to be impatient, high-spirited, and impetuous. The mule, on the other hand, is stubborn, intractable, and lazy. The psalmist says that neither animal has understanding. Both have to be controlled by bit and bridle, otherwise they will not come near to their master.

God's desire is that we be sensitive to His leading, not plunging ahead in our own wisdom, and not holding back when He has shown His will.

Here are a few rules-of-thumb that might be helpful in this regard.

Ask God to confirm His guidance in the mouths of two or three witnesses. He has said, "By the mouth of two or three witnesses every word may be established." (Mt. 18:16b). These witnesses may include a verse of Scripture, the counsel of other Christians, and the marvelous converging of circumstances. If you get two or three distinct indications of His will, you will not have any doubts or misgivings.

If you are seeking God's guidance and no guidance comes, then God's guidance is for you to stay where you are. It is still true that "darkness about going is light about staying."

Wait until the guidance is so clear that to refuse would be positive disobedience. The children of Israel were forbidden to move until the pillar of cloud and fire moved. No rationalizations on their part could excuse independent action. Their responsibility was to move when the cloud moved—not sooner and not later.

Finally, let the peace of Christ umpire in your heart. That is a free translation of Colossians 3:15. It means that when God is really guiding, He so influences our intellects and emotions that we have peace about the right way and no peace about any other way.

If we are anxious to know the divine will, and quick to obey it, we will not need the bit and bridle of God's discipline.

March 18

Do not merely look out for your own personal interests,
but also for the interests of others.
PHILIPPIANS 2:4, NASB

T he key word in Philippians 2 is "others." The Lord Jesus lived for others. Paul lived for others. Timothy lived for others. Epaphroditus lived for others. We too should live for others. We are told to do this not only because it is right but also because it is for our own good. If it is sometimes costly to live for others, it is more costly not to do so.

Our society is filled with people who live only for their own personal interests. Rather than keeping busy in serving others, they sit at home brooding. They think about every minor ache and pain and soon become confirmed hypochondriacs. In their loneliness they complain that no one takes an interest in them and soon they wallow in self-pity. The more time they have to think about themselves, the more depressed they become. Life becomes one great introspective horror of darkness. Soon they go off to the doctor and gulp enormous quantities of pills—pills that can never cure self-centeredness. Then they frequent the psychiatrist's couch to somehow find relief for their boredom and weariness with life.

The best therapy for people like that is a life of service for others. There are shut-ins to be visited. There are senior citizens who need a friend. There are hospitals that welcome volunteer help. There are people who could be cheered by a letter or a card. There are missionaries who welcome news from home (and perhaps they could use a little greenery to brighten up the scenery). There are souls to be saved and Christians to be taught. In short, there is no excuse for anyone to be bored. There is enough to do to fill one's life with productive activity. And in the very process of living for others, we widen our circle of friends, make our own lives more interesting, and find fulfillment and satisfaction. P. M. Derham said, "A heart that is full of compassion for others is less likely to be absorbed in its own sorrows and poisoned by its own self pity."

Others, yes, Lord, others,
Let this my motto be;
Help me to live for others
That I may live like Thee.

March 19

Curse Meroz, said the angel of the Lord, Curse its inhabitants bitterly,
because they did not come to the help of the Lord,
to the help of the Lord against the mighty.
JUDGES 5:23

T he Song of Deborah rehearses the curse on Meroz for staying on the sidelines while the army of Israel was locked in combat with the Canaanites. The people of Reuben also come in for withering scorn; they had good intentions but never left the sheepfolds—Gilead, Asher, and Dan receive dishonorable mention for their non-intervention.

Dante said, "The hottest places in hell are reserved for those who remain neutral in a time of great moral crisis."

The same sentiments are echoed in the book of Proverbs, where we read, "Deliver those who are drawn toward death, and hold back those stumbling to the slaughter. If you say, 'Surely we did not know this,' does not He who weighs the hearts consider it? He who keeps your soul, does He not know it? And will He not render to each man according to his deeds?" (Prov. 24:11-12). Kidner comments, "It is the hireling, not the true shepherd, who will plead bad conditions (10), hopeless tasks (10) and pardonable ignorance (12); love is not so lightly quieted—nor is the God of love."

What would we do if a great wave of anti-Semitism swept over our country, if Jewish people were herded off to concentration camps, to gas chambers, to ovens? Would we risk our own lives in order to grant them asylum?

Or if some of our fellow-Christians were being persecuted, and if it was a capital offense to shelter them, would we welcome them into our homes? What would we do?

Or perhaps we could take a less heroic but more contemporary case. Suppose you are a director of a Christian organization where a faithful employee is being railroaded to satisfy the spleen of another director who is wealthy, and influential. When the final vote is taken, would you sit on your hands and remain silent?

Suppose we had been on the Sanhedrin when Jesus was tried, or at the Cross when He was crucified? Would we have been neutral or would we have identified ourselves with Him?

"Silence is not always golden; sometimes it is just plain yellow."

March 20

Father, I have sinned.
LUKE 15:21

1 t was not until the prodigal son returned repentant that the father ran out to meet him, fell on his neck and kissed him. It would not have been righteous to administer forgiveness until first there was repentance. The scriptural principle is, "…if he repents, forgive him" (Lk. 17:3).

There is no record that the father sent help to the prodigal as long as he was in the far country. Actually, to have done so would have been to obstruct the work of God in the rebel's life. The Lord's goal was to bring the wayward one down to the dregs. He knew that the son had to come to the end of himself, that he would never look up until first he had hit bottom. The sooner the wanderer got to the husks, the sooner he would be ready to break. So the father had to commit his son to the Lord, and wait for the crisis of extremity.

This is one of the hardest things for parents to do—especially for mothers. The natural tendency is to bail out a rebellious son or daughter from every emergency that the Lord sends along. But all that such parents succeed in doing is hinder the Lord in His purpose and prolong the agony for the loved one.

Spurgeon once said, "The truest love to those who err is not to fraternize with them in their error but to be faithful to Jesus in all things." It is not love to indulge a person in his wickedness. Love rather turns the person over to the Lord and prays, "Lord, restore him, no matter what the cost may be."

One of the biggest mistakes David made was bringing Absalom back before there was any repentance. Before long, Absalom was winning the hearts of the people and plotting a revolt against his father. Finally he drove his father from Jerusalem and was anointed king in his place. Even when he set out with his army to destroy David, the latter instructed his men to spare Absalom in the event of a confrontation. But Joab thought better of it and slew Absalom.

Parents who are willing to bear the pain of watching God reduce their son or daughter to life in the pigpen are often spared a greater sorrow.

March 21

Surely the wrath of man shall praise You;
with the remainder of wrath You shall gird Yourself.
PSALM 76:10

O
ne of the fascinating features of human history is the way in which God makes man's wrath praise Him. Ever since the Fall, man has shaken the fist against God, against His people and against His cause. Instead of judging such wrath on the spot, the Lord lets it work itself out, harnessing it for His glory and for the blessing of His people.

A group of men devised evil against their brother, selling him to a band of nomads who took him to Egypt. God raised him up to be second in power and the savior of his people. Joseph later reminded his brothers, "You meant evil against me; but God meant it for good" (Gen. 50:20, NASB).

Haman's rage against the Jews resulted in his own destruction and in the exaltation of those he sought to destroy.

Three young Hebrews were thrown into a furnace of fire so hot that it consumed those who threw them in. But the Hebrews emerged unscathed and without even the smell of smoke on them. The heathen king then decreed death for anyone who said a word against the God of the Jews.

Daniel was cast into the den of lions for praying to the God of heaven. But his miraculous deliverance resulted in another decree by his pagan ruler, demanding reverence and respect for the God of Daniel.

Coming over to the New Testament era, the persecution of the church resulted in the more rapid dissemination of the gospel. The martyrdom of Stephen had within it the seeds of Saul's conversion. The imprisonment of Paul produced four letters that became part of the Holy Bible.

Later, the ashes of John Hus were thrown into the river, and everywhere the river flowed, the gospel followed shortly thereafter.

Men tear up the Bible and throw it to the wind, but someone picks up a random page, reads it and is gloriously saved. Men scoff at the doctrine of Christ's second coming, and thereby fulfill the prophecy that scoffers will come in the last days (2 Pet. 3:3-4).

So God makes the wrath of man to praise Him—and what won't praise Him He restrains.

March 22

You did well that it was in your heart.
1 KINGS 8:18

O
ne of the great desires of David's heart was to build a Temple for Jehovah in Jerusalem. The Lord sent word that he would not be permitted to build the Temple because he was a man of war, but the Lord added these significant words, "You did well that it was in your heart." It seems clear from this that God counts the desire for the act when we are unable to carry out our desires for Him.

This does not apply when our failure to perform is due to our own procrastination or inaction. Here the desire is not enough. As has been said, the streets of hell are paved with good intentions.

But there are many occasions in the Christian life when we want to do something to please the Lord but are prevented by circumstances beyond our control. A young convert, for instance, desires to be baptized but is forbidden by unbelieving parents. In such a case, God counts his unbaptism for baptism until he leaves home and can obey the Lord without being insubordinate to his parents.

A Christian wife desires to attend all the meetings of the local assembly but her drunken husband insists that she stay at home. The Lord rewards both her subjection to her husband and her desire to meet with others in His Name.

An aged sister wept as she watched others serving meals at a Bible Conference. It had been her great joy to do this for years, but now she was physically unable. As far as God is concerned she receives as rich a reward for her tears as the others do for their labors.

Who knows how many there are who have willingly offered themselves for service on the mission fields, yet they were never able to travel beyond their own hometown? God knows—and all of these holy aspirations will be rewarded at the Judgment Seat of Christ.

The principle also applies in the matter of giving. There are those who are already investing sacrificially in the work of the Lord and just wish they could give more. In a coming day, the divine ledger will show that they did give more.

The ill, the handicapped, the shut-ins, the aged, are not cut off from first-place honors, because in His mercy, God judges us, not only by our achievements, but by our dreams.

March 23

Nor will I offer burnt offerings to the Lord my God
with that which costs me nothing.
2 SAMUEL 24:24

hen David was instructed to offer burnt offerings where the Lord had stopped the pestilence, Araunah offered as an outright gift a threshing floor, oxen, and wood for the fire. But David insisted on buying these things. He would not offer to the Lord something that cost him nothing.

We know that it costs nothing to become a Christian, but we should also know that a life of genuine discipleship costs plenty. "A religion that costs nothing is worth nothing."

Too often the extent of our commitment is determined by considerations of convenience, cost, and comfort. Yes, we'll go to the prayer meeting if we aren't tired or if we don't have a headache. Yes, we'll teach the Bible Class as long as it doesn't conflict with a weekend in the mountains.

It makes us nervous to pray in public, to give a testimony, to preach the gospel—therefore, we remain silent. We have no desire to help at the rescue mission for fear of picking up lice or fleas. We shut out any thought of the mission field because of a horror of snakes or spiders.

Our giving is too often a tip instead of a sacrifice. We give what we will never miss—unlike the widow who gave all. Our hospitality is determined by the measure of expense, inconvenience and mess to our homes—unlike the soul winner who said that every rug in his house has been stained by drunks throwing up on them. Our availability to people in need ceases when we lie down on our water bed—unlike the elder who was willing to be roused at any time in order to be of spiritual or material assistance.

Very often when the call of Christ comes to us, we are prone to ask ourselves, "What's in it for me?" or "Will it pay?" The question is rather, "Is this an offering that really costs?" It has been well said, "It is better in the spiritual life that things should cost than that they should pay."

When we think of what our redemption cost our Savior, it seems a poor return that we should hold back from cost and sacrifice for Him.

March 24

To each one of us grace was given
according to the measure of Christ's gift.
EPHESIANS 4:7

 e must always remember that whenever the Lord tells us to do something, He gives us the needed power. All His commands include His
enablement, even when His commands are in the realm of the
impossible.

Jethro said to Moses, "If you do this thing, and God so commands you, then
you will be able to endure, and all this people will also go to their place in peace"
(Ex. 18:23). "The principle is that God assumes full responsibility for enabling
His man to fulfill every task to which He has appointed him" (J. O. SANDERS).

In His ministry, the Lord Jesus met at least two men who were paralyzed (Mt.
9:6; Jn. 5:9). On both occasions He told them to get up and carry their pad. As
they exercised the will to obey, power flowed into their helpless limbs.

Peter sensed that if the Lord Jesus called him to come on the water, then he
could walk on water. As soon as Jesus said, "Come," Peter went down out of the
ship and walked on the water.

It is doubtful that the man with the withered hand could stretch it out; yet when
our Lord told him to do it, he did and the hand was restored.

The idea of feeding 5,000 with a few loaves and fishes is out of the question.
But whenever Jesus said to the disciples, "Give them to eat," the impossibility
vanished.

Lazarus had lain in the grave for four days when Jesus called, "Lazarus, come
forth." The command was accompanied by the necessary power. Lazarus came
forth.

We should appropriate this truth. When God leads us, we should never cop out
with the plea that we can't do it. If He tells us to do something, He will supply the
power. It has been well said, "The will of God will never lead you where the grace
of God will not sustain you."

It is equally true that when God orders something, He pays for what He orders.
If we are sure of His leading, we need not worry about the finances. He will
provide.

The God who opened the Red Sea and the Jordan so that His people could pass
over is the same today. He is still in the business of removing impossibilities when
His people obey His will. He still supplies all needed grace to do whatever He
commands. He still works in us both to will and to do of His good pleasure.

March 25

In the beginning God...
GENESIS 1:1

1 f we separate the first four words of Genesis 1:1 from the rest of the verse, they form a sort of motto for all of life. They say, "God first."

We find this motto suggested in the first commandment, "You shall have no other gods before Me." No one and nothing must take the place of the true and living God.

We find it taught in the story of Elijah and the widow who had only enough flour and oil left to make one final loaf for her son and herself (1 Ki. 17:12). Surprisingly, Elijah said, "Make me a little loaf first." Though this might sound like gross selfishness, it wasn't. Elijah was a representative of God. He was saying, "Just put God first and your supply of the necessities of life will never fail."

The Lord Jesus taught the same thing centuries later on the Mount when He said, "Seek first the kingdom of God and His righteousness, and all these things shall be added to you" (Mt. 6:33). The central priority of life is the kingdom of God and His righteousness.

Again the Savior asserted His prior claim in Luke 14:26, "If anyone comes to Me and does not hate his father and mother, wife and children, brothers and sisters, yes, and his own life also, he cannot be My disciple." Christ must have first place.

But how do we put God first? We have our family to care for. We have our secular employment to think of. We have a multitude of duties crying out for our time and resources. We put God first by loving Him with a love beside which all other loves are hatred in comparison. By using all material things as a trust from Him, holding onto only those things which can be used in connection with His kingdom. By giving top priority to matters of eternal consequences, remembering that even good things are sometimes enemies of the best.

Man's best interests lie in a right relationship with God. The right relationship is when God is given first place. Even when man puts God first, he will have some problems, but he will find fulfillment in life. But when he puts God second, he will have nothing but problems—and a miserable existence.

March 26

What is that to you? You follow Me.
JOHN 21:22

The Lord Jesus had just told Peter that he would live to be an old man, and then die a martyr's death. Peter immediately looked across at John and wondered out loud if John would receive preferred treatment. The Lord's reply was, "What is that to you? You follow Me."

Peter's attitude reminds us of the words of Dag Hammarskjold: "In spite of everything, your bitterness because others are enjoying what you are denied is always ready to flare tip. At best it may lie dormant for a couple of sunny days. Yet, even at this unspeakably shabby level, it is still an expression of the real bitterness of death—the fact that others are allowed to go on living."

If we would take to heart the words of the Lord, they would solve many a problem among Christian people.

It is so easy to become resentful when we see others prospering more than we are. The Lord allows them to have a new home, a new car, a cottage by the lake.

Others whom we might consider less devoted have good health while we battle two or three chronic ailments.

That other family has fine looking children who excel in athletics and in academics. Our children are the common, garden variety.

We see other believers doing things that we don't have liberty to do. Even if the things are not sinful, we become resentful at their liberty.

Sad to say, there is a certain amount of professional jealousy among Christian workers. One preacher is offended because another is more popular, has more friends, is more in the public eye. Or another is piqued because his colleague uses methods he does not approve.

To all of these unworthy attitudes, the words of the Lord come with striking forcefulness, "What is that to you? You follow Me." How the Lord deals with other Christians is really none of our business. Our responsibility is to follow Him in whatever pathway He has marked out for us.

March 27

The wind blows where it wishes.
JOHN 3:8

The Spirit of God is sovereign. He moves as He pleases. We try to pour Him into our particular mold, but our attempts are invariably frustrated.

Most of the types of the Holy Spirit are fluid—wind, fire, oil, and water. We may try to hold these in our hands but they have a way of saying, "Don't fence me in."

The Holy Spirit will never do anything that is morally wrong, but in other areas He reserves the right to act in exceptional and unconventional ways. For example, while it is true that God has given headship to man, we cannot say that the Holy Spirit cannot raise up a Deborah to lead God's people if He wishes.

In days of declension, the Spirit permits behavior that ordinarily would be forbidden. Thus David and his men were allowed to eat the showbread, which was reserved exclusively for the priests. And the disciples were justified in plucking grain on the Sabbath day.

People say that there is a definite, predictable pattern of evangelism in the Book of Acts, but the only pattern I can see is the sovereignty of the Holy Spirit.

The apostles and others did not follow a textbook; they followed His leading, which was often quite different from what common sense would have dictated.

For instance, we see the Spirit leading Philip to leave a successful revival in Samaria in order to witness to a lone Ethiopian eunuch on the road to Gaza.

In our own day, we must guard against dictating to the Holy Spirit what He can and cannot do. We know that He will never do anything that is sinful. But in other areas He can be counted on to do the extraordinary. He is not limited to a certain set of methods. He is not bound by our traditional ways of doing things. He has a way of protesting against formalism, ritualism, and deadness by raising up new movements with reviving power. We should therefore be open to this sovereign working of the Holy Spirit and not be found sitting on the sidelines, criticizing.

March 28

The hatred with which he hated her
was greater than the love with which he had loved her.
2 Samuel 13:15

Amnon burned with lust for his half-sister, Tamar. She was beautiful, and he was determined to have her. He was frustrated because he knew that what he wanted to do was clearly forbidden by the law of God. But he was so consumed by desire for her that no other considerations seemed important. So he pretended to be ill, lured her into his room and violated her. He was willing to sacrifice everything for that one moment of passion.

But then lust turned to hatred. After he had selfishly exploited her, he despised her and probably wished he had never seen her. He ordered her to be thrown out and the door locked behind her.

This vignette of history is being replayed every day. In our freewheeling society, moral standards have been largely abandoned. Premarital sex is accepted as normal. Couples live together without the formality of marriage. Prostitution is legalized. Homosexuality has become an accepted alternative lifestyle.

Young and old alike see someone they like and that settles it. They recognize no higher law. They are bound by no inhibitions. They are determined to get what they want. They wave off any thought of right or wrong, and rationalize that they cannot live a normal life in any other way. So they take the plunge, as Amnon did, and think that they have achieved fulfillment.

But what had looked so beautiful in prospect often looks very hideous in retrospect. Guilt is inevitable, no matter how hotly it is denied. A mutual loss of self-respect leads to resentment. That in turn often boils over into quarreling and then into hatred. The person who once seemed so indispensable is now positively repulsive. From there it is an easy step to beatings, court-battles, and even murder.

Lust lays a rotten foundation on which to build a lasting relationship. Men ignore God's law of purity to their own loss and destruction. Only the grace of God can bring forgiveness, healing, and restoration.

March 29

No one engaged in warfare entangles himself with the affairs of this life,
that he may please him who enlisted him as a soldier.
2 TIMOTHY 2:4

T he Christian has been enlisted by the Lord, and is on active service for Him. He must not entangle himself in the affairs of everyday life. The emphasis here is on the word entangle. He cannot completely divorce himself from worldly business. He must work in order to provide the necessities of life for his family. There is a certain amount of involvement in everyday interests that is unavoidable. Otherwise he would have to go out of the world, as Paul reminds us in 1 Corinthians 5:10.

But he mustn't allow himself to become entangled. He must keep his priorities straight. Even things that are good in themselves can sometimes become the enemies of the best.

Wm. Kelly says that "to entangle oneself in the businesses of life means really to give up separation from the world by taking one's part in outward affairs as a bona fide partner in it."

I have become entangled when I become involved in the world's politics as a means of solving man's problems. That would be like spending my time "rearranging the deck chairs on the Titanic."

Or I have become entangled when I put more emphasis on social service than on the gospel as a panacea for the world's ills.

I have become entangled when business gets such a grip on me that I give my best efforts to the making of money. In thus gaining a living, I lose a life.

I have become entangled when the kingdom of God and His righteousness cease to have first place in my life.

I have become entangled when I am caught up by things that are too small for a child of eternity—like the mineral deficiencies in the tomato and cocklebur, the summer habits of Wyoming antelope, the microbic content of cotton T-shirts, the browning reaction in potato chips or the post-rotational movements of a pigeon's eye. These studies may be all right as a means of livelihood but they aren't worthy of a life passion.

March 30

*And we know that God causes all things to work together for good
to those who love God, to those who are called according to His purpose.*
ROMANS 8:28, NASB

T his is one of those verses that perplex us most when the going is roughest. As long as the wind blows gently, we have no trouble saying, "Lord, I believe." But when the storms of life arise we say, "Help my unbelief!"

And yet we know the verse is true. God does work all things together for good. We know it because the Bible says it. Faith appropriates it, even when we cannot see or understand.

We know it is true because of the character of God. If He is a God of infinite wisdom and of infinite power, then it follows that He is planning and working for our highest good.

We know it is true because of the experience of God's people. In *Choice Gleanings* the story is told of an only survivor of a wreck who was thrown on an uninhabited island. He managed to build himself a hut, in which he placed all that he saved from the wreck. He prayed to God for deliverance and anxiously scanned the horizon each day to hail any passing ship. One day he was horrified to find his hut in flames; all he had went up in smoke. But that which seemed the worst was in reality the best. "We saw your smoke signal," said the captain of the ship that came to his rescue. Let us remember that if our lives are in God's hands, "All things work together for good."

Admittedly, there are times when faith falters, when the burden seems unendurable. We ask in our extremity, "What good can possibly come out of this?" There is an answer. The good that God is working out is found in the next verse (Rom. 8:29)—that we should be "conformed to the image of His Son." It is as the sculptor's chisel wastes away the marble that the image of the man appears. And it is as the blows of life chip away all that is unworthy in us that we become changed into His blessed likeness. So if you cannot find any good in the crises of life, remember this one—conformity to Christ.

March 31

Not a novice, lest being puffed up with pride
he fall into the same condemnation as the devil.
1 TIMOTHY 3:6

In listing the qualifications of an elder, the Apostle Paul cautions against the assumption of this work by one who is young in the faith. Overseership requires the wisdom and sound judgment that come only by spiritual maturity and godly experience. Yet how often this principle is violated! A successful young businessman, politician, or professional man comes into the fellowship of the local church. We feel that if we don't get him involved immediately, he might leave and go elsewhere, so we catapult him into a place of leadership. We would be better advised to follow Paul's dictum for deacons, "...let these also first be proved."

A more glaring violation of this spiritual principle is seen in the way that newly-converted stars are publicized and glamorized in the evangelical firmament. It may be a football hero who has just come to saving faith in Christ. Some religious promoter gets a hold of him and has him billed all the way from Dan to Beersheba. As soon as word gets out that a Hollywood actress has been born again, she becomes headline news. Her opinions are sought on everything from capital punishment to premarital sex—as if conversion has given her instant wisdom on all subjects. Now it is an ex-criminal who has come to know the Lord. One fears for him as he is exploited by covetous agents who are out for a fast buck.

Says Dr. Paul Van Gorder, "I have never been in favor of getting a sinner up from his knees and showing him off in front of a crowd. Irreparable harm has been done to the cause of Christ by parading noted figures of the entertainment, sports, and political world across the evangelical platform before sufficient time has elapsed to indicate whether the seed of the Word of God has penetrated and really taken root."

It probably gives some Christians a boost to their religious ego when a drug addict or a politician is heralded as the latest addition to the faith. Perhaps they suffer from feelings of insecurity or inferiority, and every converted celebrity helps to boost their sagging confidence.

But these exploited heroes and heroines often become sitting ducks for the Devil's potshot. Unaware of his subtle devices, they fall into sin and bring enormous reproach on the testimony of the Lord Jesus.

We are thankful for everyone who is genuinely saved, whether famous or obscure. But we are mistaken if we think we can best advance the cause of Christ by pushing novices to the pulpit or TV camera.

April 1

...in Him you have been made complete.
COLOSSIANS 2:10, NASB

C ontrary to popular opinion, there are no degrees of fitness for heaven. A person is either absolutely fit or he is not fit at all. This goes counter to the common notion that at the top of God's totem pole are good, clean-living people, at the bottom are the crooks and mobsters, and in between are those with varying degrees of fitness for heaven. It is an enormous mistake. We are either fit or we aren't. There is nothing in between.

Actually none of us is fit in himself. We are all guilty sinners, deserving eternal punishment. We have all sinned and come short of the glory of God. We have all gone astray and turned to our own way. We are all unclean, and all our best works are like filthy rags.

Not only are we totally unfit for heaven, but there is nothing we can do by ourselves to make us fit. Our best resolutions and noblest endeavors cannot avail to put away our sins or to provide us with the righteousness that God demands. But the good news is that God's love provides what His righteousness demands, and He provides it as a free gift. "It is the gift of God: not of works, lest anyone should boast" (Eph. 2:8-9).

Fitness for heaven is found in Christ. Whenever a sinner is born again, he receives Christ. God no longer sees him as a sinner in the flesh; He sees him in Christ, and accepts him on that basis. God has made Christ to be sin for us, He who knew no sin, that we might be made the righteousness of God in Him (see 2 Cor. 5:21).

So what it comes down to is this: Either we have Christ or we don't. If we have Christ, we are as fit for heaven as God can make us. Christ's fitness becomes ours. We are as worthy as He is, because we are in Him.

On the other hand, if we don't have Christ, we are as lost as we can possibly be. To be without Him is the fatal deficiency. Nothing else can ever make up for this crucial lack.

It should be clear then that no believer is any more fit for heaven than another believer. All believers have the same title to glory. That title is Christ. No believer has more of Christ than another. Therefore none is more fit for heaven than another.

April 2

For we must all appear before the judgment seat of Christ,
that each one may receive the things done in the body,
according to what he has done, whether good or bad.
2 CORINTHIANS 5:10

hile it is true, as we have seen on the previous page, that there are no degrees of fitness for heaven, it is also true that there will be degrees of reward in heaven. The Judgment Seat of Christ will be a place of review and reward where some will be rewarded more than others.

Also, there will be differing capacities for enjoying the glories of heaven. Everyone will be happy, but some will have greater capacity for happiness than others. Everyone's cup will be full, but some will have bigger cups than others.

We must get away from the idea that we will all be exactly alike when we reach the glorified state. The Bible nowhere teaches such dull, faceless uniformity. Rather it teaches that crowns will be awarded for lives of faithfulness and devotedness, and that while some are being rewarded, others will suffer loss.

Here are two young men who are the same age and who are converted at the same time. One goes out and lives the next forty years by giving top priority to the kingdom of God and His righteousness. The other gives the best of his life to making money. The first talks enthusiastically about the things of the Lord, the second about activity in the market. The first has a greater capacity for enjoying the Lord now, and he will take that greater capacity to heaven. The second, though equally fit for heaven through the Person and work of Christ, is spiritually dwarfed, and he takes that reduced capacity to heaven.

Day by day we are determining the rewards that we will receive and the measure to which we will enjoy our eternal home. We determine it by our knowledge of the Bible and our obedience to it, by our prayer life, by our fellowship with God's people, by our service for the Lord, and by our faithful stewardship of all that God has given to us. As soon as we realize that we are building for eternity with every passing day, it should have a profound effect on the choices we make and the priorities we set.

April 3

As he (a man) thinks in his heart, so is he.
PROVERBS 23:7

 P. Gibbs used to say, "You are not what you think you are, but what you think—this is what you are." This means that the mind is the spring from which behavior flows. Control the source and you control the stream that flows from it.

Therefore control of the thought-life is basic. That is why Solomon said, "Keep your heart with all diligence, for out of it spring the issues of life" (Prov. 4:23). Here the heart is used as a synonym for the mind.

James reminds us that sin begins in the mind (Jas. 1:13-15). If we think about a thing long enough, eventually we'll do it.

> *Sow a thought and reap an act.*
> *Sow an act and reap a habit.*
> *Sow a habit and reap a character.*
> *Sow a character and reap a destiny.*

The Lord Jesus emphasized the importance of the thought life by equating hatred with murder (Mt. 5:21-22) and by equating the lustful look with adultery (Mt. 5:28). He also taught that it's not what a man eats that defiles him but what he thinks (Mk. 7:14-23).

We are responsible for what we think because we have the power to control it. We can think about lewd, suggestive things or we can think about what is pure and Christlike. Each one of us is like a king. The empire that we rule over is our thought life. That empire has tremendous potential for good and enormous potential for evil. We are the ones who determine which it will be.

Here are some positive suggestions as to what we can do. First, take the whole matter to the Lord in prayer, saying, "Create in me a clean heart, O God, and renew a steadfast spirit within me" (Ps. 51:10). Second, judge every thought by how it appears in the presence of Christ (2 Cor. 10:5). Third, confess every evil thought instantly and expel it (Prov. 28:13). Next, avoid having a blank, empty mind. Fill it with positive, worthy thoughts (Phil. 4:8). Fifth, exercise discipline over what you read, see, and hear. You cannot expect a pure thought life if you feed on filth and pollution. Finally, keep busy for the Lord. It's when you shift your mind into neutral that vile fantasies seek admission.

April 4

By faith we understand.
HEBREWS 11:3

"**B**y faith we understand…" These words embody one of the most basic principles of spiritual life. We believe God's Word first, then we understand. The world says, "Seeing is believing." God says, "Believing is seeing." The Lord Jesus said to Martha, "Did I not say to you that if you would believe you would see…" (Jn. 11:40). Later He said to Thomas, "Blessed are those who have not seen and yet have believed" (Jn. 20:29). And the Apostle John wrote, "These things I have written to you who believe…that you may know…and that you may continue to believe" (1 Jn. 5:13). Believe first, then you'll know.

Billy Graham tells how this principle came alive in his life: "In 1949 I had been having a great many doubts concerning the Bible. I thought I saw apparent contradictions in Scriptures. Some things I could not reconcile with my restricted concept of God. When I stood up to preach, the authoritative note so characteristic of all great preachers of the past was lacking. Like hundreds of other seminary students, I was waging the intellectual battle of my life. The outcome could certainly affect my future ministry.

"In August of that year I had been invited to Forest Home, a Presbyterian conference center high in the mountains outside Los Angeles. I remember walking down a trail, tramping into the woods, and almost wrestling with God. I dueled with my doubts, and my soul seemed to be caught in the crossfire. Finally, in desperation, I surrendered my will to the living God revealed in Scripture. I knelt before the open Bible and said, 'Lord, many things in this book I do not understand. But Thou hast said, "The just shall live by faith." All I have received from Thee, I have taken by faith. Here and now, by faith, I accept the Bible as Thy Word. I take it all. I take it without reservations. Where there are things I cannot understand, I will reserve judgment until I receive more light. If this pleases Thee, give me authority as I proclaim Thy Word, and through that authority convict men of sin and turn sinners to the Savior!'

"Within six weeks we started our Los Angeles crusade, which is now history. During that crusade I discovered the secret that changed my ministry. I stopped trying to prove that the Bible was true. I had settled in my own mind that it was ,and this faith was conveyed to the audience."

April 5

And be ye kind to one another, tender-hearted, forgiving each other,
just as God in Christ also has forgiven you.
EPHESIANS 4:32, NASB

here is a definite order to be followed in connection with scriptural forgiveness. If we would follow this order we would save ourselves a lot of headaches and heartaches.

The first thing to do when you have been wronged is to forgive that person in your heart. You don't tell him yet that he has been forgiven, but by forgiving him in your heart, you leave the matter between the Lord and him. This prevents your gastric juices from turning into sulphuric acid, and saves you from other horrible physical and emotional disorders.

Next you need to go to the brother and rebuke him (Lk. 17:3). Instead of blabbing to others about how you have been wronged, "go and tell him his fault between you and him alone" (Mt. 18:15). Try to contain the problem as much as possible, that is, try to keep it as private as you can.

If he does not confess and ask forgiveness, then go to him with one or two witnesses (Mt. 18:16). This provides adequate scriptural testimony as to the offender's attitude.

If he is still unbending, then you take the matter to the assembly, accompanied by the witnesses. If he refuses to listen to the judgment of the assembly, then, of course, he is disfellowshiped (Mt. 18:17).

But if at any point during this process, he repents, then you forgive him (Lk. 17:3). You have already forgiven him in your heart, but now you administer forgiveness to him. Here it is important not to gloss over the matter. Don't say, "Oh, that's alright. You really didn't do anything wrong." Rather say, "I very gladly forgive you. Now the whole matter is closed. Let's get down and pray together."

The shame of having to confess and repent may deter him from wronging you again. But even if he repeats his sin and then repents, you must forgive him. Even if he does it seven times in one day and repents seven times, you must forgive him—whether you think he's sincere or not (Lk. 17:4).

We must never forget that we have been forgiven millions. We must not hesitate to forgive others what amounts to a few dollars, figuratively speaking.

April 6

If anyone wants to do His will, he shall know concerning the doctrine,
whether it is from God or whether I speak on My own authority.
JOHN 7:17

Today's English Version translates the first part of this verse, "Whoever is willing to do what God wants will know." It is a wonderful promise that if a person sincerely desires to know, God will show him.

When a sinner has come to the end of himself and when he prays in deep extremity, "Oh God, reveal Yourself to me," God always does. It is a prayer that never goes unanswered.

A hippie, living in a cave in the Southwest, was ready to end it all. He had sought satisfaction in liquor, drugs, sex, and the occult. But still his life was empty, empty, empty. He could see no way out of his misery. Huddled in the cave one day, he cried out, "Oh God—if there is a God—reveal Yourself to me, or I'm going to end my life."

Within ten minutes, a young Christian, who "just happened" to be passing, stuck his head in the mouth of the cave, saw the hermit-hippie and said, "Hey, mind if I speak to you about Jesus?"

You know what happened! The hippie listened to the good news of salvation through faith in the Lord Jesus Christ. He came to the Savior and found forgiveness, acceptance, and new life. He had prayed out of the depths; God heard and answered. I have never heard of anyone who prayed like that without having a special revelation of the Lord to his soul.

Of course, the promise is true to Christians as well. If a man sincerely desires to know what the will of God for his life is, God will show it to him. If he wants to know the proper pathway as far as church fellowship is concerned, God will make it known. No matter what the need may be, God is committed to meet it, if we want His will supremely. The thing that stands between us and a true knowledge of God's mind is our own lack of desperate desire.

April 7

Indeed I have all and abound. I am full, having received from Epaphroditus
the things sent from you, a sweet-smelling aroma,
an acceptable sacrifice, well pleasing to God.
PHILIPPIANS 4:18

P aul's letter to the Philippians was really an acknowledgment of a gift which he had received from the believers at Philippi. We are probably safe in assuming that it was a gift of money. The surprising thing is the way in which the apostle magnifies the gift. He calls it "a sweet-smelling aroma, an acceptable sacrifice, well-pleasing to God." In Ephesians 5:2, he uses a similar expression to describe Christ's great gift of Himself at Calvary. He speaks of it as "an offering and a sacrifice to God for a sweet-smelling aroma." It is breathtaking to think that a gift given to a servant of the Lord should be memorialized with language similar to that which describes the Unspeakable Gift.

J. H. Jowett comments finely on this point. "How vast, then, is the range of an apparently local kindness! We thought we were ministering to a pauper, and in reality we were conversing with the King. We imagined that the fragrance would be shut up in a petty neighborhood, and lo, the sweet aroma steals through the universe. We thought that we were dealing only with Paul, and we find that we were ministering to Paul's Savior and Lord."

When we understand the true spiritual nature of Christian giving and the vast range of its influence, we are delivered from giving grudgingly or of necessity. We are immune forever to the gimmickry of professional fund-raisers who extort by cajolery, pathos, or comedy. We see that giving is a form of priestly service, not a legal enaction. We give because we love, and we love to give.

The truth that my minuscule gifts to the Great God fill the throne room of the universe with fragrance should inspire me to humble worship and hilarious giving. Never again will the offering on Sunday morning be a boring, if necessary, part of the service. It will be as truly a means of giving directly to the Lord Jesus as if He were bodily present.

April 8

For the Word of God is living and active
and sharper than any two-edged sword.
HEBREWS 4:12a, NASB

A Christian university student was witnessing to another student who was from a liberal seminary. When the believer quoted a verse, the seminarian said, "I don't believe the Bible." The Christian quoted another verse, only to be met with, "I told you I don't believe the Bible." The third time the Christian quoted a verse the seminarian became agitated and exploded, "Don't quote the Bible to me. I've already told you I don't believe it." By then the believer felt completely frustrated and defeated. He figured that he was a total failure as a soul winner.

It so happened that Dr. H. A. Ironside was a guest at his home that night. At the supper table, the Christian student shared his disappointing experience about the seminarian. Then he asked Dr. Ironside, "When you are trying to witness to someone and he says to you, 'I don't believe the Bible,' what do you do?" Dr. Ironside replied with a happy smile, "I just quote more of it."

That is excellent advice for any would-be soul winners. When people say they don't believe the Bible, just quote more of it. The Word of God is living and powerful. It has an effect on people even when they don't believe it.

Suppose two men are dueling. One says to the other, "I don't believe your sword is real steel." What happens? Does the second man lay down his sword and admit defeat? Or does he give a scientific discourse on the carbon content and malleability of the metal? Ridiculous! He gives his opponent a good sharp jab and lets him feel how real the sword is. So it is with the Bible. The Word of God is the sword of the Spirit. It needs to be used more than it needs to be defended. It is well able to defend itself.

I do not deny that there is a place for proofs of the inspiration of the Scriptures. Such proofs serve a valuable purpose in confirming the faith of those who are already saved. In a few cases, they help people come to saving faith. But generally speaking people aren't convinced by human reasonings or arguments. "A man convinced against his will is of the same opinion still." Men need to be confronted with the powerful Word of God. A single verse of Scripture is worth a thousand arguments.

This highlights the importance of Scripture memorization. If I haven't committed verses to memory, the Spirit will not be able to bring them forth at the appropriate time. But the main point is that God has not promised to honor my words, but He has promised to honor His own. So in dealing with the unsaved, I must use the sword of the Spirit generously and watch it produce conviction and conversion by a miracle of grace.

April 9

He was led as a lamb to the slaughter.
Isaiah 53:7b

1 once saw a lamb die. It was a most moving, most awful sight. As it was brought to the place of execution, it looked especially lovable. Children would have loved to cuddle it. The young of every species are darling—kittens, puppies, ducks, calves, and colts—but a lamb is especially appealing.

As it stood there, it was a picture of innocence. Its white fleece, without blemish, gave the appearance of purity. It was gentle and mild, helpless and defenseless. Its eyes were especially expressive; they spoke of fear, of pathos and poignancy. There seemed to be no reason why anything so young, so beautiful should have to die.

Now the legs were tied and the pathetic lamb was lying on its side, breathing heavily, as if aware of impending death. With one deft motion, the butcher moved the knife across the throat. The blood poured out over the ground. The little body was convulsed by the death throes, then shortly it lay still. The gentle lamb had died.

Some of the spectators had turned away from the sight; it was too sad to watch. Others were wiping away the tears. No one wanted to speak.

By faith I see another Lamb dying—the Lamb of God. It is a most blessed, most awful sight.

This Lamb is altogether lovely, the chief among ten thousand, the fairest of the fair. As He is brought to the place of execution, He is in the prime of life.

He is not only innocent—He is holy, harmless, undefiled, separate from sinners, without spot and without blemish. There seems no reason why anyone so pure should ever be put to death.

But the executioners take Him and nail Him to the Cross, hands and feet. There He suffers the concentrated torments and horrors of hell as a Substitute for sinners. Through it all His eyes are filled with love and forgiveness.

Now His suffering time is ended. He dismisses His spirit and His body hangs limp on the Cross. A soldier pierces His side and out gushes blood and water. The Lamb of God has died.

My heart is filled. Scalding tears flow freely. I fall to my knees and thank Him and praise Him! Just to think—He died for me! I will never cease to love Him.

April 10

And you do not need that anyone teach you...
1 John 2:27

t first glance this verse poses problems. If we don't need anyone to teach us, why did the risen Lord give teachers to build up the saints for the work of ministering (Eph. 4:11-12)?

In order to understand John's meaning, it helps to know the background of his letter. At the time he wrote, the church was being plagued by false teachers known as Gnostics. These heretics had once professed to be sincere believers in the Lord Jesus and had been in the fellowship of local assemblies. But then they had left to push their false views concerning the humanity and deity of Christ.

They professed to have superior knowledge, hence the name Gnostic, from the Greek word *gnosis*—"to know." They probably said something like this to the Christians: "What you have is good, but we have additional truth. We can take you beyond the simple teachings and initiate you into new and deeper mysteries. If you are going to be full-grown and fulfilled, you need our teachings."

But John warns the Christians that it is all a hoax. They don't need any of these imposters to teach them. They have the Holy Spirit. They have the Word of Truth. And they have God-ordained teachers. The Holy Spirit enables them to discern between truth and error. The Christian faith has been once for all delivered to the saints (Jude 3), and anything that claims to be in addition to it is fraudulent. Christian teachers are needed to explain and apply the Scriptures, but they must never transgress by going beyond the Scriptures.

John would be the last one to deny the need for teachers in the Church. He himself was a teacher *par excellence.* But he would be the first one to insist that the Holy Spirit is the ultimate authority, and that He leads His people into all truth through the pages of Holy Writ. All teaching must be tested by the Bible. If it professes to be in addition to the Bible, if it claims equal authority with the Bible, or if it does not agree with the Bible, then it must be rejected.

April 11

When they had assembled with the elders and consulted together,
they gave a large sum of money to the soldiers, saying, "Tell them,
'His disciples came at night and stole Him away while we slept.'"
MATTHEW 28:12-13

T he Lord Jesus had no sooner risen from the dead when His enemies began to fabricate an alibi to explain away the miracle. The best falsehood that they could concoct at that time was that the disciples came by night and stole the body. (The swoon theory, suggesting that Jesus did not really die but only swooned, didn't surface till centuries later.) Unfortunately for the theft theory, as for all the other theories, it raises more questions than it answers. For example:

Why didn't the chief priests and elders question the original report of the guards concerning the empty tomb? They accepted it as true and hastened to devise an explanation as to how it had happened.

Why were the soldiers sleeping when they should have been on watch? The Roman penalty for sleeping on duty was death. Yet they were promised immunity from punishment. Why? How could all the soldiers have fallen asleep at the same time? It taxes credulity to think they would all have risked death for a time of sleep. How could the disciples have rolled the stone without waking the guards? The stone was large and could not be moved noiselessly.

How could the disciples have moved the stone at all? In a typical Herodian-style tomb, the stone was rolled till it fell down into a lower slot. It was easier to seal such a tomb than it was to open it. Besides, the tomb had been made as "sure" as the Roman authorities were able to make it. Is it likely that the disciples, recently so fearful that they fled for their lives, would have the courage to face the Roman guards and rob the sepulcher? They would know that such an offense was punishable by a severe sentence.

If the soldiers were all asleep, how did they know that the disciples had stolen the body?

If the disciples stole the body, why did they take time to remove the grave clothes and fold the napkin? (Lk. 24:12; Jn. 20:6-7). Why would the disciples want to steal the body?

There was no reason. Actually they were surprised and incredulous when they learned He had risen.

Finally, would the disciples, honorable men that they were, go forth and preach the resurrection at great personal risk if they knew it was a lie? Paul Little said, "Men do not die for what they know is a lie." They sincerely believed that Jesus has risen. The Lord is risen! He is risen indeed!

April 12

Therefore if you have not been faithful in the unrighteous mammon,
who will commit to your trust the true riches?
LUKE 16:11

nrighteous mammon here refers to earthly riches or material treasures. No illusion is more prevalent than that the man who has a lot of material possessions is rich. We speak of houses and land as *real* estate because we think they are real wealth. We speak of stocks and bonds as *securities* because we think they provide security.

But in Luke 16:11 the Lord distinguishes between righteous mammon and true riches. The things men think are wealth aren't wealth at all.

John was a godly Christian who served as a caretaker for a wealthy aristocrat's estate. One night John had a vivid dream in which he was told that the richest man in the valley would die before midnight the following evening. When John met his employer the next morning, he shared the dream with him. At first the millionaire pretended to be completely unconcerned. He never felt better. And he didn't believe in dreams anyway.

But as soon as John left, he called his chauffeur to drive to the doctor's office. He told the doctor he wanted a complete physical checkup. As expected, the tests revealed that he was in splendid condition. And yet he was still worried about John's dream, so as he was leaving the doctor's office, he said, "By the way, Doctor, could you come to my house for supper tonight and for a visit afterwards." The doctor agreed to come.

The supper went on routinely and they talked over a wide range of subjects. Several times the doctor made a start to leave, but each time the host prevailed upon him to stay a little longer.

Finally, when the clock struck midnight, the godless rich man, greatly relieved, said good-bye to the doctor.

A few minutes later, the doorbell rang. When the gentleman opened the door, the adult daughter of old John stood there and said, "Sir, my mother wanted to let you know that my father had a heart attack and died a little while ago."

The richest man in the valley had died that night.

April 13

Therefore, whether you eat or drink, or whatever you do,
do all to the glory of God.
1 CORINTHIANS 10:31

ne of the great tests of Christian behavior is whether there is any glory for God in it. Too often we test our conduct by the question, "Is there any harm in it?" But that is not the question. What we must ask is this: "Is there any glory for God in it?"

Before engaging in any activity, we should be able to bow our head and ask the Lord to glorify Himself in what we are about to do. If God cannot be honored by it, then we should refrain from doing it.

Other religions might be satisfied with behavior that has the absence of harm in it. Christianity moves beyond the merely negative to the distinctly positive. Therefore, as Keith L. Brooks said, "If you would be a successful Christian, stop hunting for the harm there is in things, and start looking for the good. If you want your life to be happy, cast your lot among those persons who are asking for the 'good' and not the 'harm' there is in it."

Things might be harmless in themselves and yet be a dead weight in the Christian race. There is no law against an Olympic runner's toting a sack of potatoes in the 1500 meter race. He can carry the spuds but he can't win the race. So it is with the Christian. Things may be harmless and yet be a hindrance.

But usually when we ask, "Is there any harm in it?" our question betrays a hidden doubt. We don't ask that about activities that are legitimate on the face of them —such as prayer, Bible study, worship, witness, and our daily work. Incidentally, any honorable work can be done to the glory of God.

Whenever in doubt, we could follow this advice from John Wesley's mother: "If you wish to determine the lawfulness of a pleasure, follow this rule: Whatever weakens your reasons, impairs the tenderness of your conscience, obscures your sense of God, or takes away the relish of spiritual things; whatever increases the authority of your body over your mind, that thing is sin."

April 14

Whoever desires to become great among you, let him be your servant.
MATTHEW 20:26-27

W hat is true greatness?

In the kingdom of this world, the great man is the one who has risen to a place of wealth and power. He has a retinue of aides and assistants, conditioned to follow his orders. He is accorded V.I.P. treatment and receives special favors wherever he goes. People regard him with respect and awe because of his rank. He never has to stoop to anything menial; there are always others to do that for him.

But in the Kingdom of our Lord, things are quite different. Here greatness is measured by the extent to which we serve rather than the extent to which we are served. The great man is the one who stoops to become a slave for others. No service is too menial. He does not expect any special treatment or thanks. When one of George Washington's men saw him performing a menial service, he objected, saying, "General, you are too big a man to be doing that." Washington replied, "Oh, no, I'm just the right size."

Commenting on Luke 17:7-10, Roy Hession reminds us that "there are five marks of the bondslave: (1) He must be willing to have one thing on top of another put on him, without any consideration being given to him. (2) In doing this, he must be willing not to be thanked for it. (3) Having done all this, he must not charge the master with selfishness. (4) He must confess that he is an unprofitable servant. (5) He must admit that doing and bearing what he has in the way of meekness and humility, he has not done one stitch more than it was his duty to do."

When our Lord left the heights of glory to become a Man on this planet, he took "the form of a bondservant" (Phil. 2:7). He was among us as One who serves (Lk. 22:27). He said, "The Son of Man did not come to be served, but to serve, and to give His life a ransom for many" (Mt. 20:28). He girded Himself with a towel, the apron of a slave, and washed His disciples' feet (Jn. 13:1-17).

"A servant is not greater than his master" (Jn. 13:16). If He stooped so low to serve us, why should we think it beneath our dignity to serve others?

> *Wast Thou, Savior, meek and lowly,*
> *And will such a worm as I,*
> *Weak and sinful and unholy,*
> *Dare to lift my head on high?*

April 15

Through love serve one another.
Galatians 5:13

S omeone has said, "Self thinks itself great and is served. Love serves and is great."

A popular gospel singer witnessed to the man sitting next to him in a restaurant and had the joy of leading him to Christ. In the weeks that followed, he discipled this new convert. Then Fred, the new believer, was stricken with inoperable cancer and was taken to a convalescent hospital where, unfortunately, care was below standard. The gospel singer, a radio celebrity, visited faithfully, changed the bed, bathed and fed his "Timothy," and did many other things that the staff should have been doing. On the night Fred died, this well-known singer was holding him in his arms, whispering comforting verses of Scripture into his ear. "...through love serve one another."

A senior instructor at a Bible School often found the men's room awash after the morning rush. He would patiently clean the fixtures, then get down and wipe the floor dry. Not all his best teaching was done in the classroom. The students were humbled and inspired by the example of their respected teacher cleaning up after them. "...through love serve one another."

In that same Bible School, a member of the basketball team had the heart of a true servant. After a game, when all the players would rush down to be first in the showers, he would stay in the gym and see that it was set in order for the next day. He "found in the selfishness of others an opportunity to identify himself afresh with the Lord as the servant of all." "...through love serve one another."

A Christian mother from rural Turkey was taken to London to donate a kidney for her ailing son. She assumed that to give a kidney would cost her life. When the English doctor asked if she was sure she was willing to give a kidney to her son, she replied, "I am willing to give two kidneys." "...through love serve one another."

In a world dominated largely by self-interest, the pathway of selfless, sacrificial service is not overcrowded. Opportunities beckon throughout every day for innovative acts of servanthood.

April 16

...Dying, and behold we live.
2 Corinthians 6:9

T he Bible is full of paradoxes, that is, truths that seem contrary to what we could normally suppose or truths that seem to contradict one another. G. K. Chesterton maintained that a paradox is truth standing on its head to attract attention. Here are a few of the paradoxes trying to attract our attention.

We save our lives by losing them; we lose our lives by loving them (Mk. 8:35). We are strong when we are weak (2 Cor. 12:10), and powerless in our own strength (Jn. 15:5). We find perfect freedom in being Christ's slave, and bondage when we are free from His yoke (Rom. 6:17-20). We find more joy in sharing what we have than we do in getting more. Or, in the words of our Lord, "It is more blessed to give than to receive" (Acts 20:35).

We increase what we have through scattering it, and experience poverty through hoarding it (Prov. 11:24). We have a new nature that cannot sin (1 Jn. 3:9), yet everything we do is stained by sin (1 Jn. 1:8). We conquer by yielding (Gen. 32:24-28) and experience defeat by fighting (1 Pet. 5:5c).

We are abased when we exalt ourselves, but He exalts us when we abase ourselves (Lk. 14:11). We are enlarged by pressure (Ps. 4:1, JND) and shrunk by prosperity (Jer. 48:11).

We can possess all things, yet have nothing; we can be poor, yet make many rich (2 Cor. 6:10). When we are wise (in man's view) then we are fools (in God's sight), but when we are fools for Christ's sake, then we are truly wise (1 Cor. 1:20-21).

The life of faith brings freedom from care and anxiety; the life of sight brings fear of loss through moths, rust and thieves (Mt. 6:19).

The poet sees the Christian life as paradox from start to finish:

> How strange is the course that a person must steer,
> How perplexed is the path he must tread;
> The hope of his happiness rises from fear,
> And his life he receives from the dead.
> His fairest pretensions must wholly be waived,
> And his best resolutions be crossed;
> Nor can he expect to be perfectly saved
> Till he finds himself utterly lost.
> When all this is done, and his heart is assured
> Of the total remission of sins;
> When his pardon is signed and his peace is procured,
> From that moment his conflict begins. (SELECTED)

April 17

…you are not to be called rabbi, for you have one teacher, and you are all brethren. And call no man your father on earth, for you have one Father, who is in heaven. Neither be called masters, for you have, one master, the Christ.

MATTHEW 23:8-10, RSV

T he Lord Jesus warned His disciples against high-sounding titles that cater to the ego and put self in the place of the Trinity. God is our Father, Christ is our Master, the Holy Spirit is our Teacher. We should not arrogate these titles to ourselves in the assembly. In the world, of course, we have an earthly father, in our work we have a master or employer, and in school we have teachers. But in the spiritual realm, the members of the Godhead fill these roles and should be honored exclusively as such.

God is our Father in the sense that He is the Giver of life. Christ is our Master because we belong to Him and are subject to His direction. The Holy Spirit is our Teacher because He is the Author and Interpreter of Scripture; all our teaching must be guided by Him.

How strange, then, that churches perpetuate honorific titles just as if Christ had never warned against them. Priests and ministers are still called Father and Padre and are sometimes referred to as Dominie, meaning Lord. Clergymen regularly use the title "Reverend," a word that is used in the Bible only of God (see Ps. 111:9, "And reverend and holy is His name"). The title "Doctor" comes from the Latin *docere,* to teach. So *doctor* means *teacher.* The degree, whether earned or honorary, often comes from an institution that is a pesthouse of infidelity rather than a bulwark of the Christian faith. Yet when a man is introduced as "Doctor" in the assembly, the implication is that his words have added authority because of his degree. That, of course, is completely unfounded. A hunchbacked garbage collector, filled with the Holy Spirit, may speak more truly as an oracle of God.

There is a place for titles in the so-called secular world. The principle that applies in that sphere is "Render therefore to all their due…honor to whom honor" (Rom. 13:7). But the principle that applies in the assembly is laid out by the Lord in the words, "…you are all brethren" (Mt. 23:8, RSV).

April 18

For now we see in a mirror, dimly...
1 Corinthians 13:12

t few times in our Christian experience is this so evident as when we come to the Lord's Supper to remember Him in His death for us. "We see through a glass, dimly."

There seems to be a thick, impenetrable veil. We are on one side of it with all our finite limitations. On the other side is the whole great drama of our redemption—Bethlehem, Gethsemane, Gabbatha, Calvary, the empty tomb, the exalted Christ at God's right hand. We realize that there is something enormously vast there, and we try to take it in, but feel more like clods than like living beings.

We try to comprehend the Savior's sufferings for our sins. Our minds strain to take in the horror of His being forsaken by God. We know that He endured the torment that we should have endured for eternity. Yet we are frustrated to realize that there is so much more beyond. We are standing at the edge of an unexplored sea!

We think of the love that sent Heaven's best for earth's worst. We are moved when we remember that God sent His only-begotten Son into this jungle of sin to seek and to save that which was lost. But we are dealing with a love that passes knowledge. We can know only in part.

We sing of the grace of the Savior, that "though He was rich, yet for your sakes He became poor, that you through His poverty might become rich." It is enough to make angels gasp. Our eyes strain to see the vast dimensions of such grace. But it is in vain. We are limited by our human short-sightedness. We know that we should be overcome by the contemplation of His sacrifice at Calvary, but we are too often strangely unmoved. If we really entered in to what lies beyond the veil, we would be reduced to tears. Yet we have to confess...

> *Oh, wonder to myself I am,*
> *Thou loving, bleeding, dying Lamb,*
> *That I can scan the mystery o'er*
> *And not be moved to love Thee more.*

Or, in the words of Christina Rossetti, we must ask:

> *Am I a stone, and not a sheep, that I can stand*
> *O Christ, beneath Thy cross,*
> *And number drop by drop,*
> *Thy blood's slow loss,*
> *And yet not weep?*

Like the two disciples on the road to Emmaus, our eyes are holden. We long with burning desire for the time when the veil will be removed, and when we will see with better vision the awesome meaning of the broken bread and the outpoured wine.

April 19

*These things I have written to you who believe in the name of the Son of God,
that you may know that you have eternal life, and that you may continue to
believe in the name of the Son of God.*

1 JOHN 5:13

Some of us will be eternally thankful to God for this verse because it taught us that assurance of salvation comes first and foremost through the Word of God and not through feelings. The Bible was written, among other reasons, so that those who believe on the Name of the Son of God can know that they have eternal life.

We can be thankful that assurance does not come through feelings, because they fluctuate with every passing day. "God does not ask the soul to say, 'Thank God I feel so good,' but turns the eye another way, to Jesus and His Word." When someone once asked Martin Luther, "Do you feel that your sins have been forgiven?" he replied, "No, but I'm as sure of it as that there's a God in heaven."

> *For feelings come and feelings go*
> *And feelings are deceiving;*
> *My warrant is the Word of God,*
> *Naught else is worth believing.*

C. I. Scofield reminds us that "justification takes place in the mind of God and not in the nervous system of the believer." H. A. Ironside used to say, "I don't know I am saved because I feel happy, but I feel happy because I know I am saved." And he knew he was saved by the written Word of God.

When we read that the Spirit Himself bears witness with our spirit that we are the sons of God (Rom. 8:16), we must remember that the Spirit witnesses to us primarily through the Scriptures. We read John 6:47, for instance, "He who believes in Me has everlasting life." We know that we have trusted in Christ for our eternal salvation; He is our only hope for heaven. The Spirit of God therefore witnesses to us through this verse that we are sons of God.

Of course, there are other means of assurance. We know we are saved because we love the brethren; because we hate sin and practice righteousness; because we love the Word of God; and because we have the instinct of prayer. But the first and fundamental means of assurance is the surest, most dependable thing in the universe, the Word of God. George Cutting said it well in his memorable tract, *Safety, Certainty and Enjoyment:* "It's the blood that makes us safe; it's the Word that makes us sure."

April 20

If it is by grace, it is no longer on the basis of works,
otherwise grace is no longer grace.
ROMANS 11:6, NASB

W hen a person gets grounded early in the doctrine of grace, he saves himself from a host of problems in later life. It is so basic to understand that salvation is a free gift of God's grace and that it is given to those who not only do not deserve it but who in fact deserve the very opposite. There is nothing meritorious a person can do or become to earn eternal life. It is given to those who abandon any thoughts of personal worthiness but who rest their case on the worthiness of the Savior alone.

If we see that salvation is all of grace, then we can have full assurance. We can know that we are saved. If salvation depended in the slightest degree on ourselves and our miserable attainments, then we could never know for sure. We wouldn't know whether we had done enough good works or the right kind. But when it depends on the work of Christ, then there doesn't have to be any nagging doubt.

The same is true of our eternal security. If our continued safety somehow depended on our own ability to hold out, then we might be saved today and lost tomorrow. But as long as our safety depends on the Savior's ability to keep us, we can know we are eternally secure.

Those who live under grace are not helpless pawns of sin. Sin does have dominion over those under law because the law tells them what to do but doesn't give them the power to do it. Grace gives a person a perfect standing before God, teaches him to walk worthy of his calling, enables him to do it by the indwelling Holy Spirit, and rewards him for doing it.

Under grace, service becomes a joyful privilege, not a legal bondage. The believer is motivated by love, not by fear. The memory of what the Savior suffered to provide salvation inspires the saved sinner to pour out his life in devoted service.

Grace also enriches life by inspiring thanksgiving, worship, praise, and adoration. The knowledge of who the Savior is, of what sinners we are by nature and by practice, and of all He has done for us causes our hearts to overflow in loving adoration to Him.

There's nothing like the grace of God. It's the crown jewel of all His attributes. Get grounded in the truth of the sovereign grace of God and it will transfigure all of life.

April 21

A disciple is not above his teacher,
but everyone who is perfectly trained will be like his teacher.
LUKE 6:40

In this passage the Lord Jesus was reminding them that, when they went out to disciple others, they could not expect their disciples to progress further in the spiritual life than they themselves had attained. In other words, the extent of our positive influence on others is limited by what we ourselves are.

Or as O. L. Clark said:

You cannot teach what you do not know;
You cannot lead where you do not go.

The Savior went on to reinforce the lesson by the story of the mote and the beam. A man is walking by a threshing floor when a sudden gust of wind lands a tiny speck of chaff in his eye. He rubs it, pulls the top lid down over the bottom one, and tries all the well-meaning advice of his friends as to how to get the mote out of his eye. Then I come along with a telephone pole jutting out of my eye and say to him, "Here, dear friend, let me help you get that atom out of your eye." With his head at an angle, he looks up at me with his remaining good eye and says, "Don't you think you ought to take the pole out of your own eye first?"

Of course! I can't help someone who is struggling with a besetting sin if I am even more shackled by that particular sin. I can't press on him obedience to some plain command of Scripture if I have not obeyed it myself. Any spiritual failure in my life seals my lips in that particular area.

When my disciple has become perfect, that is, when I have finished training him, I cannot expect him to be one centimeter above my own spiritual stature. He may progress up to my height, but I cannot lead him beyond it.

All of which emphasizes afresh that we must take heed to ourselves. Our ministry is to be a ministry of character—it's what's inside that counts. We may be eloquent, clever, and fast-talking, but if there are blind spots in our lives, areas of neglect and disobedience, then our discipling of others is a case of the blind leading the blind.

April 22

If you confess with your mouth the Lord Jesus and believe in your heart
that God has raised Him from the dead, you will be saved.
ROMANS 10:9

T his favorite gospel verse zeroes in on the two basic truths that are so hard for fallen man to accept—the incarnation and the resurrection. There can be no salvation without accepting these doctrines and all that they signify.

First we must confess with our mouth that Jesus is Lord, that is, that the One who was born in Bethlehem's stable is none other than God manifest in the flesh. The deity of the Lord Jesus is essential to the whole plan of salvation.

Second, we must believe in our heart that God raised Him from the dead. But this means more than the simple fact of the resurrection—it includes the fact that the Lord Jesus died on the Cross as our Substitute. He paid the penalty that our sins deserved. He endured the wrath of God that we should have endured eternally. Then on the third day God raised Him from the dead as a proof of God's entire satisfaction with Christ's sacrifice for our sins.

When we receive Him as Lord and Savior, the Bible says that we are saved.

But someone may ask, "Why is confession put before believing? Don't we believe first and then confess?"

In verse 9, Paul is emphasizing the incarnation and the resurrection, and he gives the historical order in which they occurred—the incarnation first and the resurrection thirty-three years later.

In the next verse he puts believing before confessing. "For with the heart man believeth unto righteousness; and with the mouth confession is made unto salvation." Here the order is that which takes place when we are born again. First, we trust the Savior and are justified. Then we go out to confess the salvation which we have already received.

Our verse has an artless simplicity and perennial freshness about it. No wonder the children sing:

> *Romans ten and nine*
> *Is a fav'rite verse of mine;*
> *Confessing Christ as Lord,*
> *I am saved by grace divine;*
> *For there the words of promise*
> *In golden letters shine:*
> *Romans ten and nine.*

April 23

Let us go forth to Him, outside the camp, bearing His reproach.
Hebrews 13:13

W e learn first from this verse that Christ is the gathering center for His people. We don't gather to a denomination, a church, a building, or a great preacher but Christ alone. "Unto him shall the gathering of the people be" (Gen. 49:10, KJV). "Gather My saints together to Me, those who have made a covenant with Me by sacrifice" (Ps. 50:5).

A second lesson is that we must go to Him outside the camp. The camp here has been defined as "the whole earthly religious system adapted to the natural man." It is the religious sphere in which Christ is dishonored or downgraded. It is the pagan monstrosity that masquerades today as Christianity, "having a form of godliness but denying the power thereof." Christ is outside, and we must go out to Him.

We also learn that meeting to Christ alone outside the camp involves reproach. It seldom occurs to Christians that there is reproach connected with obedience to the Lord in the matter of church fellowship. More often church associations carry a measure of prestige and status. But the closer we get to the New Testament ideal, the more likely it is that we will have to share His reproach. Are we willing to pay that price?

> *He called me out, the Man with garments dyed,*
> *I knew His voice—my Lord, the crucified;*
> *He showed Himself, and oh, I could not stay,*
> *I had to follow Him—had to obey.*
> *It cast me out—this world when once it found*
> *That I within this rebel heart had crowned*
> *The Man it had rejected, spurned, and slain,*
> *Whom God in wondrous power had raised to reign.*
> *And so we are without the camp, my Lord and I,*
> *But oh, His presence sweeter is than any earthly tie*
> *Which once I counted greater than His claim;*
> *I'm out, not only from the world, but to His Name.*

April 24

If anyone defiles the temple of God, God will destroy him.
For the temple of God is holy, which temple you are.
1 CORINTHIANS 3:17

In this verse, the temple of God refers to the local assembly. Paul is not speaking to individual Christians but to believers collectively when he says "which temple you (plural) are." The saints in Corinth comprised a temple of God.

It is also true, of course, that individual believers are a temple of the Holy Spirit. The Apostle brings this out in 1 Corinthians 6:19: "Do you not know that your body is the temple of the Holy Spirit who is in you, whom you have from God, and you are not your own?" The Holy Spirit of God dwells in the body of every child of God.

But in our text for today, it is the assembly that is in view. Paul is saying that if any man destroys the assembly, God will destroy him. It is the same word that is translated "defile" and "destroy" in this verse. "It is used of marring a local church by leading it away from that condition of holiness of life and purity of doctrine in which it should abide, and of God's retributive destruction of the offender who is guilty of this sin" (W. E. VINE).

So our verse warns us that it is a serious thing to tamper with a local fellowship. In fact, it is a form of self-destruction. Yet how diffident people often are in this very area. Here is a man who doesn't get his own way in the assembly. Or he becomes involved in a violent personality clash with some other brother. Rather than make things right in a scriptural manner, he lines up people to take his side and forms a faction in the church. Things go from bad to worse and soon there is an open split.

Or perhaps it is a carnal sister who carries on a campaign of gossip and back-biting against someone else. Her slanderous tongue lashes out until the church is filled with bitterness and strife. She will not stop until a once-prosperous assembly lies in ruins.

People like this are playing a perilous game. They cannot get away with it. The Great God of the universe is committed to wreck those who wreck His assembly. Let all who are inclined to faction, beware!

April 25

But thanks be to God, who always leads us in His triumph in and manifests through us the sweet aroma of the knowledge of Him every place.
2 CORINTHIANS 2:14, NASB

I t is generally understood that Paul here borrows a figure from the victory parade of a military leader just returned from a foreign conquest. The general is at the head of the parade, savoring the sweet satisfaction of victory. Behind him are jubilant troops. Then behind them are the prisoners-of-war, slated for punishment, perhaps death. All along the parade route are incense burners, filling the air with aroma. But the aroma means different things to different people, depending on whose side they are on. To those who are loyal to the commander in chief, it is the fragrance of victory. To the captives, however, it is an omen of defeat and retribution.

The pathway of a servant of the Lord parallels this picture in several respects. The Lord always leads him in triumph. Though it might not always seem like victory, the fact is that he is on the winning side and God's cause can never fail.

Everywhere he goes, he carries the aroma of Christ with him. But this aroma means different things to different people. To those who bow to the Lord Jesus, it is the scent of everlasting life. To those who refuse the gospel, on the other hand, it is the smell of death and destruction.

But in both cases God is glorified. He is glorified in the salvation of the repentant, and he is also vindicated in the refusal of those who are perishing. When the latter stand before Christ, at the Judgment of the Great White Throne, they will not be able to blame God for their plight. They had the opportunity to be saved but refused it.

We generally judge the effectiveness of Christian service by how many people are saved. Perhaps there is a suggestion in this passage that it would be equally valid to judge it by how many people, after receiving a clear presentation of the gospel, reject it and plunge into hell.

God is glorified in both cases. To Him there is the sweet incense of grace in the first instance and of justice in the second.

Solemn issues! No wonder the Apostle asks, in closing, "Who is sufficient for these things?"

April 26

You shall never wash my feet!
JOHN 13:8

T he Lord Jesus had just girded Himself with a towel and filled a basin with water, preparatory to washing the disciples' feet. When He came to Peter, He met this emphatic refusal, "Thou shalt never wash my feet."

Why? Why didn't Peter want to submit to this gracious ministry from the Lord? On the one hand, there may have been a sense of unworthiness; he did not consider himself worthy to be served by the Lord. But there is also the real possibility that Peter's attitude was one of pride and independence. He did not want to be on the receiving end. He did not want to be dependent on others for help.

This same attitude keeps many people from being saved. They want to earn salvation or deserve it, but to receive it as a free gift of grace is beneath their dignity. They don't want to feel indebted to God. But "no one who is too proud to be infinitely in debt will ever be a Christian" (JAMES S. STEWART).

There is also a lesson here for those who are already Christians. We have all met believers who are compulsive givers. They are always doing for others. Their lives are poured out in service for their relatives and neighbors. Their generosity deserves high praise. But there is a fly in the ointment! They never want to be on the receiving end. They never want anyone to do anything for them. They have learned how to give generously but they have never learned how to receive graciously. They enjoy the blessing of ministering to others, but they deny to others that same blessing.

Paul proved himself to be a gracious recipient of gifts from the Philippians. In thanking them, he said, "Not that I seek the gift, but I seek the fruit that abounds to your account" (Phil. 4:17). He thought of their reward more than of his own need.

"It is told of Bishop Westcott that at the end of his life he said he had made one great mistake, for, while he had always been willing to do for others to the limit of his ability, he had never been willing to let others do for him, and as a result some element of sweetness and completeness was missing. He had not allowed himself the discipline of receiving many kindnesses which could not be repaid" (J. O. SANDERS).

An unknown poet summed it up well when he wrote:

> *I hold him great, who, for love's sake,*
> *Can give with generous, earnest will;*
> *But he who takes for love's sweet sake,*
> *I think I hold more generous still.*

April 27

...he began to encourage them all with resolute heart to remain true to the Lord.
ACTS 11:23, NASB

here is an alarming tendency in some Christian circles to fawn over men because they are scholars, even though they are disloyal to the Person of Christ.

Here is a man, for instance, who is a brilliant writer, a master in the use of illustrations, a commentator whose word studies are superb. But this man denies the Virgin Birth. He explains away the miracles of our Lord. He rejects the literal, bodily resurrection of the Savior. He speaks patronizingly of Jesus as one who must find a place in any gallery of the world's heroes. To him, Jesus is just one among many heroes. What this amounts to, of course, is damning the Son of God with faint praise. This man is simply not true to the Lord.

It is shocking, then, to find Christians defending a man like this for his brilliant scholarship. With mealy mouth, they extol his intellectual prowess and pass lightly over his heretical treatment of Christ. They like to quote him as a respected authority and to move in the same scholarly circles. If challenged for fraternizing with one who is an enemy of the Cross of Christ, they use weasel words to play down the seriousness of the offense. Not uncommonly, they attack fundamental, Bible-believing Christians for daring to speak out against one who is such an acknowledged authority.

It is time that Christians recapture a sense of righteous anger when their Savior is being betrayed in the halls of scholarship. This is no time for compromise. The truth concerning His Person and work is not negotiable. We must stand and be counted.

The prophets did not speak equivocally when the truth of God was at stake. They were fiercely loyal to the Lord and lashed out at those who dared to deny or belittle Him.

The apostles, too, bristled at any effort to rob the Lord of His glory. They chose loyalty to Christ over renown in the theological world.

The martyrs chose to die rather than compromise their loyalty to the Son of God. They were more interested in God's approval than man's.

Our responsibility is to be faithful to the Lord Jesus in all things, and to take an adversary relationship to anyone or anything that fails to give Him His proper place of preeminence.

April 28

Hear, my children, the instruction of a father,
and give attention to know understanding.
PROVERBS 4:1

I n the first four verses of Proverbs 4, Solomon describes how good advice can and should be passed down from one generation to another. He tells how his father had taught him, then urges his son, in turn, to pay attention to good doctrine and sound instruction.

It is sensible for young people to learn as much as possible from their earthly parents concerning the practical affairs of life. But it is also true that, in the spiritual sphere, every young Christian should have a spiritual mentor—someone to whom he can go with his questions, someone in whom he can confide, someone who will share from a rich store of experience and someone who will be candid in dealing with areas of need. If a parent can fill this role, all the better. But if not, someone else should be sought out.

Godly, mature believers have accumulated a vast amount of practical knowledge. No doubt they have experienced defeats, but they have learned valuable lessons from them and have learned how to avoid them the next time. Older Christians can often see aspects of a problem that young people might miss. And they have learned to be balanced and to avoid unreasonable extremes.

A wise young Timothy will cultivate a Paul, trying to draw on his wisdom and know-how. He will save himself from humiliations and blunders by checking first with someone who has been through it before him. Instead of treating old age with contempt, he will honor those who have fought in the conflict and have maintained a good record.

Generally speaking, older saints will not push themselves on the young. They know that no advice is as unwelcome as advice that is unsolicited. But, when asked, they are always glad to share insights that have been of help to them along the way.

So whether a young person is having a struggle with lust, or wants to know how to find God's guidance, or seeks to raise a family for the Lord, or wonders if God is calling him to the mission field, or needs help in managing his finances, or longs for a more effective prayer life—he would be wise to seek the help of a spiritual guide who can bring the light of Scripture to shine on the particular problem. Underneath those gray hairs there is often a fund of wisdom to be tapped. Why learn the hard way when you can profit from the insights and past experience of others?

April 29

Now faith is the substance of things hoped for,
the evidence of things not seen.
Hebrews 11:1

Faith is implicit trust in the Word of God. It is confidence in the trust-worthiness of God. It is the conviction that what God says is true and that what He promises will come to pass. It deals primarily in the realm of the future ("things hoped for") and the realm of the invisible ("things not seen").

Whittier said that "the steps of faith fall on the seeming void, and find the rock beneath." But not so! Faith is no leap in the dark. It demands the surest evidence, and finds that evidence in the Word of God.

Some people have the misconception that if you just believe a thing strongly enough it will come to pass. But that is credulity, not faith. Faith must have some revelation of God to lean on, some promise of God to cling to. If God promises something, then it is as sure as if it had already happened. If He foretells the future, then it is certain to be fulfilled. In other words, faith brings the future within the present and makes the invisible seen.

There is no risk in believing God. God cannot lie, He would not deceive, and He cannot be deceived. To believe God is the most rational, sane, logical thing a person can do. What is more reasonable than that the creature should believe the Creator?

Faith is not limited to possibilities but invades the realm of the impossible. Someone has said, "Faith begins where possibilities end. If it's possible then there's no glory for God in it. If it's impossible, it can be done."

> *Faith, mighty faith, the promise sees*
> *And looks to God alone;*
> *Laughs at impossibilities*
> *And cries, "It shall be done."*

Admittedly there are difficulties and problems in the life of faith. God tests our faith in the crucible of trial and affliction to see if it is genuine (1 Pet. 1:7). We often have to wait long to see the fulfillment of His promises, and sometimes we have wait till we reach the other side. But "difficulties are food for faith to feed on" (GEORGE MÜLLER).

"Without faith it is impossible to please Him" (Heb. 11:6). When we refuse to believe Him, we are saying that He is a liar (1 Jn. 5:10), and how can God be pleased by people who call Him a liar?

April 30

If you love Me, keep My commandments.
JOHN 14:15

Commandments? In the New Testament? Whenever people hear the word commandments, they immediately think legalism. But the two words are not synonymous. No one spoke more of commandments than the Lord Jesus, yet no one was less legalistic than He.

What is legalism? Though the word itself is not found in the New Testament, it describes man's ceaseless effort to earn or deserve God's favor. Basically it signifies the attempt to gain justification or sanctification by lawkeeping. That is its real meaning.

But today the word is used in a wider sense to describe what are thought of as rigid, moralistic rules. Any attempt to classify certain practices as taboo is "legalistic." In fact, the word "legalism" is now used as a handy club to beat back almost any restraints on Christian behavior or any negatives.

How, then, should a Christian think in order to avoid the danger associated with "legalism"?

First of all, it is true that a Christian is free from the law, but it is important to add quickly that he is not lawless. He is enlawed to Christ. He shouldn't do as he pleases but as Christ pleases.

Secondly, it must be remembered that the New Testament is filled with commandments, including a fair number of negatives. The difference is that these commandments are not given as law, with penalty attached. They are given as instructions in righteousness for the people of God.

Next, things may be lawful for a Christian but they may not be profitable. They may be lawful but they may also be enslaving (1 Cor. 6:12, NASB).

It is possible that a believer may have liberty to do something and yet he might stumble someone else in doing it. In that case he shouldn't do it.

Just because someone dubs a prohibition as "legalistic" doesn't mean it is bad. People also use the word "puritanical" to certain codes of conduct, but the behavior of the Puritans was more Christ-honoring than that of many who criticize them.

Very often when Christians castigate accepted patterns of behavior as "legalism," it may be a sign that they themselves are becoming more permissive and are drifting from their moorings. They naively imagine that by throwing mud at so-called legalists or Puritans, they themselves will look better.

Our safety lies in staying as close to the teachings of Scripture as possible, not in trying to see how close we can get to the edge of the precipice.

May 1

If you ask anything in My name, I will do it.
JOHN 14:14

G od answers prayer. He answers it exactly the same way we would if we had infinite wisdom, love and power. Sometimes He gives us what we want, sometimes He gives us something better, but always what we need. Sometimes He answers our prayers quickly; at other times He teaches us to wait patiently.

> *God answers prayer; sometimes when hearts are weak,*
> *He gives the very gifts His children seek.*
> *But often faith must learn a deeper rest,*
> *And trust God's silence when He does not speak;*
> *For He whose name is love will send the best.*
> *Stars may burn out, nor mountain walls endure,*
> *But God is true, His promises are sure*
> *To those who seek.*

There are conditions to prayer. Often what seems like a blank check ("if ye ask anything") has conditions attached ("in My Name"). Individual prayer promises must be considered in the light of all other Scriptures on the subject.

There are mysteries to prayer. It is easy to think up all kinds of questions about the "whys" and "wherefores." But, for the most part, they are not edifying. It is better to pray and to see God work than to solve all the mysteries connected with prayer. I like what Archbishop Temple said: "When I pray, coincidences happen. When I do not, they don't."

When we pray to God in the Name of the Lord Jesus, it is just the same as if He were making those requests to the Father. This is what gives such significance and power to our prayers. And this is why we never come closer to omnipotence than when we pray. Of course, we will never be omnipotent, even in eternity. But when we pray in the Name of the Lord Jesus, we lay hold on infinite power.

The best prayer comes from a strong, inward necessity. This means that the more we are dependent on the Lord, the more effective our prayer life will be.

When we pray, we see things happen that would never happen according to the laws of chance or probability. Our lives crackle with the supernatural. They become radioactive with the Holy Spirit. And when we touch other lives, something happens for God.

We should be like the saint who said, "I measure my influence by the number who need my prayers and the number who pray for me."

May 2

And Jesus went about all Galilee, teaching in their synagogues,
preaching the gospel of the kingdom, and healing all kinds of sickness
and all kinds of disease among the people.
MATTHEW 4:23

 recurring problem among Christians is maintaining the proper balance between evangelism and social involvement. Evangelicals are often criticized for being too concerned with people's souls and not enough with their bodies. In other words, they don't spend enough time feeding the hungry, clothing the naked, healing the sick, and educating the illiterate.

To say anything against any of these ministries would be like criticizing motherhood. The Lord Jesus certainly was concerned with man's physical needs, and He taught His disciples to be concerned also. Historically, Christians have always been out in front in compassionate causes.

But as in so many other areas of life, it is a question of priorities. Which is more important, the temporal or the eternal? Judged on this basis, the gospel is the main thing. Jesus intimated this when He said, "This is the work of God, that ye believe..." Doctrine comes before social involvement.

Some of man's most pressing social problems are the result of false religion. For example, there are people dying of starvation who won't kill a cow because they believe a relative may be reincarnated in the cow. When other nations send enormous shipments of grain, the rats eat more of it than the people, because no one will kill the rats. These people are shackled by false religion; and Christ is the answer to their problems.

In trying to strike the proper balance between evangelism and social service, there is always the danger of becoming so occupied with "coffee and doughnuts" that the gospel is crowded out. The history of Christian institutions is filled with such examples where the good has become the enemy of the best.

Certain forms of social involvement are questionable if not altogether "out." The Christian should never participate in revolutionary attempts to overthrow the government. It is doubtful that he should resort to political processes to right social injustices. Neither the Lord nor the apostles did. More can be accomplished through the spread of the gospel than through legislation.

The Christian who forsakes all to follow Christ, who sells all to give to the poor, who opens his heart and pocketbook whenever he sees a genuine case of need, need not have a guilty conscience over social unconcern.

May 3

He who sows to his flesh will of the flesh reap corruption.
GALATIANS 6:8

o one can sin and get away with it. The results of sin are not only inescapable, they are extremely bitter. Sin may look like a harmless pussy but it eventually devours like a pitiless lion.

The supposed glamour of sin receives wide coverage—we seldom hear the other side. Few leave behind a description of their downfall and subsequent misery.

One of Ireland's most brilliant authors did. This man began to dabble in unnatural vice. One thing led to another until he became embroiled in lawsuits and finally landed in prison, where he wrote the following:

"The gods had given me almost everything. I had genius, a distinguished name, high social position, brilliancy, intellectual daring; I made art a philosophy, and philosophy an art; I altered the minds of men and the colour of things; There was nothing I said or did that did not make people wonder...I treated Art as the supreme reality, and life as a mere mode of fiction; I awoke the imagination of my century so that it created myth and legend around me; I summoned up all systems in a phrase, and all existence in an epigram.

"Along with these things, I had things that were different, let myself be lured into long spells of senseless and sensual ease. I amused myself with being a flaneur, a dandy, a man of fashion. I surrounded myself with the smaller natures and the meaner minds. I became the spendthrift of my own genius and to waste an eternal youth gave me a curious joy. Tired of being on the heights I deliberately went to the depths in search for new sensations. What the paradox was to me in the sphere of thought, perversity became to me in the sphere of passion. Desire, at the end, was a malady, or a madness, or both. I grew careless of the lives of others. I took pleasure where it pleased me and passed on. I forgot that every little action of the common day makes or unmakes character, and that therefore what one has done in the secret chamber one has some day to cry aloud on the housetops...I ended in horrible disgrace."

The essay in which he wrote the above confession bears the appropriate title *De Profundis*—out of the depths.

May 4

There is a way that seems right to a man, but its end is the way of death.
PROVERBS 14:12

T wice in the book of Proverbs (14:12 and 16:25) we learn that man's judgment as to the right way is not reliable. What seems right to him ends in disaster and death.

During World War II, the Navy gave a vivid illustration of this to its flight personnel. It was trying to impress on them that when they were flying at high altitudes and did not use their oxygen, they could not trust their senses. A pilot was instructed to enter a decompression chamber and sit down at a table on which was a sheet of mathematical problems. Oxygen was withdrawn from the chamber to simulate high altitudes. When the air became less dense, the pilot was told to solve the problems. He was also told that no one had done so correctly so far.

The pilot would breeze through the problems with utmost confidence that he had beaten the system. The problems seemed easy, and he had every assurance that he would receive a perfect score. There was no doubt in his mind about it.

But when oxygen was fed back into the chamber, and he emerged to have his paper corrected, he learned that his ability to solve problems had been seriously impaired by the lack of oxygen getting to his brain. The lesson was, of course, that if he flew at high altitudes without using his oxygen, he wouldn't be able to trust his own judgment, and he would be inviting a crash.

Man's judgment has been seriously impaired by sin. He feels absolutely sure that the way to heaven is by doing the best he can. If you tell him that no one has ever been saved by good works, he still has every confidence that he will be the first to beat the system. He is certain that God would never turn him away from the gates of heaven. But he is wrong, and if he persists in his lack of "spiritual oxygen," he will perish. His safety lies in trusting the Word of God rather than his own judgment. If he does so, he will repent of his sins and receive the Lord Jesus Christ as his Lord and Savior. Because God's Word is truth, those who believe it can be confident that they are following the right route.

May 5

...Esau, who for one morsel of food sold his birthright.
HEBREWS 12:16

1t is often possible to barter life's best values for a momentary gratification of physical appetite.

That is what Esau did. He had come in from the field tired and hungry. At that moment Jacob was cooking a pot of red bean soup. When Esau asked for a bowl of the "red stuff," Jacob said, in effect, "Sure, I'll give you some if you'll sell me your birthright in return."

Now the birthright was a valuable privilege which belonged to the oldest son in a family. It was valuable because it gave him the place of eventual headship in the family or tribe and entitled him to a double portion of the inheritance.

But at that moment, Esau considered the birthright worthless. What good is a birthright, he thought, to a man who is as famished as I? His hunger seemed so overpowering that he was willing to give almost anything to satisfy it. In order to pacify a momentary appetite, he was willing to surrender something that was of enduring value. And so he made the awful bargain!

A similar drama is being reenacted almost daily. Here is a man who has maintained a good testimony for years. He has the love of a fine family and the respect of his Christian fellowship. When he speaks, his words carry spiritual authority, and his service has the blessing of God upon it. He is a model believer.

But then comes the moment of fierce passion. It seems as if he is being consumed by the fires of sexual temptation. All of a sudden nothing seems so important as the satisfaction of this physical drive. He abandons the power of rational thought. He is willing to sacrifice everything for this illicit alliance.

And so he takes the insane plunge! For that moment of passion, he exchanges the honor of God, his own testimony, the esteem of his family, the respect of his friends, and the power of a sterling Christian character. Or as Alexander Maclaren said, "He forgets his longings after righteousness; flings away the joys of divine communion; darkens his soul; ends his prosperity; brings down upon his head for all his remaining years a cataract of calamities; and makes his name and his religion a target for the barbed sarcasms of each succeeding generation of scoffers."

In the classic words of Scripture, he sells his birthright for a mess of pottage.

May 6

How long will you mourn for Saul,
seeing I have rejected him from reigning over Israel?
1 SAMUEL 16:1

T here comes a time in life when we must stop mourning over the past and get on with the work of the present.

God had rejected Saul from being king. The action was final, irreversible. But Samuel had difficulty in accepting it. He had been closely associated with Saul and he now wept to see his hopes disappointed. He continued to mourn a loss that would never be retrieved. God said, in effect, "Quit mourning. Go out and anoint Saul's successor. My program has not failed. I have a better man than Saul to step onto the stage of Israel's history."

We would like to think that Samuel not only learned the lesson for himself but that he passed it on to David, who took Saul's place as king. At any rate, David showed that he had learned the lesson well. As long as his baby was dying, he fasted and mourned, hoping that God would spare the child. But when the infant died, he bathed, changed his clothes, went to the Tabernacle to worship, then ate a meal. To those who questioned his realism, he said, "But now he is dead; why should I fast? Can I bring him back again? I shall go to him, but he shall not return to me" (2 Sam. 12:23).

This has a voice for us in our Christian life and service. Sometime it may happen that a ministry might be wrenched away from us and given to someone else. We grieve over the death of an avenue of service.

It may be that a friendship or a partnership is severed, and that, as a result, life seems empty and flat. Or that we have been cruelly disappointed by someone who was very dear to us. We mourn the death of a valued relationship.

Or it may be that some life-long dream is shattered or some ambition is frustrated. We mourn the death of a noble aspiration or vision.

There is nothing wrong about mourning, but it should not be prolonged to the extent that it cripples our effectiveness in meeting the challenges of the hour. E. Stanley Jones said he made it a point to "recover within the hour" from the griefs and blows of life. An hour may not be long enough for most of us, but we must not be forever inconsolable over circumstances that cannot be changed.

May 7

He cares for you.
1 PETER 5:7

T he Bible is fairly full of tokens of God's marvelous care for His people. During Israel's forty-year trek through the wilderness, they ate food from heaven (Ex. 16:4), had an unfailing supply of water (1 Cor. 10:4), and were equipped with shoes that never wore out (Deut. 29:5).

It is the same in our wilderness journey. To prove this, our Lord reminds us how His care for us is so much greater than His care for birds, flowers, and animals. He speaks of sparrows, for instance. He provides their food (Mt. 6:26). Not one of them is forgotten before God (Lk. 12:6). Not one falls to the ground without Him (Mt. 10:29), or, as H. A. Ironside said, "God attends the funeral of every sparrow." The moral of the story, of course, is that we are of more value to Him than many sparrows (Mt. 10:31).

If He clothes the lilies of the field more beautifully than Solomon was ever attired, He will much more clothe us (Mt. 6:30). If He makes provision for the care of oxen, how much more will He care for our needs (1 Cor. 9:9)!

As our High Priest, the Lord Jesus bears our names on His shoulders—the place of power (Ex. 28:9-12) and on His breast—the place of affection (Ex. 28:15-21). Also our names are engraved in the palms of His hands (Isa. 49:16), a fact that inevitably reminds us of the nail wounds He sustained for us at Calvary.

He knows the exact number of the hairs of our head (Mt. 10:30). He numbers our tossings at night and keeps count of our tears in His book (Ps. 56:8, RSV).

Whoever touches us, touches the apple of His eye (Zech. 2:8). No weapon formed against us can prosper (Isa. 54:17).

Whereas the heathen carry their gods on their shoulders (Isa. 46:7), our God carries His people (Isa. 46:4).

When we go through the waters, the rivers, or the fire, He is with us (Isa. 43:2). In all our afflictions, He is afflicted (Isa. 63:9).

The One who guards us neither slumbers nor sleeps (Ps. 121:3-4). Someone has called this characteristic of God "the divine insomnia."

The Good Shepherd who gave His life for us will not withhold any good from us (Jn. 10:11; Ps. 84:11; Rom. 8:32).

He cares for us from the beginning of the year to the end (Deut. 11:12). He bears us even to old age (Isa. 46:4). In fact He will never leave us or forsake us (Heb. 13:5). God really cares!

May 8

I will give you the treasures of darkness.
ISAIAH 45:3

hen God made this promise to Cyrus, He was speaking of material treasures from lands of darkness that Cyrus would conquer. But we are not doing violence to the verse when we take it and apply it in a spiritual sense.

There are treasures that are discovered in the dark nights of life that are never found in days of unrelieved sunshine.

For instance, God can give songs in the darkest night (Job 35:10) that would never have been sung if life were completely devoid of trials.

There is the darkness of what J. Stuart Holden calls "life's inexplicable mysteries—the calamities, the catastrophes, the sudden and unexpected experiences which have come into life, and which all our forethought has not been sufficient to ward off; and life is dark because of them—sorrow, loss, disappointment, injustice, misconception of motive, slander." These are often the things that make life dark.

Humanly speaking, none of us would choose this darkness, and yet its benefits are incalculable. Leslie Weatherhead wrote, "Like all men, I love and prefer the sunny uplands of experience, when health, happiness and success abound, but I have learned far more about God and life and myself in the darkness of fear and failure than I have ever learned in the sunshine. There are such things as the treasures of darkness. The darkness, thank God, passes. But what one learns in the darkness, one possesses forever."

> *He knoweth what lies in the darkness,*
> *While the light dwelleth ever with Him;*
> *And the Father in whom is no darkness*
> *Will make clear what now is so dim.*
> —SARAH FARIS

May 9

person doesn't have to be known by name in order to accomplish great exploits for God. In fact, some of the people in the Bible who won immortal fame are not identified by their names.

There were the three men who brought water to David from the well of Bethlehem (2 Sam. 23:13-17). David considered this act of devotion so remarkable that he would not drink the water but poured it out as a holy offering. But the men are unnamed.

We do not know the name of the great woman of Shunem (2 Ki. 4:8-17) but she will always be remembered for building a prophet's chamber for Elisha.

It was an anonymous Jewish maid whose advice sent Naaman to Elisha to be healed of leprosy (2 Ki. 5:3-14). God knows her name, and that is all that matters.

Who was the woman who anointed the head of Jesus (Mt. 26:6-13)? Matthew does not give her name, but her fame is announced in the words of our Lord, "Assuredly, I say to you, wherever this gospel is preached in the whole world, what this woman has done will also be told as a memorial to her" (v. 13).

The poor widow who cast her two mites into the treasury is another of "God's unknowns" (Lk. 21:2). She illustrates the truth that it's wonderful how much you can do for God if you don't care who gets the credit.

Then, of course, there was the lad who gave his five loaves and two fishes to the Lord and saw them multiplied so they fed 5,000 men plus women and children (Jn. 6:9). We don't know his name, but what he did will never be forgotten.

A final illustration! Paul sent two brothers to Corinth with Titus in connection with a collection for the poor saints in Jerusalem. He does not give their names but he eulogizes them as messengers of the churches, and the glory of Christ (2 Cor. 8:23).

As Gray looked at the tombstones of obscure people in a country churchyard, he wrote:

> *Full many a flower is born to blush unseen,*
> *And waste its sweetness in the desert air.*

With God, however, nothing is wasted. He knows the names of all those who serve Him anonymously, and He will reward in a manner that is worthy of Himself.

May 10

We are not ignorant of his devices.
2 CORINTHIANS 2:11

It is important to know the devices of our enemy, the Devil. Otherwise he is likely to take advantage of us.

We should know that he is a liar, and has been from the beginning. In fact, he is the father of lies (Jn. 8:44). He lied to Eve by misrepresenting God, and he has been doing it ever since.

He is a deceiver (Rev. 20:10). He mixes a little truth with error. He imitates or counterfeits everything that is of God. He poses as an angel of light and sends out his messengers as ministers of righteousness (2 Cor. 11:14, 15). He deceives by using great signs and lying wonders (2 Thess. 2:9). He corrupts the minds of people (2 Cor. 11:3).

Satan is a murderous destroyer (Jn. 8:44; 10:10). His goal and the goal of all his demons is to destroy. There is no exception to that statement. As a raging lion, he goes about seeking whom he may devour (1 Pet. 5:8). He persecutes God's people (Rev. 2:10) and destroys his own slaves through drugs, demonism, alcohol, immorality, and related vices.

He is the accuser of the brethren (Rev. 12:10). The word "devil" (Gr., *diabolos*) means accuser or slanderer, and as his name is, so is he. All those who slander the brethren are doing the devil's work.

He sows discouragement. Paul warned the Corinthians that if they did not forgive the repentant backslider, Satan might gain an advantage by plunging the brother into extreme discouragement (2 Cor. 2:7-11).

Just as Satan, speaking through Peter, sought to dissuade Jesus from going to the Cross (Mk. 8:31-33), so he encourages Christians to spare themselves from the shame and suffering of crossbearing.

A favorite ploy of the Wicked One is to divide and conquer. He seeks to sow strife and discord among the saints, knowing that "a house divided against itself cannot stand." Sad to say, he has been all too successful in this strategy.

He blinds the minds of unbelievers lest the light of the gospel of the glory of Christ should shine unto them and they should be saved (2 Cor. 4:4). He blinds them by amusements, false religion, procrastination, and pride. He occupies them with feelings rather than facts, and with themselves rather than Christ.

Finally, Satan attacks right after great spiritual victories or mountaintop experiences, when the danger of pride is greatest. He looks for a weak spot in our armor, and shoots straight for it.

The best defense against the Devil is to live in unclouded fellowship with the Lord, covered by the protective gear of a holy character.

May 11

Moab has been at ease from his youth; he has settled on his dregs,
and has not been emptied from vessel to vessel, nor has he gone into captivity.
Therefore his taste remained in him, and his scent has not changed.
JEREMIAH 48:11

J eremiah here takes an illustration from the art of winemaking to teach us that a life of ease does not produce strength of character.

Whenever wine is being fermented in casks or vats, lees or dregs settle to the bottom. If the wine is left undisturbed, it becomes unpalatable. So the vintner must pour out the wine from vessel to vessel, eliminating the dregs and impurities. When he does this, the wine develops strength, aroma, color, and flavor.

Moab had lived a life of ease. He had never suffered the disruption of going into captivity. He had insulated himself from troubles, trials, and privations. The result was that his life was flat and insipid. It lacked fragrance and piquancy.

What is true of wine is true of us also. We need disruption, opposition, difficulties and disturbances to rid us of impurities and to develop the graces of a Christ-filled life.

Our natural tendency is to protect ourselves from anything that would unsettle us. We strive unceasingly to nestle. But God's will for us is that our lives should be a perpetual crisis of dependence on Him. He is forever stirring up the nest.

In her biography of Hudson Taylor, Mrs. Howard Taylor wrote: "This life that was to be made a blessing the wide world over must pass through a very different process (i.e., different from being settled on his lees), including much of that emptying and re-emptying 'from vessel to vessel,' so painful to the lower nature, from which we are being refined."

When we realize what the Divine Vintner is seeking to accomplish in our lives, it saves us from rebellion and teaches us submission and dependence. We learn to say:

> *Leave to His sovereign sway*
> *To choose and to command;*
> *So shalt thou, wondering, own His way,*
> *How wise, how strong His hand.*

> *Far, far above thy thought*
> *His counsel shall appear,*
> *When fully He the work hath wrought*
> *That caused thy needless fear.*

May 12

For since, in the wisdom of God, the world through wisdom did not know God,
it pleased God through the foolishness of the message
preached to save those who believe.
1 CORINTHIANS 1:21

Some in the church in Corinth were trying to make the gospel intellectually respectable. Their preoccupation with the wisdom of this world made them sensitive to those aspects of the Christian message which were offensive to the philosophers.

There was no thought of their abandoning the faith, only of redefining it so that it would be more palatable to the scholars.

Paul came down hard on this attempt to marry the world's wisdom to God's. He knew only too well that the achieving of intellectual status would result in a loss of spiritual power.

Let's face it! There is that about the Christian message that is scandalous to Jews and foolish to Gentiles. And not only that—most Christians are not what the world would call wise, mighty, or noble. Sooner or later we have to face up to the fact that instead of belonging to the intelligentsia, we are foolish, weak, base, despised—in fact, we are nobodies as far as the world is concerned.

But the wonderful thing is that God uses that message, which seems to be foolish, in saving those who believe. And God uses non-persons like us to accomplish His purposes. In choosing such unlikely instruments, He confounds all the pomp and pretension of this world, eliminates any possibility of our boasting, and insures that He alone gets the credit.

This is not to say that there is no place for scholarship. Of course there is. But unless that scholarship is combined with deep spirituality, it becomes a deadening and dangerous thing. When scholarship sits in judgment on the Word of God, claiming, for instance, that some writers used more reliable sources than others, it represents departure from the truth of God. And when we court the approbation of scholars like that, we are vulnerable to all their heresies.

Paul did not come to the Corinthians with excellence of speech or of wisdom. He determined to know nothing among them but Jesus Christ and Him crucified. He knew that power lay in the simple, straightforward presentation of the gospel, not in occupation with knotty problems or unprofitable theories, or in the worship of intellectualism.

May 13

But whoever causes one of these little ones who believe in Me to sin,
it would be better for him if a millstone were hung around his neck,
and he were drowned in the depth of the sea.
MATTHEW 18:6

It would be difficult to imagine a more effective and foolproof method of drowning than this. The millstone here was not the small one that was operated by hand, but the great one that was turned by an ass. To have a millstone like that secured around one's neck would mean speedy and inescapable drowning.

At first we might be startled by the vehemence of the Savior's words. He seems to thunder out with unusual condemnation against the sin of offending a little one. What is it that provokes such anger?

Let us take an illustration. Here is a minister of the gospel who has a constant line of people coming to him for counseling. Among them is a young person who is enslaved by some sexual sin. This young person needs help—desperately. He (or she) looks to the minister as one in whom he can have confidence, as one who will help him find the way of deliverance. But instead of that, the minister finds himself inflamed with passion, he makes improper advances, and soon he has led his counselee back into immorality. The young person is shattered by this betrayal of trust and is thoroughly disillusioned by the religious world. It may be that he is crippled spiritually for the rest of his life.

Or the offender may be a college professor who labors tirelessly to rob his students of whatever faith they may have. By sowing doubts and denials, he undermines the authority of the Scriptures and attacks the Person of our Lord.

Again it may be a Christian whose behavior stumbles a young believer. Overstepping the fine line between liberty and license, he is seen engaging in some questionable activity. The young Christian interprets his behavior as acceptable Christian conduct and leaves the path of godly separation to plunge into a life of worldliness and compromise.

We should be solemnly warned by the words of the Savior that it is a tremendously serious thing to contribute to the ethical, moral or spiritual delinquency of a minor who belongs to Him. Better to drown in literal water than to drown in a sea of guilt, disgrace and remorse for causing one of His little ones to fall into sin.

May 14

Let there be no...silly talk, nor levity, which are not fitting.
Ephesians 5:4, RSV

E xcessive levity should be avoided because it inevitably results in a leakage of spiritual power.

The preacher deals with serious issues, with life and death, with time and eternity. He may deliver a masterpiece of a message, and yet if there is undue humor in it, people are apt to remember the jokes and forget the rest.

Oftentimes the power of a message can be dissipated by lighthearted conversation afterwards. A solemn gospel appeal may result in the hush of eternity coming over a meeting. Yet when the people rise to leave, there is the buzz of social chatter. People talk about the football scores or the business of the day. Little wonder that the Holy Spirit is grieved and nothing happens for God.

Elders who are forever cracking jokes have little real spiritual impact on young people who look to them for inspiration. They might think that their wit ingratiates them with the young, but the truth is that the latter feel a keen sense of disappointment and disillusionment.

A form of levity that is especially harmful is making puns on the Bible, using passages of Scripture to get a laugh rather than to change a life. Every time we pun on the Bible, we lower its sense of authority in our own lives and in the lives of others.

This does not mean that a believer must be a gloomy Gus, without a trace of humor showing. It means rather that he should control his humor so that it will not cancel out his message.

Kierkegaard tells of the circus clown who ran into a town to cry out that the circus tent on the outskirts was on fire. The people listened to his cries and roared with laughter. He had been clowning so much that he had lost his credibility.

Charles Simeon kept a picture of Henry Martyn in his study. Wherever Simeon went in the room, it seemed that Martyn was following him with his eyes and saying, "Be earnest, be earnest; don't trifle, don't trifle." And Simeon would reply, "Yes, I will be in earnest; I will, I will be in earnest; I will not trifle, for souls are perishing, and Jesus is to be glorified."

May 15

Nor complain, as some of them also complained,
and were destroyed by the destroyer.
1 CORINTHIANS 10:10

The Israelites were chronic complainers as they trekked through the desert. They complained about the water supply. They complained about the food supply. They complained about their leaders. When God gave them manna from heaven, they soon grew tired of it and longed for the leeks, onions, and garlic of Egypt. Although there were no food markets or shoe stores in the wilderness, God provided an unfailing supply of groceries for forty years, and shoes that never wore out. Yet instead of being grateful for this miraculous provision, the Israelites complained without letup.

Times haven't changed. Men today complain about the weather: it's either too hot or too cold, too wet or too dry. They complain about the food, like lumpy gravy or burnt toast. They complain about their work and wages, then about unemployment when they have neither. They find fault with the government and its taxes, at the same time demanding ever-increasing benefits and services. They are unhappy with other people, with their car, with service in the restaurant. They complain about minor pains and aches, and wish they were taller, thinner, better looking. No matter how good God has been to them, they say, "What's He done for me lately?"

It must be a trial to God to have people like us on His hands. He has been so good to us, providing not only the necessities of life, but luxuries which His own Son did not enjoy when He was here upon earth. We have good food, pure water, comfortable homes, clothes in abundance. We have sight, hearing, appetite, memory, and so many other mercies that we take for granted. He has protected us, guided us, and sustained us. Best of all, He has given us eternal life through faith in the Lord Jesus Christ. And what thanks does He receive? Too often He hears nothing but a tirade of complaints.

I had a friend in Chicago years ago who had a good answer when asked, "How are you?" He would always reply, "It would be a sin to complain." I often think of that when tempted to murmur. It's a sin to complain. The antidote to complaining is thanksgiving. When we remember all that the Lord has done for us, we realize that we have no reason to complain.

May 16

Do not love the world or the things in the world.
If anyone loves the world, the love of the Father is not in him.
1 JOHN 2:15

T he world is presented in the New Testament as a kingdom that is opposed to God. Satan is its ruler, and all non-believers are subjects. This kingdom makes its appeal to man through the lust of the eyes, the lust of the flesh, and the pride of life. It is a society in which man tries to make himself happy without God, and in which the name of Christ is unwelcome. Dr. Gleason L. Archer Jr. says that the world is "the organized system of rebellion, self-seeking, and enmity toward God which characterizes the human race in opposition to God."

The world has its own amusements, politics, art, music, religion, thought-patterns and lifestyle. It seeks to force everyone to conform and hates those who refuse. This explains its hatred of the Lord Jesus.

Christ died to deliver us from the world. Now the world is crucified to us and we to it. It is positive treason for believers to love the world in any of its forms. In fact, the Apostle John says that those who love the world are the enemies of God.

Believers are not of the world, but they are sent into it to testify against it, to denounce its works as evil, and to preach salvation from it through faith in the Lord Jesus Christ.

Christians are called to walk in separation from the world. In the past, this may have been too narrowly limited to dancing, theaters, smoking, drinking, card playing, and gambling. But it includes much more. Much of what comes over the TV is worldly, appealing to the lust of the eyes and the lust of the flesh. Pride is worldly, whether it be pride of titles, degrees, salary, heritage, or a big name. Luxurious living is worldly, whether palatial homes, gourmet foods, attention-getting clothing and jewelry, or prestige cars. So is a life of ease and pleasure, spent largely on travel cruises, shopping sprees, sports and recreation. Our ambitions for ourselves and for our children may be worldly, even while we appear to be spiritual and pious. Finally, sex outside of marriage is a form of worldliness.

The more devoted we are to the Savior and the more sold out we are to Him, the less time we will have for worldly pleasures and amusements. C. Stacey Woods said, "The measure of our devotion to Christ is the measure of our separation from the world."

We are but strangers here, we do not crave
A home on earth, which gave Thee but a grave;
Thy cross has severed ties which bound us here,
Thyself our treasure in a brighter sphere.
—J. G. DECK

May 17

Whether in pretense or in truth, Christ is preached;
and in this I rejoice, yes, and will rejoice.
PHILIPPIANS 1:18

It is a common failing among men to acknowledge no good beyond their own private circle. It is as if they have a monopoly on excellence and refuse to admit that anyone else can be or do anything comparable. They remind us of the humorous bumper sticker, "I'm O.K. You're so-so." Even this would be a grudging admission for some of them to make.

Their church is the only right one. Their service for the Lord is what really counts. Their views on all subjects are the only authoritative ones. They are the people, and wisdom will die with them.

Paul did not belong to that school. He recognized that others were also preaching the gospel. True, some were doing it out of jealousy, hoping to annoy him. But he could still give them the credit for proclaiming the gospel and could still rejoice that Christ was being preached.

In his commentary on the Pastoral Epistles, Donald Guthrie wrote, "It takes great grace for independent thinkers to acknowledge that truth can flow in channels other than their own."

It is a distinctive feature of the cults that their leaders profess to speak the last word on all matters of faith and morals. They demand unquestioning obedience to their pronouncements, and seek to isolate their followers from contact with any dissenting views.

In the seldom-read introduction to the King James Version of the Bible, the translators wrote of "self-conceited brethren, who run their own ways, and give liking unto nothing, but what is framed by themselves, and hammered on their anvil."

The lesson for us is to be large-souled, to be willing to acknowledge good wherever we find it, and to realize that no believer or Christian fellowship can afford to claim that they are the only right ones, or that they have a corner on the truth.

May 18

...he spoke rashly with his lips.
PSALM 106:33

W hen the people of Israel grumbled about the lack of water at Kadesh, God told Moses that water would flow if he would speak to the rock. But Moses was fed up with the people by now, so he lashed out at them, saying, "Hear now, ye rebels; must we fetch you water out of the rock?" Then he smote the rock twice with his rod. By his angry words and disobedient action, he misrepresented God to the people. The result was that he forfeited the privilege of leading the children of Israel into the promised land (Num. 20:1-13).

It is easy for a man of burning zeal to be intemperate with other believers. He is so self-disciplined whereas they need to be forever babied along. He is so knowledgeable and they so ignorant.

But what he must learn is that they are still God's beloved people, and that the Lord will not tolerate any verbal abuse of them. It is one thing to preach the Word of God in such power that people are convicted and torn up. But it is quite another thing to scold them severely as an expression of personal irritation. This will cut a man off from God's best rewards.

When David's illustrious men are listed in 2 Samuel 23, there is one name that is conspicuous by its absence. It is the name of Joab, David's commander-in-chief. But why is his name missing? It has been suggested that the reason is that Joab used the sword on some of David's friends. If so, the incident is full of warning for us when we are tempted to use our tongues as a sword on God's people.

When James and John, the sons of thunder, wanted to call down fire from heaven on the Samaritans, Jesus said, "You do not know what manner of spirit you are of" (Lk. 9:55). How *apropos* the rebuke is to us when we speak unadvisedly with our lips to those who are His not only by creation (as the Samaritans were), but by redemption as well.

May 19

The judgment of God is according to truth.
ROMANS 2:2

G od is the only One in the universe who is perfectly qualified to judge. We can be everlastingly thankful that He has not entrusted the final judgment to us. Think of some of the disabilities under which an earthly judge works. It is impossible for him to be completely objective. He may be influenced by the prominence of the defendant or by his appearance. He may be influenced by bribes or by other more subtle considerations. He can not always know if a witness is lying. Or if not lying, the witness may be withholding the truth. Or again, he may be shading the truth. Or finally, he may be sincere but inaccurate.

The judge cannot always know the motives of those with whom he deals-and it is important to establish motives in many legal cases.

Even the polygraph or lie detector can be fooled. Hardened criminals can sometimes control their physiological reactions to guilt.

But God is the perfect Judge. He has absolute knowledge of all acts, thoughts and motives. He can judge the secrets of men's hearts. He knows all the truth; nothing can be withheld from Him. He is not a respecter of persons but treats each one impartially. He knows the mental ability with which each one is endowed; an imbecile may not be as responsible as others for his actions. He knows the differing moral strengths of His subjects; some may resist temptation more easily than others. He knows the differing privileges and opportunities each one has, and the extent to which a person sins against light. He detects sins of omission as easily as sins of commission, secret sins as easily as public scandal.

Therefore we need not fear that the heathen who has never heard the Gospel will be treated unjustly. Or that those who have suffered wrongfully through life will be unavenged. Or that wicked tyrants who have escaped in this life will go unpunished.

The Judge on the bench is a perfect Judge, and His justice will be according to truth and therefore absolutely perfect.

May 20

No one puts new wine into old wineskins; or else the new wine
will burst the wineskins and be spilled, and the wineskins will be ruined.
But new wine must be put into new wineskins, and both are preserved.
LUKE 5:37, 38

T he bottles referred to here were actually containers made from the hides of animals. When these wineskins were new, they were pliable and somewhat elastic. But when they became old, they were stiff and inflexible. If new wine was placed in old skins, the fermenting action of the wine would build up too much pressure for the old wineskins, to accommodate, and they would burst.

Here in Luke 5, Jesus uses this to illustrate the clash between Judaism and Christianity. He is saying that "the outmoded forms, ordinances, traditions and rituals of Judaism were too rigid to hold the joy, the exuberance and the energy of the new dispensation."

This chapter contains dramatic illustrations. In verses 18-21, we see four men tearing up the roof of a house in order to bring a paralyzed man to Jesus for healing. Their innovative, unconventional method is an illustration of the new wine. In verse 21, the scribes and Pharisees begin to find fault with Jesus; they are the old wineskins. Again, in verses 27-29 we have Levi's enthusiastic response to Christ's call, and the banquet he held to introduce his friends to Jesus. That is the new wine. In verse 30, the scribes and Pharisees grumble again. They are the old wineskins.

We see this in all of life. People get set in traditional ways of doing things and find it hard to adjust to change. The housewife has her own way of doing the dishes and finds it irritating to see someone else fumbling around in her sink. The husband has his own ideas as to how a car should be driven, and nearly loses his senses when wife or children drive.

But the great lesson for all of us is in the spiritual realm. We should be flexible enough to allow for the joy, the effervescence, the enthusiasm of the Christian faith, even if it comes in unconventional ways. We neither want nor need the stodginess and cold formalism of the Pharisees, who sat on the sidelines criticizing when God was working.

May 21

Unless a grain of wheat falls into the ground and dies, it remains alone;
but if it dies, it produces much grain.
JOHN 12:24

O ne day some Greeks came to Philip with the noble request, "Sir, we would see Jesus!" But why did they want to see Him? Perhaps they wanted to take Him back to Athens as a popular new philosopher. Or perhaps they wanted to save Him from crucifixion and death, which now seemed inevitable.

Jesus answered with one of the great laws of harvest: a kernel of grain must fall into the ground and die if it is to become productive. If He were to save Himself from death, He would abide alone. He would enjoy the glories of heaven by Himself; there would be no saved sinners there to share His glory. But if He died, He would provide a way of salvation by which many would enjoy eternal life. It was imperative for Him that He die a sacrificial death rather than live a comfortable life.

T. G. Ragland once said, "Of all plans of ensuring success, the most certain is Christ's own, becoming a grain of wheat, falling into the ground and dying. If we refuse to become grains of wheat...if we will neither sacrifice prospects, nor risk character, and property and health; nor, when we are called, relinquish home, and break family ties, for Christ's sake; then we shall abide alone. But if we wish to be fruitful, we must follow our blessed Lord Himself, by becoming a corn of wheat, and dying. Then we shall bring forth much fruit."

Years ago I read of a group of missionaries in Africa who had labored tirelessly for years without seeing any lasting fruit for God. In desperation, they finally announced a conference where they would get before God in prayer and fasting. In the discussion that followed, one of the missionaries said, "I don't think we'll ever see blessing until a corn of wheat falls into the ground and dies." Shortly afterward, that same missionary took sick and died. Then the harvest began—the blessing which he had predicted.

Samuel Zwemer wrote:

There is no gain but by a loss,
You cannot save but by a cross;
The corn of wheat to multiply
Must fall into the ground and die.
Wherever you ripe fields behold,
Waving to God their sheaves of gold,
Be sure some corn of wheat has died,
Some soul there has been crucified;
Someone has wrestled, wept, and prayed,
And fought hell's legions undismayed.

May 22

Sever yourselves from such a man, whose breath is in his nostrils;
For of what account is he?
ISAIAH 2:22

hen we give a man or woman the place in our life that only God should have, we are in for a bitter disappointment. We will soon learn that the best of men are men at best. Although they might have some very fine qualities, yet they still have feet of iron and clay. This may sound like cynicism, but it is not. It is realism.

When the invaders were threatening Jerusalem, the people of Judah looked to Egypt for deliverance. Isaiah denounced them for this misplaced trust, saying, "Look! You are trusting in the staff of this broken reed, Egypt, on which if a man leans, it will go into his hand and pierce it. So is Pharaoh king of Egypt to all who trust in him" (Isa. 36:6). And Jeremiah said later, under similar circumstances, "Thus says the Lord: Cursed is the man who trusts in man and makes flesh his strength, whose heart departs from the Lord" (Jer. 17:5).

The psalmist showed genuine insight on this subject when he wrote, "It is better to trust in the Lord than to put confidence in man. It is better to trust in the Lord than to put confidence in princes" (Ps. 118:8-9). And again, "Do not put your trust in princes, nor in a son of man, in whom there is no help. His spirit departs, he returns to his earth; in that very day his plans perish" (Ps. 146:3-4).

Of course, we must realize that there is a certain sense in which we have to trust one another. What would a marriage be, for instance, without a certain measure of trust and respect? In business life, the use of checks as money is based on a system of mutual trust. We trust doctors to diagnose and prescribe properly. We trust the labels on cans and packages in the food market. It would be almost impossible to live in any society without some confidence in our fellows.

The danger comes when we trust man to do what only God can do, when we take the Lord off the throne and put man on it. Anyone who displaces God in our affections, who takes His place as our confidence, who usurps any of His prerogatives in our lives—that one is certain to disappoint us bitterly. We will realize too late that man is not worthy of such trust.

May 23

That they all may be one, as You, Father, are in Me, and I in You;
that they also may be one in Us, that the world may believe that You sent Me.
JOHN 17:21

T wice in His great high priestly prayer, our Lord prayed that His people might be one (vv. 21 and 22-23). This prayer for unity has been seized as scriptural support for the ecumenical movement—a great organizational union of all professing Christian churches. Unfortunately, this ecumenical union is achieved through abandoning or reinterpreting fundamental Christian doctrines. As Malcolm Muggeridge wrote, "By one of our time's larger ironies, ecumenicalism is triumphant just when there is nothing to be ecumenical about; the various religious bodies are likely to find it easy to join together only because, believing little, they correspondingly differ about little."

Is this the kind of unity that the Lord Jesus was praying for in John 17? We think not. He said that the unity He had in mind would result in the world's believing that God had sent Him. It is extremely doubtful that any external federation would have this effect.

The Lord defined the unity He had in mind when He said, "as You, Father, are in Me, and I in You; that they also may be one in Us." He also said, "…just as We are one: I in them, and You in Me; that they may be made perfect in one" What unity does the Father and Son share which we can also have a part in? Not the fact of Their common deity; we can never share in that. I would suggest that the Lord Jesus was referring to a unity based on common moral likeness. He was praying that believers might be one in exhibiting the character of God and of Christ to the world. This would mean lives of righteousness, holiness, grace, love, purity, long-suffering, self-control, meekness, joy and generosity. Ronald Sider suggests in *Rich Christians in an Age of Hunger* that the unity for which Christ prayed was manifested when the early Christians shared freely with one another whenever there was need. They had a true spirit of *koinonia* or community. "Jesus' prayer that the loving unity of His followers would be so striking; that it would convince the world that He had come from the Father has been answered—at least once! It happened in the Jerusalem church. The unusual quality of their life together gave power to the apostolic preaching" (see Acts 2:45-47; 4:32-35).

Such unity today would have a profound impression on the world. As Christians presented a united testimony in radiating the life of the Lord Jesus, unbelievers would be convicted of their own sinfulness and would thirst for the living water. Today's tragedy is that many Christians are scarcely distinguishable from their worldly neighbors. Under such circumstances, there is little inducement for unbelievers to be converted.

May 24

Wealth gained by dishonesty will be diminished,
PROVERBS 13:11

Y ou may have already won $100,000!" With this and similar come-ons, we are constantly barraged by the temptation to participate in some form of gambling. The housewife shopping in the supermarket is enticed by the latest sweepstakes. The average citizen is encouraged to send his name (together with a subscription for a magazine) to participate in an upcoming lottery involving millions. Or it may be a bingo contest in which you are almost assured of being a winner.

Then, of course, there are the more obvious forms of gambling—roulette, horse-racing, dog-racing, the numbers game, etc.

What does the Bible have to say about all this? Nothing good.

It says, "Wealth gained by dishonesty will be diminished, but he who gathers by labor will increase" (Prov. 13:11).

It says, "A man with an evil eye hastens after riches, and does not consider that poverty will come upon him" (Prov. 28:22).

It says, "Like a partridge that hatches eggs it did not lay is the man who gains riches by unjust means. When his life is half gone, they will desert him, and in the end he will prove to be a fool" (Jer. 17:11, NIV).

While the Ten Commandments do not explicitly say, "Thou shalt not gamble," They do say, "You shall not covet" (Ex. 20:17), and what is gambling but a form of covetousness?

Gambling will always have an evil connotation for believers when they remember that Roman soldiers gambled for the Savior's seamless robe at the scene of His crucifixion.

Consider also the poverty and grief that chronic gamblers have brought to their families, the crimes that have been committed to recoup losses, and the evil associations frequently linked with gambling, and it will be seen that it should have no place in a Christian's life.

After reminding Timothy that the believer should be content with food and raiment, Paul warned that those who "desire to be rich fall into temptation and a snare, and into many foolish and harmful lusts, which drown men in destruction and perdition" (1 Tim. 6:9).

May 25

Go and tell him his fault between you and him alone.
MATTHEW 18:15B

 omeone has done or said something which has offended you or bothered you in some way. The Bible says to go and tell him his fault, but you don't want to do it; it's too difficult.

So you start brooding about it. You begin rehearsing what he has done, how he was utterly in the wrong. When you should be working, your mind is going over all the details, and your gastric juices work overtime. When you should be sleeping, you resurrect the unpleasant incident, and the pressure builds up in the boiler. The Bible says to go and tell him his fault, but you just can't face up to it.

You try to think of some way in which you can get the message across to him anonymously. Or you hope that something will happen to shame him for what he has done. It doesn't happen. You know what you ought to do, but you dread the trauma of a face to face confrontation.

By this time, the ordeal is harming you a lot more than it is harming him. People can tell by your glum appearance that something is bothering you. When they talk to you, your mind is off in another hemisphere. Your work suffers because you are preoccupied. In general, you are too distracted to be effective. And the Bible still says, "Go and tell him his fault between you and him alone." By a tremendous display of will power, you have refrained from talking to anyone else about it, but finally the pressure becomes unbearable. You break down and tell one person—just for his prayer fellowship, of course. Instead of giving you the expected sympathy, he says, "Why don't you go and talk to the one who has offended you?"

That does it! You decide to bite the bullet. After rehearsing your speech, you obey the Word by telling him his fault. He takes it surprisingly well, is sorry that it has happened, and asks your forgiveness. The interview is terminated by prayer.

As you walk away, a great load is lifted from your shoulders. Your stomach quits churning and your metabolism returns to normal. You kind of hate yourself for not having had the sense to obey the Scriptures more promptly.

May 26

Behold, to obey is better than sacrifice, and to heed than the fat of rams.
1 SAMUEL 15:22

 od's instructions to King Saul were clear enough. Slay the Amalekites and destroy all their possessions. All of them. Don't take any spoil. But Saul spared King Agag and the choicest of the sheep, oxen, fatlings, and lambs.

When Samuel met Saul in the morning at Gilgal, Saul confidently announced that he had done exactly what the Lord commanded. But at that very moment, a barnyard choir began its oratorio—sheep bleating and oxen lowing. Very embarrassing!

Samuel wanted to know, of course, how the sheep were bleating if Saul had killed them all. The king then tried to cover his disobedience by blaming the people and by excusing them on religious grounds. He said, "The people spared the best of the sheep and oxen to sacrifice to the Lord."

It was then he heard God's prophet thunder out the convicting words, "Behold, to obey is better than sacrifice, and to heed than the fat of rams. For rebellion is as the sin of witchcraft, and stubbornness is as iniquity and idolatry" (1 Sam. 15:22-23).

Obedience is more important than rituals, sacrifices, and offerings. I heard once of a family who treated their mother with cool contempt and disobedience during her lifetime. But when she died, they dressed her corpse in a Dior original. A despicable and futile attempt to atone for years of rebellion and discourtesy!

We often hear people defending an unscriptural position or unscriptural associations on the ground that they can have a wider influence in this way. But God is not deceived by such specious rationalizations. He wants our obedience—He will take care of our sphere of influence. The truth is that when we are disobedient, our influence is negative. Only when we are walking in fellowship with the Lord can we exert a godly influence on others.

William Gurnall said, "Sacrifice without obedience is sacrilege." And it becomes even worse when we cloke our disobedience with some pious, religious excuse. God is not hoodwinked.

May 27

Which is greater, the gold or the temple that sanctifies the gold?
MATTHEW 23:17

The scribes and Pharisees of Jesus' day taught that if a man swore by the Temple, he wasn't necessarily obligated to do what he promised. But if he swore by the gold of the Temple, then that was a different story. He was bound by that oath. They made the same false distinction between swearing by the altar and swearing by the sacrifice on it. The former oath could be broken; the latter was binding.

The Lord told them that their sense of values was completely twisted. It is the Temple that gives the gold special value, and it is the altar that sets apart the sacrifice in a special way.

The Temple was the dwelling place of God on earth. The highest honor that any gold could have was to be used in that dwelling. Its connection with the House of God set it apart in a unique way. So it was with the altar and the sacrifice on it. The altar was an integral part of the divine service. No animal could be more highly honored than to be sacrificed on the altar. If animals could have ambitions, they would have all aimed for that destiny.

A tourist bought an inexpensive amber necklace in a secondhand shop in Paris. He became curious when he had to pay heavy customs in New York. He went to a jeweler to have it appraised and was offered $25,000. A second jeweler offered $35,000. When he asked why it was so valuable, the jeweler put it under a magnifying glass. The tourist read, "From Napoleon Bonaparte to Josephine." It was the name of Napoleon that made the necklace so valuable.

The application should be clear. In ourselves we are nothing and can do nothing. It is our association with the Lord and with His service that sets us apart in a special way. As Spurgeon said, "Your connection with Calvary is the most wonderful thing about you."

You may have an unusually brilliant mind. That is something to be thankful for. But remember this: It is only as that mind is used for the Lord Jesus Christ that it ever reaches its highest destiny. It is Christ that sanctifies your intellect.

You may have talents for which the world is willing to pay a high price. You may even think that the Church is too insignificant for them. But it is the Church that sanctifies your talents, and not your talents that sanctify the Church.

You may have bundles of money. You can hoard it, spend it on self-indulgence, or use it for the Kingdom. The greatest use to which it can be put is to spend it in furthering the cause of Christ. It is the Kingdom that sanctifies your wealth, not vice versa.

May 28

But we all, with unveiled face, beholding as in a mirror the glory of the Lord,
are being transformed into the same image from glory to glory,
just as by the Spirit of the Lord.
2 CORINTHIANS 3:18

T he Bible teaches that we become like what we worship. That important insight is found in today's text. Let's break it down this way:

But we all—that is, all true believers;

with open or *unveiled face*—sin causes a veil between our faces and the Lord. When we confess and forsake the sin, we have an open or unveiled face;

beholding as in a glass—the glass or mirror is the Word of God, in which we behold

the glory of the Lord—meaning His moral excellence. In the Bible we gaze upon the perfection of His character, the beauty of all His works and ways;

are changed into the same image—we become like Him. We are changed by beholding. The more we are occupied with Him, the more like Him we become. This change is

from glory to glory—from one degree of glory to another. The change does not take place all at once. It is a process that continues as long as we behold Him. The transformation of our character is effected

even as by the Spirit of the Lord—the Holy Spirit produces likeness to Christ in all those who gaze by faith upon the Savior as He is revealed in the Bible.

In *The Tales of Nathaniel Hawthorne,* it wasn't Mr. Gathergold or General Blood and Thunder or Old Stony Phiz or the poet, but Ernest—who, gazing in quiet meditation on the Great Stone Face, eventually came to resemble it.

I heard once of a man who went daily to a Buddhist temple and sat with legs akimbo and arms folded, gazing upon the green statue. It was said that after years of this meditation, he actually came to resemble the Buddha. Whether that is true, I don't know, but I do know that reverent occupation with the Son of God produces moral resemblance to Him.

The way to holiness is through gazing upon the Lord Jesus. It is not ordinarily possible to think of Christ and of sin at the same time. During those moments when we are taken up with Him, we are most free from sin. Our goal then should be to increase the percentage of our time when we are beholding Him.

May 29

Not that I speak in regard to need...
Philippians 4:11

I t is noteworthy that Paul never made his own financial needs known. His was a life of faith. He believed that God had called him into His service, and was utterly convinced that God pays for what He orders.

Should Christians today publicize their needs or beg for money? Here are a few considerations:

There is no scriptural justification for this practice. The apostles made known the needs of others, but never asked for money for themselves.

It seems more consistent with the life of faith to look to God alone. He will provide the needed funds for anything He wants us to do. When we see Him providing in just the right amount at just the right time, our faith is greatly strengthened. And He is greatly glorified when the provision is undeniably miraculous. On the other hand, He does not get the credit when we manipulate our own finances through clever fund-raising techniques.

By using appeals and solicitation, we can carry on works "for God" that might not be His will at all. Or we can perpetuate a work long after the Spirit has departed from it. But when we are dependent on His supernatural provision, we can continue only as long as He supplies.

High-pressure solicitation introduces a new way of measuring success in Christian work. The one who is most clever in public relations is the one who gets the most money. It may be that worthy works suffer because the fund campaigns siphon off the money. This often gives rise to jealousy and disunity.

C. H. Mackintosh took a dim view of publicizing one's own personal needs. "To make known my wants, directly or indirectly, to a human being is departure from the life of faith, and a positive dishonor to God. It is actually betraying Him. It is tantamount to saying that God has failed me, and I must look to my fellow for help. It is forsaking the living fountain and turning to a broken cistern. It is placing the creature between my soul and God, thus robbing my soul of rich blessing, and God of the glory due to Him."

In similar vein, Corrie Ten Boom wrote in *Tramp for the Lord,* "I would much rather be a trusting child of a rich Father, than a beggar at the door of worldly men."

May 30

No one knows the Son except the Father.
MATTHEW 11:27

T here is deep mystery connected with the Person of the Lord Jesus Christ. Part of the mystery is the combination of absolute deity and full humanity in one Person. There is the question, for instance, how One who has the attributes of God can at the same time have the limitations of finite Man. No mere man can comprehend the Person of Christ. Only God the Father understands.

Many of the most serious heresies that have racked the Church have centered on this subject. Heedless of their own frailty, men have occupied themselves with that which is too deep for them. Some have overemphasized the deity of our Lord at the expense of His humanity. Others have so stressed His humanity as to detract from His Godhood.

William Kelly once wrote, "The point where error comes in is as to the Son of God becoming a man; for it is the complex person of the Lord Jesus that exposes persons to break down fatally. There are those, no doubt, who dare to deny His divine glory. But there is a far more subtle way in which the Lord Jesus is lowered; where, although He is owned to be divine, the manhood of the Lord is allowed to swamp His glory, and neutralize the confession of His person. Thus, one is soon perplexed, and one lets that which puts Him in association with us here below work so as to falsify that which He has in common with God Himself. There is but one simple safeguard that keeps the soul right as to this, which is, that we do not venture to pry and never dare to discuss it, fearing to rush in human folly on holy ground, and feeling that on such ground as this we should be only worshippers. Wherever this is forgotten by the soul, it will invariably be found that God is not with it—that He allows the self-confident one, who of himself ventures to speak of the Lord Jesus to prove his own folly. It is only by the Holy Ghost that he can know what is revealed about the Only-begotten."

A venerable servant of the Lord once advised his students to stick to the language of Scripture itself when discussing the dual nature of our Lord. It is when we inject our own ideas and speculations that errors creep in.

No man knows the Son. Only the Father knows Him.

The high myst'ries of His fame
The creature's grasp transcend.
The Father only—glorious claim
The Son can comprehend.
—JOSIAH CONDER

May 31

But the natural man does not receive the things of the Spirit of God, for they are foolishness to him; nor can he know them, because they are spiritually discerned.
1 CORINTHIANS 2:14

T he natural man is the one who has never been born again. He does not have the Spirit of God. He is disinclined to receive spiritual truths because they sound like nonsense to him. But that is not all! He cannot understand spiritual truths because they can only be understood by the illumination of the Holy Spirit.

This must be emphasized. It is not just that the unsaved man doesn't want to understand the things of God. He cannot understand them. He has a native incapacity for doing so.

This helps me in properly evaluating the scientists, philosophers, and other professional people of the world. As long as they speak about mundane matters, I respect them as experts. But as soon as they start intruding into the spiritual realm, I write them off as unqualified to speak with any authority.

I am not unduly surprised if some college professor or even some liberal clergyman grabs the headlines with doubts or denials concerning the Bible. I have come to expect that and disregard it. I realize that the unregenerate have gone beyond their depth when they talk about the things of the Spirit of God.

F. W. Boreham likened the great men of science and philosophy to second-class passengers on an ocean liner, barred from the first-class promenade. "Scientists and philosophers—as such—are, so to speak, 'second-class passengers,' and they must be kept on their own side of the barrier. They are not authorities on the Christian faith...The fact is that we have a faith which cannot be shocked by the contempt of second-class passengers, and which derives no real support from their corroboration and patronage."

Of course, there is the occasional scientist or philosopher who is a saint. In such a case, Boreham said, "I always discover a 'first-class ticket' peeping out of his pocket; and as I stroll the promenade in his delightful company, I no more think of him as a scientist than I think of Bunyan as a tinker. We are fellow passengers—first-class."

Said Robert G. Lee, "Men may be critical and scholarly and scientific, knowing all about rocks and molecules and gases, and yet be utterly incompetent to sit in judgment upon Christianity and the Bible."

June 1

The Lord was with Joseph, and he was a successful man.
Genesis 39:2

1 have heard that one of the earliest versions of the English Bible translated this verse, "And the Lord was with Joseph, and he was a lucky fellow." Perhaps "lucky" at that time had a different meaning. At any rate we are glad that later translators removed Joseph from the realm of luck.

For the child of God there is no luck. His life is controlled, guarded, and planned by a loving heavenly Father. Nothing happens to him by chance.

That being so, it is inconsistent for a Christian to wish "Good luck" to someone else. Nor should he say, "I lucked out." Such expressions are a practical denial of the truth of divine providence.

The unbelieving world associates various things with good luck—a rabbit's foot, a wishbone, a four-leaf clover, a horseshoe (always with ends pointing upward so the luck won't spill out!). Men cross their fingers and knock on wood, as if those actions could affect events favorably, or avert misfortune.

The same people associate other things with bad luck—a black cat, Friday the 13th, walking under a ladder, the number 13 on a room or on the floor of a building. It is sad to think of people living in bondage to such superstitions, a bondage that is both needless and fruitless.

In Isaiah 65:11 (NASB), God threatened punishment for those in Judah who, it seems, were worshiping the god of chance.

> *But you who forsake the Lord,*
> *Who forget My holy mountain,*
> *Who set a table for Fortune,*
> *And who fill cups with mixed wine for Destiny.*

We cannot be positive as to the particular sin involved but it sounds suspiciously as if the people were bringing offerings to idols that were associated with luck and chance. God hated it and still does.

What confidence it gives us to know that we are not the helpless pawns of blind chance, or of the rolling of cosmic dice, or of Lady Luck. Everything in life is planned, is meaningful, and is purposeful. For us it is our Father, not fate; Christ, not chance; love, not luck.

June 2

It is enough! Now, Lord, take my life, for I am no better than my fathers.
1 KINGS 19:4b

It is not uncommon for God's people to suffer from nervous depression, just as Elijah did. Moses and Jonah also wished they could die (Ex. 32:32; Jonah 4:3). The Lord has never promised believers exemption from this type of trouble. Neither does the presence of this affliction necessarily indicate a lack of faith or spirituality. It could happen to anyone of us.

When it does strike, it is something like this. You feel that God has forsaken you, even though you know very well that He never forsakes His own. You go to the Word of God for comfort, and invariably you turn to a passage on the unpardonable sin or the hopeless condition of an apostate. You experience the frustration of having an affliction that cannot be removed by surgery and cannot be cured by medicines. Your friends suggest that you should "snap out of it," but they never tell you how. You pray and long for some quick remedy, but find that while nervous prostration comes in pounds, it leaves in ounces. All you can think about is yourself and your own misery. In your despondency, you wish you could die by some dramatic act of God.

Depression like this can have several different causes. There may be a physical problem: anemia, for instance, can cause your mind to play tricks on you. There may be a spiritual cause: sin unconfessed or unforgiven can do it. There may be an emotional basis: the unfaithfulness of a spouse can bring it on. Overwork or extreme mental stress can lead to nervous exhaustion. Or it may be caused by a medication to which a certain individual may react unfavorably.

What can be done? First, go to God in prayer, asking Him to work out His wonderful purposes. Confess and forsake all known sin. Forgive anyone who may have wronged you. Then have a thorough medical checkup to rule out any physical ailment as a possible reason. Take drastic action to eliminate causes of overwork, worry, stress, and anything else that might be bothering you. Regular rest, good food, and physical work out of doors all provide good therapy.

From then on, you must learn how to pace yourself, daring to say "no" to claims on you that might push you over the brink again.

June 3

*This being so, I myself always strive to have a conscience
without offense toward God and men.*
ACTS 24:16

I n a society like ours, and with a corrupt old nature like ours, we are constantly faced with problems of ethics that test the sincerity of our commitment to Christian principles.

The student, for instance, is tempted to cheat on his exams. If all diplomas earned dishonestly were returned, the schools and colleges would scarcely contain them.

The taxpayer is forever tempted to understate his income, overstate his expenses, or withhold some pertinent information altogether.

The name of the game in business, politics, and law is payola. Bribes are used to pervert justice. Gifts change hands to get orders. Kickbacks keep business coming. Payoffs appease local inspectors who often make extreme and sometimes ridiculous demands.

Almost every profession has its own pressures to be dishonest. The Christian doctor is called on to sign his name to insurance claims that are patently false. The lawyer must decide whether to defend a criminal whom he knows to be guilty, or to handle a divorce case where both parties are Christians. The used car dealer fights a battle within whether to adjust the odometer to show a lower mileage. The laborer faces the decision, in joining a union, of committing himself to violence in the event of a strike. Should a Christian flight attendant serve liquor (or, choosing that job, does she have any choice)? Should a Christian athlete play on the Lord's Day? Should a Christian grocer sell cigarettes, which are known to produce cancer?

Is it worse for a Christian architect to design a nightclub or a modernistic, liberal church building? Should a Christian organization accept gifts from a brewery? Or from a Christian who is living in sin? Should a buyer accept a crate of oranges or a box of jams and jellies from one of his suppliers at Christmas time?

The best deciding rule is the one in our text—"to have always a conscience void of offense toward God, and toward men."

June 4

Great is the Lord, and greatly to be praised; and His greatness is unsearchable.
PSALM 145:3

T he thought of God is undoubtedly the greatest thought that can occupy the human mind. Great thoughts of God ennoble all of life. Small thoughts of God destroy those who hold them.

God is very great. After a magnificent description of the power and majesty of God, Job said, "Lo, these are but the outskirts of His ways: and how small a whisper do we hear of Him! but the thunder of His power who can understand?" (Job 26:14, RV). We see only the fringes, and hear only a whisper!

The Psalmist reminds us that the glance of God produces an earthquake and His touch precipitates volcanic eruptions (Ps. 104:32).

The Lord has to humble Himself to behold things in heaven (Ps. 113:6). He is so great that He calls the stars by name (Ps. 147:4).

When Isaiah tells us that the train of God's glory fills the Temple (Isa. 6:1), he leaves us to imagine how great the full display of His glory must be. Later he pictures God as measuring the oceans in the hollow of His hand and measuring the skies by the width of His spread hand (Isa. 40:12). To Him, the nations are a drop of a bucket or the dust on the scales (40:15). All the forests of Lebanon and all its animals would not be sufficient to make a suitable burnt offering to Him (40:16).

The prophet Nahum says, "The Lord has His way in the whirlwind and in the storm, and the clouds are the dust of His feet" (Nahum 1:3).

In the midst of another breathtaking description of the glory of God, Habakkuk says, "and there His power was hidden" (Hab. 3:4). All of which says that human language breaks down in any attempt to picture the greatness of God.

As we contemplate some of the attributes of God in the next few days, they should lead us to:

Wonder—because He is wonder-ful.

Worship—because of who He is and all He has done for us.

Trust—because He is worthy of our full, undivided confidence.

Serve—because it is one of life's greatest privileges to serve such a Master.

Imitate—because His will is that we should be more and more like Him.

(However, there are some attributes of God, such as His wrath, that we should not imitate, and others, such as His infinity, that we cannot imitate.)

June 5

God is greater than our heart, and knows all things.
1 JOHN 3:20

T he omniscience of God means that He has perfect knowledge of everything. He has never learned and can never learn.

One of the great passages on the subject is Psalm 139:1-6, where David wrote: "O Lord, You have searched me and known me. You know my sitting down and my rising up; You understand my thought afar off. You comprehend my path and my lying down, and are acquainted with all my ways. For there is not a word on my tongue, but behold, O Lord, You know it altogether. You have hedged me behind and before, and laid Your hand upon me. Such knowledge is too wonderful for me; it is high, I cannot attain it."

In Psalm 147:4, we learn that God counts the number of the stars and calls them all by name. The wonder of this increases when Sir James Jeans tells us that "the total number of stars in the universe is probably something like the total number of grains of sand on all the sea shores of the world."

Our Lord reminded His disciples that not a sparrow falls to the ground unnoticed by our Father. And in the same passage He said that the very hairs of our head are all numbered (Mt. 10:29-30).

It is clear then that "all things are naked and open to the eyes of Him to whom we must give account" (Heb. 4:13), causing us to join with Paul in saying "Oh, the depth of the riches both of the wisdom and knowledge of God! How unsearchable are His judgments and His ways past finding out!" (Rom. 11:33).

The omniscience of God is filled with practical meaning for everyone of us. There is warning. God sees everything we do. We can't keep anything secret from Him.

There is comfort. He knows what we are going through. As Job said, "He knows the way that I take" (Job 23:10). He counts our tossings and numbers our tears in His bottle (Ps. 56:8, RSV).

There is encouragement. He knew all about us and yet He saved us anyway. He knows what we feel in worship and prayer but cannot express.

There is wonder. Although God is omniscient, yet He can forget the sins He has forgiven. As David Seamands said, "I don't know how divine omniscience can forget but it does."

June 6

Do I not fill heaven and earth? says the Lord.
Jeremiah 23:24b

When we speak of God's omnipresence, we mean that He is present in all places at one and the same time. A Puritan named John Arrowsmith told of a heathen philosopher who once asked, "Where is God?" The Christian answered, "Let me first ask you, "Where is He not?"

An atheist wrote on a wall, "God is nowhere." A child came along and changed the spacing to read, "God is now here."

We are indebted to David for a classic passage on the omnipresence of God. He wrote, "Where can I go from Your Spirit? Or where can I flee from Your presence? If I ascend into heaven, You are there; If I make my bed in hell, behold, You are there. If I take the wings of the morning, And dwell in the uttermost parts of the sea, Even there Your hand shall lead me, And Your right hand shall hold me" (Ps. 139:7-10).

When we speak of omnipresence, we must be careful not to confuse it with pantheism. The latter says that all is God. In some of its forms, men worship trees or rivers or the forces of nature. The true God controls the universe and fills the universe, but He Himself is separate from the universe and is greater than it.

What practical influence should the truth of God's omnipresence have in the life of His people?

There is the solemn reminder, of course, that we cannot hide from God. He is inescapable.

There is unspeakable comfort in knowing that God is always with His people. He never leaves us. We are never alone.

Then there is challenge! Because He is always with us, we should walk in holiness and in separation from the world.

He has promised His presence in a special way when two or three are gathered together in His Name: He is in the midst. This should inspire deep reverence and solemnity in the gatherings of the Saints.

June 7

For the Lord God Omnipotent reigns!
REVELATION 19:6

T he omnipotence of God means that He can do anything that is not inconsistent with His other attributes. Hear the uniform testimony of Scripture! "I am Almighty God" (Gen. 17:1). "Is anything too hard for the Lord?" (Gen. 18:14). "I know that Thou canst do all things, and that no purpose of Thine can be thwarted" (Job 42:2 NASB). "There is nothing too hard for You" (Jer. 32:17). "With God all things are possible" (Mt. 19:26). "For with God nothing will be impossible" (Lk. 1:37). But it is understood that God cannot do anything that is inconsistent with His own character. For instance, it is impossible for God to lie (Heb. 6:18). He cannot deny Himself (2 Tim. 2:13). He cannot sin because He is absolutely holy. He cannot fail because He is absolutely dependable.

The omnipotence of God is seen in His creation and sustaining of the universe, in His providence, in the salvation of sinners, and in the judgment of the impenitent. The greatest display of His power in the Old Testament was the Exodus; in the New Testament, the Resurrection of Christ.

If God is omnipotent, then no man can fight successfully against Him. "There is no wisdom or understanding or counsel against the Lord" (Prov. 21:30).

If God is omnipotent, then the believer is on the winning side. One with God is a majority. "If God is for us, who can be against us?" (Rom. 8:31).

If God is omnipotent, then in prayer we can deal in the realm of the impossible. As the chorus says, we can laugh at impossibilities and cry, "It shall be done."

If God is omnipotent, then we have the unutterable comfort that:

> *The Savior can solve every problem,*
> *The tangles of life can undo.*
> *There is nothing too hard for Jesus,*
> *There is nothing that He cannot do.*

"When my weakness leans on His might, all seems light."

June 8

To God, alone wise, be glory through Jesus Christ forever.
ROMANS 16:27

T he wisdom of God is a thread that runs all through the Bible. For example: "With Him are wisdom and strength, He has counsel and understanding...With Him are strength and prudence. The deceived and the deceiver are His" (Job 12:13, 16). "O Lord, how manifold are Your works! In wisdom You have made them all. The earth is full of Your possessions" (Ps. 104:24). "The Lord by wisdom founded the earth; by understanding He established the heavens" (Prov. 3:19). "Blessed be the name of God forever and ever, for wisdom and might are His" (Dan. 2:20). "For since, in the wisdom of God, the world through wisdom did not know God, it pleased God through the foolishness of the message preached to save those who believe" (1 Cor. 1:21). "Christ Jesus, who became for us wisdom from God..." (1 Cor. 1:30).

The wisdom of God refers to His perfect insight, His unerring discernment, and His infallible decisions. Someone has defined it as His ability to produce the best possible results by the best possible means. It is more than knowledge. It is the ability to use that knowledge properly.

All the works of God express His wisdom. The marvelous design of the human body, for instance, bears eloquent tribute to it.

And God's wisdom is seen in the plan of salvation. The gospel tells us how sin's penalty is paid, God's justice is vindicated, His mercy is dispensed righteously, and the believer in Christ is better off than he ever could have been if Adam had not fallen.

Now that we are saved, the wisdom of God speaks tender comfort to our souls. We know that our God is too wise to make a mistake. Though there are things in life that are hard to understand, we know that He cannot err.

We can have utmost confidence in His guidance. He knows the end from the beginning. He knows pathways of blessing of which we are completely unaware. His way is perfect.

Finally, He wants us to grow in wisdom. We should be wise unto that which is good (Rom. 16:19). We should walk circumspectly, as wise men, redeeming the time, because the days are evil (Eph. 5:15-16). We should be wise as serpents, and harmless as doves (Mt. 10:16).

June 9

Holy, holy, holy, Lord God Almighty, who was and is and is to come!
REVELATION 4:8

hen we speak of the holiness of God, we mean that He is spiritually and morally perfect in His thoughts, deeds, motives, and in every other way. He is absolutely free from sin and defilement. He cannot be anything but pure.

The scriptural testimony to His holiness is abundant. Here are a few examples: "I the Lord your God am holy" (Lev. 19:2). "No one is holy like the Lord" (1 Sam. 2:2). "O Lord my God, my Holy One…You are of purer eyes than to behold evil, and cannot look on wickedness" (Hab. 1:12-13). "God cannot be tempted by evil, nor does He Himself tempt anyone" (Jas. 1:13). "God is light and in Him is no darkness at all" (1 Jn. 1:5b). "You alone are holy" (Rev. 15:4).

Even the stars are not pure in His sight (Job 25:5).

The priesthood and the sacrificial system of the Old Testament taught, among other things, the holiness of God. They taught that sin had brought distance between God and man, that there must be a go-between to bridge the gap, and that a holy God can be approached only on the basis of the blood of a sacrificial victim.

The holiness of God was also demonstrated in a unique way at the Cross. When He looked down and saw His Son bearing our sins, God forsook His Well-beloved for those three terrible hours of darkness.

The application of all this to us is clear. The will of God is that we should be holy, "For this is the will of God, your sanctification" (1 Thess. 4:3). "As He who called you is holy, you also be holy in all your conduct" (1 Pet. 1:15).

Thoughts of the holiness of God should also produce in us a profound sense of reverence and awe. As He said to Moses, "Take your sandals off your feet, for the place where you stand is holy ground" (Ex. 3:5).

T. Binney marveled at the holiness required to stand in the presence of God.

> *Eternal light! Eternal light!*
> *How pure the soul must be*
> *When, placed within Thy searching sight,*
> *It shrinks not, but with calm delight*
> *Can live, and look on Thee.*

Our hearts overflow with worship when we realize that we have that necessary purity imputed to us through faith in the Lord Jesus.

June 10

I am the Lord, I do not change.
MALACHI 3:6

T he attribute of God which describes Him as changeless is called His immutability. He does not change in His essential being. He does not change in His attributes. He does not change in the principles by which He operates.

The psalmist contrasted the changing destiny of the heavens and earth with God's changelessness: "They will be changed. But You are the same" (Ps. 102:26-27). James describes the Lord as "the Father of lights, with whom there is no variation or shadow of turning" (Jas. 1:17).

There are other scriptures that remind us that God does not repent. "God is not a man, that He should lie, nor a son of man, that He should repent" (Num. 23:19). "The Strength of Israel will not lie nor relent" (1 Sam. 15:29).

But what, then, do we do with verses that say that God does repent? "The Lord was sorry that He had made man on the earth" (Gen. 6:6). "The Lord regretted that He had made Saul king over Israel (1 Sam. 15:35). See also Exodus 32:14 and Jonah 3:10.

There is no contradiction. God always acts on these two principles: He always rewards obedience and always punishes disobedience. When man shifts from obedience to disobedience, God must still be true to His own character by shifting from the first principle to the second. This seems like repentance to us, and it is so described in what we might call the language of human appearance. But it does not indicate regret or changeableness.

God is always the same. In fact, that is one of His names. "…Thou art the Same, Thou alone art the God of all the kingdoms of the earth" (Isa. 37:16, DARBY). That name is also found in 2 Samuel 7:28, marg., Psalm 102:27 and Isaiah 41:4, marg., all in Darby's translation.

The immutability of God has been a comfort to His saints in all ages, and a theme of their song. We celebrate it in the immortal lines of Henry F. Lyte:

> *Change and decay in all around I see—*
> *O Thou who changest not, abide with me!*

It is also a quality for us to imitate. We should be stable, constant, and steadfast. If we are vacillating, fickle, and mercurial, we misrepresent our Father to the world.

"Therefore, my beloved brethren, be steadfast, immovable, always abounding in the work of the Lord, knowing that your labor is not in vain in the Lord" (1 Cor. 15:58).

June 11

In this is love, not that we loved God, but that He loved us
and sent His Son to be the propitiation for our sins.
1 JOHN 4:10

ove is that quality in God which causes Him to lavish unbounded affection on others. His love is manifest in giving good and perfect gifts to the beloved.

We can give only a few of the myriad of verses that speak of that love! "I have loved you with an everlasting love; therefore with lovingkindness I have drawn you" (Jer. 31:3). "God demonstrates His own love toward us, in that while we were still sinners, Christ died for us" (Rom. 5:8). "But God, who is rich in mercy, because of His great love with which He loved us" (Eph. 2:4). And, of course, the best known of all, "For God so loved the world that He gave His only begotten Son, that whoever believes in Him should not perish but have everlasting life" (Jn. 3:16).

When John says "God is love" (1 Jn. 4:8), he is not defining God, but insisting that love is a key element in the divine nature. We do not worship love, but the God of love.

His love had no beginning and can have no end. It is limitless in its dimensions. It is absolutely pure, without taint of selfishness or any other sin. It is sacrificial, never minding the cost. It seeks only the welfare of others, and nothing in return. It goes out to the unlovely as well as to the lovely, to enemies as well as to friends. It is not drawn out by any virtues in its objects, but only by the goodness of the Giver.

The practical implications of this sublime truth are obvious. "Therefore be imitators of God," said Paul, "as beloved children. And walk in love, as Christ loved us and gave Himself for us" (Eph. 5:1-2a, NASB). Our love should ascend to the Lord, should flow out to our brethren, and should extend to the unsaved world.

Contemplation of His love should also inspire deepest worship. As we fall at His feet, we must say repeatedly:

How Thou canst love me as Thou dost
And be the God Thou art
Is darkness to my intellect
But sunshine to my heart.

June 12

The God of all grace, who called us to His eternal glory by Christ Jesus.
1 PETER 5:10

he grace of God is His favor and acceptance to those who do not deserve it; who, in fact, deserve the very opposite; but who trust Jesus Christ as Lord and Savior.

Four of the better known verses on grace are these: "The law was given through Moses, but grace and truth came through Jesus Christ" (Jn. 1:17). "Being justified freely by His grace through the redemption that is in Christ Jesus" (Rom. 3:24). "For you know the grace of our Lord Jesus Christ, that though He was rich, yet for your sakes He became poor, that you through His poverty might become rich" (2 Cor. 8:9). "For by grace you have been saved through faith, and that not of yourselves; it is the gift of God, not of works, lest anyone should boast" (Eph. 2:8-9).

Some extol God's grace as the chief of all His virtues. Samuel Dades, for instance, wrote:

> *Great God of wonders! all Thy ways*
> *Display Thine attributes divine;*
> *But the bright glories of Thy grace*
> *Above Thine other wonders shine:*
> *Who is a pard'ning God like Thee?*
> *Or who has grace so rich and free?*

But who can say that one of God's attributes is greater than another?

God has always been a God of grace—in the Old Testament as well as in the New. But that aspect of His character was revealed in a new and arresting way with the coming of Christ.

Once we come to understand something of the grace of God, we become worshippers forever. We ask ourselves, "Why should He have chosen me? Why should the Lord Jesus have shed His life's blood for one so unworthy? Why should God not only save me from hell, but bless me with all spiritual blessings in the heavenlies now, and destine me to spend eternity with Him in heaven?" No wonder we sing of the amazing grace that saved such wretches!

Then, too, God wants His grace to be reproduced in our own lives and to flow through us to others. He wants us to be gracious in our dealings with others. Our speech should be always with grace, seasoned with salt (Col. 4:6). We should impoverish ourselves that others might be enriched (2 Cor. 8:9). We should grant favor and acceptance to the unworthy and the unloved.

June 13

God...is rich in mercy.
EPHESIANS 2:4

T he mercy of God is His pity, lovingkindness, and compassion on those who are guilty, failing, distressed or needy. The Scriptures emphasize that God is rich in mercy (Eph. 2:4) and plenteous in mercy (Ps. 86:5). His mercy is abundant (1 Pet. 1:3); it is great unto the heavens (Ps. 57:10). "For as the heavens are high above the earth, so great is His mercy toward those who fear Him" (Ps. 103:11). God is spoken of as "the Father of mercies" (2 Cor. 1:3), One who is "very compassionate and merciful" (Jas. 5:11). He is impartial in bestowing mercy: "for He makes His sun rise on the evil and on the good, and sends rain on the just and on the unjust" (Mt. 5:45). Men are not saved by works of righteousness (Titus 3:5) but by His sovereign mercy (Ex. 33:19; Rom. 9:15). His mercy endures forever to those who fear Him (Ps. 136:1; Lk. 1:50), but for the impenitent it is for this life only.

There is a difference between grace and mercy. Grace means that God showers me with blessings which I do not deserve. Mercy means that He does not give me the punishment that I do deserve.

Every doctrine of the Scripture has duty attached. The mercies of God require, first of all, that we should present our bodies a living sacrifice, holy, acceptable unto God (Rom. 12:1). It is the most reasonable, rational, sane, sensible thing we can do.

Then, too, God would have us to be merciful to one another. A special reward is promised to the merciful: "they shall obtain mercy" (Mt. 5:7). The Lord would rather have mercy than sacrifice (Mt. 9:13), that is, great acts of sacrifice are unacceptable if they are divorced from personal godliness.

The good Samaritan is the one who shows mercy to his neighbor. We show mercy when we feed the hungry, clothe the poor, nurse the sick, visit the widows and orphans, and weep with those who weep.

We are merciful when we refuse the opportunity to take vengeance on someone who has wronged us, or when we show compassion on those who have failed.

Remembering what we are, we should pray for mercy for ourselves (Heb. 4:16) and for others (Gal. 6:16; 1 Tim. 1:2).

Finally, the mercies of God should tune our hearts to sing His praise.

When all thy mercies, O my God,
My rising soul surveys,
Transported with the view I'm lost,
In wonder, love, and praise.
—JOSEPH ADDISON

June 14

*For the wrath of God is revealed from heaven against all ungodliness
and unrighteousness of men, who suppress the truth in unrighteousness.*
ROMANS 1:18

T he wrath of God is His fierce anger and retributive punishment directed against unrepentant sinners in time and in eternity. A.W. Pink has
pointed out that it is as much a divine perfection as is His faithfulness,
power, and mercy. We need make no apology for it.

In pondering the wrath of God, there are a few facts we should keep in mind.

There is no conflict between God's love and His wrath. True love punishes sin,
rebellion, and disobedience.

If men refuse God's love, what is left but His wrath? There are only two eternal abodes, heaven and hell. If men refuse heaven, they thereby choose hell.

God did not create hell for men, but for the devil and his angels (Mt. 25:41).
The Lord does not desire the death of the wicked (Ezek. 33:11). But there is no
alternative for the Christ-rejecter.

Judgment is spoken of as God's strange work (Isa. 28:21). The suggestion is
that He prefers to show mercy (Jas. 2:13b). There is no vindictiveness or spite in
God's wrath. It is righteous wrath, without any stain of sin.

The wrath of God is an attribute we are not called to imitate. It is peculiarly His
in the sense that He alone can exercise it with absolute justice. Thus Paul writes
to the Romans, "Never take your own revenge, beloved, but leave room for the
wrath of God, for it is written, 'Vengeance is mine, I will repay,' says the Lord"
(Rom. 12:19, NASB).

The Christian is called on to display righteous anger, but it must be righteous.
It must not overflow into sinful wrath (Eph. 4:26). And it should be exercised only
when God's honor is at stake, never in self-defense or self-justification.

If we really believe in the wrath of God, it should move us out to share the
gospel with those who are still on the broad road that leads to destruction. And
when we preach the wrath of God, it should be with tears of compassion.

June 15

His compassions fail not. They are new every morning;
great is Your faithfulness.
LAMENTATIONS 3:22-23

God is faithful and true. He cannot lie or deceive. He cannot go back on His word. He is absolutely trustworthy. No promise of His can ever fail. "God is not a man, that He should lie, nor a son of man, that He should repent. Has He said, and will He not do? Or has He spoken, and will He not make it good?" (Num. 23:19). "Therefore know that the Lord your God, He is God, the faithful God" (Deut. 7:9). "Your faithfulness endures to all generations" (Ps. 119:90).

God's faithfulness is seen in His calling us into the fellowship of His Son (1 Cor. 1:9). It is seen in not allowing us to be tempted beyond what we can bear (1 Cor. 10:13). It is seen in the way He establishes us and keeps us from evil (2 Thess. 3:3). Even if some do not believe, yet He remains faithful: He cannot deny Himself (2 Tim. 2:13).

The Lord Jesus is truth incarnate (Jn. 14:6). The Word of God is sanctifying truth (Jn. 17:17). "Let God be true, but every man a liar" (Rom. 3:4).

The knowledge that God is faithful and true floods our souls with confidence. We know that His Word cannot fail, that He will do as He has promised (Heb. 10:23). We know, for instance, that we are eternally secure, because He said that no sheep of His will ever perish (Jn. 10:28). We know that we will never want because He has promised to supply all our needs (Phil. 4:19).

God wants His people to be faithful and true. He wants us to be true to our word. He wants us to be dependable in keeping appointments. We should not be given to lies, exaggeration, or half-truths. We should be faithful in keeping our promises. Christians, above all people, should be faithful to their marriage vows. They should be faithful in discharging their commitments in the assembly, in business, and in the home.

How we should praise and thank the Lord for His faithfulness. He is the God who cannot fail.

> *He cannot fail—for He is God;*
> *He cannot fail—He gave His Word.*
> *He cannot fail—He'll see you through;*
> *He cannot fail—He'll answer you.*
> —C. E. MASON, JR.

June 16

Our God is in heaven; He does whatever He pleases.
PSALM 115:3

God is sovereign. That means that He is the supreme Ruler of the universe, and that He can do as He pleases. But having said that, we must quickly add that what pleases God is always right. His way is perfect.

Isaiah quotes the Lord as saying, "My counsel shall stand, and I will do all My pleasure" (Isa. 46:10). When Nebuchadnezar was restored to his right mind, he said, "He does according to His will in the army of heaven and among the inhabitants of the earth. No one can restrain His hand or say to Him, "What have You done?" (Dan. 4:35). The Apostle Paul insists that man has no right to question God's actions: "But indeed, O man, who are you to reply against God? Will the thing formed say to him who formed it, Why have you made me like this?" (Rom. 9:20). And in another place he speaks of God as the One "who works all things according to the counsel of His will" (Eph. 1:11).

To put it very simply, the doctrine of the sovereignty of God is a doctrine that allows God to be God.

It is a truth that fills me with reverence and awe. I cannot comprehend all its ramifications, but I can worship and adore.

It is a truth that moves me to submit myself to Him. He is the Potter; I am the clay. He has rights to me by creation and redemption. Under no circumstances should I talk back to Him or question His decisions.

It is a truth that is full of comfort. Since He is the supreme Ruler, I know that He is working out His purposes and that they will reach their desired end.

Though there are things in life I can't understand, I can be sure that the dark threads are as necessary for His weaving as the threads of gold and silver.

June 17

Can you search out the deep things of God?
Can you find out the limits of the Almighty?
JOB 11:7

T here are other attributes of God that must be mentioned, even if only briefly. Contemplation of these divine perfections lifts the soul from earth to heaven, from the petty to the sublime.

God is righteous, that is, He is just, equitable, and fair in all His dealings. He is "a just God and a Savior" (Isa. 45:21).

God is incomprehensible (Job 11:7-8). He is too great to be understood by the human mind. As Stephen Charnock said, "It is visible that God is. It is invisible what He is." And Richard Baxter said, "You may know God, but not comprehend Him."

God is eternal—without beginning or end (Ps. 90:1-4). Eternity is His lifetime.

God is good (Nahum 1:7). He is "good to all, and His tender mercies are over all His works" (Ps. 145:9).

God is infinite (1 Ki. 8:27). He has no limits or boundaries. "His greatness is beyond calculation, measurement, or human imagination."

God is self-existent (Ex. 3:14). He did not receive His existence from any out-side source. He is the Fountain of His own life as well as of all other life.

God is self-sufficient, that is, He has within the Trinity all that He could ever need.

God is transcendent. He is far above the universe and time, and is separate from the material creation.

A final attribute of God is His foreknowledge. Christians are divided on whether God's foreknowledge determines who will be saved, or whether it is merely a prior knowledge of who will trust the Savior. Judging from Romans 8:29, I believe that God sovereignly selected certain individuals and decreed that all whom He thus foreknew would eventually be glorified.

And so we come to the end of our consideration of the attributes of God. But it is a subject that in another sense has no end. God is so great, so majestic, so awesome that we only see through a glass darkly. Because He is infinite, He never can be fully known by finite minds. Throughout eternity we will dwell on the won-ders of His Person and will still have to say, "The half has not been told."

June 18

Pure and undefiled religion before God and the Father is this: to visit orphans and widows in their trouble, and to keep oneself unspotted from the world.
JAMES 1:27

W hen James wrote these words, he didn't mean to suggest that if a believer did these things, he did all that was required of him. Rather he was saying that two outstanding examples of ideal religion are to visit orphans and widows and to keep oneself pure.

We might have thought that he would have zeroed in on expository preaching, or missionary work, or personal soul winning. But no! He thinks first of visiting those in need.

The Apostle Paul reminded the Ephesian elders how he had visited "from house to house" (Acts 20:20). J. N. Darby considered visiting "the most important part of the work." He wrote, "The clock strikes the hours and the passersby hear it, but the works inside make the clock go, and keep the striking and the hands right. I think that visiting should be your substantive work, and take all else as it comes. I dread much public testimony: and especially so, if there be no private work" (from a letter to G. V. Wigram, Aug. 2, 1839).

An elderly widow, living alone, reached the stage where she depended on help from neighbors and friends. With time on her hands, she kept a diary of anything and everything that happened during the day—especially of contacts with the outside world. One day neighbors realized that they hadn't seen any signs of life around her house for several days. The police were called to enter the house, and they found that she had been dead for several days. For three days prior to her death, the only entry in her diary was: "No one came," "No one came," "No one came."

In the busyness of our everyday lives, it is all too easy to forget the lonely, the needy, the infirm. We give priority to other matters, and often to those forms of service that are more public and glamorous. But if we want our religion to be pure and undefiled, we will not neglect the orphans and widows, the aged and shut-ins. The Lord has a special concern for those who need help, and a special reward for those who step forward to fill the need.

June 19

As your days, so shall your strength be.
DEUTERONOMY 33:25

 od promises to give His people strength according to their needs at any particular time. He does not promise it in advance of the need, but when the crisis comes, the grace is there to meet it.

Perhaps you are called to go through a patch of sickness and suffering. If you knew in advance how great the testing would be, you would say, "I know I could never bear it." But all the divine support comes with the testing, to your amazement and everyone else's.

We live in fear of the time when our loved ones will be called away by death. We are sure our little world will fall apart and that we ourselves will be utterly unable to cope. But it isn't that way at all. We are conscious of the Lord's presence and power in a way we never knew before.

Many of us have close scrapes with death in "accidents" and situations of extreme peril. We find our hearts flooded with peace when ordinarily we would be in panic. We know it is the Lord, coming alongside to help.

As we read the stories of those who have heroically laid down their lives for the sake of Christ, we realize afresh that God gives "martyr grace for martyr days." Their cool courage was beyond human bravery. Their bold witness was obviously empowered from on high.

Now it should be obvious that worrying in advance of the need produces nothing but ulcers. The fact is that God doesn't give the grace and strength until they are needed. As D. W. Whittle said,

> *I have nothing to do with tomorrow,*
> *The Savior will make that His care;*
> *Its grace and its strength I can't borrow,*
> *Then why should I borrow its care?*

Annie Johnson Flint's memorable lines are ever *apropos.*

> *He giveth more grace when the burdens grow greater;*
> *He sendeth more strength when the labors increase.*
> *To added affliction He addeth His mercy;*
> *To multiplied trials, His multiplied peace.*

> *When we have exhausted our store of endurance,*
> *When our strength has failed ere the day is half done,*
> *When we reach the end of our hoarded resources,*
> *Our Father's full giving is only begun.*

June 20

Who can find a virtuous wife? For her worth is far above rubies.
PROVERBS 31:10

What are some of the things that a Christian husband desires in his wife? The following is a suggested list. Hopefully no one will be so immature as to expect all this in any one woman.

First of all, she should be a godly woman—one who is not only born again but spiritually minded as well. This woman puts Christ first in her life. She is a woman of prayer and active in the service of the Lord. A woman of Christian character and integrity whom he can respect spiritually; and who respects him in return.

She is a woman who takes her God-given place of subjection and who actively assists her husband to take his proper place as head…She is faithful to her marriage vows…She is a good wife and mother of her children…She is personally neat and attractive, one who does not go to extremes in dress, one who is feminine and ladylike but not prissy.

This ideal wife is a good homemaker, who keeps the place neat and clean and who manages its affairs efficiently. She serves good meals on a regular schedule and loves to show hospitality to others…It goes without saying that she should share the same goals and interests as her husband.

When differences arise, she is willing to bring her problems to the surface rather than clam up, pout, or sulk. She is willing to negotiate differences and is able to apologize and confess if necessary.

She is not a gossip nor a busybody, meddling in other people's affairs. She has a meek and a quiet spirit and is not contentious or a nagger.

This wife cooperates in living within the family income. She is not obsessed with a desire for fancy things, and does not strive to keep up with the Joneses.

She is willing to accept adversity, if necessary.

She renders her husband his conjugal rights joyfully, not passively nor disinterestedly.

She has a good temperament, is a good sport, is not a social climber, and is entirely trustworthy.

Husbands should be grateful when they find a majority of these traits in their wives, and wives can use these as a checklist to help them climb higher.

June 21

Husbands, love your wives, just as Christ also loved the church and gave Himself for her.
EPHESIANS 5:25

W hat does a Christian wife desire in her husband? Her first concern should be with his spiritual life, not with his physical appearance. He should be a man of God, one who seeks first the kingdom of God and His righteousness. His objective is to serve the Lord and to be active in the local fellowship. In the home he should maintain a family altar, and be an example of the believer.

This man takes his proper place as head of the house, but he is not a tyrant.

He loves his wife and thereby wins her subjection rather than demanding it. He is respectful to her, treating her like a lady at all times. He is faithful, understanding, longsuffering, kind, thoughtful, considerate, and joyful.

The ideal husband is a good provider, one who is diligent in business. But money is not his first priority. He is not covetous or greedy.

He is one who loves his children, trains them, spends time with them, plans social activities for them, is a good example for them and gives each one individual attention.

He is a lover of hospitality. His home is open to the Lord's servants, to all Christians, and to the unsaved as well.

He keeps lines of communication open with his wife and family. He understands and accepts their limitations and can laugh good-naturedly at their blunders. He shares with them on a social and intellectual basis. When he does or says something wrong, he is quick to admit his mistake and apologize. He is always open to suggestions from the family. It is highly desirable that he be able to keep on top when his wife is down.

Other desirable traits are that he be clean and well-groomed, unselfish, honest, gentle, dependable, loyal, generous, and appreciative. He should have a good sense of humor and be neither grouchy nor complaining.

Few if any men embody all these virtues and it is unrealistic to expect them all. A wife should be grateful for those which she does find and lovingly help her husband to develop others.

June 22

Test all things; hold fast what is good.
1 Thessalonians 5:21

Sometimes it seems that Christians are especially prone to accept passing fads and winds of doctrine. John Blanchard wrote of two tour-bus drivers who were comparing notes. When one mentioned that he had a bus full of Christians, the other said, "Really? What do they believe?" To which the first replied, "Anything I tell them!"

One minute it may be a food fad. Certain foods are denounced as poison and others are credited with almost magical properties. Or it may be a medicinal fad, claiming spectacular results for some strange weed or extract.

Christians can be gullible when it comes to financial appeals. In this country, at least, they respond readily to publicity involving orphans or anti-Communist crusades without investigating the integrity of the sponsoring agency.

Impostors have a heyday among believers. No matter how ridiculous their sob story, they are able to rake in the money.

Perhaps the problem is that we fail to distinguish between faith and gullibility. Faith believes the surest thing in the universe, that is, the Word of God. Gullibility accepts things as fact without evidence and sometimes in the face of evidence to the contrary.

God never intended His people to abandon their powers of discernment or their critical faculty. Interspersed in the Bible are such exhortations as the following:

"Test all things; hold fast what is good" (1 Thess. 5:21), "take out the precious from the vile" (Jer. 15:19), "And this I pray, that your love may abound still more and more in real knowledge and all discernment" (Phil. 1:9, NASB).

"Beloved, do not believe every spirit, but test the spirits to see whether they are from God; because many false prophets have gone out into the world" (1 Jn. 4:1, NASB).

The danger is especially great, of course, in connection with doctrinal fads and novelties. But in many other areas as well it is possible for Christians to get sidetracked or duped with schemes or crazes that they pursue with exaggerated zeal.

June 23

...those who have fallen asleep in Jesus.
1 THESSALONIANS 4:14, NASB

How are we to react when one of our loved ones dies in the Lord? Some Christians fall apart emotionally. Others, while sorrowful, are able to bear up heroically. It depends on how deep our roots are in God and how fully we appropriate the great truths of our faith.

First of all, we should view the death from the Savior's standpoint. It is an answer to His prayer in John 17:24, "Father, I desire that they also whom You gave Me may be with Me where I am, that they may behold My glory..." When our loved ones go to be with Him, "He shall see the labor of His soul, and be satisfied" (Isa. 53:11). "Precious in the sight of the Lord is the death of His saints" (Ps. 116:15).

Then we should appreciate what it means to the one who has died. He has been ushered in to see the King in His beauty. He is forever free from sin, sickness, suffering, and sorrow. He has been taken away from the evil to come (Isa. 57:1). "Nothing compares with the homegoing of a saint of God...to go home, to leave these old clods of clay, to be loosed from the bondage of the material—welcomed by the innumerable company of angels." Bishop Ryle wrote, "The very moment that believers die, they are in paradise. Their battle is fought. Their strife is over. They have passed through that gloomy valley we must one day tread. They have gone over that dark river we must one day cross. They have drunk that last bitter cup which sin has mingled for man. They have reached that place where sorrow and sighing are no more. Surely we should not wish them back again! We should not weep for them, but for ourselves." Faith appropriates this truth and is enabled to stand firm like a tree planted by rivers of water.

For us, the death of a loved one always involves sadness. But we sorrow not as others who have no hope (1 Thess. 4:13). We know that our loved one is with Christ, which is far better. We know that the separation is only for a little while. Then we will be reunited on the hillsides of Immanuel's land, and will know each other under better circumstances than we have ever known down here. We look forward to the Lord's coming when "the dead in Christ shall rise first, we who are alive and remain shall be caught up together with them in the clouds to meet the Lord in the air, and so shall we ever be with the Lord" (1 Thess. 4:16-17). This hope makes all the difference.

And so the consolations of God are not too small for us (Job 15:11). Our sorrow is mingled with joy, and our sense of loss is more than compensated by the promise of eternal blessing.

June 24

Let the little children come to Me, and do not forbid them;
for of such is the kingdom of God.
MARK 10:14

he death of children is always an especially severe trial of the faith of God's people, and it is important to have some solid moorings to hold us at such a time.

The general belief among Christians is that children who die before they reach the age of accountability are safe through the blood of Jesus. The reasoning goes something like this: the child himself has never had the capacity to either accept or reject the Savior, so God reckons to him all the value of the work of Christ on the Cross. He is saved through the death and resurrection of the Lord Jesus, even though he himself has never fully understood the saving value of that work.

As far as the age of accountability is concerned, no one but God knows what that is. It is clearly different in each case since one child may mature earlier than another.

While there is no Scripture that says specifically that children who die before the age of accountability go to heaven, there are two lines of Scripture that support this view. The first is our verse for today: "Let the little children come to Me, and do not forbid them; for of such is the kingdom of God" (Mk. 10:14). Speaking of children, Jesus said, "...of such is the kingdom of God." He didn't say that they had to become adults to enter the kingdom of God, but that they themselves are characteristic of those who are in the kingdom of God. This is a very strong argument for the salvation of little children.

Another line of proof is as follows. When Jesus was speaking of adults, He said, "The Son of Man has come *to seek and to save* that which was lost" (Lk. 19:10). But when He was speaking of children, He omitted any mention of seeking. He simply said, "The Son of man is come *to save* that which was lost" (Mt. 18:11). The implication here is that children have not wandered away as adults have, and that the Savior sovereignly gathers them into His fold at the time of their death. Although they have never known about the work of Christ, God knows about it and reckons all the saving value of that work to their account.

We should not question the providence of God when He takes children away from us. As Jim Elliot wrote, "I must not think it strange if God takes in youth those whom I would have kept on earth till they were older. God is peopling eternity, and I must not restrict Him to old men and women."

June 25

O my son Absalom—my son, my son Absalom—if only I had died in your place!
O Absalom, my son, my son!
2 SAMUEL 18:33

hether Absalom was a saved man or not, his father's wail mirrors the grief of many believers who mourn the death of an unsaved relative for whom they may have prayed for many years. Is there any balm in Gilead for such an occasion? What is the scriptural attitude to take?

Well, first of all, we cannot always be sure whether the person actually did die without Christ. We have heard of the testimony of one man who was thrown by a horse and who trusted Christ, "Between the stirrup and the ground, he mercy sought and mercy found." Another man slipped off a gangplank and was converted before he hit the water. If either had died in these mishaps, no one would have known that he died in faith.

We believe that it is possible for a person to be saved in a coma. Medical authorities tell us that a person in a coma can often hear and understand what is being said in the room, even if he himself cannot speak. If he can hear and understand, why can he not receive Jesus Christ by a definite act of faith?

But let us suppose the worst. Let us suppose that the person actually did die unsaved. What should be our attitude then? We should very clearly take sides with God against our own flesh and blood. It is not God's fault if anyone dies in his sins. At stupendous cost, God has provided a way by which people can be saved from their sins. His salvation is a free gift, quite apart from debt or merit. If men refuse the gift of eternal life, what more can God do? He certainly cannot populate heaven with people who don't want to be there, for then it would not be heaven.

So if some of our loved ones do go into eternity without hope, all we can do is share the grief and heartbreak of the Son of God, who, weeping over Jerusalem, said, "How often I wanted to gather your children together, as a hen gathers her brood under her wings, but you were not willing!" (Lk. 13:34).

We know that the Judge of all the earth will do right (Gen. 18:25), so we vindicate Him in the punishment of the lost as much as in the salvation of repentant sinners.

June 26

He said to them, "Come aside by yourselves to a deserted place"...So they departed to a deserted place...But the multitudes saw them departing, and many knew Him and ran there on foot from all the cities. They arrived before them.... Jesus...was moved with compassion. MARK 6:31-34

It is easy for us to be annoyed by interruptions. I blush to think how often I have chafed at unexpected demands that prevented me from accomplishing some self-appointed task. Perhaps I was writing, and the words were flowing easily. Then the phone rang or someone was at the door in need of counsel. It was an unwelcome intrusion.

The Lord Jesus was never upset by interruptions. He accepted them all as part of His Father's plan for that day. This gave tremendous poise and serenity to His life.

Actually, the extent to which we are interrupted is often an index of our usefulness. A writer in the *Anglican Digest* said, "When you are exasperated by interruptions, try to remember that their very frequency may indicate the valuableness of your life. Only the people who are full of help and strength are burdened by other people's need. The interruptions which we chafe at are the credentials of our indispensability. The greatest condemnation that anyone could incur—and it is a danger to guard against—is to be too independent, so unhelpful, that nobody ever interrupts us and we are left uncomfortably alone."

We all smile nervously when we read the experience of a busy housewife. One day when she had planned an unusually full schedule, she looked up from her work to see her husband come home earlier than usual. "What are you doing here?" she asked with thinly-veiled annoyance. "I live here," he replied with a pained smile. She wrote later, "Since that day I've made it a point to lay aside my work when my husband comes home. I give him a loving welcome and let him know he's really tops."

Every morning we should turn the day over to the Lord, asking Him to arrange every detail. Then if someone interrupts us, it is because He has sent that person. We should find out the reason and minister to it. That could be the most important thing we do all day, even if it came disguised as an interruption.

June 27

Nevertheless she will be saved in childbearing...
1 TIMOTHY 2:15

From some of the restrictions Paul places on woman's ministry in the church, it might seem that she is reduced to a nonentity. For instance, she is not permitted to teach or to usurp authority over the man, but must be in silence (v. 12). Some might conclude that she is relegated to an inferior place in the Christian faith.

But verse 15 clears up any such misconception. "She will be saved in childbearing..." Clearly this is not referring to the salvation of her soul, but rather to the salvation of her position in the church. To her is given the tremendously important privilege of raising sons and daughters for God.

William Ross Wallace said, "The hand that rocks the cradle is the hand that rules the world." Behind almost every great leader is a great mother.

It is doubtful that Susannah Wesley ever ministered from a pulpit, but her ministry in the home has had a worldwide outreach through two of her sons, John and Charles.

In our society, it is fashionable for many women to desert the home in order to carve out more glamorous careers in the business or professional world. To them housework is drab and raising a family is a dispensable chore.

At a Christian women's luncheon, the conversation had drifted to the subject of careers. Each one was rhapsodizing about her position and her salary. There is no question that there was a spirit of rivalry! Finally one turned to a housewife who had three stalwart sons and asked, "And what is your career, Charlotte?" Charlotte replied humbly, "I raise men for God."

Pharaoh's daughter said to the mother of Moses, "Take this child away, and nurse him for me, and I will give you your wages" (Ex. 2:9). Perhaps one of the greatest surprises at the Judgment Seat of Christ will be the high wages the Lord pays to those women who have devoted themselves to raising boys and girls for Him and for eternity.

Yes, "she will be saved in childbearing..." Woman's place in the church is not one of public ministry, but perhaps the ministry of godly childbearing is of far greater importance in the eyes of God.

June 28

He who believes and is baptized will be saved;
but he who does not believe will be condemned.
MARK 16:16

I f this were the only verse in the Bible on the subject, we might justifiably conclude that salvation is by faith plus baptism. But when there are 150 verses in the New Testament that condition salvation on faith alone, we must conclude that those 150 verses cannot be contradicted by one or two like this one.

However, although baptism is not essential for salvation, it is essential for obedience. God's will is that all who have trusted His Son as Lord and Savior should publicly identify themselves with Him in the waters of believer's baptism.

The New Testament does not contemplate any such anomaly as an unbaptized believer. It assumes that when a person is saved, he will be baptized. In the book of Acts, the disciples practiced what we might call "instant baptism." They didn't wait for a formal service in a church setting, but baptized immediately on the basis of a person's profession of faith.

The sequence of belief and baptism is so close that the Bible speaks of them in the same breath— "He that believes and is baptized…"

In our desire to avoid the unscriptural teaching of baptismal regeneration, we often allow the pendulum to swing too far in the opposite direction. People are apt to go off with the false idea that it doesn't really matter whether they are baptized. But it does matter.

We hear some saying glibly, "I can go to heaven without being baptized." I always answer them, "Yes, that is true. You can go to heaven without being baptized, but if you do, you'll be unbaptized for all eternity." There will be no opportunity for baptism in heaven. It is one of those acts in which we can obey the Lord now or never.

All who have trusted Jesus Christ as Lord and Savior should lose no time in being baptized. In this way they publicly identify themselves with Him in His death and resurrection and they publicly commit themselves to walk with Him in newness of life.

June 29

Most assuredly, I say to you, he who hears My word and believes in Him who sent Me has everlasting life, and shall not come into judgment, but has passed from death into life.

JOHN 5:24

ere is an insight that has revolutionized and transformed many a life. The duplication of "verily" or "truly" at the outset alerts us to expect something momentous. We will not be disappointed.

"I say to you." The "I" is the Lord Jesus; we know that from verse 19. What we must also know is that when He says something, it is absolutely and invariably true. He cannot lie. He cannot deceive. He cannot be deceived. Nothing can be more sure and dependable than what He says.

To whom is He speaking? "I say unto you." The Eternal Son of God is speaking to you and to me. We never had anyone so illustrious speak to us before and never will. We ought to listen!

"He that hears My word." The "he" means "anyone." It has the same force as "whoever." To hear His word means not just to hear it with the ears, but to hear and believe, to hear and receive, to hear and obey.

"...and believes on Him that sent Me." We know that it was God the Father who sent Him. But the important question is, "Why did He send Him?" I must believe that the Father sent His Son to die as my Substitute, to pay the penalty I deserved, to shed His blood for the remission of my sins.

And now comes the threefold promise. First, "has everlasting life." As soon as a person believes, he possesses eternal life. It's just as plain as that. Second, he "shall not come into judgment." This means he will never be consigned to hell because of his sins, because Christ has paid the debt, and God will not demand payment twice. Third, he "is passed from death into life." He passes from a condition in which he is spiritually dead as far as his relation to God is concerned, and is born again into a new life that will never end.

If you have truly heard His Word and if you have believed on the Father who sent Him, then the Lord Jesus Christ assures you that you are saved.

No wonder it is called "Good News."

June 30

And so it was, when Moses held up his hand, that Israel prevailed;
and when he let down his hand, Amalek prevailed.
EXODUS 17:11

srael was in conflict with the forces of Amalek. Moses was on top of the hill, overlooking the battlefield. The position of Moses' hand spelled the difference between victory and defeat. The uplifted hand turned Amalek back. The lowered hand turned Israel back.

As long as Moses' hand was raised, he pictured the Lord Jesus as our Intercessor, "for us His hands uplifting in sympathy and love." It is through His intercession that we are saved to the uttermost. But from then on, the type breaks down, because our Intercessor's hand is never lowered. No fatigue causes Him to need outside help. He always lives to make intercession for us.

There is a second way in which we may apply this incident, namely, to ourselves as prayer warriors. The uplifted hand pictures our faithful intercession for those believers who are engaged in the spiritual conflict on the mission fields of the world. When we neglect the ministry of prayer, the enemy prevails.

A missionary and his party on safari had to spend the night in an area infested by brigands. They committed themselves to His care, then retired. Months later, when a brigand chief was brought to a mission hospital, he recognized the missionary. "We intended to rob you that night out in the open country, but we were afraid of your twenty-seven soldiers."

Later, when the missionary related this in a newsletter to his home church, one of the members said, "We had a prayer meeting that same night and there were twenty-seven of us present."

> *When our God beholds us there,*
> *Pleading in the place of prayer,*
> *Then the tide of battle turns,*
> *Then the flame of conquest burns,*
> *Then the flag of truth prevails,*
> *Foes slink back and Satan quails!*
> *Then the faltering wail of fear*
> *Turns to victory's ringing cheer!*
> *Bring us, Lord, O bring us there,*
> *Where we learn prevailing prayer.*

Then we can see another insight in this incident. The Lord swore that He will have war with Amalek from generation to generation. Amalek is a picture of the flesh. The Christian must wage warfare against the flesh. Prayer is one of his principal weapons. The faithfulness of his prayer life often spells the difference between victory and defeat.

July 1

Then I shall know just as I also am known.
1 CORINTHIANS 13:12

1 t is quite normal and understandable for us as Christians to wonder if we will know our loved ones in heaven. While there is no Scripture that deals specifically with the subject, there are several lines of reasoning that lead us to a positive conclusion.

First of all, the disciples recognized Jesus in His resurrected, glorified body. His physical appearance was unchanged. There was no mistaking that it was "this same Jesus." This suggests that we too will have our own distinctive features in heaven, though in a glorified form. There is no suggestion that we will all look alike. When it says in 1 John 3:2 that we shall be like the Lord Jesus, it means morally like Him, i.e., forever free from sin and its consequences. But certainly we will not look like Him so as to be mistaken for Him. Never!

Second, there is no reason to believe that we will know less in heaven than we know down here. We recognize one another down here; why should it be thought strange that we should recognize each other up there? If we shall know then as we are now known, that should be decisive.

Paul expected to know the Thessalonians in heaven. He said that they would be his hope, joy, and crown of rejoicing (1 Thess. 2:19).

There are indications in the Bible that people have been given and will be given the ability to identify people they have never seen before. Peter, James, and John recognized Moses and Elijah on the Mount of Transfiguration (Mt. 17:4).

The rich man in Hades recognized Abraham (Lk. 16:24). Jesus told the Jews that they would see Abraham, Isaac, Jacob, and all the prophets in the Kingdom of God (Lk. 13:28). We are told to make friends through the wise stewardship of our money so that these friends will welcome us to the everlasting habitations—which assumes that they will recognize us as their benefactors (Lk. 16:9).

But one word of caution should be added! While it seems clear that we will know our loved ones in heaven, we will not know them in the same relationships that existed on earth. For instance, the husband-wife relationship will no longer be in effect. That seems to be the clear meaning of the Savior's words in Matthew 22:30 "...in the resurrection, they neither marry, nor are given in marriage."

July 2

Martha, Martha, you are worried and troubled about many things.
But one thing is needed, and Mary has chosen that good part,
which will not be taken away from her. •
LUKE 10:41-42

Mary sat quietly at Jesus' feet and heard His word. Martha was flustered and upset in her service, and resented the fact that Mary didn't pitch in to help. The Lord Jesus didn't correct Martha for her service but for the spirit in which she was doing it. Also there is a suggestion that Martha's priorities were wrong; she shouldn't have put service above worship.

Many of us are like Martha. We are achievers, who would rather be doing than sitting. We pride ourselves on being organized, efficient, able to accomplish. We are so preoccupied with our work that our morning Bible reading is often interrupted by the memory of sixty things that have to be done. Our prayers tend to be helter-skelter because our mind wanders from Dan to Beersheba, planning out the day. It is easy for us to resent it when others don't grab a towel and help. We feel that everyone should be doing what we are doing.

Then there are those who are like Mary. They are lovers. Their lives exude affection for others. To them, people are more important than pots and pans. One Person in particular is the Object of their affection. They are not lazy, though it might seem that way to us Marthas. It's just that they have different priorities.

We ourselves appreciate a person who is warm and loving more than one who is coldly capable and efficient. Our hearts are captured by a child who showers us with hugs and kisses more than by one who is too busy with his toys to pay much attention to us.

Someone has well said that God is more interested in our worship than in our service; the heavenly Bridegroom is wooing a bride, not hiring a servant.

> *Christ never asks of us such busy labor*
> *As leaves no time for sitting at His feet;*
> *The patient attitude of expectation*
> *He often counts a service most complete.*

Mary chose that good part, which shall not be taken away from her. May we all do the same!

July 3

Do not forget to entertain strangers,
for by so doing some have unwittingly entertained angels.
HEBREWS 13:2

 ospitality is not only a sacred duty (Be not forgetful to entertain strangers); it carries within it the promise of glorious surprises (for thereby some have entertained angels unawares).

It had started out as just another ordinary day for Abraham. Suddenly three men appeared before him as he sat by the door of his tent. The patriarch reacted in the typical Middle-Eastern manner—he washed their feet, arranged a cool resting place for them under a tree, went out to the herd for a calf, asked Sarah to bake some bread, then served them a sumptuous meal.

Who were these men anyway? Two of them were angels; the third was the Angel of the Lord. We believe that the Angel of the Lord was the Lord Jesus appearing as a Man (see Genesis 18:13 where the angel is called "the Lord").

So Abraham entertained not only angels; he entertained the Lord Himself in one of His many pre-incarnate appearances. And we may have the same privilege, startling as it may seem!

How many Christian families can testify to the blessing received from entertaining godly men and women in their homes. Impressions for God have been made on children that followed them all through their lives. Zeal for the Lord has been rekindled, sorrowing hearts have been comforted, problems have been resolved. How much we owe to these "angels" whose very presence was a benediction in the home!

But it is also our incomparable privilege to have the Lord Jesus as a guest. Whenever we receive one of His people in His Name, it is the same as if we received Him (Mt. 10:40). If we really believe this, we will spend and be spent in the wonderful ministry of hospitality as never before. We will "be hospitable to one another without grumbling" (1 Pet. 4:9). We will treat every guest the same as we would treat Christ Himself. And our homes will be like the home of Mary and Martha in Bethany—where Jesus loved to be.

July 4

Will You not revive us again, that Your people may rejoice in You?
PSALM 85:6

A backslidden condition is often like cancer; we don't know we have it. We can grow spiritually cold so gradually that we don't realize how carnal we have actually become. Sometimes it takes a tragedy, a crisis, or the voice of some prophet of God to awaken us to our desperate need. Only then can we claim God's promise, "I will pour water on him who is thirsty, and floods on the dry ground" (Isa. 44:3).

I am in need of revival when I have lost my enthusiastic zest for the Word of God, when my prayer life has lapsed into a dull routine (or lapsed altogether), when I have left my first love. I need a fresh touch from God when I am more interested in TV programs than in the meeting of the local fellowship, when I am punctual for work but late for meetings, when I am regular at my job but spasmodic at the assembly. I need reviving when I am willing to do for dollars what I am unwilling to do for the Savior, when I spend more money on self-indulgence than I do on the work of the Lord.

We need revival when we harbor grudges, resentments, bitter feelings. When we are guilty of gossiping and backbiting. When we are unwilling to confess wrongs we have committed or to forgive others when they confess their faults to us. We need reviving when we fight like cats at home, then appear in the assembly as if all were sweetness and light. We need to be revived when we have become conformed to the world in our talk, our walk, our whole lifestyle. How great is our need when we are guilty of the sins of Sodom—pride, fullness of bread, and prosperous ease (Ezek. 16:49)!

As soon as we realize our coldness and barrenness, we can claim the promise of 2 Chronicles 7:14, "If My people who are called by My name will humble themselves, and pray and seek My face, and turn from their wicked ways, then I will hear from heaven, and will forgive their sin and heal their land."

Confession is the road to revival!

O Holy Ghost, revival comes from Thee;
Send a revival—start the work in me.
Thy Word declares Thou wilt supply our need;
For blessings now, O Lord, I humbly plead.
—J. EDWIN ORR

July 5

Do not quench the Spirit. Do not despise prophecies.
1 THESSALONIANS 5:19-20

 e usually think of quenching in connection with a fire. We quench the fire when we throw water on it. In so doing, we either douse it completely or greatly reduce its scope and effectiveness.

Fire is used in the Scriptures as a type of the Holy Spirit. He is fervent, burning, enthusiastic. When people are under the control of the Spirit, they are glowing, ardent, and overflowing. We quench the Spirit when we suppress the manifestation of the Spirit in the gatherings of God's people.

Paul says, "Do not quench the Spirit; do not despise prophecies." The way in which he links the quenching of the Spirit with the despising of prophecies leads us to believe that quenching has to do primarily with meetings of the local church.

We quench the Spirit when we make a man ashamed of his testimony for Christ, whether in prayer, worship, or ministry of the Word. Constructive criticism is one thing, but when we carp at a man over words or nitpicking details, we are apt to discourage or stumble him in his public ministry.

We also quench the Spirit when we have services so over-organized that He is effectively in a straitjacket. If arrangements are made in prayerful dependence on the Holy Spirit, then no one can object. But arrangements that are made on the basis of human cleverness have the effect of leaving the Holy Spirit as a Spectator instead of as the Leader.

God has given many gifts to the Church. He uses different gifts at different times. Perhaps a brother has a word of exhortation for the fellowship. If all public ministry is centralized in some other man, then the Spirit does not have liberty to bring forth the needed message at the appropriate time. This is another way of quenching the Spirit.

Finally, we quench the Spirit when we refuse His promptings in our own lives. Perhaps we are powerfully moved to minister on a certain subject but we hold back because of the fear of man. We feel impelled to lead in public prayer but remain seated because of shyness. We think of a hymn that would be especially appropriate but we lack the courage to give it out.

The net result is that the fire of the Spirit is quenched, our meetings lose their spontaneity and power, and the local body is impoverished.

July 6

And do not grieve the Holy Spirit of God,
by whom you were sealed for the day of redemption.
EPHESIANS 4:30

J ust as it is possible for us to quench the Spirit in the meetings of the church, so it is possible for us to grieve Him in our private lives.

There is a certain tenderness about the word "grieve." We can only grieve someone who loves us. The neighborhood brats don't grieve us, but our own naughty children do.

We hold a special place of nearness and dearness to the Holy Spirit. He loves us. He has sealed us until the day of redemption. He can be grieved by us.

But what grieves Him? Any form of sin brings sorrow to His heart. It is not by accident that Paul here calls Him the Holy Spirit. Anything that is unholy bows Him down with grief.

The exhortation "grieve not" comes in the middle of a series of sins against which we are warned. The list is not intended to be exhaustive but merely suggestive.

Lying grieves the Spirit (v. 25)—white lies, black lies, fibs, exaggerations, half-truths, and shaded truths. God cannot lie and He cannot give that privilege to His people.

Anger that overflows into sin grieves the Spirit (v. 26). The only time that anger is ever justified is when it is in God's cause. All other anger gives the devil a beachhead (v. 27).

Stealing is grievous to the Holy Spirit (v. 28), whether from mother's purse or from our employer's time, tools, or office supplies.

Unwholesome speech grieves the Holy Spirit (v. 29). This runs the gamut from dirty, suggestive jokes to idle chatter. Our conversation should be edifying, appropriate, and gracious.

Bitterness, wrath, anger, clamor, slander, and malice complete the list in chapter 4.

One of the favorite ministries of the Holy Spirit is to occupy us with the Lord Jesus Christ. But when we sin, He has to turn from this ministry in order to restore us to proper fellowship with the Lord.

But even then He is never grieved away. He never leaves us. We are sealed by Him unto the day of redemption. However, this should not be used as an excuse for carelessness but should be one of the greatest motives for holiness.

July 7

*For I consider that the sufferings of this present time are not worthy
to be compared with the glory which shall be revealed in us.*
ROMANS 8:18

T aken by themselves, the sufferings of this present time can be appalling. I think of the gruesome sufferings of the Christian martyrs. I think of what some of God's people have had to endure in the concentration camps. What shall we say concerning the horrible sufferings associated with war? The cruel dismemberment and paralysis connected with accidents? The unspeakable pain of human bodies racked by cancer or other diseases?

And yet physical suffering isn't the whole story. It seems at times that bodily pain is easier to bear than mental torture. Isn't that what Solomon meant when he wrote, "The spirit of a man will sustain him in sickness, but who can bear a broken spirit?" (Prov. 18:14)? There is the suffering that comes with unfaithfulness in the marriage relationship, or with the death of a loved one, or with disappointment over a broken dream. There is the heartbreak of being forsaken, of being betrayed by a close friend. We wonder oftentimes at the ability of the human frame to endure the blows, the agonies, the crushing griefs of life.

Viewed by themselves, these sufferings are overwhelming. But when seen alongside the coming glory, they are only pinpricks. Paul says they are "not worthy to be compared with the glory which shall be revealed in us." If the sufferings are so great, how much greater must be the glory!

In another passage, the Apostle Paul indulges in a delightful burst of spiritual imagery when he says that "our light affliction, which is but for a moment, is working for us a far more exceeding and eternal weight of glory" (2 Cor. 4:17). Seen on the scales, the afflictions are feather-light while the glory is infinitely heavy. Judged by the calendar, the sufferings are momentary while the glory is eternal.

When we see the Savior at the end of the journey, the sufferings of this present time will fade into insignificance.

> *It will be worth it all when we see Jesus,*
> *Life's trials will seem so small when we see Christ;*
> *One glimpse of His dear face all sorrow will erase,*
> *So bravely run the race till we see Christ.*
> —ESTHER K. RUSTHOI

July 8

They made me the keeper of the vineyards,
But my own vineyard I have not kept.
SONG OF SOLOMON 1:6B

T he brothers of the Shulamite maiden had sent her to work in the vineyard. She kept so busy tending the vines that she neglected her own vineyard, that is, her personal appearance. Her skin had become swarthy and dried, and no doubt her hair was unkempt.

There is always the danger of neglecting our own vineyard by becoming overly occupied with someone else's. There is the peril, for instance, of becoming so engrossed with the evangelization of the world that one's own family is lost. If God gives us children, those children are our number one mission field. When we stand before the Lord, one of the greatest joys will be to be able to say, "Here am I and the children whom God has given Me" (Heb. 2:13). Not all the accolades from appreciative audiences will compensate for the loss of our own sons and daughters.

It does seem from the Scriptures that responsibility begins at home. After Jesus had driven the demons out of Legion, He charged him, "Go home to your friends, and tell them what great things the Lord has done for you, and how He has had compassion on you" (Mk. 5:19). It often seems that the most difficult place to evangelize is in our own backyard, but that is where we should start.

Again when the Lord commissioned His disciples, He said, "You shall be witnesses to Me in Jerusalem, and in all Judea and Samaria, and to the end of the earth" (Acts 1:8). Begin in "Jerusalem" (your home base)!

Andrew was determined not to neglect his own vineyard. We read of him, "He first found his own brother Simon, and said to him, We have found the Messiah (which is translated, the Christ)" (Jn. 1:41).

There are, no doubt, cases where a believer is faithful in seeking to win his loved ones to the Lord Jesus, and yet they persist in their unbelief. We cannot guarantee the eternal salvation of our relatives and friends. But what we must guard against is the possibility of being so preoccupied in ministering to others that we neglect our own family circle. Our own vineyard, in such cases, should have priority.

July 9

For whoever calls on the name of the Lord shall be saved.
ROMANS 10:13

N o one can ever really call on the Name of the Lord without being saved. This call of desperate earnestness never goes unanswered. When we get to the end of our own resources, when we abandon all hope of saving ourselves, when we have nowhere to turn but up, if at that time we send a distress call to the Lord, He will hear and answer.

A young Sikh named Sadhu Sundar Singh determined that if he could not find peace, he would commit suicide. He prayed, "Oh God, if there is a God, reveal Thyself to me tonight." If he didn't get an answer in seven hours, he was going to put his head on the railroad track as the next train rushed to Lahore.

In the early hours of the morning, he had a vision of Jesus coming into his room and saying in Hindustani, "You were praying to know the right way. Why do you not take it? I am the way."

He rushed into his father's room and said, "I am a Christian. I can serve no one else but Jesus. Till the day I die, my life is His."

I have never known of anyone who called on the Name of the Lord in blood-earnestness without being heard. Of course, there are those who pray to the Lord when they are in a tight spot, who promise to live for Him if He will deliver them, and who then quickly forget once the pressure has been lifted. But God knows their hearts; He knows they were only fox-hole opportunists who never made a genuine heart-commitment to Him.

The fact remains that God will always reveal Himself to the one who is desperate to find Him. In countries where the Bible is not readily available, He may do it in a vision. Elsewhere He may do it through a Scripture portion, through personal witness, through Christian literature or through the miraculous converging of circumstances. So in a real sense it is true that "he who seeks God has already found Him." It's that sure!

July 10

If you know these things, blessed are you if you do them.
JOHN 13:17

Those who teach and preach the Christian faith should practice what they preach. They should present to the world a living example of the truth. The will of God is that the Word should become flesh in the lives of His people.

The world is more impressed by action than by talk. Wasn't it Edgar Guest who wrote, "I'd rather see a sermon than hear one any day"? And there is the well-known jibe, "What you are speaks so loud, I can't hear what you say."

It was said of one preacher that when he was in the pulpit, the people wished he would never leave it; but when he was out of the pulpit, the people wished he would never enter it again.

H. A. Ironside said, "Nothing locks the lips like the life." In similar vein, Henry Drummond wrote, "The man is the message." Carlyle added his testimony: "Holy living is the best argument that tells for God in an age of fact…Words have weight when they have a man behind them." E. Stanley Jones said, "The Word has to become flesh in us before it can become power through us." "If I preach the right thing but do not live it, I am telling an untruth about God," said Oswald Chambers.

Of course we know that the Lord Jesus Christ is the only One who perfectly embodies what He teaches. There is absolutely no contradiction between His message and His life. When the Jews asked Him, "Who are you?" He replied, "Just what I have been claiming all along" (Jn. 8:25, NIV). His conduct corresponded to His claims. Ours should do so increasingly

Two brothers were doctors, one a preacher and the other an M.D. One day a troubled woman came to see the preacher, but she was not sure which of the doctors lived there. When the preacher opened the door, she asked, "Are you the doctor who preaches or the one who practices?" The question impressed him afresh with the necessity of being a living example of what he taught.

July 11

Not that I have already attained, or am already perfected.
PHILIPPIANS 3:12

I n yesterday's study we saw that our conduct should correspond to our creed. But in order to balance the subject we must add two postscripts. First, we have to acknowledge that we will never fully and completely live out the truth of God as long as we are in this world. After we have done our best, we still have to say that we are unprofitable servants. But we must not use this fact to excuse failure or even mediocrity—our obligation is to continually try to close the gap between our lips and our lives.

The second consideration is this: The message is always greater than the messenger, no matter who he is. Andrew Murray said, "We who are the Lord's servants will sooner or later have to preach words which we ourselves are unable to fulfill." Thirty-five years after he wrote the book, *Abide in Christ,* he wrote, "I would like you to understand that a minister or Christian author may often be led to say more than he has experienced. I had not then (when he wrote *Abide in Christ*) experienced all that I wrote of. I cannot say that I have experienced it all yet."

The truth of God is superlative and sublime. It is so supernal that, as Guy King wrote, it "causes one to fear lest one should in any wise spoil it by touching it." But must it go forever unheralded simply because we do not reach its loftiest summits? On the contrary, we will proclaim it, even if in so doing we condemn ourselves. To whatever extent we fail to experience it ourselves, we will make it the aspiration of our hearts.

Once again we emphasize that these considerations must never be used to excuse behavior that is unworthy of the Savior. But they should keep us from unwarranted condemnation of a true man of God just because his message sometimes leaps to heights which he himself has not attained. And it should not keep us ourselves from holding back the full counsels of God, even if we have not experienced them in full. God knows our hearts. He knows whether we are practicing hypocrites or passionate aspirants.

July 12

The battle is not yours, but God's.
2 CHRONICLES 20:15

If a man is a soldier of the Cross, he can expect to be attacked sooner or later. The more courageously he declares the truth of God and the more accurately he exemplifies the truth in his own life, the more he will be subjected to assault. An old Puritan said, "He that standeth near his Captain is a sure target for the archers."

He will be accused of wrongs he did not do. He will be savaged by gossip, slander, and backbiting. He will be ostracized and ridiculed. This treatment will come from the world and, sadly enough, it may sometimes come from fellow-Christians.

At such times, it is important to remember that the battle is not ours, but God's. And we should claim the promise of Exodus 14:14: "The Lord will fight for you, and you shall hold your peace." What this means is that we don't have to defend ourselves or fight back. The Lord will vindicate us at the proper time.

F. B. Meyer wrote, "How much is lost by a word! Be still; keep quiet; if they smite thee on one cheek, turn the other also. Never retort. Never mind your reputation or character—they are in His hands, and you mar them by trying to retain them."

Joseph stands out as an example of one who did not try to vindicate himself when falsely accused. He committed his cause to God, and God cleared his name and promoted him to great honor.

An aged servant of Christ testified that he had been wronged many times over the years. But he prayed in the words of Augustine, "Lord, deliver me from the lust of always vindicating myself." He said that the Lord had never failed to justify him and to expose his accusers.

The Lord Jesus, of course, is the supreme Example. "...when He suffered, He did not threaten, but committed Himself to Him who judges righteously" (1 Pet. 2:23).

This, then, is the message for today. We don't have to defend ourselves when we are falsely accused. The battle is the Lord's. He will fight for us. We should hold our peace.

July 13

Beloved, do not believe every spirit, but test the spirits to see whether they are from God; because many false prophets have gone out into the world.

1 JOHN 4:1, NASB

e live in a day when cults are multiplying with amazing rapidity. Actually there are no new cults; they are just variations of heretical groups that sprang up in New Testament days. It is their variety that is new, not their basic tenets.

When John says that we should test the spirits, he means that we should test all teachers by the Word of God so that we can detect those that are false. There are three fundamental areas where the cults expose themselves as being counterfeits. No cult can pass all three of these tests.

Most of the cults are fatally defective in their teaching concerning the Bible. They do not accept it as the inerrant Word of God, the final revelation of God to man. They give equal authority to the writings of their own leaders. They claim new revelations from the Lord and boast of "new truth." They publish their own translation of the Scripture which twists and perverts the truth. They accept the voice of tradition on a par with the Bible. They handle the Word of God deceitfully.

Most of the cults are heretical in their teachings concerning our Lord. They deny that He is God, the Second Person of the Holy Trinity. They might admit that He is the Son of God, but by this they mean something less than equality with God the Father. Often they deny that Jesus is the Christ, teaching that the Christ is a divine influence that came upon the man Jesus. Often they deny the true, sinless humanity of the Savior.

A third area in which the cults stand condemned is in what they teach concerning the way of salvation. They deny that salvation is by grace through faith in the Lord Jesus alone. Every one of them teaches another gospel, namely, salvation by good works or good character.

When propagators of these cults come to our door, what should be our response? John leaves us in no doubt: "Don't have him inside your house; don't even greet him. For to greet such a man is to share in the evil that he is doing." (2 Jn. 10-11, PHILLIPS).

July 14

We have renounced the hidden things of shame, not walking in craftiness nor handling the Word of God deceitfully, but by manifestation of the truth commending ourselves to every man's conscience in the sight of God.

2 CORINTHIANS 4:2

On the previous page, we noted three areas in which the cults expose themselves as being untrue to the Christian faith that has been once-for-all delivered unto the saints. There are other characteristics of the cults of which we should not only be aware but which we should carefully avoid in our own Christian fellowships

For instance, their leaders build up what we might call a personality cult, setting themselves forth as virtual messiahs and wonder-men. Men with charisma often exercise harsh, autocratic control over the laity, demanding submission and threatening dire punishment for failure to obey.

They often claim to be exclusive possessors of the truth, make prideful claims to certain distinctives, and criticize all other groups that disagree. Some claim to combine the best of other doctrines and thus to be the final word. They imply that no one can be fully happy until he is initiated into their mysteries.

They try to isolate their members from all other teachers, from all others who profess to be believers, and from books written by others than their own leaders.

They often prescribe a legalistic lifestyle, that becomes a system of bondage. They equate holiness with certain rituals and observances which men can do by their own strength rather than by divine life.

They exploit the people financially by a system of clever psychological manipulations. The leaders live in splendor and luxury, while many of the people are reduced to near poverty.

Many of the cults are sheep-stealers, conducting raids on other religious institutions rather than trying to reach the unchurched.

They overemphasize one doctrine or a few doctrines, completely neglecting vital areas of divine revelation.

They treat those who teach the truth as enemies. Thus Paul asked the legalistic Galatians, "Have I therefore become your enemy because I tell you the truth?" (Gal. 4:16).

It is unfortunate that any of these attitudes or acts should ever creep into sound Christian fellowships, but as long we are in the body, we all have to guard against them zealously.

July 15

But go and learn what this means: I desire mercy and not sacrifice.
MATTHEW 9:13

G od is far more interested in how we treat other people than in how many religious ceremonies we go through. He prefers mercy to sacrifice. He places practical morality above ritual. It might seem strange to read that God doesn't desire sacrifice, because it was He who instituted the sacrificial system in the first place.

But there is no contradiction. While it is true that He ordered the people to bring sacrifices and offerings, He never intended these to take the place of justice and kindness. "To do righteousness and justice is more acceptable to the Lord than sacrifice" (Prov. 21:3). The Old Testament prophets thundered out against people who observed all the proper rituals, yet who cheated and oppressed their neighbors. Isaiah told them that God was fed up with their burnt offerings and religious holidays as long as they oppressed the fatherless and widows (Isa. 1:10-17). He told them that the fast God desired was to treat their employees fairly, to feed the hungry, and clothe the poor (Isa. 58:6-7). Unless their lives were right, they might as well offer a dog's head or swines' blood (Isa. 66:3).

Amos told the people to stop their religious observances because God would continue to hate these rituals until justice and mercy flowed like a mighty torrent (Amos 5:21-24). And Micah warned that what God wants more than ritual is reality—the reality of fairness, justice, mercy, and humility (Micah 6:6-8).

In our Lord's day, the Pharisees earned His scorn by pretending to be religious with long, public prayers while evicting widows from their homes (Mt. 23:14). They were careful to give God a tenth of the mint in their garden, but this could never take the place of justice and faith (Mt. 23:23). It is futile for us to bring our offering to the Lord if our brother has a valid grievance against us (Mt. 5:24); the gift is acceptable only after the wrong has been righted. Attending church regularly will never serve as a cover-up for dishonest business practices during the week. There is no use giving mother a box of chocolates on Mother's Day if we treat her hatefully during the year. Or a shirt to father on Father's Day if we do not show love and respect to him the rest of the time. God is not fooled by externals or rituals. He sees the heart and our day-by-day behavior.

July 16

Help, Lord, for the godly man ceases!
For the faithful disappear from among the sons of men.
PSALM 12:1

aithful people are an endangered species; they are rapidly vanishing from the human race. If David mourned their demise in his day, we often wonder how he would feel if he lived today.

When we speak of a faithful person, we mean one who is trustworthy, reliable, dependable. If he makes a promise, he keeps it. If he has a responsibility, he fulfills it. If he has honorable allegiances, he is staunchly loyal to them.

The unfaithful man makes an appointment, then either fails to keep it or is inexcusably late. He agrees to teach a Sunday School class, yet fails to arrange for a replacement when he cannot be present. You can never depend on him. His word means nothing. No wonder Solomon said, "Confidence in an unfaithful man in time of trouble is like a bad tooth and a foot out of joint" (Prov. 25:19).

God is looking for faithful men and women. He wants stewards who are faithful in caring for His interests (1 Cor. 4:2). He wants teachers who are faithful in passing on the great truths of the Christian faith (2 Tim. 2:2). He wants believers who are faithful to the Lord Jesus, sharing His rejection and bearing the cross. He wants people who are uncompromisingly loyal to His inspired, inerrant, infallible Word. He wants Christians who are loyal to the local assembly, instead of wandering from church to church like religious gypsies. God wants saints who are faithful to other believers and faithful to the unsaved as well.

As in all other virtues, the Lord Jesus is our glorious example. He is the faithful and true Witness (Rev. 3:14), a merciful and faithful High Priest in things pertaining to God (Heb. 2:17), faithful and just to forgive us our sins and to cleanse us from all unrighteousness (1 Jn. 1:9). His words are true, His promises are unfailing, and His ways are utterly dependable.

Although men might not put a high premium on faithfulness, God does. The Lord Jesus commended the faithfulness of His disciples with the words, "You are those who have continued with Me in My trials. And I bestow upon you a kingdom, just as My Father bestowed one upon Me" (Lk. 22:28-29). And the ultimate reward for faithfulness will be to hear His accolade, "Well done, good and faithful servant:...enter into the joy of your Lord" (Mt. 25:21).

July 17

I will bless those who bless you, and I will curse him who curses you.
GENESIS 12:3

W hen God first called Abraham to be the head of His chosen earthly people, He promised to bless the friends of that nation and to curse its enemies. In the intervening centuries the Jewish people have suffered untold hostility and discrimination, but the curse of God has never been lifted on anti-Semitism.

Haman plotted the destruction of the Jewish people in Persia. He inveigled the king into signing an unalterable decree. For a while everything seemed to be moving in his favor. But then snags developed. The arch-conspirator staggered from disappointment to failure till finally he was hanged on the gallows he had built for Mordecai, the Jew.

Failing to learn from history, Adolph Hitler was doomed to relive it. He inaugurated a vicious program to wipe out the Jews with his concentration camps, gas chambers, ovens, and mass shootings. It seemed that nothing could stop him. But then the tide turned and he died ignominiously with his mistress in a Berlin bunker.

Anti-Semitism will reach its most horrendous climax during the Great Tribulation. The Jews will be delivered up to be afflicted and killed; they will be hated by all the Gentile nations. Vast numbers will be massacred. But the pogrom will be interrupted by the personal advent of the Lord Jesus Christ. Those who have persecuted His people will be destroyed; those who have befriended Christ's Jewish brethren will enter the Kingdom.

No true believer should ever allow his soul to be tainted with a trace of anti-Semitism. His Lord, his Savior, his best and truest Friend, was and is a Jew. God used the Jewish people to give and preserve the Scriptures. Although God has temporarily set aside the nation because of its rejection of the Messiah, He still loves Israel for the Father's sake. No one who hates the Jews can expect the blessing of God on his life and service.

"Pray for the peace of Jerusalem: May they prosper who love you" (Ps. 122:6). They shall also prosper who love the Jewish people.

July 18

Therefore Michal the daughter of Saul had no children to the day of her death.
2 SAMUEL 6:23

D avid was ecstatic when he brought the ark to Jerusalem and when it was placed in the tent that he had specially prepared for it. Sensing that this was one of his greatest achievements and one of the most glorious moments in his career, the king danced before the Lord with all his might. His wife, Michal, ridiculed him for what she thought was shameful behavior. As a direct result of her critical attitude, she had no child unto the day of her death.

We learn from this that a critical spirit produces barrenness. Of course, when we say that, we are not speaking about constructive criticism. If criticism is true, we should welcome it and benefit from it. There are few friends in life who love us enough to give helpful criticism.

But destructive criticism can be devastating. It can destroy the work of God in someone's life, and can undo the progress of years in a few minutes.

In the incident involving David, the ark represents Christ and the ark given its place in Jerusalem speaks of Christ enthroned in the human heart. When that happens, the Spirit-filled believer cannot help but express his exuberance and enthusiasm. This often stirs up the hostility of unbelievers and sometimes the scorn of other Christians. But that critical spirit inevitably leads to barrenness.

It can lead to barrenness not only in an individual life but in a local assembly as well. Take, for example, a fellowship where the young people are subjected to a continual torrent of criticism. They are taken to task for the way they dress, for their hair styles, for their public prayers, for their music. Instead of patiently training them, the leadership expects them to be instantly full-grown. Soon the young people drift away to more congenial fellowships, and the assembly is left to die on the vine.

Let us be warned by the example of Michal that censoriousness not only harms its victims but takes its revenge on the one who practices it. That revenge is spiritual barrenness.

July 19

As He is, so are we in this world...
1 JOHN 4:17B

H ere is one of those New Testament truths that shocks us by its sheer audacity. We would not dare to utter the words if we did not see them in the Bible. But they are; gloriously true, and we can revel and rejoice in them.

In what sense are we like Christ in this world? Our minds almost automatically think first of the ways we are not like Him. We do not share with Him the attributes of deity, such as omnipotence, omniscience, and omnipresence. We are full of sin and failure whereas He is absolutely perfect. We do not love as He loves, or forgive as He forgives.

How, then, are we like Him? The verse explains. "Herein has love been perfected with us that we may have boldness in the day of judgment, that even as He is, we also are in this world" (DARBY). God's love has so worked in our lives that we will not be terrified when we stand before the Judgment Seat of Christ. The reason for our confidence is that we have this in common with the Savior— judgment is behind us. We are like Him with respect to judgment. He bore the judgment of our sins on the Cross of Calvary and settled the sin question once for all. Because He took the punishment of our sins, we will never have to take it. We can confidently sing,

Death and judgment are behind me, Grace and glory lie before, All the billows rolled o'er Jesus, There they spent their utmost power.

Just as judgment is forever past for Him, so it is past for us also, and we can say, *"There is no condemnation, There is no hell for me, The torment and the fire, Mine eyes shall never see. For me there is no sentence, For me death has no sting: Because the Lord who loves me Will shield me with His wing."*

We are like Him not only with respect to judgment but also with respect to acceptance before God. We stand before God with the same favor that the Lord Jesus does, because we are in Him. *"Near, so very near to God, I could not nearer be, For in the Person of His Son, I am as near as He."*

And finally, we are like Christ because we are loved by God the Father, just as Christ is. In His high-priestly prayer, the Lord Jesus said, "…You…have loved them as You have loved Me" (Jn. 17:23b). Thus, it is no exaggeration for us to say, *"Dear, so very dear to God, I could not dearer be; The love wherewith He loves His Son, Such is His love to me."*

So it is blessedly true that as Christ is, so are we in this world.

July 20

24 A man that hath friends must shew himself friendly:
and there is a friend that sticketh closer than a brother.
PROVERBS 18:24, KJV

Even though all modern versions translate this verse differently, the King James Version enshrines the valuable truth that friendships must be cultivated. They thrive on attention but die through neglect.

An editorial in *Decision* magazine said, "Friendships don't just happen; they have to be cultivated—in short, we have to work at them. They are not built on just taking, they are built on giving. They are not just for the good times, they are for the bad times as well. We do not hide our needs from a true friend. Neither do we hold onto a friend only to have his help."

A good friend is worth keeping. He stands by you when you are falsely accused. He commends you for whatever is praiseworthy, and is frank to point out areas that need improvement. He keeps in touch over the years, sharing your joys and sorrows.

That is important—keeping in touch. It can be done by letters, cards, phone calls, visits. But friendship is a two-way street. If I consistently fail to answer letters, I am saying that I don't consider the friendship worth continuing. I am too busy. Or I can't be bothered. Or I hate writing letters. Few friendships can survive on continued neglect.

Our refusal to communicate is often a form of selfishness. We are thinking of ourselves—of the time, effort, and cost involved. True friendship thinks of others— how we can encourage or comfort or cheer or help; how we can minister spiritual food to them.

How much we owe to friends who have come alongside with the Spirit-given word when it was most needed! There was a time in my life when I was feeling very low over a deep disappointment in Christian service. A friend who could not have known of my discouragement wrote a cheery letter in which she quoted Isaiah 49:4, "Then I said, I have labored in vain, I have spent my strength for nothing and in vain; yet surely my just reward is with the Lord, and my work with my God." It was just the word I needed to pick me up and set me to work again.

Charles Kingsley wrote,

> *Can we forget one friend,*
> *Can we forget one face,*
> *Which cheered us to the end,*
> *Which nerved us for our race?*
> *To godlike souls, how deep our debt!*
> *We would not, if we could, forget.*

Most of us have only a few close friends in life. That being so, we should do all in our power to keep those friendships strong and healthy.

July 21

Casting all your care upon Him, for He cares for you.
1 Peter 5:7

1 t is possible to live a long, long life as a believer and yet never learn to cast our care on the Lord. We can memorize the verse and even preach it to others, yet never really practice it in our own lives. We know theologically that God cares for us, that He is concerned with our affairs, and that He is well able to take care of the greatest anxieties we could imagine. Yet we insist on tossing and turning in our beds at night, fretting, worrying, and imagining the worst.

It doesn't have to be that way. I have a friend who faces more problems and headaches than most of us have ever known. If he had to bear them himself, he would be a spiritual basket-case. What does he do? He takes them to the Lord and leaves them there, gets up from his knees, crawls into bed, sings a few verses of a hymn, and is off to sleep in no time.

Bill Bright once said to LeRoy Eims, "LeRoy, I have found great comfort in 1 Peter 5:7. I have concluded in my own life that either I carry my burdens or Jesus does. We cannot both carry them, and I've decided to cast them on Him."

Eims decided to try it. He wrote, "I went to my room and began to pray. To the best of my ability I did what Bill had said. For months I had carried a heavy knot in my stomach. I could actually feel the thing leaving. I experienced the deliverance of God. No, the problem did not go away, and hasn't to this day. But the burden is gone. I no longer spend sleepless nights or cry myself to sleep. I can honestly face the burdens with a joyful spirit and thankfulness of heart."

Most of us can identify with the one who wrote:

It is God's will that I should cast
My care on Him each day.
He also asks me not to cast
My confidence away.
But oh! how stupidly I act
When taken unawares,
I cast away my confidence
And carry all my cares.

And all the time the Savior is saying to us:

Bear not a single care thyself,
One is too much for thee.
The work is Mine and Mine alone.
Thy work is 'Rest in Me.'

213

July 22

*Look, Lord...if I have taken anything from anyone
by false accusation, I restore fourfold.*
LUKE 19:8

As soon as Zacchaeus had opened his heart to the Lord Jesus, a divine instinct told him that he should make restitution for the past. It might sound from the text that there was a question whether he had ever cheated anyone but it is reasonable to believe that the "if" really means "since" in the case of this rich tax collector. He had gotten money dishonestly, he knew it, and he was determined to do something about it.

Restitution is good Bible doctrine and good Bible practice. When we are converted, we should restore to the rightful owner things we have taken wrongfully. Salvation doesn't relieve a person from making right the wrongs of the past. If money was stolen before salvation, a true sense of the grace of God requires that this money be repaid. Even legitimate debts contracted during one's unconverted days are not cancelled by the new birth.

Years ago, when hundreds of people were saved in Belfast under the preaching of W. P. Nicholson, the local factories had to build huge sheds to hold the stolen tools that were returned by the new converts.

Mammoth warehouses would be needed in this country to house the loot taken from the Armed Services alone. To say nothing of the steady leak of tools, supplies, and merchandise that flows illegally from factories, offices, and stores.

Ideally, when restitution is made by a believer, it should be done in the Name of the Lord Jesus. For example, "I stole these tools when I worked for you years ago, but I was saved recently and my life has been transformed by the Lord Jesus Christ. He has put it on my heart to return the tools and to ask your forgiveness." In this way, the glory goes to the Savior, where it belongs.

There are circumstances where, as a matter of Christian testimony, interest should be paid on money that was stolen. The trespass offering in the Old Testament foreshadowed this. It required the payment of damages plus one-fifth.

Admittedly, there are situations where, because of the passing of time or because of changed conditions, it is no longer possible to make restitution. The Lord knows about this. If the sin is confessed, He accepts the sincere desire for the actual act —but only in those cases where restitution is impossible.

July 23

They brought the sick out into the streets and laid them on beds and couches,
that at least the shadow of Peter passing by might fall on some of them.
ACTS 5:15

The people recognized that Peter's ministry was a ministry of power. Wherever he went, the sick were healed. No wonder the crowd wanted to get into his shadow! He wielded a tremendous influence.

Everyone of us casts a shadow. Inevitably we influence the lives of those we contact. Herman Melville wrote: "We cannot live for ourselves alone. Our lives are connected by a thousand invisible threads, and along these sympathetic fibers, our actions run as causes and return to us as results."

> *You are writing a Gospel, a chapter each day,*
> *By the deeds that you do, by the words that you say.*
> *Men read what you write whether faithless or true:*
> *Say! What is the Gospel according to you?*

When asked which of the Gospels was his favorite, one man answered, "The Gospel according to my mother." And John Wesley once said, "I learned more about Christianity from my mother than from all the theologians of England."

It is sobering to realize that someone looks at each one of us and thinks, "That's just what a Christian should be." It may be a son or daughter, a friend or neighbor, a teacher or student. You are his hero, his model, his ideal. He watches you more closely than you think. Your business life, your church life, your family life, your prayer life—all these set the pattern for him to imitate. He wants your shadow to overshadow him.

Generally we think that shadows are nothings. But the spiritual shadow we cast is something real. Therefore we must ask ourselves this question:

> *When to the last great reckoning the lives I meet must go,*
> *Shall this wee, fleeting touch of mine have added joy or woe?*
> *Shall He who looks their records o'er—of name and time and place—*
> *Say, "Here a blessed influence came" or "Here is evil's trace"?*
> —STRICKLAND GILLILAN

Robert G. Lee wrote: "You can no more prevent what you are, what you say, and what you do from affecting other people than you can prevent your body from casting a shadow in sunlight. What you are within you shows without, with no ambiguous expression. You exert an influence which mere language and strong persuasion are feeble to express."

July 24

One person esteems one day above another; another esteems every day alike.
Let each be fully convinced in his own mind.

ROMANS 14:5

The word "alike" should be omitted from this verse; it was added by the translators. It should read, "another esteems every day," that is, he looks upon every day as sacred.

To Jews, living under law, the Sabbath or seventh day was especially sacred. The law forbade labor on that day and restricted travel. Additional offerings were required.

Christians, living under grace, are never commanded to keep the Sabbath. To them all days are sacred, even though they believe that there is a principle in the Word of one day of rest in seven. They cannot be condemned for failing to keep the Sabbath (Col. 2:16).

The first day of the week, that is, the Lord's Day, stands out in the New Testament for several reasons. The Lord Jesus arose on that day (Jn. 20:1). After His resurrection He met with His disciples on two successive Sundays (Jn. 20:19, 26). The Holy Spirit was given at Pentecost on the first day; Pentecost occurred seven Sundays after the Feast of Firstfruits (Lev. 23:15-16; Acts 2:1), which symbolizes Christ's resurrection (1 Cor. 15:20, 23). The disciples gathered to break bread on the first day of the week (Acts 20:7). And Paul gave instructions to the Corinthians to take a special offering on the first day of the week (1 Cor. 16:1-2). However, it is not a day of special obligation, like the Sabbath, but a day of special privilege. Because we are released from our normal employment on Sunday, we are able to devote it to the worship and service of our Lord in a way we are not able to devote the other days.

While we have liberty to regard all days as equally sacred, we do not have liberty to do anything on Sunday that might stumble others. If working around the house, repairing the car or playing football would stumble a brother, then we should forego what we might consider to be a legitimate right. As Paul said, "Therefore let us not judge one another anymore, but rather resolve this, not to put a stumbling block or a cause to fall in our brother's way" (Rom. 14:13).

Jews under law had their day of rest at the end of a week of work. Christians under grace begin their week with a day of rest, because Christ has finished the work of redemption.

C. I. Scofield pointed out that the true character of the Lord's Day is illustrated by the way our Lord used it: "He comforted weeping Mary; walked seven miles with two perplexed disciples, giving a Bible reading by the way; sent messages to other disciples; had a private interview with backslidden Peter; and imparted the Holy Spirit to the men in the upper chamber."

July 25

When the Lord saw that Leah was unloved, He opened her womb;
but Rachel was barren.
GENESIS 29:31

There is a law of compensation in life. According to that law, people who are deficient in one respect are given some counter-balancing benefit in another. The law prevents anyone from having everything. What one person lacks in beauty, she may make up for in practical wisdom. A man who is not well coordinated in athletics may have a better disposition than if he were. Poets are not always practical, and artists are not always good managers of their finances.

When God saw that Jacob loved Rachel more than Leah, He caused Leah to be more prolific. Years later the law of compensation worked in the same way with Hannah and Peninnah. Elkanah loved Hannah more than Peninnah, but Peninnah had children and Hannah did not (1 Sam. 1:1-6).

Though Fanny Crosby did not have the gift of sight, she had the gift of song to a superlative degree. Her hymns are one of the Church's great legacies. Alexander Crudens suffered from severe depression but he had the strength to produce the concordance that bears his name.

Here is a humble Christian who cannot preach for sour apples; he has no public gift at all. But he is a mechanical genius, and thankfully can keep the preacher's car in operating condition. The preacher is hopeless in mechanics. When anything goes wrong with his car, all he can do is raise the hood, put his head under it and pray.

If someone objects that the law of compensation does not work perfectly in this life, we would have to agree. There are inequalities and injustices. But this life is not all. The last chapter has not been written. When God pulls back the curtain and lets us see the world beyond, we realize that the scores are evened and the tables turned. We hear Abraham, for example, say to the rich man, "Son, remember that in your lifetime you received your good things, and likewise Lazarus evil things; but now he is comforted and you are tormented" (Lk. 16:25).

In the meantime, it's good for us to take a balanced view of life. Instead of concentrating on our deficiencies, we should remember that God has given us some qualities and abilities that others who seem to be more favored do not have. This will save us from feelings of worthlessness, inadequacy, and envy.

July 26

For I have come to set a man against his father, a daughter against her mother,
and a daughter-in-law against her mother-in-law,
and a man's enemies will be those of his own household.
MATTHEW 10:35-36

O ur Lord is not speaking here about the direct purpose of His coming but rather about its almost inevitable result. He is saying that whenever people would follow Him, they could expect bitter opposition from their relatives and friends. In that sense, He did not come to bring peace but a sword (v. 34).

History has fulfilled the prophecy. Wherever people have turned to the living, loving Savior, they have met with abuse and hostility. They have been ridiculed, disinherited, thrown out of the home, fired from their jobs, and, in many cases, murdered.

The opposition is completely irrational. Here is a father whose son was a dope addict. But now that son has turned his back on drugs and is actively serving Christ. You'd think the father would be pleased. But no! He's furious. He frankly admits he would rather have his son the way he was before.

Others are saved from alcoholism, from crime, from sex perversion, from the occult. They naively think that their relatives will not only be ecstatic but will want to become Christians themselves. It doesn't work that way. The coming of the Lord Jesus brings division into the family.

To forsake the religion of one's parents for Christ inflames the deepest passions. For instance, a family may be Jewish in name only, yet for a member of that family to become a Christian provokes violent emotional outbursts. The offender is called a renegade, a traitor, and is even associated with Hitler, as an enemy of the Jews. Christian pleas and protests fall on deaf ears.

In many Muslim countries, conversion to Christ is punishable by death. The sentence is carried out not by the government but by the immediate family. The wife, for instance, may put ground glass in her husband's food.

And yet through the bold confession of new converts and through their patient, Christ-like endurance of hatred and persecution, others come to realize the emptiness of their own lives and their own religion, and turn to the Lord Jesus Christ in repentance and faith. And so the ranks grow through opposition, and thrive through persecution.

July 27

*Indeed you are to them as a very lovely song of one who has a pleasant voice
and can play well on an instrument; for they hear your words,
but they do not do them.*

EZEKIEL 33:32

ne of the ironies of declaring the word of the Lord is that people are often intrigued with the speaker but not with the message that requires action on their part.

This is true with public preaching. The people admire the preacher. They remember his jokes and his illustrations. They hang on his enunciation. Like the woman who said, "I could almost weep every time my minister says that blessed word 'Mesopotamia.'" But they are paralyzed as far as obedience is concerned. They are immunized against action. They are anesthetized by the pleasant voice.

This is a familiar syndrome to those who carry on a counseling ministry. There are some people who get a secret satisfaction out of being counseled. They thrive on being the center of attention for that brief hour or so. They enjoy the fellowship of the counselor so much that they become chronic counselees.

Presumably they have come to get advice. But they don't really want advice. Their minds are already made up. They know what they want to do. If the counselor's advice agrees with their own desire, then they are fortified. If not, they will reject his advice and continue on in their stubborn way.

King Herod belonged to this class of dilettantes. He used to enjoy listening to John the Baptist (Mk. 6:20) but he was a superficial dabbler. He had no intention of letting the message change his life.

Erwin Lutzer writes, "I've discovered that the most frustrating problem in helping those who come for counsel is simply that most people do not want to change. Of course, they are prepared to make minor adjustments—particularly if their behavior is getting them into trouble. But most of them are comfortable with their sin as long as it doesn't get out of hand. And often they'd prefer to have God keep His activity in their lives to a minimum."

Some counselors have developed a stratagem to bridge the gap between hearing and doing. They give the counselee a specific assignment—something that he must do before he appears for another session. This tends to eliminate those who are not serious. It prevents wasting time for them both.

It is a serious thing to reach the stage in life where we can hear God's Word and not be moved by it. We must pray for continued sensitivity to the voice of the Lord and a readiness to perform whatever He says.

July 28

Let the wicked forsake his way, and the unrighteous man his thoughts;
let him return to the Lord, and He will have mercy on him;
and to our God, for He will abundantly pardon.
ISAIAH 55:7

T he trembling sinner fears that God will not receive him. The penitent backslider doubts that God can ever forget. But our verse reminds us that those who return to the Lord are greeted with bounteous mercy and abundant pardon.

This is illustrated by a story that surfaces periodically over the years—a story in which the details change but the message lives on. It is about a rebellious son who left home, went to New York, lived in sin and shame, and finally landed in jail. After four years in prison, he was paroled and desperately wanted to go home. But he was tortured by the fear that his father would not receive him. He couldn't face the disappointment of being rejected.

Finally he wrote his dad giving no return address. He said that he would be on the train the following Friday. If the family wanted him, they should tie a white handkerchief on the oak tree in the front yard. If he saw no handkerchief as the train passed, he would keep going.

Now he is on the train, sullen and withdrawn, fearing the worst. As it happens, a Christian is sitting beside him. After several unsuccessful tries, the Christian finally gets him to open up and tell his story. They are now fifty miles from his home. The returning prodigal fluctuates between fear and hope. Forty miles. He thinks of the disgrace he has brought on his parents, and how he has broken their hearts. Thirty miles. The wasted years pass before his mind. Twenty miles. Ten miles. Five miles.

At last the house comes into view. He sits there stunned. The oak tree is covered with white strips of cloth, fluttering madly in the breeze. He gets up, brings down his suitcase and prepares to get off at the station.

The tree, of course, speaks of the Cross. With arms outstretched and decked with innumerable promises of pardon, it beckons the repentant sinner to come home. What a welcome to the Father's house! What unbounded forgiveness when the wanderer returns!

July 29

Should you help the wicked and love those who hate the Lord?
Therefore the wrath of the Lord is upon you.
2 CHRONICLES 19:2

King Jehoshaphat had joined wicked King Ahab in war against the Syrians. It was an unholy alliance that almost cost his life. The Syrians mistook Jehoshaphat for Ahab and were about to kill him when they realized their mistake. Although Jehoshaphat escaped death, he didn't escape a stinging rebuke from the prophet Jehu. God is angry when His people love those who hate Him and cooperate with the ungodly.

Where could such a thing happen today? It could happen when professed evangelical Christians join with avowed liberals in great religious crusades. These liberals deny the great fundamental doctrines of the Christian faith. They seek to undermine the authority of the Scriptures with their doubts and denials. Although posing as Christians, they are actually enemies of the Cross of Christ. Their god is their belly. Their glory is in their shame. They mind earthly things (see Phil. 3:18-19). The cause of Christ cannot possibly benefit from their patronage. It can only suffer.

As the ecumenical movement gains momentum, Bible believing Christians will face increasing pressure to close ranks with every ungodly element in Christendom. If they refuse, they will be ridiculed and denounced, and their liberties will be curtailed. Yet faithfulness to Christ will require them to walk a path of separation.

One of the unkindest cuts of all comes when real Christians are contemptuous of their brothers who refuse to work with the ungodly. It is not unknown for Christian leaders to speak with appreciation of the modernists while assailing the fundamentalists. They fawn over liberal scholarship, quote liberal writers approvingly and show a lovely tolerance of liberal heresies. But they have nothing but scornful epithets for their fundamentalist brothers who seek to maintain clear-cut lines of demarcation between the righteous and the ungodly.

To court the favor of God's enemies or seek their help is a policy of treachery. Loyalty to Christ demands that we stand with His uncompromising followers against the foe.

July 30

As his part is who goes down to the battle,
so shall his part be who stays by the supplies; they shall share alike.
1 SAMUEL 30:24

hen David recovered the city of Ziklag from the Amalekites, some of his men did not want to share the spoil with 200 who had stayed behind at the brook Besor. David ruled that those who stayed by the supplies should share equally with those who went into the battle.

For every soldier who engages in combat, there are several who work behind the lines. In the U.S. Army in World War II, only about 30% of the troops were in combatant units. The others were support personnel, serving in such units as engineer, quartermaster, ordnance, communications, chemical, transportation, and military government.

There is a parallel to this situation in the work of the Lord. Although all Christians are soldiers, not all are in the front line of battle. Not all are preachers, or evangelists, or teachers, or pastors. Not all are missionaries serving on the battle fronts of the world.

God has support personnel in His army too. There are His faithful prayer warriors who agonize daily until the tide of battle turns. There are His devoted stewards who live sacrificially so that they can send more money to the front. There are those who provide food and accommodations for those who are in face-to-face conflict with the enemy. Then think of those who type manuscripts that will one day carry the message to distant lands. Think of those who edit, translate, and print Christian literature. Think of the women of excellence who minister in the home, raising sons and daughters for the service of the King. For everyone in the thick of the battle, there are several others serving as support personnel.

When the rewards are passed out, those who had supportive roles will share equally with those who were acclaimed as war heroes. Those who served quietly behind the lines will share equal honors with the evangelical celebrities.

God is able to sort it all out. He can accurately measure the importance of everyone's contribution. There will be plenty of surprises. Inconspicuous people whom we thought to be fairly unimportant will be seen to have occupied crucial positions. Without them, we ourselves would have been powerless.

July 31

There is no one who has left house or brothers or sisters or father or mother or wife or children or lands, for My sake and the gospel's, who shall not receive a hundred-fold now in this time...and in the age to come, eternal life.

MARK 10:29-30

T he greatest of all investments is the investment of one's life for Jesus Christ. The important considerations in any investment are the safety of the principal and the rate of return. Judged on this basis, no investment can compare with the life that's lived for God. The principal is absolutely safe because He is able to keep that which we have committed unto Him (2 Tim. 1:12). As for the income, it boggles the mind by its immensity.

In today's passage, the Lord Jesus promises to repay one hundredfold. That amounts to a 10,000% rate of interest—something that is unheard of in the world. But that is not all!

Those who have forsaken the comforts of a home in order to serve the Lord Christ are promised they shall receive "an hundredfold now in this time, houses"—the warmth and conveniences of many homes, where they are shown the kindness of God for Jesus' sake.

Those who forego the delights of marriage and a family, or who sever other tender earthly ties for the gospel's sake, are promised brothers, and sisters, and mothers, and children—a worldwide family, many of whom actually become closer than blood-relatives.

Those who forsake lands are promised "lands." They leave behind the privilege of owning a few acres of real estate, and gain the immeasurably greater privilege of claiming countries and even continents for the precious Name of Jesus.

They are also promised "persecutions." At first this seems to be a sour note in an otherwise harmonious symphony. But Jesus includes persecutions as a positive return on one's investment. To share the reproach of Christ is greater treasure than all the wealth of Egypt (Heb. 11:26).

Those are the dividends in this life. Then the Lord adds, "...and in the age to come, eternal life." This looks forward to eternal life in its fullness. Though eternal life itself is a gift received by faith, there will be differing capacities for enjoying it. Those who have left all to follow Jesus will share a greater degree of reward in the City Foursquare.

When we consider the transcendent returns from a life invested for God, it's strange that more people do not participate. Investors can be extremely shrewd when it comes to stocks and bonds, yet strangely dense when it comes to the best investment of all.

August 1

A word fitly spoken is like apples of gold in settings of silver.
PROVERBS 25:11

T he combination of golden apples in a setting of silver is pleasingly appropriate. The two go together well. It is the same with a golden word spoken at just the proper time. "A man has joy by the answer of his mouth, and a word spoken in due season, how good it is!" (Prov. 15:23).

A veteran missionary lady is dying in the cancer ward, still conscious but too weak to talk. A godly elder goes to her bedside just as the evening visiting hours are closing. Leaning over her bed, he quotes Song of Solomon 8:5, "Who is this coming up from the wilderness, leaning upon her beloved?" She opens her eyes and smiles. That is her last contact with this sobbing, suffering world. Before dawn breaks, she has left this wilderness, leaning on her Beloved. It was just the right word!

A family is numb with grief over the loss of a loved one. Friends crowd around with messages of condolence, but none seem to assuage the heartache. Then a letter comes from Dr. H. A. Ironside, quoting Psalm 30:5, "Weeping may endure for a night, but joy comes in the morning." That proves to be the right word from the Lord to snap the chain of sorrow.

As a group of young Christians are on a long trip, one starts to share some doubts concerning the Scriptures which he has picked up in one of his college courses. After listening for a while, one of the quieter, more forgettable passengers startles the group by quoting Proverbs 19:27 from memory: "Cease listening to instruction, my son, and you will stray from the words of knowledge." It was an apple of gold in a setting of silver!

Then there is the familiar story of how Ingersoll, standing before a large audience, defied God to strike him dead in five minutes—if there was a God. The five minutes passed, heavy with suspense. The fact that Ingersoll was still alive was supposed to demonstrate that no God exists. Just then a nondescript Christian arose in the audience and asked, "Mr. Ingersoll, do you think you can exhaust the mercy of God in five minutes?" It was a word on target.

The proper word, spoken at the proper time, is truly a gift from God. We might well covet the gift so that the Spirit of God can use us to speak the appropriate word of comfort, encouragement, warning, or rebuke.

August 2

They were fearful as they entered the cloud.
LUKE 9:34

Peter, James, and John were on the mount with Jesus. Sensing that this was a significant moment in history and desiring to somehow preserve its glory, Peter proposed erecting three booths—one each for Jesus, Moses, and Elijah. This, of course, would have put the Lord on the same level as the two Old Testament saints. God thwarted the project by enveloping them in a cloud. Luke tells us that "they were fearful as they entered the cloud."

They shouldn't have feared. It was a cloud of glory, not of judgment. It was a temporary phenomenon, not a permanent fact of life. God was in the cloud, even though He was not visible.

Oftentimes clouds come into our lives and, like the apostles, we fear as we enter into one of these clouds. When God calls us to a new sphere of service, for instance, there is often the fear of the unknown. We imagine the worst in the way of dangers, discomforts, and disagreeable situations. Actually we are just being afraid of a blessing. When the cloud lifts, we find that God's will is good and acceptable and perfect.

We fear as we enter the cloud of sickness. Our minds run wild with alarm. We interpret every word and facial movement of the doctor as an omen of doom. We diagnose every symptom as pointing to a terminal disease. But when the illness passes, we find ourselves saying with the psalmist, "It is good for me that I have been afflicted" (Ps. 119:71). God was in the cloud and we did not know it.

We fear when we enter the cloud of sorrow. What good, we ask, could ever come out of such tears, anguish, and bereavement? Our whole world seems to collapse in ruins around us. But there is instruction in the cloud. We learn how to comfort others with the comfort with which the Lord comforts us. We come to understand the tears of the Son of God in a way we could never have known otherwise.

We needn't fear as we enter the clouds of life. They are educative. They are temporary. They are not destructive. They may hide the Lord's face but not His love and power. So we should take to heart the words of William Cowper:

> *Ye fearful saints, fresh courage take;*
> *The clouds ye so much dread*
> *Are big with mercy, and shall break*
> *In blessings on your head.*

August 3

He takes no pleasure in the legs of a man.
PSALM 147:10

What an interesting insight! The great, transcendent God doesn't take pleasure in the legs of a man!

We can think of this in connection with the world of athletics. The track star, lithe and swift, crossing the finish line with hands flung high in victory. The basketball player, streaking down the court to sink the winning basket. The football hero, muscular and strong, irresistibly plunging through the line.

The crowd goes wild. They are jumping, shouting, cheering (or alternately booing and catcalling). They are fanatics, emotionally involved in every play. You might say that they take pleasure in the legs of a man—that is, in his ability to play the game.

Our verse is not intended to prohibit an interest in athletics. The Bible elsewhere speaks well of the value of bodily exercise. But God's disinterest in the legs of a man should remind us to keep our priorities in balance.

It is easy for a young believer to become so engrossed in some sport that it becomes the passion of his life. All his best efforts are aimed toward achieving excellence. He disciplines his time, his food intake, his sleep. He practices endlessly, perfecting skill in every conceivable play. He maintains an exercise regimen, designed to keep him in top physical condition. He thinks and talks about this sport as if it were his life. Perhaps it actually is.

Sometimes a young Christian like this is brought up short when he realizes that God doesn't take pleasure in the legs of a man. If he wants to walk in fellowship with God, he must adopt God's perspective.

What, then, does God take pleasure in? The eleventh verse of Psalm 147 tells us: "The Lord takes pleasure in those who fear Him, in those who hope in His mercy." In other words, God is more interested in the spiritual than in the physical. The Apostle Paul mirrors this same value system when he says that "bodily exercise profits a little, but godliness is profitable for all things, having promise of the life that now is, and of that which is to come" (1 Tim. 4:8).

One hundred years from today, when the cheers have died away, when the stadium is empty, and the score is forgotten, the thing that will really count is a life that first sought the kingdom of God and His righteousness.

August 4

The Lord is righteous, He loves righteousness.
PSALM 11:7

T he Lord Himself is righteous and loves to see His people acting in a righteous manner. He is pleased when believers instinctively make choices that are consistent with divine or moral law.

But it is not always easy in a world such as ours. We are constantly tempted to compromise in the areas of morals and ethics. Some of the temptations are blatant; others are insidious. It takes both discernment and backbone to walk a straight line.

It would not be possible to catalog all the problem areas, but perhaps a selective list will provide a base for future decision-making.

Bribes and kickbacks are forms of unrighteousness. So are gifts made to a purchasing agent in order to prejudice his judgment...It is wrong to kite checks, that is, to issue them without sufficient funds in the account in the hope that you can deposit enough money before the checks are collected...It's illegal to mail a package of merchandise with writing enclosed and not pay the extra postage for the letter...A form of deceit is to tell a caller that the boss is not in when, in fact, he is sitting in the adjacent office...Any misuse of company time or expense account with personal expenditures that are not related to the business...And then, of course, there is the widespread practice of falsifying income tax returns, either by understating income or padding contributions and expenses...The filing of fraudulent insurance claims has reached epidemic proportions...Work slowdowns and work that is below standard are wrong...And perhaps one of the most frequent abuses is the unauthorized use of an employer's time to transact personal business. It is not right to stand up for relatives or friends when they are clearly in the wrong. This is misguided affection and false loyalty. The cause of righteousness is served when we stand for truth against sin, no matter who the guilty person is.

Similarly, it is wrong to side in with an ex-communicated person on the sentimental notion that someone has to befriend the offender. This only succeeds in creating division in the church and hardening the offender in his wickedness.

Finally, it is never right for someone to shoulder the blame for something he hasn't done. There are some peace-loving souls who are willing to take the blame when the guilty refuses to come forward and confess. Peace cannot be won by the sacrifice of truth.

Courage, brother! do not stumble,
Though thy path is dark as night;
There's a star to guide the humble:
"Trust in God, and do the right."
—NORMAN MACLEOD

August 5

The wrath of man does not produce the righteousness of God.
JAMES 1:20

T he picture is not an unfamiliar one. A church business meeting is in progress. A decision must be made. It is not about some great doctrine of the faith, but perhaps about building an addition, or painting the kitchen, or distributing some funds. A disagreement develops, anger rises, tempers flare and shouting erupts. A few strong-minded, vocal individuals finally prevail, then leave with the delusion that they have forwarded the work of God. Whatever else they have forwarded, they have not advanced God's work or accomplished His will. Man's wrath does not work the righteousness of God.

The story is told that Emerson rushed out of some committee meeting where there had been a lot of argument and mental strife. While he was still seething with anger, he seemed to hear the stars say to him, "Why so hot, little man?" To which Leslie Weatherhead comments: "How wonderfully the silent stars in their majesty and remote beauty, hush our spirits, as if they were really saying, 'God is great enough to take care of you', and 'Nothing troubling you is as important as it seems.'"

We know, of course, that there is a time for righteous anger. That time is when the honor of God is at stake. But James is not thinking of that when he speaks of the wrath of man. He is thinking of the man who insists on having his own way, and who, when blocked, explodes in anger. He is thinking of the proud person who considers his own judgment infallible and who is therefore intolerant of dissent.

To the man of this world, an explosive temper is a sign of strength. To him it is a badge of leadership, a means of commanding respect. He thinks that meekness is weakness.

But the Christian knows better. He knows that when he loses his temper, he loses respect. Every outburst of temper is a failure. It is the work of the flesh, not the fruit of the Spirit.

Christ has taught him a better way. It is the way of self-control, of giving place to God's wrath, of showing all meekness to all men. It is the way of patiently enduring wrong, of turning the other cheek. The Christian knows that he hinders the work of God by displays of temper; he obscures any visible difference between himself and the unconverted, and he seals his lips as far as testimony is concerned.

August 6

Is it nothing to you, all you who pass by? Behold and see if there is any sorrow like my sorrow, which has been brought on me, which the Lord has inflicted in the day of His fierce anger.
LAMENTATIONS 1:12

Sometimes as I sit at the Lord's Supper, I have to ask myself, "What is the matter with me? How can I sit here and contemplate the passion of the Savior and not be melted in tears?"

> *Am I a stone, and not a sheep,*
> *That I can stand, O Christ, beneath Thy cross,*
> *To number drop by drop Thy blood's slow loss*
> *And yet not weep?*
> *Not so the sun and moon*
> *Which hid their faces in a starless sky,*
> *A horror of great darkness at broad noon—I, only I.*
> *Yet give not o'er but seek Thy sheep,*
> *True Shepherd of the flock;*
> *Greater than Moses, turn and look once more,*
> *And smite a rock.* —CHRISTINA ROSSETTI

Another wrote: *"O wonder to myself I am, Thou loving, bleeding, dying Lamb, That I can scan the mystery o'er, and not be moved to love Thee more.*

I admire those sensitive souls who are so moved by the sufferings of the dying Redeemer that they break down and cry. I think of my Christian barber, Ralph Ruocco. Often as he stood over me, he would talk about the agonies which the Savior endured. Then with his tears falling on the cloth cover, he would say, "I don't know why He was willing to die for me. I am such a wretch. Yet He bore the penalty of my sins in His body on the Cross."

I think of the sinful woman who washed the Savior's feet with her tears and wiped them with her hair, and kissed His feet, and anointed them with ointment (Lk. 7:38). Although living on the other side of the Cross, she was more attuned emotionally than I with all my superior knowledge and privilege.

Why am I such a block of ice? Is it that I have been brought up in a culture where it is considered unmanly to weep? If so, then I wish I had never known that culture. It is not a disgrace to weep in the shadow of Calvary; the disgrace lies in not weeping.

Borrowing Jeremiah's words, I must henceforth pray, "Oh, that my head were waters, and my eyes a fountain of tears, that I might weep day and night" (Jer. 9:1); weep, that is, over the sufferings and death which my sins brought on the sinless Savior. And I take as my own the immortal words of Isaac Watts: *"Well might I hide my blushing face while His dear cross appears; dissolve my heart in thankfulness, and melt my eyes to tears."*

Lord, deliver me from the curse of a dry-eyed Christianity!

August 7

...To give them beauty for ashes, the oil of joy for mourning, the garment of praise for the spirit of heaviness.
ISAIAH 61:3

1 n this exalted passage, the Messiah is describing some of the marvelous exchanges which He brings to those who receive Him. He gives beauty for ashes, joy for mourning, praise for heaviness.

We bring Him the ashes of a life burned out with pleasure, the ashes of a body ruined by liquor or drugs. We bring Him the ashes of wasted years in the wilderness, or the ashes of frustrated hopes and shattered dreams. And what do we get? He gives us beauty, the beauty of a dazzling bridal diadem. What an exchange! "The poor wearied drudge of sin is honored by becoming the consort of the holy God" (J. H. JOWETT). Mary Magdalene, controlled by seven demons, is not only delivered but becomes a daughter of the King. The Corinthians come to Him in all their degradation and are washed, sanctified, and justified.

We bring Him the tears of mourning. These are tears brought on by sin, defeat and failure. Tears caused by tragedy and loss. Tears over shattered marriages and wayward children. Can He do anything with these briny, scalding tears? Yes, He can wipe them away and give us the oil of joy in their place. He gives us the joy of forgiveness, the joy of acceptance, the joy of His family, the joy of finding the reason for our existence. In short, He gives us "the joy of the bridal feast for heavy-footed woe."

Finally, He takes from us the spirit of heaviness. We all know what this spirit is like—the burden of guilt, remorse, shame, and humiliation. The spirit of loneliness, of rejection, of betrayal. The spirit of fear and anxiety. He takes them all away and gives us the garment of praise. He puts a new song in our mouth, even praise to our God (Ps. 40:3). The grumbler is filled with thanksgiving, the blasphemer with worship.

Something beautiful, something good,
All my confusion He understood.
All I had to offer Him was brokenness and strife,
And He made something beautiful of my life.
—WM. GAITHER

August 8

Do good, and lend, hoping for nothing in return; and your reward will be great.
LUKE 6:35

These commandments of our Lord refer to our behavior toward all men, converted and unconverted, but we shall be thinking of them particularly in regard to financial dealings among individual Christians. It is sadly true that some of the most serious conflicts among believers arise over money matters. It shouldn't be so, but unfortunately the old adage still holds: "When money comes in the door, love goes out the window."

A simple solution might be to forbid all financial dealings among the saints, but we cannot do this as long as the Bible says, "Give to everyone who asks of you" and "Lend, hoping for nothing in return" (Lk. 6:30, 35). So we must adopt various guidelines that enable us to obey the Word and yet avoid strife and broken friendships.

We should give to any genuine case of need. The gift should be unconditional. It should not obligate the other person in any way either to vote with us in a church meeting or to defend us when we are wrong. We must not try to "buy" people with our kindnesses.

The commandment to give to every man who asks has certain exceptions. We should not give to anyone to finance gambling, drinking, or smoking. We should not give to underwrite some foolish, get-rich scheme that caters to man's covetousness.

When we lend for a worthy cause, we should do so with the attitude that we don't care if the money is never returned. Non-payment will not affect our friendship. And we should not charge interest on the loan. If a Jew, living under law, could not collect interest from a fellow-Jew (Lev. 25:35-37), how much less should a Christian, living under grace, collect interest from a fellow-believer?

If a case arises where we are not quite sure whether the need is genuine, it is generally better to seek to meet the need. If we must err, it is better to do so on the side of grace.

In giving to others, we must face the fact that recipients of charity often feel resentment toward the donor. This is a price we must be willing to pay. When Disraeli was once reminded that a certain man hated him, he said, "I don't know why. I haven't done anything for him lately."

August 9

So he left all, rose up, and followed Him.
LUKE 5:28

 icture Levi sitting at a table beside the highway, collecting taxes from those who passed by. If he was a typical tax-collector, he pocketed considerable sums of money instead of turning them in to the despised Roman government.

On this particular day Jesus passed by and said, "Follow Me." A tremendous spiritual awakening took place in Levi's life. He saw his sins exposed. He realized the emptiness of his life. He heard the promise of better things. His response was immediate. "He left all, rose up, and followed Him." In doing so, he anticipated Amy Carmichael's pregnant lines:

> I heard His call, 'Come, follow!'
> That was all.
> My earthly gold grew dim,
> My soul went after Him,
> I rose and followed:
> That was all.
> Who would not follow
> If they heard Him call?

But Levi, or Matthew as he is better known, little realized on that day when he answered the call of Christ the great things that would flow from his obedience.

First of all, of course, he experienced the priceless blessing of salvation. From then on he wore out his sandals on the toes instead of on the heels. From then on he had more joy even when he was sad than he formerly had when he was glad. From then on he could say in the words of George Wade Robinson, "Something lives in every hue, Christless eyes have never seen."

Then too, Matthew became one of the twelve Apostles. He lived with the Lord Jesus, heard His incomparable teachings, became a witness of His resurrection, went forth with the message glorious, and finally laid down His life for the Savior.

To Matthew was given the unspeakable privilege of writing the first Gospel. We said that he left all, but the Lord allowed him to keep his pen. That pen was used to portray the Lord Jesus as the true King of the Jews.

Yes, Matthew left all, but in doing so, he gained all, found the real reason for his existence.

There is a sense in which the call of Christ comes to every man, woman, boy, and girl. We can answer or we can refuse. If we respond, He blesses us beyond our wildest dreams. If we refuse, He finds others to follow Him. But we can never find a better Christ to follow.

August 10

The people who stood by and heard it said that it had thundered.
JOHN 12:29

od had just spoken from heaven in clear, articulate tones. Some said that it thundered. They gave a naturalistic explanation for what was divine and miraculous.

That is one attitude we can take toward miracles today. We can try to explain them away as nothing more than natural occurrences.

Or we can say flatly that the age of miracles has passed. We can conveniently relegate them to a dispensational pigeonhole.

A third attitude is to go to the other extreme and claim to experience miracles which, in fact, are nothing but the product of a vivid imagination.

The proper approach is to acknowledge that God can and does perform miracles in our day. As the Sovereign Lord, He can do as He pleases. There is no scriptural reason why He should have abandoned miracles as a means of revealing Himself.

A miracle occurs every time someone is born again. It is a mighty demonstration of divine power, delivering that person from the kingdom of darkness and translating him into the kingdom of the Son of God's love.

There are miracles of healing when medical science has given up and all human hope is gone. Then, in answer to believing prayer, God sometimes chooses to touch the body and restore the person to health.

There are miracles of provision, when the wallet is all but empty. And miracles of guidance, when we stand at the crossroads and don't know which way to go.

There are miracles of preservation when, for example, someone walks away without a scratch from a tangled mass of steel that used to be an automobile.

Yes, God still works miracles, but not necessarily the same ones. He has never chosen to repeat the ten plagues which He sent on Egypt. Though Jesus Christ is the same, yesterday, today, and forever, it does not follow that His methods are the same. The fact that He raised the dead when He was on earth does not mean that He raises the dead today.

One final word! Not all miracles are divine. The devil and his agents can perform miracles. In a coming day, the second beast of Revelation 13 will deceive the earth dwellers by the miracles he will perform. Even today we must test all purported miracles by the Word of God and by the direction in which they lead people.

August 11

For if we are beside ourselves, it is for God.
2 CORINTHIANS 5:13

G od has irregulars in His army, and very often these are the ones who win the greatest victories. In their zeal for the Lord they seem eccentric. They use original methods instead of sticking to the traditional ones. They are always saying and doing the unexpected. They can murder the English language and violate every known rule of preaching and teaching, yet see great gains for God's kingdom. Often they are dramatic, even electrifying. People are shocked, but they never forget them.

These irregulars are a constant source of embarrassment to the staid and conventional, to those who shudder at the thought of violating cultural norms. Other Christians try to change them, to make them more normal, to put out the fire. But fortunately for the Church, their efforts are usually in vain.

It is hard for us to believe that our Lord seemed peculiar to His contemporaries. "So zealous was He in His work that often He had no time even to eat, and His mother and brothers wanted to take Him home because they thought He was going 'off his head.' They said, 'He is beside himself.' But it was Jesus who was the sane man, not his brothers" (W. MACKINTOSH MACKAY).

It is apparent that people accused the Apostle Paul of being strange. His answer to the charge was: "For if we are beside ourselves, it is for God" (2 Cor. 5:13).

We have all heard of one of God's irregulars who wore a sandwich board with writing on the front and back. On the front it said, "I'm a fool for Christ's sake." Then on the back it read, "Whose fool are you?"

The trouble with most of us is that we are too much like the ordinary to create any stir for God in society. As someone has said, "We leave the average where it is. We are like Peter, standing outside the judgment hall where Christ was on trial, just 'warming himself.'"

Rowland Hill, the great London preacher, was eccentric. So was C. T. Studd. And Billy Bray. And W. P. Nicholson, the Irish evangelist. Would we want them to have been any different? No, when we consider how God used them, we only wish we were more like them. "Better a thousand times effective peculiarity than ineffective ordinariness. First love may sometimes be peculiar, but, thank God, it is effective; and some of us have lost it" (FRED MITCHELL).

August 12

Reject a divisive man after the first and second admonition,
knowing that such a person is warped and sinning, being self-condemned.
TITUS 3:10-11

When we think of a heretic, we usually think of someone who holds and propagates views that are contrary to the great fundamental truths of the faith. We think of men like Arius, Montanus, Marcion, and Pelagius who lived in the second and third centuries AD.

I do not propose to reject that definition of heretic but to broaden it. A heretic, in the New Testament sense, also includes anyone who obstinately promotes a teaching, even of secondary importance; that causes division in the church. He may be true to the fundamentals and yet push some other teaching that causes strife because it differs from the accepted belief of the fellowship he is in.

Most modern translations read "factious man" instead of "heretic." A factious man is stubbornly determined to ride his doctrinal hobby horse, even if it will cause a split in the church. His conversation inevitably reverts to this pet subject. No matter where he turns in the Bible, he thinks he finds support for his view. He cannot minister the Word publicly without introducing it. He is a Johnny-one-note. He has only one string on his violin, and plays only one note on that string.

His behavior is utterly perverse. He completely disregards the thousand and one teachings in the Bible that would build up the saints in their faith, and majors on one or two deviant doctrines that serve only to create a schism. It may be that he harps on some particular aspect of prophecy. Or he may overemphasize a gift of the Spirit. Or his obsession may be with the five points of Calvinism.

When the church leaders warn him against pursuing his self-willed crusade, he is unrepentant. He insists that he would not be faithful to the Lord if he did not teach these things. He will not be silenced. He has a "super-spiritual" answer for every argument that is used against him. The fact that he is creating strife and division in the church does not deter him in the least. He seems unmoved by the divine decree, "If any man destroys the temple of God, God will destroy him" (1 Cor. 3:17, NASB).

The Scripture says that this person is subverted, is sinning, and is self-condemned. He is subverted in the sense that he has a "moral twist" (PHILLIPS), a "distorted mind" (NEB), is "warped" (NIV). He is sinning because the Bible condemns such behavior. And he knows it in spite of his pious protestations. After two warnings the fellowship should shun him, hoping by this social ostracism to cause him to abandon his factiousness.

August 13

For where two or three are gathered together in My name,
I am there in the midst of them.
MATTHEW 18:20

W hen Jesus spoke these words, He was referring to a meeting of the church convened to deal with a sinning member who refuses to repent. Other efforts to handle the offender have failed and now he is brought before the church. If he still refuses to repent, he must be disfellowshipped. The Lord Jesus promises His presence at such a meeting called to deal with a matter of church discipline.

But the verse surely has a wider application. It is true wherever and whenever two or three are gathered in His Name. To gather in His Name means to meet as a Christian assembly. It means to gather together by His authority, acting on His behalf. It means to gather with Him as the attraction. It means to gather in accordance with the practice of the early Christians for "the apostles' doctrine and fellowship, and in breaking of bread, and in prayers" (Acts 2:42). It means to gather with Christ as the center, to gather to Him (Gen. 49:10; Ps. 50:5).

Wherever believers are thus gathered to the Person of the Lord Jesus, He promises to be present. But someone may ask, "Isn't He present everywhere? As the omnipresent One, is He not in all places at one and the same time?" The answer is, of course, that He is. But He promises to be present in a special way when saints gather in His Name.

"…there am I in the midst." That is, in itself, the strongest single reason why we should be faithful in attending all the meetings of the local assembly. The Lord Jesus is there in a special way. Many times we may not be conscious of His promised presence. At those times we accept the fact by faith, based upon His promise. But there are other times when He manifests Himself to us in an unusual way. Times when heaven seems to bend very low. Times when all hearts are bowed beneath the influence of the Word. Times when the glory of the Lord so fills the place that a deep sense of reverential awe grips the people and tears flow freely. Times when our hearts burn within us.

We never know the times of these sacred visitations. They come unannounced and unexpectedly. If we are not present, we miss them. Then we share a loss similar to that of Thomas. He was not present when the risen, glorified Lord Jesus appeared to the disciples on the evening of His resurrection (John 20:24). It was a moment of glory that could never be recaptured.

If we really believe Christ is present when His people gather in His Name, we will be much more determined to attend than if the President were going to be there. Nothing short of death or terminal illness would hinder our presence.

August 14

The sacrifices of God are a broken spirit, a broken and a contrite heart—
these, O God, You will not despise.
PSALM 51:17

T here is nothing more beautiful in God's spiritual creation than a believer who demonstrates a true spirit of brokenness. Even God Himself finds such a person irresistible; He can resist the proud and haughty (Jas. 4:6), but He can't resist the broken and humble.

In our natural condition, none of us is broken. We are like a wild donkey's colt—rebellious, stubborn, impetuous. We resist the bit, the bridle, and the saddle of God's will. We refuse to be harnessed, wanting only our own way. As long as we are unbroken, we are unfit for service.

Conversion is like the beginning of the breaking process. The penitent sinner can say, *"The proudest heart that ever beat, Has been subdued in me; The wildest will that ever rose To scorn Thy cause or aid Thy foes Is quelled, my God, by Thee!"* In conversion, we take the yoke of Christ upon us.

But it is possible to be a believer and still behave very much like an unbroken colt that wants to roam the range as it pleases. We must learn to turn over the reins of life to the Lord Jesus. We must submit to His dealings in our life without kicking, bucking, or jumping. We must be able to say:

> *His way is best*
> *We cease from needless scheming*
> *And leave the ruling of our life to Him.*

We need to practice brokenness not only toward God but toward our fellow men as well. This means that we will not be proud, assertive, arrogant. We will not feel compelled to stand up for our rights or to defend ourselves when accused unjustly. When we are insulted, ridiculed, abused or slandered, we will not fight back. Broken people are quick to apologize when they have said or done something wrong. They don't carry grudges or keep a count of wrongs against them. They look upon others as better than themselves. When they encounter delays, interruptions, breakdowns, accidents, schedule changes, and disappointments, they do not respond with frenzy, panic, hysteria, or ruffled feathers. They display poise and equanimity in the crises of life.

If a married couple is truly broken, they will never need to go to the divorce court. Broken parents and children never experience a generation gap. Broken neighbors never need to erect fences. Churches with people who have learned the way of brokenness experience continual revival.

When we come to the Lord's Supper and hear the Savior say, "This is My body, broken for you," the only proper response is, "This is my life, Lord Jesus, broken for You."

August 15

Take heed and beware of covetousness.
LUKE 12:15

ovetousness is the excessive desire for wealth or possessions. It is a mania that grips people, causing them to grasp for more and more. It is a fever that drives them to crave things they don't actually need.

We see covetousness in the businessman who is never satisfied. He says he will stop when he has accumulated a certain amount, but when that time comes, he is greedy for more.

We see it in the housewife whose life is one unending shopping spree. She squirrels away tons of miscellany till her attic, garage, and storage area bulge with the loot.

We see it in the tradition of Christmas gifts and birthday gifts. Young and old alike judge the success of the occasion by the amount of booty they are able to accumulate.

We see it in the disposition of an estate. When someone dies, his relatives and friends shed a ritual tear, then descend like vultures to divide the prey, often starting a civil war in the process.

Covetousness is idolatry (Eph. 5:5; Col. 3:5). It puts self-will in the place of God's will. It expresses dissatisfaction with what God has given, and is determined to get more, no matter what the cost may be.

Covetousness is a lie, creating the impression that happiness is found in the possession of material things. The story is told of a man who could have anything he wanted by merely wishing for it. He wished for a mansion, servants, a Cadillac, a yacht and presto! they were there instantly. At first it was exhilarating, but then as he began to run out of new ideas, he became dissatisfied. Finally he said, "I want to get out of here. I want to create something, to suffer something. I'd rather be in hell than here." The attendant answered, "Where do you think you are?"

Covetousness tempts people to compromise, to cheat, to sin in order to get what they want.

It unfits a man for leadership in the church (1 Tim. 3:3). Ronald Sider asks, "Would it not be more biblical to apply church discipline to people whose greedy acquisitiveness has led to 'financial success' than to elect them to the board of elders?"

When greed leads to embezzlement, extortion, or other public scandals, it calls for ex-communication (1 Cor. 5:11).

And if covetousness is not confessed and forsaken, it leads to exclusion from the Kingdom of God (1 Cor. 6:10).

August 16

Having food and clothing, with these we shall be content.
1 TIMOTHY 6:8

Few Christians take these words seriously, yet they are as truly the Word of God as John 3:16. They tell us to be satisfied with food and covering. That word "covering" includes a roof over our heads as well as the clothes we wear. In other words, we should be content with the minimum essentials and put everything above that into the work of the Lord.

The man who has contentment has something that money cannot buy. E. Stanley Jones said, "Everything belongs to the man who wants nothing. Having nothing, he possesses all things in life, including life itself…He is rich in the fewness of his wants rather than in the abundance of his possessions."

Years ago, when Rudyard Kipling spoke to a graduating class at McGill University, he warned the students against putting a great premium on material wealth. He said, "Some day you'll meet a man who cares for none of these things and then you'll realize how poor you are."

"The happiest state of a Christian on earth seems to be that he should have few wants. If a man has Christ in his heart, heaven before his eyes, and only as much of temporal blessings as is just needful to carry him safely through life, then pain and sorrow have little to shoot at; such a man has little to lose" (WILLIAM C. BURNS).

This spirit of contentment seems to have characterized many of God's giants. David Livingston said, "I am determined not to look upon anything that I possess except as in relation to the Kingdom of God." Watchman Nee wrote, "I want nothing for myself; I want everything for the Lord." And Hudson Taylor said that he enjoyed "the luxury of having few things to care for."

To some, the idea of contentment means the lack of drive and ambition. They picture the contented person as a drone or a freeloader. But that is not godly contentment. The contented Christian has plenty of drive and ambition, but they are directed toward the spiritual, not the material. Rather than being a freeloader, he works so that he can give to those who are in need. In Jim Elliot's words, the contented person is the one for whom God has "loosed the tension of the grasping hand."

August 17

Those who honor Me I will honor.
1 SAMUEL 2:30

O ne of the many ways in which we can honor the Lord is by standing true to divine principles and by steadfastly refusing to compromise.

During his early years, Adam Clarke worked for a silk merchant. One day his boss showed him how he should stretch the silk when measuring it out for a customer. Adam said, "Sir, your silk may stretch but my conscience won't." Years later God honored that honest clerk by enabling him to write the Bible commentary that bears his name.

Eric Liddell was scheduled to run in the 100 meters event in the Olympic Games. But when he found that the heats for this event were scheduled for Sunday, he told the manager that he wouldn't run. He felt that by dishonoring the Lord's Day, he would be dishonoring the Lord Himself. A great storm of criticism broke. He was accused of being a spoilsport, of letting his country down, of being a straightlaced religious fanatic. But he would not go back on his decision.

When he noticed that the heats for the 220 meters were scheduled for a weekday, he asked his manager for permission to run, even if that wasn't his distance. He won the first heat, the second heat, then the semi-finals. On the day of the finals he strode to the starting place, someone pressed a small piece of paper in his hand. He glanced down and saw the words, "…them that honor Me I will honor." That day he not only won the race but set a new world's record.

The Lord gave him the greater honor of serving as one of His ambassadors in the Far East. During World War II, he was interned by the Japanese and died in a concentration camp, thus winning the martyr's crown.

Adam Clarke and Eric Liddell followed in the illustrious line of men like Joseph who honored God by his sterling character and was honored by God by becoming the savior of his people in a time of famine. Men like Moses whose loyalty to his God was honored by his leading the nation of Israel out of Egyptian bondage. Men like Daniel whose refusal to compromise brought him a place of distinction in the Persian Kingdom. And—greatest of all—the Lord Jesus who honored His Father as no one else, and has been given the Name above every name.

August 18

Let not him who girds on his armor boast like him who takes it off.
1 KINGS 20:11, NASB

Although these words were spoken by a wicked king, Ahab, they are words of truth. Even ungodly men sometimes lapse into truth.

The king of Syria had made insulting, degrading demands of Ahab, threatening military disaster if he did not obey. But in the battle that followed, the Syrians were forced to retreat and their king had to flee for his life. His performance didn't match his boast.

Today's text would have been good advice for Goliath also. When he saw David approaching, he said, "Come to me, and I will give your flesh to the birds of the air and the beasts of the field!" (1 Sam. 17:44). But David easily felled him with a single stone from his sling. The giant had boasted too soon.

When we are young Christians, it is easy for us to overestimate our own ability. We act as if we could take on the world, the flesh, and the devil single-handed. We might even reproach older Christians for their failure to evangelize the world. We will show them how to do it! But our boasting is premature. The battle has only started and we are acting as if it were all over.

In an informal gathering of believers one evening, the spotlight was shining on a brilliant young preacher who was present. He found it quite satisfying to be the center of interest. Also in the group was a Sunday School teacher who had had a profound influence on his life. Someone said to this teacher, "You must be quite proud of your former student." His reply was, "Yes, if he goes on well to the end." At the time, the young preacher thought that that was a rather sour note to inject into an otherwise pleasurable evening. But later, given the perspective of years, he realized that his old teacher was right. It isn't how you put on your armor that counts. It's how you finish the battle.

Actually the battle is never over in this life. It will not be over until we stand before our great Captain in heaven. Then we will hear His appraisal of our service —the only appraisal that really counts. And no matter what His appraisal might be, we will have no grounds for boasting. We will say with heartfelt humility, "We are unprofitable servants: we have done that which was our duty to do" (Lk. 17:10).

August 19

You shall not revile God, nor curse a ruler of your people.
EXODUS 22:28

W hen God gave the Law to Moses, He included a specific prohibition against speaking reproachfully or disrespectfully of those who hold positions of authority. The reason for this is clear. These rulers and leaders are representatives of God. "There is no authority except from God, and the authorities that exist are appointed by God" (Rom. 13:1). The ruler is "God's minister to you for good" (Rom. 13:4). Even though the leader may not know the Lord personally, still he is the Lord's man officially.

The link between God and human rulers is so close that He sometimes refers to them as gods. Thus in today's verse we read, "You shall not revile the gods," which may mean governmental authorities. And in Psalm 82:1, 6, the Lord refers to judges as gods—not meaning that they are deities but simply that they are agents of God.

In spite of King Saul's murderous attacks on David, the latter would not allow his men to harm the king in any way because he was the Lord's anointed (1 Sam. 24:6).

When the Apostle Paul unknowingly reproached the high priest, he quickly repented and apologized, saying, "I did not know, brethren, that he was the high priest; for it is written, You shall not speak evil of a ruler of your people" (Acts 23:5).

Respect for authorities applies even in the spirit realm. This explains why Michael, the archangel, did not dare to bring a railing accusation against Satan, but simply said, "The Lord rebuke you" (Jude 9).

One of the marks of latter-day apostates is that they despise governments and are not afraid to speak evil of dignitaries (2 Pet. 2:10).

The lesson for us is clear. We are to respect our rulers as official servants of God even though we might not agree with their policies or approve of their personal character. Under no circumstances should we ever say what one Christian said in the heat of a political campaign, "The president is a lowdown scoundrel."

Further, we are to pray "for kings and all who are in authority, that we may lead a quiet and peaceable life in all godliness and reverence" (1 Tim. 2:2).

August 20

If you endure chastening, God deals with you as with sons;
for what son is there whom a father does not chasten?
HEBREWS 12:7

T he words *chastening, chasteneth, chastisement* and *chastened* occur seven times in the first 11 verses of Hebrews 12. As a result, it is easy for the casual reader to get a wrong impression. He might easily picture God as an angry Father who is forever whipping His children. This misconception arises from thinking of chastening as nothing but punishment.

It is a great relief to learn that chastening in the New Testament has a much broader meaning than that. It really means child-training, and includes all parental activity that is involved in raising a child. Kittel defines it as "the upbringing and handling of the child which is growing up to maturity and which needs direction, teaching, instruction, and a certain measure of compulsion in the form of discipline or even chastisement."

The Christians to whom the book of Hebrews was written were suffering persecution. The writer speaks of this persecution as part of the chastening of the Lord. Does this mean that God had sent the persecution? Certainly not! It was inspired by enemies of the gospel. Was God punishing the Christians because of their sins? No, the persecution was probably brought on because of their faithful witness for Him. In what sense, then, could persecution be said to be the chastening of the Lord? In the sense that God allowed it to take place, and then used it as part of His educative program in the lives of His people. In other words, He used the persecution to refine, mature, and conform His children to the image of His Son.

It goes without saying that this type of chastening is not pleasant at the time. The chisel deals roughly with the marble. The furnace subjects the gold to intense heat. But it is all worthwhile when the face of the man appears in the marble and when the gold is purified from dross.

It is self-defeating to despise the chastening of the Lord or to faint under it. The only proper attitude is to remember that God is using it as a training device, then to try to get the maximum benefit from it. That is what the writer means when he says that "it yields the peaceable fruit of righteousness to those who have been trained by it" (Heb. 12:11b).

August 21

...I would rather speak five words that can be understood,
in order to teach others, than speak thousands of words in strange tongues.
1 CORINTHIANS 14:19, TEV

T he subject here, of course, is the use of tongues without interpretation in the meetings of the church. Paul is opposed to the practice. He insists that what is spoken must be intelligible, otherwise no one is edified.

But the verse can be applied in a broader sense. When we speak, we should speak loudly enough for everyone to hear, otherwise we might just as well be speaking in a foreign language. In almost every audience there are people who are hard of hearing. It is a great trial to them when a speaker's voice is so soft that they miss the train of thought. Because love thinks of others, not self, it speaks with sufficient volume for all to hear.

Love also uses words that are simple enough for the average person to understand. We have a great message—the greatest message in all the world. It is important that people hear and understand the message. If we use involved, obscure, technical jargon, we defeat our own purpose.

A preacher went to the Far East to minister to the people, using an interpreter, of course. The first sentence of his message was, "All thought may be divided into two categories—concrete and abstract." Looking down at the audience of toothless grandmothers and restless children, the interpreter translated it as, "I have come all the way from America to tell you about the Lord Jesus." From that point on, it is said, the message was firmly in the hands of the angels.

In a recent issue of a Christian magazine, I came across such expressions as: normative datum of a trans-historical category; work that is not eclectic but that has existential relevance; a vertical continuum of consciousness; the canonical language of affirmation; classical causality at the extreme limits of measurement. Pity the poor people who are asked to wade through such religious gobbledegook! Spare us all from those who have a ponderous way of saying nothing in infinite sentences!

We hear that the average TV or radio program is beamed at those with a third-grade education. That should be a cue to Christians who want to reach the world with the message of redemption. We should "make the message clear and plain: Christ receiveth sinful men." Better to speak five words and be understood than 10,000 words in a language no one can understand.

August 22

Do not cling to Me, for I have not yet ascended to My Father.
JOHN 20:17

ne of the much-loved hymns for children says,

> *I think when I read that sweet story of old,*
> *When Jesus was here among men,*
> *How He called little children as lambs to His fold,*
> *I should like to have been with Him then.*

Probably most of us have shared that sentimental desire at one time or another. We think how nice it would have been to enjoy the personal companionship of the Son of God during His earthly ministry.

But what we should realize is that it is better to know Him today, as He is revealed by the Spirit through the Word. Instead of being at a disadvantage, we are actually more privileged than the disciples. Look at it this way: Matthew saw Jesus through Matthew's eyes, Mark through Mark's eyes, Luke through Luke's eyes, and John through John's eyes. But we see Him through the eyes of all four evangelists. And, to carry the thought a step farther, we have a fuller revelation of the Lord Jesus in the entire New Testament than any of the disciples had when they were on earth.

There is an additional sense in which we are more privileged than the contemporaries of Jesus. When He was mingling with the crowd in Nazareth or Capernaum, He was necessarily closer to some than to others. In the Upper Room, John leaned on His bosom, whereas the other disciples reclined at varying distances. But all that is changed now. The Savior is equally close to all believers. He is not only with us; He is in us.

When Mary met the resurrected Lord, she wanted to cling to Him in the same way she had previously known Him. She did not want to lose His physical, bodily presence. But Jesus said to her, "Do not cling to Me, for I have not yet ascended to My Father..." (Jn. 20:17). He was saying, in effect, "Mary, don't cling to Me in an earthly, physical sense. When I ascend to My Father, the Holy Spirit will be sent to the earth. Through His ministry you will know Me in a fuller, clearer, more intimate way than you have ever known Me before."

So the conclusion is this: Instead of wishing we had been with Jesus when He was on earth, we should realize, rejoicingly, that it is better to be with Him now.

August 23

For My people have committed two evils: They have forsaken Me,
the fountain of living waters, And hewn themselves cisterns—
broken cisterns that can hold no water.
JEREMIAH 2:13

It is a bad bargain to exchange a fountain for cisterns, and especially for broken cisterns. A fountain is a spring of cool, pure, refreshing water, gushing forth from the earth. A cistern is an artificial reservoir for storing water. The water in it may become stagnant and foul. When the cistern is broken, the water leaks out and pollution seeps in.

The Lord is a Fountain of living waters. His people can find lasting satisfaction in Him. The world is a cistern, and a broken cistern at that. It offers the hope of pleasure and happiness, but those who seek satisfaction in it are inevitably disappointed.

Mary was brought up in a Christian home where the Word of God was read and memorized. But she rebelled against her parents' lifestyle and left home, determined to live it up. Dancing became the passion of her life. Trying to repress all memories of her Christian background, she lived from one dance to the next.

One night while gliding across the dance floor with her partner, she was arrested by a verse of Scripture which she had learned as a girl: "For My people have committed two evils: They have forsaken Me, the fountain of living waters, and hewn themselves cisterns—broken cisterns that can hold no water." In the middle of the dance, she was convicted of her sin. Realizing the emptiness of her life, she turned to the Lord and was converted. She excused herself from continuing the dance, left the hall and never returned.

From that moment she could identify with the poet who wrote:

> I tried the broken cisterns, Lord,
> But ah! the waters failed!
> E'en as I stooped to drink they'd fled,
> And mocked me as I wailed.
> Now none but Christ can satisfy,
> None other name for me;
> There's love, and life, and lasting joy,
> Lord Jesus, found in Thee.

Mary experienced the truth of the Savior's words, "Whoever drinks of this water will thirst again, but whoever drinks of the water that I shall give him will never thirst. But the water that I shall give him will become in him a fountain of water springing up into everlasting life" (Jn. 4:13-14).

August 24

Thus says the Lord: Refrain your voice from weeping, and your eyes from tears;
for your work shall be rewarded, says the Lord,
And they shall come back from the land of the enemy.
JEREMIAH 31:16

S tephen had been brought up on the mission field. He professed faith in Christ at an early age and had been the means of leading several to the Lord. When he first came back to the States to attend college, he maintained a good testimony. But then he began to drift. Coldness set in. He compromised with sin. Soon he began to dabble in Eastern religions.

When his parents came home on furlough, they were heartsick. They pled, reasoned, and entreated, but he was adamant. Finally they went to visit him where he lived with three others. What they saw there utterly crushed them. They went home and wept bitterly.

They went to bed and tried to sleep but it was useless. Finally at 4 A.M. they decided to get up and have their morning devotions. Ordinarily they would have been reading Jeremiah 31 on that day, but the husband said, "Not Jeremiah," thinking that the weeping prophet would have no comfort for them. But the Lord overruled and they turned to Jeremiah 31. When they got to the 16th verse, they read, "Refrain your voice from weeping, and your eyes from tears; for your work shall be rewarded, says the Lord, and they shall come back from the land of the enemy."

Thousands of Christian parents today are brokenhearted, mourning over rebel sons and daughters. When they pray, the heavens seem like brass. They begin to wonder if God ever can or will restore the backslider.

They should remember that no case is too hard for the Lord. They should continue in prayer, watching in the same with thanksgiving. They should plead the promises of God's Word.

When the mother referred to above wondered if she had been justified in claiming Jeremiah 31:16, she read in Isaiah 49:25, "For I will contend with him who contends with you, and I will save your children."

August 25

Yes, we had the sentence of death in ourselves,
that we should not trust in ourselves but in God who raises the dead.
2 CORINTHIANS 1:9

aul had a narrow scrape with death in the province of Asia. We cannot be sure exactly what happened, but it was so serious that if we had asked him, "Is it going to be life or death?" he would have said, "Death."

Most people whom God uses have had a similar experience at one time or another in their lives. Biographies of great men of God record marvelous deliverances from disease, from accidents, from personal attacks.

Sometimes God uses this kind of experience to get a man's attention. Perhaps he is riding the crest of the wave as far as material prosperity is concerned. Everything is going his way. Then suddenly he is laid low with illness. The surgeon removes yards of cancerous intestines. This causes him to reevaluate his life and to rethink his priorities. Realizing how short and uncertain life is, he determines to give the rest of it to the Lord. God raises him up and gives him many additional years of fruitful service.

It was different in Paul's case. He had already yielded his life to the Lord for service. But there was the dangerous possibility that he might try to serve in his own strength, and by his own cleverness. So the Lord brought him to the brink of the grave in order that he might not trust in himself but in the God of resurrection. There would be many times in his tumultuous career when he would face predicaments beyond human solution. Having already proved the sufficiency of the God of the impossible, he would not be daunted.

These close encounters with death are blessings in disguise. They show us how frail we are. They remind us of the folly of this world's values. They teach us that life is a short story that can end very unexpectedly. When we face death, we realize that we must work the works of Him that sent us while it is day, for the night is coming when no man can work. In a sense we all have the sentence of death in ourselves—a healthy reminder to put Christ's interests first and to depend upon His power and wisdom.

August 26

Establish the work of our hands for us; yes, establish the work of our hands.
PSALM 90:17

T he margin of the New American Standard Bible reads "...give permanence to the work of our hands." Now that is a thought worth pondering and a request worth praying! We should make it our ambition to
spend our lives doing that which will last.

This finds an echo in the New Testament when the Lord Jesus said, "I chose
you and appointed you that you should go and bear fruit, and that your fruit should
remain" (Jn. 15:16).

F. W. Boreham said that each of us should provide himself with some honorable occupation that he can do while his body is lying in the grave. But we should
advance the thought beyond the grave and say that each of us should be building
for eternity.

So much of modern activity is of transient importance and of fleeting value.
The other day I heard of a man who was devoting his life to a chemical analysis
of fifty volatile chemicals in the skin of a Bartlett pear. Even Christians can fall
into the trap of building castles in the sand, of chasing bubbles, and of becoming
experts in trivia. As someone has said, we can be guilty of spending our lives
straightening pictures in a burning house.

There are many types of work that are of eternal significance, and we should
concentrate on these. First is the development of Christian character. Our character is one of the few things we will take to heaven. It needs cultivating now.

Souls won to Christ are of abiding importance. They will be worshippers of the
Lamb of God forever and ever.

Those who teach the Word of Truth, who disciple young believers, who feed
the sheep of Christ, are making a deposit in lives that will last indefinitely.

Parents who raise their sons and daughters for the service of the Kingdom are
assured that their work will endure.

Faithful stewards who invest their money for Christ and His cause are engaged
in a ministry that cannot fail.

Those who devote themselves to the work of prayer will see some day how
every prayer was answered in God's own time and way.

Anyone who serves God's people is engaged in a work for eternity. The humblest servant of Christ has superior vision to the wisest men of the world. His work
will last while theirs will go up in a mushroom cloud.

August 27

Lord, who may abide in Your tabernacle? Who may dwell in Your holy hill?...
He who swears to his own hurt and does not change.
PSALM 15:1, 4

I n Psalm 15, David is describing the person who is qualified to be a companion of the Great God. One of the aspects of this man's character is that he stands by his word, even at great personal cost to himself. If he makes a promise or a commitment, he remains faithful to it.

Here, for example, is a Christian who is selling his house. A buyer comes along and agrees to pay the asking price. The seller agrees to the deal. Before any papers are signed, someone else offers $5,000 more for the house. Legally, perhaps, the seller can reject the first offer and thus make $5,000 more on the transaction. But morally he is obligated to be true to his spoken word. His testimony as a dependable Christian is at stake.

Or here is a believer who has an infected wisdom tooth. His dentist refers him to an oral surgeon who treats the tooth with an antibiotic, then makes an appointment for the extraction. After witnessing to the surgeon, the Christian leaves the office. On the way home he meets a friend who tells him where he can get the extraction done for half the amount. No doubt he could pay the surgeon for the work already done, then go to the other dentist. But should he?

Sue has just accepted a supper invitation from an older couple. Then the phone rings and she is invited to a potluck supper with a group of young people her own age. She is between a rock and a hard place. She doesn't want to disappoint the older couple, yet she desperately wants to be with the young people.

The decision is often most difficult when large amounts of money are at stake. But no amount of money should induce us to break a promise, to go back on a commitment, to discredit our Christian testimony and to bring dishonor on the Name of the Lord. No matter what the cost may be, we must disprove Voltaire's snide remark that "when it comes to money, all men are of the same religion."

The man of God "always does what he promises, no matter how much it may cost" (TEV); he "keeps a promise even if it ruins him" (LB).

August 28

Be sure your sin will find you out.
NUMBERS 32:23

od has built certain unalterable principles into this world of ours, and all man's ingenuity cannot escape the outworking of these principles. One of them is that you can't sin and get away with it.

Some of us learned this early when we swiped jam or other foods which left their telltale marks which mother easily discovered. But the truth applies to all of life, and is attested by every newspaper.

The poem, "The Dream of Eugene Aram," is a remarkable illustration of the point. Thinking he could commit a "perfect crime," Aram murdered a man and threw his body into the river—"a sluggish water, black as ink, the depth was so extreme." The next morning he went down to the riverbank where he had committed the crime:

> *And sought the black accursed pool,*
> *With a wild misgiving eye;*
> *And he saw the dead in the riverbed*
> *For the faithless stream was dry.*

He tried to cover the body with a huge pile of leaves, but that night a great wind blew through the area, leaving the corpse plainly visible.

> *Then down I cast me on my face,*
> *And first began to weep,*
> *For I knew my secret then was one*
> *That earth refused to keep,*
> *On land or sea, though it should be*
> *Ten thousand fathoms deep.*

Finally he buried his victim in a remote cave, but years later the skeleton was discovered; he was tried for the crime, and executed. His sin had found him out.

But there is another way in which sin catches up with us. E. Stanley Jones reminds us that "It registers itself in inner deterioration, in the inner hell of not being able to respect yourself, in compelling you to live underground in blind labyrinths."

And even if a man's sin could somehow remain undetected in this life, it will surely overtake him in the next. Unless that sin has been cleansed through the blood of Jesus, it will be brought to light in the Day of Judgment. Whether it be acts, thoughts, motives or intents, it will be charged against him and the penalty announced. That penalty, of course, is eternal death.

August 29

Christis all.
COLOSSIANS 3:11

T here is a tendency for us Christians to spend a great deal of our time looking for new spiritual experiences that will somehow guarantee permanent victory or freedom from the ups and downs of daily living. We rush around to conventions, conferences, seminars, and workshops in search of the elusive magic formula that will smooth out the rough places of life. Glossy brochures assure us that Dr. So-and-So will share a great new breakthrough that will make us radioactive with the Spirit. Or some zealous neighbor insists on dragging us to the Municipal Auditorium to hear about a recently discovered shortcut to the abundant life.

The lures are legion. One preacher offers the royal road to fulfillment. Another advertises the threefold secret of victory. Now we go to a seminar on keys to the deeper life. The next week there is a convention on five easy steps to holiness. We surge forward for an altar call experience by which we will receive the filling of the Spirit. Or we become obsessed with healing of the body as if that were the most important thing in life. One minute we are off on a Christian psychology kick, the next on healing of the memories. We compass land and sea for some new spiritual high.

There is no doubt that many of these speakers are sincere and that there is value in some of the things that they say. But we return to the nitty-gritty of life to find that there is no shortcut to holiness, that the problems are still there, and that we must live day by day in dependence on the Lord.

Eventually we should learn that it is better to be occupied with the Lord Jesus than with experiences. There is no disappointment in Him. We have all we need in Him. He is the all-sufficient One.

A. B. Simpson spent the early part of his life in the quest for experiences, but he found that they didn't satisfy. Then he wrote the lovely hymn entitled "Himself," the first verse and chorus of which are as follows:

Once it was the blessing, now it is the Lord;
Once it was the feeling, now it is His Word;
Once His gifts I wanted, now the Giver own;
Once I sought for healing, now Himself alone.
All in all forever, Jesus will I sing;
Everything in Jesus,
And Jesus everything.

August 30

Take heed to yourself and to the doctrine.
1 TIMOTHY 4:16

One of the many noteworthy features of the Word of God is that it never isolates doctrine from duty. Take Philippians 2:1-13, for example. It is one of the classic passages in the New Testament on the doctrine of Christ. We learn there of His equality with God the Father, His self-emptying, His incarnation, His servanthood, His death, and His subsequent glorification. But this is introduced, not as a doctrinal treatise, but as an appeal to the Philippians and to us to have the mind of Christ. If we live for others as He did, this will eliminate strife and vainglory. If we take the low place as He did, God will exalt us in due time. The passage is intensely practical.

I often think of this when I read books on systematic theology. In these books the authors seek to gather together all that the Bible teaches on the doctrines of the faith—whether of God, Christ, the Holy Spirit, angels, man, sin, redemption, etc. While this has definite value, it can be very cold when isolated from godly living. A person can be intellectually proficient in the great doctrines and yet be sadly deficient as to his Christian character. If we study the Bible as God has given it to us, we never get a dichotomy between doctrine and duty. The two are always beautifully balanced and woven together.

Perhaps the doctrinal subject that has been most divorced from our personal responsibility is prophecy. Too often it has been presented in such a way as to cater to curiosity. Sensational speculations concerning the identity of the Antichrist may draw the crowds but they don't develop holiness. Prophecy was never intended to tickle itching ears but rather to shape Christian character. George Peters lists 65 ways in which the Second Advent is calculated to affect our doctrine, duty, and character; and I don't doubt that there are many more than that.

The lesson for us is that we should never divorce theology from practical godliness. In our own personal study and in teaching the Word to others, we should emphasize Paul's exhortation to Timothy, "Take heed to yourself, and to the doctrine…"

August 31

What things were gain to me, these I have counted loss for Christ. Yet indeed I also count all things loss for the excellence of the knowledge of Christ Jesus my Lord, for whom I have suffered the loss of all things, and count them as rubbish, that I may gain Christ. PHILIPPIANS 3:7-8

It is always eminently fine when a believer makes great renunciations for Jesus' sake. Here is a man whose talents have brought him wealth and fame, yet in obedience to the divine call, he lays them at the Savior's feet. Or a woman whose voice has opened doors to the world's great concert halls. But now she feels she must live for another world, so she gives up her career to follow Christ. After all, what are reputation or fortune or earthly distinctions when compared to the incomparable gain of winning Christ?

Ian MacPherson asks, "Is there anywhere a sight more deeply moving than that of a man laden with gifts, laying them all humbly and adoringly at the Redeemer's feet?" And that, after all, is where they were meant to be. In the words of a wise old Welsh divine, "Hebrew, Greek and Latin are all very well in their place; but their place is not where Pilate put them, over Jesus' head, but rather at His feet."

The Apostle Paul renounced wealth, culture, and ecclesiastical status and counted them loss for Christ. Jowett comments that "when the Apostle Paul regarded his aristocratic possessions as great gains, he had never seen the Lord; but when 'the glory of the Lord' blazed upon his wondering eyes, these things faded away into shadow and even eclipse. And it was not only that the Apostle's former gains were cheapened in the effulgence of the Lord, and stood revealed as contemptible nothings in his hands; it was that he ceased to think of them at all. They vanished entirely from the mind where they had been treated as supreme and sacred deposits."

It is strange, then, that when a man forsakes all to follow Christ, some think that he has lost his mind. Some are shocked and uncomprehending. Some weep and offer alternate routes. Some argue on the basis of logic and common sense. A few approve and are stirred to their depths. But when a person walks by faith, he is able to appraise the opinions of others properly.

C. T. Studd forsook a private fortune and fine prospects at home to devote his life to missionary service. John Nelson Darby turned his back on a brilliant career to become an unctionized evangelist, teacher, and prophet of God. The five martyrs of Ecuador renounced the comforts and materialism of the United States to bring Christ to the Auca tribe.

People call it a great sacrifice but it is no sacrifice. When someone tried to commend Hudson Taylor for the sacrifices he had made for Christ, he said, "Man, I never made a sacrifice in my life." And Darby said, "It is no great sacrifice to give up refuse."

September 1

You shall consecrate the fiftieth year, and proclaim liberty throughout all the land to all its inhabitants. It shall be a Jubilee for you; and each of you shall return to his possession, and each of you shall return to his family.

LEVITICUS 25:10

Every fiftieth year in Israel's calendar was known as the year of jubilee. The soil was supposed to lie fallow. Land reverted to its original owner. Slaves were set free. It was a joyous time of freedom, grace, redemption and rest.

When someone bought a piece of property, he had to take into account the nearness of the year of jubilee. For instance, the land would be more valuable if forty-five years remained before the next year of jubilee. But if there was only one year left, the land would hardly be worth buying. The buyer would be able to raise only one crop.

There is a sense in which the Lord's coming will be the year of jubilee for believers. They will enter into the eternal rest of the Father's house. They will be set free from the shackles of mortality, and receive their glorified bodies. And all the material things that have been entrusted to them as stewards will revert to their original owner.

We should take this into account in valuing our material possessions. We may have thousands of dollars worth of real estate, investments, and bank deposits. But if the Lord should come today, they would be worth nothing to us. The closer we get to His coming, the less real value they have. This means, of course, that we should put them to work today in the advancement of the cause of Christ and in the alleviation of human need.

Just as the year of jubilee was ushered in by the blowing of a trumpet, so the Lord's return will be announced by the sound of "the last trump."

"All this teaches us a fine lesson. If our hearts are cherishing the abiding hope of the Lord's return, we shall set light by all earthly things. It is morally impossible that we can be in the attitude of waiting for the Son from heaven, and not be detached from this present world...One who lives in the habitual expectation of Christ's appearing must be separated from that which will be judged and broken up when He comes...May our hearts be affected and our conduct in all things influenced by this most precious and sanctifying truth" (C. H. MACKINTOSH).

September 2

Lord, I will follow You wherever You go.
Luke 9:57

Sometimes I think we talk and sing too glibly about the Lordship of Christ, about total commitment, and about absolute surrender. We parrot neat little cliches like, "If He's not Lord of all, then He's not Lord at all." We sing, "All to Jesus I surrender, all to Him I freely give." We act as if total commitment involved little more than attending church every Sunday.

It isn't that we are insincere; it's just that we don't realize all that's involved. If we acknowledge the Lordship of Christ, it means that we are willing to follow Him in poverty, rejection, suffering, and even death.

"Some faint at the sight of blood. One day a young enthusiast came to Jesus with the finest of all possible purposes in his heart. 'Lord,' he said, 'I will follow You wherever You go.' Nothing could be finer than that. But Jesus did not thrill. He knew that the young man did not understand all that was involved in his promise. Therefore He told him that He Himself was more homeless than the foxes, that he might have to sleep supperless upon the mountainside. He showed him a cross with a bit of crimson on it, and at that he who was all eagerness fell into a dead faint. While he yearned for the goods, the price was greater than he was willing to pay. It is too often the case. Some of you are not in the fight, not because the call of Christ makes no appeal, but rather because you are afraid of a little bloodletting. Therefore you say whiningly: 'But for these vile guns, I would have been a soldier'" (CHAPPELL).

If Jesus didn't thrill when the young man in Luke 9 volunteered to go with Him all the way, I'm sure He did thrill when Jim Elliot wrote in his diary "If I would save my life blood—forbear to pour it out as a sacrifice in opposition to the example of my Lord—then must I feel the flint of the face of God set against my purpose. Father, take my life, yea, my blood, if Thou wilt, and consume it with Thine enveloping fire. I would not save it, for it is not mine to save. Have it, Lord, have it all. Pour out my life as an oblation for the world. Blood is only of value as it flows before Thine altars."

When we read words like those, and remember that Jim did pour out his blood as a martyr in Ecuador, some of us realize how little we know about absolute surrender.

September 3

But the free gift is not like the offense. For if by the one man's offense many died, much more the grace of God and the gift by the grace of the one Man, Jesus Christ, abounded to many.

ROMANS 5:15

I n Romans 5:12-21, Paul contrasts the two federal heads of the human race, Adam and Christ. Adam was the head of the first creation; Christ is the head of the new creation. The first was natural; the second is spiritual. Three times Paul uses the words "much more" to emphasize that the blessings flowing from Christ's work superabound over the losses incurred by Adam's sin. He is saying that "in Christ the sons of Adam boast more blessings than their father lost." Believers are better off in Christ than they ever would have been in an unfallen Adam.

Let us suppose, for a moment, that Adam hadn't sinned—that instead of eating of the forbidden fruit, he and his wife decided to obey God. What would have been the result in their lives? As far as we know, they would have continued to live indefinitely in the Garden of Eden. Their reward would have been long life on earth. And this would have been true of their offspring.

As long as they too continued without sinning, they would have lived indefinitely in Eden. They would not have died.

But in that state of innocence, they would have no prospect of ever going to heaven. There would be no promise of being indwelt and sealed by the Holy Spirit. They would never become heirs of God, and joint-heirs with Jesus Christ. They would never have the hope of being conformed to the image of God's Son. And there would always be the terrible possibility that they might sin and forfeit the earthly blessings they enjoyed in Eden.

Think, by contrast, of the infinitely superior position which Christ has won for us by His atoning work. We are blessed with all spiritual blessings in heavenly places in Christ. We are accepted in the Beloved, complete in Christ, redeemed, reconciled, forgiven, justified, sanctified, glorified, made members of the body of Christ. We are indwelt and sealed by the Spirit and He is the earnest of our inheritance. We are eternally secure in Christ. We are children of God, and sons of God, heirs of God, and joint-heirs with Jesus Christ. We are as near to God and as dear to God as His own beloved Son. And there is much, much more. But that is enough to show that believers are better off today in the Lord Jesus Christ than they would have ever been in an innocent Adam.

September 4

Then I restored that which I took not away.
PSALM 69:4, KJV

T he speaker in Psalm 69 is the Lord Jesus. In verse 4 He is saying that in His glorious work of redemption, He made restitution to God for losses that had been caused by man's sin. No doubt He is picturing Himself as the true trespass offering.

When a Jew stole from another Jew, the law of the trespass offering required him to repay the amount that was stolen and to add one-fifth of that value.

Now God was robbed through man's sin. He was robbed of service, worship, obedience, and glory. He was robbed of service because man turned to serve self, sin, and Satan. He was robbed of worship because man bowed down to carved images. He was robbed of obedience because man rejected God's authority. He was robbed of glory because man failed to give Him the honor that was His due.

> *The Lord Jesus came to restore what He did not take away.*
> *Aside He threw His most divine array,*
> *And veiled His Godhead in a robe of clay,*
> *And in that garb did wondrous love display,*
> *Restoring what He never took away.*

He not only restored what had been stolen through man's sin but added more. For God has received more glory through the finished work of Christ than He lost through the sin of Adam. "He lost creatures through sin, He gained sons through grace." We may go so far as to say that God has been more glorified through the Savior's work than He ever could have been even in an eternity of unfallen Adams.

Perhaps we have here an answer to the question, "Why did God allow sin to enter?" We know that God could have made men without the power of free moral choice. But He chose to make them with the ability to love and worship Him of their own volition. And that, of course, means that they also had the ability to disobey Him, to reject Him, to turn away from Him. Man chose to disobey Him, bringing in a great holocaust of sin. But God is not defeated by the sin of His creatures. In His death, burial, resurrection and ascension, the Lord Jesus triumphed over sin, hell, and Satan. Through His work, God has received greater glory; and redeemed man has received richer blessings than if sin had never entered this world of ours.

September 5

He was in the world, and the world was made through Him, and the world did not know Him. He came to His own, and His own did not receive Him. But as many as received Him, to them He gave the right to become children of God, to those who believe in His name. JOHN 1:10-12

He was in the world. It was incredible grace that the Lord of life and glory would ever come to live on this tiny planet. It would not be newsworthy to say of anyone else, "He was in the world." That is something over which man has no control. But for Him, it was a deliberate choice, an act of wonderful compassion.

...and the world was made through Him. The wonder increases! The One who was in the world is the One who made the world. He who fills the universe compressed Himself into the body of a baby, a youth, a man, and in that body dwelt all the fullness of the Godhead.

...and the world did not know Him. This was a case of inexcusable ignorance. The creatures should have recognized their Creator. Sinners should have been struck by His sinlessness. They should have known by His words and works that He was more than just a man.

He came to His own. Everything in the world belonged to Him. As Creator, He had inalienable rights to it all. He did not trespass on someone else's property.

...and His own did not receive Him. Here was the ultimate insult. The Jewish people rejected Him. He had all the credentials of the Messiah, but they didn't want Him to rule over them.

But as many as received Him. An unrestricted invitation goes out. It is for Jews and Gentiles alike. The sole condition is that they must receive Him.

...to them He gave the right to become children of God. What an undeserved honor—that rebel sinners should become children of God through a miracle of love and grace!

...to those who believe in His name. The terms could not be simpler. Authority to become children of God is granted to all those who, by a definite act of faith, receive Jesus Christ as Lord and Savior.

So there is sad news and glad news. First the sad news: "the world did not know Him" and "His own did not receive Him." Then the glad news: "But as many as received Him, to them He gave the right to become children of God, to those who believe in His name." If you have not already received Him, why not believe on His Name today?

September 6

Then the Lord God took the man and put him in the garden of Eden
to tend and keep it.
GENESIS 2:15

C ontrary to the attitude of some, work is not a curse; it is a blessing. Before sin ever entered into the world, God assigned Adam to tend the Garden of Eden. It was after man had sinned that God cursed the ground—but not work itself. He decreed that, in trying to make a living from the ground, man would encounter sorrow, frustration, and sweat (Gen. 3:17-19).

One old worthy said, "Blest work! if thou dost bear God's curse, what must His blessing be?" But work does not bear His curse. It is part of our essential being. It is part of our need for creativity and for self-significance. It is when we succumb to idleness that the danger of sinning is greatest. And it is often when we retire from an active life that we begin to fall apart.

We should not forget that God commanded His people to work (Six days you shall labor" Ex. 20:9). Men tend to overlook that and to emphasize the other part that commands them to rest on the seventh day.

The New Testament labels the loafer as "disorderly" or "unruly" and decrees that if a man won't work, he should be allowed to go hungry (2 Thess. 3:6-10).

The Lord Jesus is our supreme example of a hard Worker. "What days of toil were His! What nights of laboring prayer! Three years in the ministry made an old man of Him. 'Thou art not yet fifty years old,' they said, making a rough guess at his age. Fifty? He was only thirty! I will make no secret of it." (IAN MACPHERSON).

Some people develop an allergy to work because their job has some disagreeable feature. They should realize that no job is completely ideal. Every occupation has some drawback. But the Christian can do it to the glory of God, "not somehow, but triumphantly."

The believer labors, not only to supply his own needs but to help others who are in need (Eph. 4:28). This adds a new, unselfish motive to work.

Even in eternity we will work for "His servants shall serve Him" (Rev. 22:3).

In the meantime we should follow Spurgeon's advice: "Kill yourselves with work, and then pray yourselves alive again."

September 7

Come out from among them and be separate, says the Lord.
Do not touch what is unclean, and I will receive you. I will be a Father to you,
and you shall be My sons and daughters, says the Lord Almighty.
2 CORINTHIANS 6:17-18

What should a Christian do when he finds himself in a church that has become increasingly liberal and modernistic? This church was founded by men who believed in the inerrancy of the Bible and in all the other fundamental doctrines of the faith. It had a glorious history of evangelical fervor and of missionary endeavor. Many of its ministers were well-known scholars and faithful preachers of the Word. But the denominational seminaries have been taken over by a new breed, and now the ministers coming out of them preach a social gospel. They still use biblical phraseology but they mean something completely different by it. They undermine the major Bible doctrines, give natural explanations for the miracles, and scoff at biblical morality. They are out front in advocating radical politics and subversive causes. They speak contemptuously of fundamentalists.

What should a Christian do? Perhaps his family has been associated with this church for generations. He himself has contributed generously over the years. His closest friends are in the church. He wonders what would happen to the young people in his Sunday School class if he should leave. Shouldn't he remain in the church and be a voice for God as long as possible?

His arguments seem plausible to him. And yet it vexes his righteous soul to see people coming to the church for bread week after week and getting nothing but a stone. He values his associations there and yet it grieves him to hear his Savior condemned with faint praise.

There is no doubt what he should do. He should leave the church. That is the clear command of God's Word. If he removes himself from this unequal yoke, God will take care of all the consequences. God will assume responsibility for those Sunday School students. God will provide new friendships. In fact, God Himself promises to be a Father to him in a closeness that can only be known by those who are unquestioningly obedient. The blessedness of true separation is nothing less than the glorious companionship of the great God Himself.

September 8

When you make a vow to God, do not delay to pay it;
for He has no pleasure in fools. Pay what you have vowed.
ECCLESIASTES 5:4

W e have all heard of the man who, when he finds himself in a tight spot, makes a vow to God. He promises that if God delivers him, he will trust, love, and serve Him forever. But when he escapes from the crisis, he forgets all about the vow and goes on living the same old life.

What place do vows have in the life of a Christian, and what guidelines are given in the Word on this subject?

First of all, it is not necessary to make vows. They are not commanded, but are generally voluntary promises made to the Lord in gratitude for His favors. Thus we read in Deuteronomy 23:22, NIV: "But if you refrain from making a vow, you will not be guilty."

Second, we should be careful not to make rash vows, that is, vows that we won't be able to fulfill or that we might later regret. Solomon warns us, "Do not be rash with your mouth, and let not your heart utter anything hastily before God. For God is in heaven, and you on earth; therefore let your words be few" (Eccl. 5:2).

But if we do make a vow, we must be careful to keep it. "If a man makes a vow to the Lord, or swears an oath to bind himself by some agreement, he shall not break his word; he shall do according to all that proceeds out of his mouth" (Num. 30:2). "When you make a vow to the Lord your God, you shall not delay to pay it; for the Lord your God will surely require it of you, and it would be sin to you." (Deut. 23:21).

It is better not to vow than to vow and not pay. "Better not to vow than to vow and not pay" (Eccl. 5:5).

There may be exceptional cases where it would be better to break a vow than to continue in it. Before his conversion, a man may have taken vows in a false religion or in a secret fraternal order. If it would be contrary to God's Word to fulfill those vows, then he must obey the Scriptures, even at the cost of breaking the vows. If they were simply vows not to divulge certain secrets, then he could remain silent concerning them the rest of his life, even after severing his ties with the order.

Perhaps the vow that is most commonly broken today is the marriage vow. Solemn promises made in the presence of God are treated as of no great importance. But God's verdict stands: "The Lord your God will surely require it of you and you will be guilty of sin" (Deut. 23:21, NIV).

September 9

A good man leaves an inheritance to his children's children.
PROVERBS 13:22

W hen we read this verse, we should not jump to the conclusion that a financial inheritance is intended. It is far more likely that the Spirit of God is referring to a spiritual heritage. A person could have been brought up by parents who were poor, yet godly; and that person might be everlastingly grateful for the memory of a mother and father who read the Bible daily, prayed together as a family, and raised him in the fear and admonition of the Lord—even though they didn't leave him a cent when they died. A spiritual inheritance is the best kind.

Actually, a son or daughter could be ruined spiritually by inheriting a large amount of money. Sudden wealth often proves intoxicating. Few are able to manage it wisely. Few who inherit fortunes go on well for the Lord.

Another consideration is that families are often torn apart by jealousy and strife when an estate is divided. It is true that "where there's a will, there are a lot of relatives." Family members who have lived peacefully for years suddenly become enemies over a few bits of jewelry or china or furniture.

Oftentimes Christian parents leave their wealth to unsaved children, to relatives in false religions, or to ungrateful children, when that money could have been better used for the spread of the gospel.

Sometimes this business of leaving money to children is a veiled form of selfishness. The parents actually want to hold onto it for themselves as long as they can. They know that death will one day tear it from their grip, so they then follow the tradition of bequeathing it to their children.

But no will has yet been devised that cannot be broken or eroded by legal fees. A parent can't be sure that his wishes will be carried out after he is gone.

Therefore the best policy is to give generously to the work of the Lord while one is still alive. As the saying goes, "Do your giving while you're living; then you're knowing where it's going."

And the best way to make out a will is to say, "Being of sound mind I put my money to work for God while I was alive. I leave my children the heritage of a Christian background, a home where Christ was honored, and where God's Word was revered. I commend them to God and to the word of His grace, which is able to build them up and give them an inheritance among all those who are sanctified."

September 10

Pray for those who spitefully use you and persecute you.
MATTHEW 5:44

S ometimes an illustration is the best commentary on a verse.

Captain Mitsuo Fuchida was the Japanese pilot who directed the attack on Pearl Harbor on December 7, 1941. He sent back the message, "Tora, Tora, Tora," indicating the complete success of his mission. But World War II was not over. As the conflict raged on, the tide of battle turned until finally the United States was victorious.

During the war, the Japanese executed an elderly missionary couple in the Philippines. When their daughter in the U.S. got the news, she decided to visit Japanese prisoners of war and share with them the good news of the gospel.

When they asked her why she was so kind to them, she would reply, "Because of the prayer my parents prayed before they were killed." But that is all she would say.

After the war, Mitsuo Fuchida was so bitter that he decided to bring the United States before an international tribunal to be tried for war atrocities. In an attempt to collect evidence, he interviewed Japanese prisoners of war. When he debriefed those who were held in the U.S., he was chagrined to hear, not of atrocities, but of the kindness shown by a Christian lady whose parents had been killed in the Philippines. The prisoners told how she supplied them with a book called the New Testament and mentioned that her parents had prayed some unknown prayer before they were executed. This was not exactly what Fuchida wanted to hear but he made a mental note of it anyway.

After hearing the story numerous times, he went out and bought a New Testament. When he read the Gospel of Matthew, his attention was arrested. He read through Mark and his interest deepened. When he came to Luke 23:34, light flooded his soul. "Father, forgive them; for they know not what they do." Instantly he knew the prayer that the elderly missionary couple had prayed before they were killed.

"He no longer thought of the American woman or the Japanese prisoners of war, but of himself, a fierce enemy of Christ, whom God was prepared to forgive in answer to the prayer of the crucified Savior. At that very moment he sought and found forgiveness and eternal life by faith in Christ."

Plans for the international tribunal were scrapped. Mitsuo Fuchida spent the rest of his life proclaiming the unsearchable riches of Christ in many countries.

September 11

Beware that you do not forget the Lord your God...
when all that you have is multiplied.
DEUTERONOMY 8:11, 13

s a general rule, God's people cannot stand material prosperity. They thrive much better under adversity. In his parting song, Moses predicted that Israel's prosperity would ruin them spiritually: "But Jeshurun grew fat and kicked; you grew fat, you grew thick, you are obese! Then he forsook God who made him, and scornfully esteemed the Rock of his salvation" (Deut. 32:15).

The prophecy was fulfilled in Jeremiah's day, when the Lord complained, "When I had fed them to the full, then they committed adultery and assembled themselves by troops in the harlots' houses" (Jer. 5:7).

Again we read in Hosea 13:6, "When they had pasture, they were filled; they were filled and their heart was exalted; therefore they forgot Me."

After returning from exile, the Levites confessed that Israel had not responded properly to all that the Lord had done for them: "So they ate and were filled and grew fat, and delighted themselves in Your great goodness. Nevertheless they were disobedient and rebelled against You, cast Your law behind their backs and killed Your prophets, who testified against them to turn them to Yourself; and they worked great provocations" (Neh. 9:25-26).

We tend to look upon material prosperity as an undeniable evidence of the Lord's approval of what we are and do. When profits in our business soar, we say, "The Lord is really blessing me." It would probably be more accurate to look upon those profits as a test. The Lord is waiting to see what we will do with them. Will we spend them on self-indulgence? Or will we act as faithful stewards, using them to send the good news to the uttermost parts of the earth? Will we hoard them in an effort to amass a fortune? Or will we invest them for Christ and His cause?

Said F. B. Meyer, "If it should be debated as to whether sunshine or storm, success or trial, were the severer test for character, the shrewdest observers of human nature would probably answer that nothing so clearly shows the real stuff of which we are made as prosperity, because this of all tests is the severest."

Joseph would have agreed. He said, "God has caused me to be fruitful in the land of my affliction" (Gen. 41:52). He profited more from adversity than he did from prosperity, although he conducted himself favorably under both circumstances.

September 12

Supposing Him to have been in the company, they went a day's journey.
LUKE 2:44

When Jesus was twelve, His parents and He went from Nazareth to Jerusalem to keep the Feast of the Passover. Doubtless they traveled with a large crowd of other pilgrims. It was inevitable that boys of the same age would pal together during the festivities. Therefore, on the return trip to Nazareth, Joseph and Mary assumed that Jesus was with the other young people somewhere in the caravan. But He wasn't. He had stayed behind in Jerusalem. They traveled for a full day before they missed Him. Then they had to backtrack to Jerusalem where they found Him after three days.

There is a lesson in this for us all. It is possible for us to suppose Jesus is in our company when He is not. We may think that we are walking in fellowship with Him when actually sin has come between our souls and the Savior. Spiritual decline is subtle. We are not conscious of our coldness. We think that we are the same as ever.

But other people can tell. They can tell by our talk that we have drifted away from our first love and that worldly interests have taken precedence over the spiritual. They can detect that we have been feeding on the leeks, the onions, and the garlic of Egypt. They notice that we have become critical whereas once we were loving and kind. They notice that we use a lot of street talk instead of the language of Zion. Whether they notice it or not, we have lost our song. We are unhappy and miserable ourselves and tend to make other people miserable too. Nothing seems to go right. Money leaks out of our pockets. If we try to witness for the Savior, we have little impact on others. They don't see that much difference between themselves and us.

Usually it takes a crisis of some kind to reveal to us that Jesus is not in our company. It may be that we hear God's voice speaking to us through some anointed preaching. Or a friend might put an arm around us and confront us with our low spiritual condition. Or it may be a sickness, the death of a loved one, or some tragedy that brings us to our senses.

When that happens, we have to do what Joseph and Mary did—go back to the place where we last saw Him. We have to go back to the place where some sin broke our fellowship with Him. By confessing and forsaking our sin, we find forgiveness, and begin traveling with Jesus in our company once more.

September 13

*Moses did not know that the skin of his face shone
because of His speaking with him.*
EXODUS 34:29, NASB

When Moses came down from Mount Sinai with the stone tablets containing the Ten Commandments, there were two remarkable features. First of all, his face shone. He had been in the presence of the Lord, who revealed Himself in a bright, shining glory cloud known as the Shekinah. The radiance on the face of Moses was a borrowed glow. After speaking with God, the lawgiver carried away some of the splendor and effulgence of the glory. It was a transfiguring experience.

The second notable feature was that Moses did not know that his face was luminous. He was totally unconscious of the unique cosmetic he carried away from communion with the Lord. F. B. Meyer comments that that was the crowning glory of that transfiguration—the fact that Moses was unaware of it.

There is a sense in which Moses' experience can be ours. When we spend time in the presence of the Lord, it shows. It may actually show in our faces, because there is a close link between the spiritual and the physical. But I do not press the physical, because some cultists often have very benign faces. The important point is that communion with God transfigures a person morally and spiritually. That is what Paul teaches in 2 Corinthians 3:18: "But we all, with unveiled face, beholding as in a mirror the glory of the Lord, are being transformed into the same image from glory to glory, just as by the Spirit of the Lord."

But the crowning glory of that transfiguration is that we ourselves are not conscious of it. Others can tell. They take knowledge of us that we have been with Jesus. But the change is hidden from our own eyes.

How is it that we are blissfully unaware that the skin of our face is shining? The reason is this: The closer we are to the Lord, the more we are aware of our sinfulness, our unworthiness, our wretchedness. In the glory of His presence, we are led to self-abhorrence and deep repentance.

If we were conscious of our own radiance, that would lead to pride and the radiance would instantly be replaced with repugnance, because pride is repugnant.

So it is a blessed circumstance that those who have been on the mount with the Lord and who carry away the borrowed glow do not realize that the skin of their face is shining.

September 14

As the Lord lives, there shall no punishment come upon you for this thing.
1 SAMUEL 28:10, NASB

Earlier in his reign, Saul had decreed that all mediums and spiritists should be cut off from the land. But then things went from bad to worse in his personal and public life. After Samuel's death, the Philistines massed against Saul's army at Gilboa. When he couldn't get any word from the Lord, he consulted a witch in Endor. She fearfully reminded him that he had ordered the removal of all witches from the land. It was then that Saul reassured her, "As the Lord lives, there shall no punishment come upon you for this thing" (1 Sam. 28:10, NASB).

The lesson is clear. People have a tendency to obey the Lord only as long as it suits them. When it no longer suits them, they can always think up excuses for doing whatever they want.

Did I say "they"? Perhaps I should have said "we." We all tend to evade Scriptures, bend them, or explain them away when we don't want to obey.

For example, there are some plain instructions concerning the role of women in the church. But they seem to clash with the current feminist movement.

So what do we do? We say that those commandments were based on the culture of that day and do not apply to us today. Of course, when we once admit that principle, we can get rid of almost anything in the Bible.

Sometimes we come to some hard-hitting statements of the Lord Jesus concerning the terms of discipleship. If we feel they demand too much of us, we say, "Jesus didn't mean that we should do it, but only that we should be willing to do it." We deceive ourselves that we are willing, when we have no intention of ever doing it.

We can be very firm in demanding that offenders be disciplined according to the stern demands of the Word. But when an offender turns out to be our relative and friend, we can insist that the demands be relaxed or overlooked altogether.

Another device we have is to classify Scripture commandments as "important" or "not important." Those in the "not important" category can be disregarded—or at least that is what we tell ourselves.

In all of these false reasonings, we are actually wresting the Scriptures to our own destruction. God wants us to obey His Word whether it suits us or not. That is the pathway to blessing.

September 15

Now hope does not disappoint, because the love of God
has been poured out in our hearts by the Holy Spirit who was given to us.
ROMANS 5:5

Sometimes words in the Christian vocabulary have a different meaning than they have in ordinary usage. "Hope" is one of those words.

As far as the world is concerned, to hope often means to look forward to something unseen but with no certainty of fulfillment. A man in deep financial trouble may say, "I hope everything will turn out all right," but he has no assurance that it will. His hope may be nothing but wishful thinking. The Christian hope also looks forward to something unseen, as Paul reminds us in Romans 8:24: "Hope that is seen is not hope; for why does one still hope for what he sees?" All hope deals in the realm of the future.

But what makes the Christian hope different is that it is based on the promise of the Word of God and is therefore absolutely certain. "We have this hope as an anchor for the soul, firm and secure" (Heb. 6:19, NIV). Hope is "faith laying hold of God's Word and living in the present assurance of what God has promised or predicted" (WOODRING).

"Notice that I am using hope to mean 'certainty.' Hope in Scripture refers to future events that will happen, come what may. Hope is not a delusion to buoy our spirits and keep us going forth blindly to an inevitable fate. It is the basis of all Christian living. It represents ultimate reality" (JOHN WHITE).

Because the believer's hope is based on God's promise, it can never lead to shame or disappointment (Rom. 5:5). "Hope without God's promises is empty and futile, and often even presumptuous. But based on the promises of God, it rests upon His character and cannot lead to disappointment" (WOODRING).

The Christian hope is spoken of as a good hope. Our Lord Jesus and God our Father have loved us and have given us "everlasting consolation and good hope by grace" (2 Thess. 2:16).

It is called a blessed hope, referring particularly to the coming of Christ: "Looking for the blessed hope and glorious appearing of our great God and Savior Jesus Christ" (Titus 2:13).

And it is called a living hope. "In His great mercy He has given us new birth into a living hope through the resurrection of Jesus Christ from the dead" (1 Pet. 1:3, NIV).

The Christian's hope enables him to endure seemingly endless delays, tribulation, persecution, and even martyrdom. He knows that these experiences are only pinpricks compared to the coming glory.

September 16

Discipline your son while there is hope, and do not desire his death.
PROV. 19:18, NASB

We live in a permissive society. Especially in the area of child-training, people listen to the advice of psychologists and sociologists rather than to the teachings of God's Word. Many adults who were brought up by parents who dared to discipline them, determine to allow their children freedom and self-expression. What are the results?

Such children grow up with a deep sense of insecurity. They are misfits in society. They find it difficult to cope with problems and troubles, and seek release in drugs and liquor. A few years of discipline would have made the rest of life much easier for them.

Not surprisingly, they live undisciplined lives. Their personal appearance, their living quarters, their personal habits all betray their careless and disorderly mindset.

They are satisfied with mediocrity or less. They lack the drive to excel in sports, music, art, business, and other areas in life.

Such children become alienated from the parents. These parents thought they would win the undying love of their children by withholding punishment. Instead they won the hatred of their offspring.

Their rebellion against parental authority extends to other areas of life—to school, employment, and government. If their parents had only broken their wills early in life, they would have made it easier for their children to submit in other areas of life.

Rebellion spreads to moral standards set forth in the Scriptures. Young rebels flout the divine commands concerning purity and abandon themselves to loose and reckless living. They manifest a deep loathing for whatever is good, and a love for whatever is unnatural, obscene, and hideous.

Finally, parents who fail to break the will of a child through discipline make it harder for that child to be saved. Conversion involves the breaking of the will in its rebellion against the rule of God. That is why Susannah Wesley said, "The parent who studies to subdue self-will in his child works together with God in the renewing and saving of a soul. The parent who indulges it does the Devil's work, makes religion impractical, salvation unattainable, and does all that in him lies to damn his child, soul and body, forever."

September 17

He causes all, both small and great, rich and poor, free and slave, to receive a mark on their right hand or on their foreheads, and that no one may buy or sell except one who has the mark or the name of the beast, or the number of his name. REVELATION 13:16-17

The mark of the beast! During the Tribulation period a powerful and evil ruler will arise, ordering all people to receive a mark in their forehead or in their right hand. Those who refuse will suffer the wrath of the beast. Those who submit will suffer the wrath of God. Those who refuse will reign with Christ in His millennial glory. Those who submit will be tormented with fire and brimstone in the presence of the holy angels, and in the presence of the Lamb.

As we read this, we can feel quite detached from it all, knowing that it belongs to the future, and believing that the Church will be raptured home to heaven in the meantime. And yet there is a sense in which the mark of the beast is with us now. There are times in life when we are forced to choose between loyalty to God and bowing to a system that is opposed to God.

There are times when, in order to gain employment, for instance, we are asked to accept conditions that are clearly contrary to divine principles. It is easy to rationalize at such times. Unless we can work, we can't buy groceries. And unless we can get food, we can't survive. And we have to live, don't we? Under this false excuse, we agree to the demands and, in effect, take the mark of the beast.

Whatever threatens our food supply or our continued existence throws us into panic, and we are tempted to sacrifice almost anything to avert that threat. The same arguments that men will use to justify worshiping the image in the Tribulation period are the arguments that present themselves to us today when we must choose between God's truth and our own lives.

The idea that we must live is false. What we must do is obey God and love not our lives unto death.

F. W. Grant wrote, "On the coin for which we sell the truth, there is at all times, faint as it may be, the image of Antichrist." So the question is not, "Would I refuse to take the mark of the beast if I were living in the Tribulation?" but rather "Do I refuse to sell the truth now?"

September 18

Were there not ten cleansed? But where are the nine?
LUKE 17:17

The Lord Jesus healed ten lepers but only one returned to thank Him, and that one was a despised Samaritan.

One of the valuable experiences for us in life is to encounter ingratitude, for then we can share in a small degree the heartbreak of God. When we give generously and do not receive so much as an acknowledgment, we have a greater appreciation of Him who gave His beloved Son for a thankless world. When we pour out ourselves in tireless service for others, we join the fellowship of the One who took the place of a slave for a race of ingrates.

Unthankfulness is one of the unlovely traits of fallen man. Paul reminds us that when the pagan world knew God, they glorified Him not as God, neither were thankful (Rom. 1:21).

A missionary to Brazil discovered two tribes who had no words for "Thank you." If a kindness was shown to them, they would say "That is what I wanted" or "That will be useful to me." Another missionary, working in North Africa, found that those to whom he ministered never expressed gratitude because they were giving him the opportunity of earning merit with God. It was the missionary who should be grateful, they felt, because he was acquiring favor through the kindness he showed them.

Ingratitude permeates all of society. A radio program called "Job Center of the Air" succeeded in finding jobs for 2500 people. The emcee later reported that only ten ever took time to thank him.

A dedicated school teacher had poured her life into fifty classes of students. When she was eighty, she received a letter from one of her former students, telling how much he appreciated her help. She had taught for fifty years and this was the only letter of appreciation she had ever received.

We said that it is good for us to experience ingratitude because it gives us a pale reflection of what the Lord experiences all the time. Another reason why it is a valuable experience is that it impresses on us the importance of being thankful ourselves. Too often our requests to God outweigh our thanksgiving. We take His blessings too much for granted. And too often we fail to express our appreciation to one another for hospitality, for instruction, for transportation, for provision, for numberless deeds of kindness. We actually come to expect these favors almost as if we deserved them.

The study of the ten lepers should be a constant reminder to us that while many have great cause for thanksgiving, few have the heart to acknowledge it. Shall we be among the few?

September 19

For when we were still without strength,
in due time Christ died for the ungodly.
ROMANS 5:6

hrist did not come to call the righteous nor did He die for good people. It was not for decent, respectable, refined people that He went to the Cross. He died for the ungodly.

Of course, from God's standpoint, all mankind is ungodly. We were all born in sin and shaped in iniquity. Like lost sheep, we have gone astray and turned to our own way. In God's pure eyes, we are depraved, unclean, and rebellious. Our best efforts to do what is right are nothing but filthy rags.

The trouble is that most people are not willing to admit that they are ungodly. By comparing themselves with the criminal elements in society, they imagine that they are quite fit for heaven. They are like the distinguished upper-class matron who prided herself on her social involvement and donations to charity. When a Christian neighbor witnessed to her, she said she felt no need of being saved; her own good works were sufficient. She reminded him that she was a church member and that she came from a long line of "Christians." The Christian took a slip of paper, wrote UNGODLY on it in capital letters, then turned to her and asked, "Would you mind if I pinned this to your blouse?" When she saw the word UNGODLY, she bristled. "Of course, I would mind," she said. "No one is going to tell me I'm ungodly." He then explained to her that by refusing to admit her sinful, lost, hopeless condition, she cut herself off from any benefit in the saving work of Christ. If she wouldn't confess she was ungodly, then Christ didn't die for her. If she wasn't lost, then she couldn't be saved. If she was well, then she didn't need the Great Physician.

A special party was once held in a large civic auditorium. It was for children who were blind, crippled, or otherwise impaired. The youngsters came in wheelchairs, on crutches, and led by the hand. While the party was under way, a patrolman found a little boy crying on the front steps of the building. "Why're you crying," he asked sympathetically?

"Because they won't let me in."

"Why won't they let you in?"

The little fellow sobbed, "Because there's nothing the matter with me."

That's the way it is with the gospel feast. If there's nothing the matter with you, you can't get in. In order to gain admittance, you have to prove that you are a sinner. You have to acknowledge that you are ungodly. It was for the ungodly that Christ died. As Robert Munger said, "The Church is the only fellowship in the world where the one requirement for membership is the unworthiness of the candidate."

September 20

Do not set your mind on high things, but associate with the humble.
ROMANS 12:16

T he natural tendency is to want to hobnob with the upper crust. In every human heart there is the lust to associate with those who are prominent, wealthy, and aristocratic. So Paul's advice in Romans 12:16 really cuts across the grain of nature. He says, "Do not be proud but be willing to associate with people of low position" (NIV). There are no castes in the Church. Christians should live above class distinctions.

A story that illustrates this is told of Fred Elliot. One morning he was having family devotions at the breakfast table when he heard a noisy clatter in the yard. He realized that the garbage collector had arrived. So he put down his open Bible on the table, went to the window, opened it, called out a cheery greeting to the scavenger, then returned to the table to resume the devotions. To him it was just as sacred to greet the garbage collector as it was to read the Bible.

There was another servant of the Lord who took our text quite literally. Jack Wyrtzen conducted a Bible camp each summer at Schroon Lake, N.Y. At one of the adult conferences, a guest showed up with a serious physical impairment. Because he could not control the muscles of his mouth, he was not able to swallow all his food. Much of it came back out and fell down on the newspapers with which he covered his chest and lap. The scene was not conducive to pleasant eating and as a result, this man usually sat at a table by himself.

Because of the pressures of his work, Jack Wyrtzen was often late arriving at the dining hall. Whenever he appeared at the door, people would wave to him excitedly, beckoning him to come and sit at their table. But Jack never did. He always went to the table where this guest was eating alone. He condescended to a man of low estate.

"A Christian general was once seen talking to a poor old woman. Friends remonstrated with him, saying, 'You ought to consider your rank.' The general answered, 'What if my Lord had considered His rank?'" (*Choice Gleanings*).

In his poem, "For A' That and A' That," Robert Burns reminds us that in spite of a lowly position in life, a man's a man for all that. He says that the man of independent mind can laugh at the tinsel show of fools in silk.

When we think of how our Savior condescended to us in our low estate, it is absurd that we should fail to do so with others.

September 21

Finally, there is laid up for me the crown of righteousness, which the Lord,
the righteous Judge, will give to me on that Day, and not to me only
but also to all who have loved His appearing.

2 TIMOTHY 4:8

"Also to all who have loved His appearing." For many years I thought that this expression referred to those believers who had kindly, sentimental feelings about the coming of the Lord. They would be rewarded with a crown of righteousness because their hearts glowed warm when they thought about the Rapture.

But surely it means more than this. To love His appearing means to live in the light of His coming, to behave as if He were coming today.

Thus, to love His appearing means to live in moral purity. For, as John reminds us, "everyone who has this hope in Him purifies himself, just as He is pure" (1 Jn. 3:3).

It means to stay disentangled from the things of this life. We should set our affections on things above, not on things on the earth (Col. 3:2).

It means to serve God's people, giving them "food in due season" (Mt. 24:45). The Lord pronounces a special blessing on those who are doing that when He comes.

In short, it means that we won't do anything that we would not want to be found doing when He appears. We would not go anywhere that would cause shame at His coming. We would not say anything that would be offensive in His presence.

If you knew Christ were coming in a week, how would you spend the intervening days? Does it mean you would give up your job, go to a mountaintop and spend all day reading the Bible and praying? Does it mean you would go into "full-time Christian work," preaching and teaching day and night?

If we are really walking with the Lord today and living in the center of His will, it would mean carrying on as usual. If, however, we are living for self, then it would require some revolutionary changes.

It is not enough to have kind thoughts about the Savior's return. The crown of righteousness is reserved for those who love it enough to let the truth mold their lives. It is not enough to hold the truth about His coming; the truth must hold us.

September 22

...say Amen.
1 CORINTHIANS 14:16

Amen is an extremely useful word with which to express hearty approval of what is being said. Many congregations could afford to use it more often in their services.

The word is found 68 times in the Bible. From 1 Corinthians 14:15-16, it is clear that it was used in the meetings of the early church. So we can be assured that the use of the Amen is eminently scriptural.

Not only so, it is imperative. The sublime nature of the truths we deal with require the intelligent expression of enthusiastic appreciation. It seems like ingratitude to hear such truths and never make a vocal response.

It is always an encouragement to the speaker when his audience says, "Amen" at those places in his message where he has made an effective point. It tells him that the people are following him and that they share his spiritual and emotional exuberance.

And it is good for the person who says the Amen. It keeps him involved as an attentive listener. It keeps him from becoming apathetic when he should be amazed.

I would suggest that it is good for outsiders who may be present. They sense that the Christians are enthusiastic, that they enjoy their faith, that they believe what they believe. The use of the Amen expresses life and fervor. Its absence speaks of dullness and deadness.

Amen is one of three Bible words that are practically universal. In most languages these words are the same. So you can go almost anywhere and say, "Maranatha! Hallelujah! Amen!" and people will understand you as saying, "The Lord is coming! Praise the Lord! So be it.'"

Of course, the word "Amen" should be used discerningly. It would be inappropriate to use it to express enthusiasm over misfortune, tragedy, or sorrow.

It is a shame that some bodies of Christians have stopped using the Amen because it has been abused in meetings given over to extreme emotionalism. Like all good things, it can be used or overdone. But we should not be robbed of this scriptural practice just because some have used it undiscerningly. Amen?

September 23

O my soul, come not thou into their secret.
GENESIS 49:6, KJV

T hese words are found in Jacob's blessing of his sons. When he thought of the cruelty which Simeon and Levi showed to the men of Shechem, he said, "O my soul, come not thou into their secret."

I would like to borrow the words and use them in a broader sense. There are secrets connected with sin which it is better never to know.

Temptation puts on its best face and suggests that we can never be happy until we have been initiated into its mysteries. It offers thrills, physical gratification, emotional highs, and the lure of the unknown.

Many people, especially those who have lived sheltered lives, are stirred by these appeals. They feel that they have missed out on true pleasures. They consider themselves disadvantaged. They think they can never be satisfied until they get a taste of the world.

The trouble is that sin does not come alone. There are built-in hazards and enduring consequences. When we come to experience any sin for the first time, we unloose a flood of pain and remorse.

Yielding to temptation lowers our resistance to sin. Once we have committed a sin, it is always easier to do it the next time. Soon we become expert in the sin. We even become slaves to it, bound by the chains of habit.

The moment we give in to temptation, our eyes are opened to a sense of guilt that we never had before. The exhilaration of breaking the code of sin is followed by a terrible sense of moral nakedness. It is true that the sin can be confessed and forgiven, but all through life there is the embarrassment of meeting former partners in transgression. There is the stabbing of memory when we unavoidably revisit the places of our folly. There are unwanted occasions when the whole sordid episode flashes back during our most holy moments—when our bodies actually pulsate and our lips muffle a groan.

While it is wonderful to experience the forgiveness of God for these sins, it is still better not to enter into their secrets in the first place. What poses as an attractive secret proves to be a nightmare. Pleasure soon turns to horror, and a moment of passion results in a lifetime of regret.

In the hour of trial, our response should be, "O my soul, come not thou into their secret."

September 24

I have learned by experience.
GENESIS 30:27

aban had learned by experience that the Lord had blessed him for Jacob's sake. It was a good lesson to learn. Experience is a great teacher.

I am impressed by the way that experience often helps us to understand verses in the Bible. We may be acquainted with the verses intellectually, but when we pass through some new experience, the verses come alive. They seem to stand out in neon lights. We have a new appreciation of them.

Martin Luther's wife said that she would never have known what certain verses in the Psalms meant if God had not brought her under certain afflictions.

When Daniel Smith and his wife were missionaries in China, a robber band cut a wide hole through the side of their house one night. While the Smith's slept, the robbers cleaned out the drawers and cupboards. If the missionaries had not slept soundly, they might have been killed. Later, in describing the incident, Mr. Smith said, "I never understood Habakkuk 3:17-18 until that morning. 'Though the fig tree may not blossom, nor fruit be on the vines; though the labor of the olive may fail, and the fields yield no food; though the flock may be cut off from the fold, and there be no herd in the stalls—yet I will rejoice in the Lord, I will joy in the God of my salvation.'" What it means, of course, is that you can't fully enter into Habakkuk's joy in calamity until you have experienced the kind of loss that he described.

When Corrie Ten Boom was in a concentration camp, she had to appear before the judge. "The judge...still had his job to do, and there came a day when he showed me papers that could mean not only my death sentence but also the death sentence of family and friends.

"'Can you explain these papers?' he asked. 'No, I can't,' I admitted. Suddenly he took all the papers and threw them in the stove! When I saw the flames destroy those condemning papers, I knew I had been guarded by divine power, and understood as never before Colossians 2:14: 'Having wiped out the handwriting of requirements that was against us, which was contrary to us. And He has taken it out of the way, having nailed it to the cross.'"

The new insights we gain in the sacred Scriptures through the experiences of life make those experiences tremendously worthwhile.

September 25

Have I therefore become your enemy because I tell you the truth?
GALATIANS 4:16

Paul's experience with the Christians in Galatia reminds us that we often make enemies of our friends when we tell them the truth. The apostle had introduced these people to the Lord and nurtured them in the faith. But later when false teachers infiltrated their Christian assemblies, Paul had to warn believers that they were forsaking Christ for the law. That caused them to become hostile toward their father in the faith.

It was also true in Old Testament times. Elijah was always honest and forthright in his messages to Ahab. Yet one day when Ahab met him, he said, "Is that you, O troubler of Israel?" (1 Ki. 18:17). "Troubler of Israel"? Why, Elijah was one of the best friends Israel had! But his thanks for being faithful was to be denounced as a troublemaker.

Micaiah was another fearless prophet. When Jehoshaphat asked if there was a prophet of the Lord whom they could consult, the king of Israel said, "There is still one man, Micaiah the son of Imlah, by whom we may inquire of the Lord; but I hate him, because he does not prophesy good concerning me, but evil" (1 Ki. 22:8). The king didn't want the truth, and hated the one who spoke it to him.

In the New Testament we find John the Baptist telling Herod, "It is not lawful for you to have your brother's wife" (Mk. 6:18, NIV). It was true, but such courageous handling of the truth soon led to John's execution.

Our Lord stirred up the hatred of the unbelieving Jews. What caused this hatred? It was because He had told them the truth. He said, "But now you seek to kill Me, a Man who has told you the truth" (Jn. 8:40).

Thomas Jefferson wrote, "If you meant to escape malice, you should have confined yourself within the sleepy line of regular duty. There are two sides to every question, and if you take one with decision and act on it with effect, those who take the other will, of course, be hostile in proportion as they feel that effect."

The truth often hurts. Instead of bowing to it, men often curse the one who speaks it. The true servant of the Lord has already counted this cost. He must speak the truth or die. He knows that the wounds of a friend are faithful, but the kisses of an enemy are deceitful (Prov. 27:6).

September 26

I have reserved for Myself seven thousand men
who have not bowed the knee to Baal.
ROMANS 11:4

G od never leaves Himself without a witness. In the darkest days, a voice sounds out for Him in clear, articulate tones. Often in the most unusual circumstances, He raises up some unexpected confessor to speak His Name boldly.

In the days before the flood, the earth was gripped by violence and immorality. But Noah was there to take a valiant stand for the Lord.

It seemed to Elijah that all Israel had sunk in idolatry, but God had 7,000 men that had not bowed to Baal.

In the midst of spiritual deadness and moral decline, John Hus, Martin Luther, and John Knox stepped forth on the stage of history to defend the cause of the Most High.

More recently, God was acknowledged when the telegraph was discovered. The first message to be transmitted was: "What hath God wrought!"

When Apollo 8 was returning to the earth after the first manned flight to the moon, on Christmas Eve, 1968, three astronauts took turns reading from Genesis 1:1-10, then concluded, "And from the crew of Apollo 8 we close with...God bless you, all of you on the good earth."

In spite of the enraged protests of infidels, the United States Postal Service issued an Apollo 8 stamp with words from Genesis 1:1, "In the beginning..."

The currency of the United States bears the motto, "In God we trust."

The calendar abbreviation AD reminds us that this is the year of our Lord (*Anno Domini*).

Is it a coincidence that the stellar heavens feature a virgin, a man-child, a serpent and a cross—all important participants in the drama of redemption? Is it the gospel in the stars?

Even atheists sometimes slip by acknowledging the Lord. An atheistic ruler said at a summit meeting in Austria in 1979, "God will not forgive us if we fail."

There is a certain moral imperative in the universe that our God be publicly acknowledged. When the disciples praised the Lord Jesus as the King that had come in the Name of the Lord, the Pharisees demanded that Christ rebuke them. But He said to them, "I tell you that if these should keep silent, the stones would immediately cry out" (Lk. 19:40).

We need not fear that God's name will ever be unsung or His honor neglected. At the very time when men pronounce Him dead, He will raise up some witness to confound His enemies and comfort His friends.

September 27

*But the cowardly, unbelieving, abominable, murderers, sexually immoral,
sorcerers, idolaters, and all liars shall have their part in the lake which burns
with fire and brimstone, which is the second death.*
REVELATION 21:8

I t probably comes as a shock to anyone reading this verse that the cowardly and unbelieving are listed together with what we would think of as outrageous, vile sinners, and that they will share the same punishment for all eternity.

It probably comes as an added surprise to note that the cowardly are listed first. This should be tremendously sobering to any who excuse their timidity as a trifling matter. Perhaps they are afraid to accept the Lord Jesus because of what their friends might say, or because they are of a naturally retiring disposition. God does not excuse it as a trifle; He views it as culpable cowardice.

It should also be sobering to those who are listed second—the unbelieving. We hear people say, "I can't believe" or "I wish I could believe." But those are insincere statements. There is nothing about the Savior that makes it impossible for men to believe in Him. The trouble does not lie in man's intellect but in his will. Unbelievers don't want to believe on Him. The Lord Jesus said to the unbelieving Jews of His day, "...you refuse to come to Me to have life" (Jn. 5:40, NIV).

No doubt many of the fearful and unbelieving think of themselves as decent, cultured, and moral people. In this life they would want nothing to do with murderers, with the immoral, or with those who practice magic arts. But the irony is that they will spend eternity together because they never came to Christ for salvation.

Their doom is "the lake which burns with fire and brimstone, which is the second death." This is, of course, the supreme tragedy. People may argue about the existence of hell and the fact of eternal punishment, but the Bible is very explicit. Hell does exist at the end of a Christless life.

What makes it especially sad is that neither the fearful or the unbelieving or any of the others listed in our verse have to go to the lake of fire. It is completely unnecessary. If they would just repent of their fears and doubts and other sins, and turn to the Lord Jesus in simple, trusting faith, they would be forgiven, cleansed, and made fit for heaven.

September 28

Do not be overcome by evil, but overcome evil with good.
ROMANS 12:21

If this verse had been written by uninspired men, it would have said, "Don't let people walk all over you. Give them back a dose of their own medicine." The world thinks in terms of retaliation and of revenge. But we learn a different lesson in the school of Christ. We should not allow ourselves to be overpowered by evil. Rather we should use good to defeat evil.

A story attributed to Francis of Assisi illustrates the point. As a little boy was playing in the neighborhood of his home, he discovered that there was an echo when he shouted. It was his first experience with echoes, so he began to experiment. He shouted, "I hate you," and the message came back, "I hate you." Raising his volume, he hollered, "I hate you," and the words came back with greater intensity: "I hate you." The third time he cried out with all his strength, "I hate you," and the words bounced back with great vehemence, "I hate you." This was all he could take. He ran back to his house, sobbing convulsively. His mother had heard the loud yelling out in the yard, but still she asked, "What's the matter, dear?" He answered, "There's a little boy out there who hates me." She thought for a moment, then said, "I'll tell you what to do. You go outside and tell that little boy that you love him."

So the youngster ran out and called out, "I love you." Sure enough, the words came back, clear and gentle, "I love you." He called again with greater emphasis, "I love you," and once again he heard the answering, "I love you." A third time he cried out with deep sincerity, "I love you," and the words came back to him tenderly, "I love you."

As I write this, people all over the world are shouting, "I hate you" at one another and wondering why tensions keep mounting. Nations are expressing hatred of other nations. Religious groups are locked in combat. Races are striving against one another. Neighbors are quarreling over the back fence. And homes are torn by quarrels and bitterness. These people are allowing themselves to become conquered by evil, because hate breeds hate. If they would just change their strategy by repaying hatred with love, they would conquer evil with good. They would discover that love breeds love.

We can never be too careful
What the seeds our hands shall sow;
Love from love is sure to ripen,
Hate from hate is sure to grow.

September 29

Salvation is of the Lord.
JONAH 2:9

W e are all familiar with the zealous "soul winner" who dashes around, buttonholing unsuspecting prospects, leading them through a salvation formula, and badgering them until they finally make a profession in order to get rid of him. He chalks up another convert and then looks around for more heads to count. Is this evangelism?

We would have to admit that it is not. It is a form of religious harassment. Like any service performed in the energy of the flesh, it does more harm than good.

John Stott was right when he wrote: "Christ has the keys. He opens the doors. Then let us not barge our way unceremoniously through doors which are still closed. We must wait for Him to make openings for us. Damage is continually being done to the cause of Christ by rude or blatant testimony. It is indeed right to seek to win for Christ our friends and relatives at home and at work. But we are sometimes in a greater hurry than God. Be patient! Pray hard and love much, and wait expectantly for the opportunity of witness."

We may not agree with much of Dietrich Bonhoeffer's doctrine, but we might well take to heart the following words of his: "The word of salvation has its limits. He has neither power nor right to force it on other men…Every attempt to impose the gospel by force, to run after people and proselytize them, to use our own resources to arrange the salvation of other people, is both futile and dangerous…We shall only meet with the blind rage of hardened and darkened hearts, and that will be useless and harmful. Our easy trafficking with the word of cheap grace simply bores the world to disgust, so that in the end it turns against those who try to force on it what it does not want."

Real conversion is a work of the Holy Spirit. It is "not of the will of man" in the sense that a man cannot produce it by his own efforts, however well intended. People who are pressured into a profession of Christ without the full consent of their will become disillusioned, disaffected and often become enemies of the Cross of Christ.

It is one of the great experiences of life when the Holy Spirit uses us in the salvation of another person. But it is bizarre and grotesque when we try to do it in our own strength.

September 30

He (Andrew) first found his own brother Simon...and he brought him to Jesus.
JOHN 1:41-42

T he normal method of personal evangelism is for Christians to witness for Christ within the context of their daily lives. This does not mean that God never uses the "cold turkey" approach—that is, walking up to total strangers and presenting the gospel to them. He does! But it is far more convincing when a believer witnesses to people who know him and who can see that Christ makes a difference in his life. This is what Simon did.

Walter Hennchsen tells of a young man who was extremely apprehensive about witnessing on his college campus. Henrichsen asked him, "Joe, how many students on campus do you know personally? By that I mean when they see you they know you by name." After being there for a couple of months, he knew only two or three men.

"I said, 'Joe, in the next four weeks, I want you to get to know as many students on campus as you can. Let's set our goal at fifty students. You don't have to witness to them. You don't even have to tell them you are a Christian. All you have to do is get to know them. Stop by their rooms and chat with them. Play ping-pong with them. Go to athletic events with them. Go to meals together. Do anything you want, but get to know fifty men so that one month from today, when I return, you can introduce me to each one of them by name.'"

When Henrichsen met the young man a month later, this fellow had led six men to Christ. "We didn't talk about whether he had gotten to know fifty people. We didn't have to. He had discovered for himself that as he became friends with 'the publicans and sinners,' the Lord naturally provided opportunities for him to share his faith."

With regard to this method of evangelizing within the context of our daily lives, two observations should be made. First, the life of the personal worker is important. It makes a difference whether he is walking close to the Lord. He may be ever so glib in presenting a pre-packaged message, but if his life isn't holy, it cancels out his message.

The second observation is that this method doesn't put the emphasis on instant results, and that is in its favor. Jesus likened the salvation process to the growth of grain; you don't harvest the crop the same day you plant the seed. It is true that some people are saved the first time they hear the gospel, but they represent a small fraction of the total. Generally speaking, conversion is preceded by a period of hearing the message, of being convicted of sin, and of resisting the voice of the Holy Spirit.

October 1

For what is your life? It is even a vapor that appears for a little time
and then vanishes away.
JAMES 4:14

The insistent voice of the Holy Spirit reminds mortal man frequently in the Scriptures of the brevity of his life. By the repeated use of similes, the Spirit of the Lord impresses on us that our days are limited and passing swiftly.

For instance, He likens life to a weaver's shuttle (Job 7:6), the device that darts back and forth in the loom almost faster than the eye can follow.

Job speaks of life as wind (Job 7:7), here one minute and gone the next, never to return. The psalmist echoes the sentiment, speaking of "A breath that passes away and does not come again" (Ps. 78:39).

Bildad unnecessarily reminds Job that "our days on earth are a shadow" (Job 8:9), a picture that is repeated in Psalm 102:11, "My days are like a shadow that lengthens, and I wither away like grass." A shadow is ephemeral—lasting a very short time.

Job compares his life to a leaf (Job 13:25), fragile, frail, and fading; and to dry stubble, driven away by the winds. Isaiah appeals to the Lord's pity by reminding Him that "we all fade as a leaf" (Isa. 64:6).

David describes his days as handbreadths (Ps. 39:5), as narrow as the width of his hand. Viewing life as a journey, it would be about four inches long.

Moses, the man of God, depicts life as a sleep (Ps. 90:5), in which time passes without our being conscious of it.

In the same place, Moses speaks of people and their lives as grass: "In the morning they are like grass which grows up; in the morning it flourishes and grows up; in the evening it is cut down and withers" (Ps. 90:5-6). Centuries later David used the same figure in describing our transiency: "As for man, his days are like grass; as a flower of the field, so he flourishes. For the wind passes over it, and it is gone, and its place remembers it no more" (Ps. 103:15-16). As Spurgeon said, the grass is "sown, grown, blown, mown, gone." And that is life in a nutshell!

Finally James adds his testimony that life is as evanescent as vapor (Jas. 4:14). It appears for a brief moment, then vanishes away.

This accumulation of similes is designed to do two things. First, it should motivate the unconverted to consider the shortness of time and the importance of being ready to meet God. Second, it should cause believers to number their days so that they might apply their hearts to wisdom (Ps. 90:12). This will result in lives of devotion and dedication to Christ, in lives that are lived for eternity.

October 2

There shall not be found among you...that useth divination,
or an observer of times, or an enchanter, or a witch, or a charmer,
or a consulter with familiar spirits, or a wizard, or a necromancer.
DEUTERONOMY 18:10-11, KJV

God warned His people Israel against any dabbling in the world of the occult. All the activities listed in today's verses are connected with demonism and must therefore be avoided. The warning is just as applicable to believers today as it was in the Old Testament.

Divination is fortune-telling. It includes the use of the crystal ball, clairvoyance, palm reading, phrenology, reading tea leaves, and every other similar effort to foretell the future.

An observer of times is an astrologer, one who uses the position of the stars and planets to project their influence on human affairs. The daily horoscope in the newspaper is connected with astrology, as is the use of the signs of the zodiac.

An enchanter is one who influences others by charms and incantations.

A witch is a woman who exercises supernatural power through contact with demons. The contacts are ultimately evil and injurious.

A charmer is one who pronounces bans or curses on others and who has demonic power to make them come to pass. (Such curses are ineffective on believers).

Consulters with familiar spirits are mediums who are able to contact the world of evil spirits. These spirits often impersonate dead relatives of those who consult the mediums.

A wizard is one who uses magical arts in the realm of spiritism. Sometimes "wizard" is the male form of the word "witch."

A necromancer is a person who professes to conjure the spirits of the dead in order to reveal the future or influence events.

Christians should avoid all these and also such modern manifestations of spiritism as yoga, transcendental meditation, Hare Krishna, seances, black magic, white magic, hypnotism, water-divining, spiritistic healing, numerology, and praying to the dead. They should also know that the following items are stock-in-trade for spiritists: mind-expanding drugs, the ouija board, playing cards, Tarot cards, dice, pendants, medallions, amulets, dominos, sticks and bones (when used for mystical purposes).

October 3

*And He healed many who were ill with various diseases,
and cast out many demons.*
MARK 1:34, NASB

S ome Christians tend to think of demon-possession as a phenomenon that existed when our Lord was on earth but is no longer present today. That is a misconception that should be corrected. Almost every day's newspaper contains accounts of mindless crimes that give every indication of being demon-inspired. There are certain symptoms of demon-possession that help us to identify it and to distinguish it from mental illness.

First of all, a demon eventually leads his victim into violence and destruction. The purpose of a demon is always to destroy.

A person who is demon-possessed has two or more personalities—his own and that of the demon(s). He may speak with different voices and identify himself with different names.

This person is capable of supernatural feats of strength or supernatural powers of knowledge.

Although he may speak patronizingly of the Lord Jesus at times, his normal behavior will be to blaspheme or react violently to any mention of the Lord, or of prayer, or of the blood of Christ, or of the Word of God.

His behavior is extremely strange, erratic, and restless. Others can neither understand him, control him, nor rehabilitate him. He may be suicidal, and may live in bondage to fear and superstition.

Demon-possession is often closely associated with the use of hallucinogenic drugs. These drugs usher the person into the transcendental realm and open his being to the entrance of demons. The word translated "witchcraft" (KJV) or "sorcery" (NASB) comes from the Greek word *pharmakia* meaning drugs.

The demon-possessed person is often sadistic, exhibiting unusual mental or physical cruelty, and sometimes mutilating and dismembering the bodies of his victims.

Other demon-possessed people may be morbid, frequenting cemeteries, collecting skulls or other bones, or obsessed with gruesome stories.

The sun and the moon, especially the new moon, exercise profound influence in the world of demonism. Hence the reassuring promise of the Word to believers, "The sun shall not strike you by day, Nor the moon by night" (Ps. 121:6).

Demons can be exorcised by prayer and by the authority of the Name of the Lord Jesus. But lasting deliverance for the person is only found when that person is born again through faith in the Savior.

October 4

Turn away mine eyes from beholding vanity.
PSALM 119:37, KJV

T he first and last words of this short prayer begin with the letters TV, and the verse is especially appropriate when applied to television. Most of the programs on TV are vanity. They picture a world that doesn't exist and a life that is far removed from reality.

Television is a robber of precious time. Watchers squander hours that can never be retrieved. Generally speaking, TV has caused a decline in Bible reading, thus tuning out the voice of God and lowering the spiritual temperature of viewers without their realizing it.

The harmful effects of TV on children are well known. Their morals are corrupted because violence is glorified, sex is glamorized, and pornography is publicized. The children suffer educationally, finding neither time nor desire to read or to write. Their values are determined by what they see on the screen, and their entire thinking is molded by anti-Christian propaganda.

The humor that is served up on the tube is filthy, and most of the rest of the script is filled with vile innuendos.

The advertising is not only stupid but morally destructive as well. It seems that nothing can be sold without a bevy of Hollywood harlots exposing vast portions of their anatomy and using body language to incite lust.

In many families, TV has caused a breakdown of communications. Members are so captivated by the programs that they no longer carry on constructive conversations with one another.

In the area of music, the lyrics are often highly objectionable. They glorify lust, treat adultery and homosexuality as valid lifestyles, and make a hero of the violent man.

If it be objected that there are wholesome Christian programs on the TV, the answer is that these are only the sugar coating on a poison pill. The plain fact is that the overall effect of TV is destructive of spiritual vitality.

A Christian had ordered a television set to be delivered to his home. When he saw the truck pull up out front, he noticed the advertising on the side of the truck, "TV brings the world into your living room." That was all he needed. He had the set returned to the store.

No one who sits glued to the television set will ever make history for God. It is one of the principle causes of spiritual decline in our day.

October 5

*Every place that the sole of your foot will tread upon I have given you,
as I said to Moses.*
JOSHUA 1:3

G od had given the land of Canaan to the people of Israel. It was theirs by divine promise. But they still had to make it their own. They had to occupy it. The rule of possession was, "Every place that the sole of your foot will tread upon, I have given you."

God has given us many great and precious promises. The Bible is full of them. But we must appropriate them by faith. Only then are they really ours.

Take, for instance, the promises concerning salvation. The Lord repeatedly promises that He will give eternal life to those who repent of their sins and receive Jesus Christ as Lord and Savior. And yet the promise does us no good until we claim it by trusting the sinner's Savior.

Let us go a step further! A person may genuinely believe on the Lord Jesus Christ and yet not enjoy the assurance of salvation. For instance, he may think that it is presumption to say that he is saved. And so he may go on in doubt and darkness. The Word promises that those who believe on the Name of the Son of God have eternal life (1 Jn. 5:13), but this must be appropriated by faith in order to be enjoyed.

God loves to be trusted. He is pleased when we take Him at His Word. He is honored when we claim the most improbable promises and reckon on them as being fulfilled.

One day when Napoleon was reviewing his troops, his horse bolted so violently that the Emperor was in danger of being thrown. A private rushed forward, seized the reins and quieted the horse.

Fully aware that his helper was a lowly private, Napoleon said, "Thank you very much, Captain."

Taking him at his word, the private replied, "Of which regiment, sir?"

Later, when the former private rehearsed the incident to his friends, they mocked his confidence in thinking he was now a Captain. But it was true! The Emperor had said so, and he had claimed the promotion on the spot.

The believer's situation is somewhat similar. He can be a Captain or remain a private. He can enjoy the riches that are his in Christ Jesus or live in virtual poverty. "We can have as much of God as we wish. Christ puts the key of the treasure-chamber in our hand, and bids us take all that we want. If a man is admitted into the bullion vault of a bank, and told to help himself, and comes out with one cent, whose fault is it that he is poor? Whose fault is it that Christian people generally have such scanty portions of the free riches of God?" (MCLAREN).

October 6

T he devoted, loyal, steadfast love of the Shulamite maiden for her beloved pictures the kind of love which we should have for the Eternal Lover of our souls. Notice the following particulars:

First, she loved everything about him. She extols the beauties of his complexion, head, hair, eyes, cheeks, lips, hands, body, legs, countenance, and mouth (5:10-16). We, of course, do not think of the physical features of the Lord Jesus, but we should be just as articulate in extolling His moral excellencies.

She thought of him day and night. Whether she was working in the vineyard or retiring for the night, or even when she was dreaming, he was the one who filled her vision and occupied her mind. It is good for us if our love for the Lord Jesus is so great that He fills our hearts from morning to evening.

She had eyes only for him. Others might try to woo and win her with words of glowing admiration, but she would redirect the praise and apply it to her beloved. So, when the voice of the world seeks to allure us, we should say,

> *O worldly pomp and glory, your charms are spread in vain;*
> *I've heard a sweeter story, I've found a truer gain.*
> *Where Christ a place prepareth, there is my loved abode.*
> *There shall I gaze on Jesus. There shall I dwell with God.*

She could talk about him most readily. Her mouth spoke out of the abundance of her heart. Her lips were the pen of a ready writer. Ideally we should be able to talk about our Lord more readily and eloquently than any other subject. Unfortunately it is not always so.

She felt her own unworthiness very keenly. She apologized for her unkempt appearance, for her ordinariness, and for her unresponsiveness to him. When we think of our sinfulness, our proneness to wander, and our disobedience, we have even more cause to wonder that Christ would ever be interested in us.

Her great delight was to be with him. She ardently longed for the time when he would come to claim her as his bride. With how much greater longing should we look forward to the coming of the Heavenly Bridegroom, that we might be with Him for all eternity.

In the meantime, her heart seemed to be a helpless captive, and she confessed that she was sick with love. She did not feel she could contain any more. Let us aspire to have hearts that are captivated by Jesus, and that are filled to overflowing with love for Him!

October 7

Brethren, I do not count myself to have apprehended.
PHILIPPIANS 3:13

T he Apostle Paul did not think that he had arrived, and neither should we. We are all in need of change. Liu Shao-chi said, "Men should regard themselves as being in need of and capable of being changed. They should not look upon themselves as something unchanging, perfect, holy, and beyond reform…Otherwise men cannot make progress."

The trouble is that most of us resist change in ourselves. We are desperately anxious to see others change. Their personality quirks annoy us and we wish they would reform. But we are either oblivious to our own idiosyncrasies or satisfied to perpetuate them. We want to remove the splinter from someone else's eye but rather admire the pole in our own. Their faults and failures are hideous, whereas ours are darling.

The problem lies in our own wills. We can change if we really want to. If we face up to the fact that we have some undesirable traits in our character, we have made a start toward becoming better persons.

But how can we know what changes are needed? One way is for us to let the Word of God act as a mirror. As we read and study it, we see what we should be, and how far we fall short of the standard. When the Bible condemns something of which we are guilty, we should face the fact bravely and determine to do something about it.

Another help in learning where we are unChristlike is to listen carefully to our relatives and friends. Sometimes their suggestions come in a velvet glove; sometimes they come like a sledgehammer. Whether the remarks are veiled or blatant, we should get the message and accept it gratefully.

In fact, it is a very good practice to cultivate the loving criticism of friends. For instance, we could say, "I hope you will feel free to let me know of any undesirable traits in my personality or any ways I have that prove irritating to others." A real friend will do just that.

It is sad to think of people who go through life, making pests of themselves in the church, in the home, and in society, just because no one was willing to level with them or they were not willing to change.

If we take the time and trouble to find out the areas where we rub people the wrong way, and if we then take positive steps to eliminate these areas, we will be better people to live with.

October 8

Do not speak evil of one another.
JAMES 4:11

hile the word "gossip" is not found in the King James Version of the Bible, the idea is certainly included in such words as backbiting, evil speaking, and whispering. And it goes without saying that the practice is uniformly condemned.

To gossip means to reveal information about another person that is designed to put him in a bad light. In other words, the information is mean or unkind. Usually there is the element of secrecy or confidentiality; the person doing the gossiping would not want to be quoted.

Two women in Brooklyn were talking. One said, "Tilly told me that you told her what I said about her and I told you not to tell her." The other replied, "She's a mean thing. I told Tilly not to tell you I told her." The first speaker responded, "Well, I told Tilly I wouldn't tell you she told me—so don't tell her I did."

There are rare souls in the world who never say anything negative about another person. I have known such, and admire them beyond my powers of description. One told me that if he couldn't say anything good about someone else, he would say nothing. Another said he always tried to see something in other believers which reminded him of the Lord Jesus. A third started to say something negative about a third party, then he interrupted himself in the middle of the sentence and said, "No, it wouldn't be edifying." (I've been dying of curiosity ever since.)

Paul had heard that there were contentions among the Corinthians. In confronting them with the fact, he said that he had been told by the household of Chloe (1 Cor. 1:11). Clearly Chloe's family was not gossiping. They were sharing the information so that the problem might be solved.

The Apostle also wrote some strong words against Hymeneus, Alexander, and Philetus (1 Tim. 1:20; 2 Tim. 2:17), because they were harming the cause of Christ. He also warned Timothy about Phygellus, Hermogenes, and Demas (2 Tim. 1:15; 4:10), men who seemingly turned back after putting their hand to the plow. But this was not gossip. It was important intelligence for believers engaged in a common warfare.

When someone came to a noted preacher with a juicy bit of gossip, he took out a black notebook and told the gossip that he would write it down, have the talebearer sign it, and pass the information on to the person involved. It is said that he opened the book hundreds of times but never made a single entry.

October 9

Keep the commandments of the Lord and His statutes
which I command you today for your good.
DEUTERONOMY 10:13

Notice the last three words of today's verse—"for your good." All the commandments of the Lord are for our good. Many people do not realize this. They think of God as a stern Judge who imposes rules and regulations that take all the fun out of life. But it isn't so! He is interested in our welfare and pleasure, and designs all His laws toward that end.

Let us take a few of the Ten Commandments, for example. Why does God say that we should have no other gods? Because He knows that men become like the objects of their worship, and false gods lead to depravity.

Why does He say that we should not make graven images? Because idolatry is closely linked with demonism. "The things which the Gentiles sacrifice, they sacrifice to demons" (1 Cor. 10:20, NASB), and the purpose of demons is always to destroy.

Why does God set apart one day in seven for rest? Because He created man and knows that man's constitution requires rest from labor. Nations that have tried to enforce seven-day work weeks found that productivity slumped, and they had to abandon the experiment.

Why does God command children to obey their parents? Because it saves the children from lives of recklessness and riot, and even from premature death.

Why does God forbid adultery? Because He knows that it destroys the home and the family as well as the happiness of those involved.

Why does God forbid murder? Because it leads to guilt and remorse, to imprisonment and sometimes to capital punishment.

Why does God condemn coveting? Because sin begins in the mind. If we indulge it there, eventually we will commit the act. Unless we can control the fountain, we won't be able to control the stream that flows from it.

And so it is with other sins—taking God's Name in vain, stealing, bearing false witness, etc. We can't get away with them. They take their toll in our spirits, souls, and bodies. Every sin sets painful reflex actions in motion, robbing the sinner of peace, joy, and satisfaction. We reap what we sow. Our chickens come home to roost.

Years ago, someone wrote a book entitled, *The Kindly Laws of God.* They really are kindly because they are designed for our own good.

October 10

*Let all bitterness, wrath, anger, clamor, and evil speaking
be put away from you, with all malice.*
EPHESIANS 4:31

L ife brims with provocative situations that tempt a person to lose his temper. Perhaps you can identify with some of the following scenarios. A waiter spills hot coffee on you or makes you wait interminably for your food. You arrive home with your latest purchase only to find that the merchandise is defective. When you try to get a refund, the salesman is insolent. Or perhaps you have been given wrong information that causes you to miss your plane. The first week you have your new car, some careless driver puts a dent into the side of it. Then a store promises to deliver an appliance on a certain date. You stay home but no appliance arrives! Repeated delivery promises are broken. The clerk at the supermarket overcharges you, then is rude when you speak to him about it. Your neighbor hassles you over some minor squabble between her child and yours—and her child was obviously to blame. Another neighbor drives you up the wall with loud stereo music and wild parties. A fellow employee heckles you constantly, probably because of your Christian testimony. The computer makes an error on your monthly account, then in spite of your repeated protests by phone, the error reappears month after month. In your favorite sport, the referee makes a grossly bad call. Or the problem may be a clash of wills over TV programs in the living room of your home.

There is no way of avoiding some of these irritating situations. But for the believer, the important thing is how he reacts to them. The natural way is to explode in anger, to tell off the offender in a few well-chosen words. But when a Christian loses his temper, he loses his testimony also. There he stands, livid with rage, his eyes like piercing steel, his lips quivering. There is no way he can speak a word for the Lord Jesus. He is behaving like a man of the world. He is no longer a Bible but a libel.

The tragedy is that the person who has wronged him probably needs the gospel. Perhaps his annoying behavior is because of some crisis in his personal life. If he were just shown love and consideration, he might be won over to the Savior.

Eruptions of temper have done much to nullify the witness of believers and to bring dishonor on the name of the Lord. A mad Christian is a poor advertisement for the faith.

October 11

If you have run with the footmen, and they have wearied you, then how can you contend with horses? And if in the land of peace, in which you trusted, they wearied you, then how will you do in the floodplain of the Jordan?

JEREMIAH 12:5

This is a good verse to challenge us when we are tempted to give up too quickly and too easily. If we can't face minor difficulties, how can we expect to face major ones? If we buckle under the petty blows of life, how will we bear up under the sledgehammer blows?

We hear of Christians who sulk and pout because someone has offended them. Others turn in their resignation because someone has criticized them. Still others get their nose out of joint because some pet idea has been voted down.

Folks with minor physical ailments often howl like a wounded bear. One wonders what they would do with a catastrophic illness. If a businessman can't cope with day to day problems, it is unlikely he will be able to face the big ones.

We all need a certain amount of tough-mindedness. By that we do not mean that we should be harsh or insensitive. Rather we mean that we should be able to bend with the punches. We need the resiliency that bounces back and carries on.

Perhaps you are facing a crisis today. At the moment it seems monumental. You are tempted to quit. And yet a year from now it won't seem important at all. This is the time when you should say with the psalmist, "For by Thee I can run upon a troop; and by my God I can leap over a wall" (Ps. 18:29, NASB).

The unidentified writer of Hebrews makes an interesting observation to those whom he was challenging to endure. He says, "You have not yet resisted to bloodshed" (Heb. 12:4). In other words, you have not paid the ultimate price—martyrdom. If Christians go to pieces over a broken dish or a lost cat or a disappointed love affair, what would they do if they were faced with martyrdom?

Most of us would have quit long ago if we gave in to our feelings. But you don't quit in the Christian warfare. You pick yourself up from the ground, shake off the dust, and move forward into the conflict. Victory in the minor skirmishes will help us win the major battles.

October 12

Look, all you who kindle a fire, who encircle yourselves with sparks:
walk in the light of your fire and in the sparks you have kindled—
this you shall have from My hand: you shall lie down in torment.
ISAIAH 50:11

There is a right and a wrong way of doing everything, and this is certainly true in the matter of obtaining guidance. Today's verse describes the wrong way. It pictures a man building a bonfire, then using the fire and the sparks to provide illumination for his path.

Notice that there is no mention of consulting the Lord. There is no suggestion that the man has made it a matter of prayer. He has unbounded confidence that he knows the best way. In his arrogant independence, he leans on his own understanding. In Henley's words, he is the master of his own fate and the captain of his own soul.

But notice the aftermath! "This you shall have from My hand; you shall lie down in torment." The man who manufactures his own guidance is heading for trouble. Anyone who is that headstrong and willful will live to regret it. He will learn by experience that God's way is the best way.

The preceding verse (v. 10) gives us the right way of obtaining guidance. It says, "Who among you fears the Lord? Who obeys the voice of His Servant? Who walks in darkness and has no light? Let him trust in the name of the Lord and rely upon his God." Notice three things about this man. First of all, he fears the Lord in the sense that he fears displeasing Him or walking in independence of Him. Second, he obeys the voice of God's Servant, the Lord Jesus. Third, he is willing to admit that he walks in darkness and has no light. He acknowledges that he does not know which way to go.

What should such a person do? He should trust in the name of the Lord and rely on his God. In other words, he should acknowledge his own ignorance, ask the Lord to guide him, and depend completely on the divine guidance.

Our God is a God of infinite wisdom and love. He knows what is best for us and designs only what is for our good.

> *He knows, He loves, He cares;*
> *Nothing this truth can dim;*
> *He does the very best for those*
> *Who leave the choice to Him.*

October 13

Or what man is there among you who, if his son asks for bread,
will give him a stone?
MATTHEW 7:9

he question calls for a negative answer. Ordinarily a father wouldn't give his son a stone in place of bread. Certainly the Heavenly Father would never do it.

But the sad fact is that we sometimes do that very thing. People come to us in deep spiritual need. Perhaps we are insensitive to what is really troubling them. Or we put them off with some surface panacea instead of sharing the Lord Jesus with them.

E. Stanley Jones illustrates this with a story he tells on himself (it takes a great man to tell a story that discloses a personal failure). "When the (Indian) Congress members in their newly acquired powers were sometimes using these powers for themselves instead of the country's good, it was proving too much for Jawaharlal Nehru to bear. He said he was thinking of resigning the Prime Ministership and going off to regain his inner spirit. I saw him at that time, and at the close of the interview I offered him a bottle of tablets of the cereal grasses, containing all the known vitamins. He took the bottle with thanks but added, 'My problem is not physical,' implying that it was spiritual. Instead of offering him grace, I offered him grass. He asked for bread, and I gave him a stone...I knew I had the answer, but I didn't know how to say it. I was afraid of offending the great man. I should have remembered the motto on the Sat Tal Ashram wall: 'There's no place in which Jesus Christ is out of place.' But I didn't. I remembered my hesitations and they prevailed.

"I offered him grass tablets when he really wanted grace—the grace and power that would heal him at the heart. Then he could have said, 'I am healed at the heart. Now let the world come on—the world of impossible problems. I'm ready.'"

I am afraid that the experience of Dr. Jones is all too familiar to many of us. We encounter people who have deep spiritual needs. They drop some word that provides a wide open door for us to minister Christ to them. But, we fail to take advantage of it. We either suggest some band-aid remedy for a spiritual wound or we change the subject to something of trivial value.

Prayer: *Lord, help me to seize every opportunity to witness for You, to enter every opened door. Help me to overcome my hesitations, giving bread and grace where they are needed.*

October 14

You shall know the truth, and the truth shall make you free.
JOHN 8:32

People often quote this verse, forgetting that it is part of a conditional promise. The previous verse says, "Then Jesus said to those Jews who believed Him, If you abide in My word, you are My disciples indeed." Then follows the promise, "And you shall know the truth, and the truth shall make you free." In other words, the liberating power of the truth depends on our continuing in His Word.

It is not enough just to know the truth in an intellectual sense. We must obey it and practice it. As we live by the precepts of the Bible, we are freed from innumerable evils.

As soon as we obey the gospel call, we are freed from guilt and condemnation and introduced into the liberty of the sons of God.

Then we are freed from sin as master. It no longer holds the upper hand in our lives.

We are free from the law. Not that we become lawless, but we are now enlawed to Christ. We are henceforth motivated to holiness by love to the Savior rather than by the fear of punishment.

We enjoy freedom from fear because perfect love casts out fear. God is now our loving heavenly Father, not a stern Judge.

We are free from the bondage of Satan. He no longer leads us about at will.

We are freed from sexual immorality, having escaped the corruption that is in the world through lust.

We are free from false teaching. God's Word is truth, and the Holy Spirit leads His people into all truth, and teaches them to discern truth from error. Those who continue in His Word are freed from superstition and from the dominion of evil spirits. What an emancipation this is—to be set free from the power of demonic forces!

We are freed from the fear of death. No longer the king of terrors, death ushers the soul into the presence of the Lord. To die is gain.

We are freed from enslaving habits, from the love of money and from hopelessness and despair. Henceforth the language of our heart is:

> *Low at Thy feet, Lord Jesus; this is the place for me;*
> *There I have learned sweet lessons, truth that has set me free.*
> *Free from myself, Lord Jesus, free from the ways of men;*
> *Chains of thought that once bound me never will bind again.*

October 15

O Jerusalem, Jerusalem...How often I wanted to gather your children together, as a hen gathers her chicks under her wings, but you were not willing!
MATTHEW 23:37

1 t has been called "the passing of religious opportunity." It means that people are favored with a marvelous visitation, a glorious opportunity, but they fail to seize it.

That is what happened to Jerusalem. The Incarnate Son of God walked its dusty streets. Its ochre-tinted buildings looked down on the Creator and Sustainer of the universe. The people heard His matchless words and saw Him perform miracles that no other man had ever performed. But they failed to appreciate Him. They would not receive Him.

Things would have been so much better for them if they had. Conditions would have been like those described in Psalm 81:13-16: "Oh, that My people would listen to Me, that Israel would walk in My ways! I would soon subdue their enemies, and turn My hand against their adversaries. The haters of the Lord would pretend submission to Him, but their fate would endure forever. He would have fed them also with the finest of wheat; and with honey from the rock I would have satisfied you."

Isaiah also describes what might have been. "Oh, that you had heeded My commandments! Then your peace would have been like a river, and your righteousness like the waves of the sea" (Isa. 48:18).

Bret Harte wrote, "Of all the words of tongue or pen, the saddest are, 'It might have been.'"

Think of those who have rejected the gospel call. Jesus of Nazareth passed by but they missed Him. Now they are living empty lives and facing an eternity of doom.

Or think of those believers who heard the call of Christ to some specific sphere of service but failed to respond. They have no idea of the present blessings and eternal rewards which they have missed.

It is true that sometimes opportunity knocks only once. Though it is laden with choicest treasures, it may seem at the moment to conflict with personal plans or to involve personal sacrifice. It represents God's very best for us, but for reasons of our own we let the opportunity pass. We refuse His best and settle for His second best. All the time He is saying, "I would, but you would not."

October 16

For the wrath of God is revealed from heaven against all ungodliness
and unrighteousness of men, who suppress the truth in unrighteousness
ROMANS 1:18

A t selected times in human history, God has burst forth in judgment on men in order to show His extreme displeasure at certain sins they have committed. Obviously He does not strike men dead every time these sins are committed. If He did, the population of the world would be drastically reduced. But He has gone on record on isolated occasions to warn mankind that such ungodliness and unrighteousness will not go unpunished. If He does not deal with it in time, He most surely will in eternity.

When God looked down and saw that the earth was corrupt and filled with violence, He sent a cataclysmic flood, destroying the world (Gen. 6:13). Only eight people escaped with their lives.

Later the cities of Sodom and Gomorrah became centers of homosexuality (Gen. 19:1-13). Sodom was also guilty of pride, fullness of bread, and prosperous ease (Ezek. 16:49). God revealed His wrath from heaven by raining fire and brimstone on these cities, consigning them to perpetual extinction.

"Nadab and Abihu died before the Lord, when they offered strange fire" (Num. 3:4). They should have used fire from the altar (Lev. 16:12), but they decided to approach God in some other way. By smiting them with instant death, the Lord warned future generations against attempts to approach Him in any way other than the way He has appointed.

Nebuchadnezzar, King of Babylon, failed to acknowledge the Most High who rules in the affairs of men. Instead he claimed full credit for all the glory of Babylon. God punished him with madness. The king was driven away from men to live like an animal in the field. He ate grass like oxen, his body was wet with the dew of heaven, his hair had grown like eagles' feathers, and his nails like birds' claws (Dan. 4:33).

Ananias and Sapphira pretended to make a total sacrifice of their property to the Lord, but they secretly held back part for themselves (Acts 5:1-11). They both died suddenly as a warning against insincerity in worship and in service.

Some time later, Herod accepted worship instead of giving God the glory. He was consumed by worms and died (Acts 12:22-23).

Sinful men should not presume on the seeming silence and inaction of God. Just because He doesn't always punish sin instantly doesn't mean that He won't punish it ultimately. In isolated instances down through the years, He has given His verdict and revealed the penalties that follow.

October 17

Buy the truth, and do not sell it.
PROVERBS 23:23

here is often a price to be paid in obtaining the truth of God, and we should be willing to pay the price, whatever it may be. Once having obtained the truth, we should not give it up.

The verse is not to be taken with such strict literalness that we would buy Bibles and Christian literature, but would not sell them under any circumstances. Buying the truth here means making great sacrifices to achieve the knowledge of divine principles. It may mean hostility from one's family, loss of employment, separation from religious ties, financial loss, or even physical abuse.

To sell the truth means to compromise it or abandon it altogether. We should never be willing to do that.

In his book, *Church in the House,* Arnot wrote: "It is a general law of human nature that what comes lightly, goes lightly. What we gain by a hard struggle, we retain with a firmer grasp, whether it be our fortune or our faith. Those men who have obtained great wealth without any trouble or toil of their own, often scatter it and die in poverty. It is seldom that the man who gains a fortune by gigantic labor wastes the wealth he has won. In like manner, give me the Christian who has fought his way to his Christianity. If it is through fire and water that he has reached the wealthy place, he will not lightly leave his rich inheritance."

Saints of all ages have turned their back on family, fame, and fortune in order to enter the strait gate and walk the narrow way. Like the Apostle Paul, they have counted all else but loss for the excellency of the knowledge of Christ Jesus the Lord. Like Rahab they have renounced the idols of paganism and acknowledged Jehovah as the only true God, even if it seemed like betrayal of their own people. Like Daniel, they have refused to sell the truth, even if it meant being thrown into a den of bloodthirsty lions.

We live in a society when the spirit of the martyrs is largely gone. Men would rather compromise their faith than suffer for it. The voice of the prophet is missing. Faith is flabby. Convictions concerning the truth are condemned as dogmatism. In order to achieve a show of unity, men are willing to sacrifice fundamental doctrines. They sell the truth and buy it not.

But God will always have those choice souls who so value the hidden treasure of truth that they are willing to sell all that they have to buy it, and having bought it, they are unwilling to sell it at any price.

October 18

I have more understanding than all my teachers,
For Your testimonies are my meditation. I understand more than the ancients.
PSALM 119:99-100

 When we first read these verses, they sound like the words of an immature braggart or a full grown egotist. In fact, we might almost be surprised to find such boasts in the Bible. They seem rather sub-Christian.

However, as we study the verses more closely, we find a key that removes the difficulty. The psalmist gives a reason for his superior understanding. He says, "...for Your testimonies are my meditation." In other words, he is saying that he has more understanding than all his teachers who do not know the Scriptures. He understands more than the ancients whose knowledge was purely secular. He is not contrasting himself with other believers, but only with the men of this world.

And, of course, he is right! The humblest believer can see more on his knees than the most learned unbeliever can see on his tiptoes. Let us consider a few illustrations:

Here is a governmental leader assuring the people that there will be peace in the world if a certain course of action is followed. In a remote village, a Christian farmer hears the speech on his radio. He knows that there will never be peace until the Prince of Peace sets up His Kingdom on earth. Not till then will men beat their swords into plowshares and learn war no more. The farmer has more understanding than the diplomat.

Now meet a renowned scientist who teaches that the universe as we know it came into being without divine agency. Sitting in his class is a recent convert to Christ. Through faith this student understands that the worlds were framed by the word of God so that what is seen was not made out of things that are visible (Heb. 11:3). The student has insight that the scientist does not possess.

Then again we think of the psychologist who seeks to explain human behavior but who is unwilling to accept the fact of inborn sin. The believer who knows God's Word realizes that every man inherits an evil, corrupt nature, and that failure to recognize this can only lead to worthless solutions to man's problems.

So the psalmist was not indulging in idle boasting when he said he had more understanding than all his teachers. Those who walk by faith have better vision than those who walk by sight. Those who meditate on God's testimonies see truths that are hidden from the wise and prudent.

October 19

What shall I render to the Lord for all His benefits toward me?
I will take up the cup of salvation, and call upon the name of the Lord.
PSALM 116:12-13

n the matter of our soul's salvation, there is nothing we can do to earn or deserve it. We cannot put God in our debt or reimburse Him in any way, because salvation is a gift of grace.

The proper response to God's free offer of eternal life is first to take the cup of salvation, that is, to accept it by faith. Then we should call upon the name of the Lord, that is, thank and praise Him for the unspeakable gift.

Even after we are saved there is nothing we can do to repay the Lord for all His benefits toward us. *"Were the whole realm of nature mine, that were an offering far too small."* However, there is a fitting response we can make, and that is the most reasonable thing we can do. *"Love so amazing, so divine, demands my soul, my life, my all."*

If the Lord Jesus gave His body for us, the least we can do is give our bodies for Him.

Pilkington of Uganda said, "If He is King, He has a right to all." C.T. Studd said, "When I came to see that Jesus Christ had died for me, it didn't seem hard to give up all for Him."

Borden of Yale prayed, "Lord Jesus, I take hands off as far as my life is concerned. I put Thee on the throne in my heart."

Betty Scott Stam prayed, "I give myself...my life, my all, utterly to Thee, to be Thine forever."

Charles Haddon Spurgeon said, "In that day, when I surrendered myself to my Savior, I gave Him my body, my soul, my spirit; I gave Him all I had, and all I shall have for time and for eternity. I gave Him all my talents, my power, my faculties, my eyes, my ears, my conscience, my limbs, my emotions, my judgment, my whole manhood, and all that could come of it, whatever fresh capacity or new capability I might be endowed with."

Finally, Isaac Watts reminded us that *"drops of grief can ne'er repay the debt of love I owe,"* then added, *"Dear Lord, I give myself away, 'tis all that I can do."*

The passion of Jesus—His bleeding hands and feet, His wounds, His tears—demand one fitting response: the sacrifice of our lives for Him.

October 20

And David said with longing, Oh, that someone would give me a drink of water
from the well of Bethlehem, which is by the gate!
1 CHRONICLES 11:17

Bethlehem was David's hometown. He knew all its streets and lanes, the marketplace, and the community well. But now the Philistines had a garrison in Bethlehem and David was holed up in the Cave of Adullam. When three of his men heard David yearn for a drink of water from the well at Bethlehem, they broke through the enemy lines and brought the water to him. He was so moved by this courageous act of love and devotion that he could not drink the water, but rather poured it out as a libation to the Lord.

We may think of David here as a picture of the Lord Jesus. Just as Bethlehem was David's place, so the entire "earth is the Lord's and the fullness thereof." David should have been on the throne but instead he was in the cave. Similarly our Lord should be enthroned by the world but instead He is rejected and disowned. We can liken David's longing for water to the Savior's thirst for the souls of men all over the world. He longs to be refreshed by seeing His creatures saved from sin, self, and the world. David's three courageous men picture those intrepid soldiers of Christ who throw aside considerations of personal comfort, convenience and safety in order to fulfill the desire of their Commander in chief. They carry the good news to all the world, then offer their converts to the Lord as a sacrifice of love and devotion. David's emotional reaction suggests the Savior's response when He sees His sheep crowding to Him from every tribe and nation. He sees of the travail of His soul, and is satisfied (Isa. 53:11).

In David's case, he didn't have to command, coax, or cajole his men. The slightest hint was all they needed; they welcomed it as an order from their commander.

What then shall we do when we know the longing of the heart of Christ for those whom He purchased with His precious blood? Must we have high pressure missionary appeals and altar calls? Is it not enough to hear Him ask, "Whom shall I send, and who will go for us?" Shall it be said of us that we are unwilling to do for our Commander what David's men were willing to do for him? Or shall we say to Him, "Your slightest longing is my command"?

October 21

Enter by the narrow gate; for wide is the gate and broad is the way that leads to destruction, and there are many who go in by it. Because narrow is the gate and difficult is the way which leads to life, and there are few who find it.

MATTHEW 7:13-14

When you look out at the religious world today, you see numerous religions, denominations and cults. And yet basically there are only two religions, as suggested in today's text. On the one hand there is the wide gate and the broad, well-traveled way that leads to destruction. On the other is the strait gate and sparsely traveled, narrow way that leads to life. All religions can be classified under one or the other. The feature that distinguishes the two is this: one religion tells what man must do to earn or deserve salvation; the other tells what God has done to provide salvation for man.

The true Christian faith is unique in that it calls on men to receive eternal life as a gift by faith. All other religions tell men that they must earn their salvation by works or by character. The gospel tells how Christ finished the work necessary for our redemption. All other systems tell men what they must do to redeem themselves. It is the difference between DOING and DONE.

The popular idea is that good people go to heaven and bad people go to hell. But the Bible teaches that there are no good people, and that the only ones who go to heaven are sinners saved by God's grace. The Christian gospel eliminates boasting; it tells man that there are no meritorious deeds he can do to win God's favor because he is dead in trespasses and sins. All other religions cater to man's pride by implying that there is something he can do to save himself or to assist in his salvation.

All false religions are "a way that seems right to a man" but are also the way which ends in death (Prov. 14:12). Salvation by believing on the Lord Jesus Christ seems "too easy" to men, but this is the way that leads to life. In false religions Christ is nothing or only something. In the true Christian faith Christ is everything.

In other religions there can be no real assurance of salvation because a person never knows whether he has done enough good works or the right kind. The believer in Christ can know he is saved because it isn't a question of his works but rather of Christ's work for him.

Only two religions—one of law, the other of grace. One of works, the other of faith. One of doing, the other of believing. One of trying, the other of trusting. The first leads to condemnation and death, the second to justification and life.

October 22

Now Joshua the son of Nun was full of the spirit of wisdom,
for Moses had laid his hands on him; so the children of Israel heeded him,
and did as the Lord had commanded Moses.
DEUTERONOMY 34:9

O ne important insight we gather from this verse is that Moses appoint-ed Joshua as his successor, knowing that his own ministry would be coming to an end. In doing so, he set a good example for others who are in places of spiritual leadership. Some may think that this is too elementary to emphasize, but the fact is that there is often gross failure to train successors and to turn work over to them. There seems to be an innate resistance to the idea that we are replaceable.

Sometimes this is a problem that faces an elder in a local fellowship. Perhaps he has served faithfully for many years, but the day is approaching when he will no longer be able to shepherd the flock. Yet it is hard for him to train a younger man to take his place. He may see young men as threats to his position. Or he may contrast their inexperience with his own maturity and conclude that they are quite unsuitable. It is easy for him to forget how inexperienced he was at one time, and how he came to his present maturity by being trained to do the work of an overseer.

This can also be a problem on the mission field. The missionary knows that he should train nationals to assume places of leadership. But he rationalizes that they cannot do it as well as he. And they make so many mistakes...and attendance at the meetings will drop if he does not do all the preaching. And anyway, they don't know how to lead. The answer to all these arguments is that he should look upon himself as being expendable. He should train the nationals and delegate authority to them until he works himself out of a job in that particular area. There are always untilled fields elsewhere. He never needs to be unemployed.

When Moses was replaced by Joshua, there was a smooth transition. There was no vacuum of leadership. The cause of God did not suffer trauma. That's the way it should be.

All God's servants should rejoice to see younger men raised up to places of leadership. They should count it a great privilege to share their knowledge and experience with these disciples, then turn the work over to them before they are forced to do so by the hand of death. They should have the selfless attitude that Moses displayed on another occasion when he said, "Would God that all the Lord's people were prophets."

October 23

He will not speak on His own authority, but whatever He hears He will speak;
and He will tell you things to come. He will glorify Me,
for He will take of what is Mine and declare it to you.
JOHN 16:13-14

W hen the Lord Jesus said that the Holy Spirit would not speak of Himself, He did not mean that the Spirit would never make any reference to Himself. Rather, the thought is that the Spirit would not speak on His own authority or independently of God the Father. This is borne out by the words that follow: "…whatsoever He shall hear, that shall He speak." The New American Standard Bible reads, "He will not speak on His own initiative."

But having said that, we should add that the Holy Spirit does not ordinarily talk about Himself. One of His characteristic ministries is to glorify Christ. Jesus said, "He shall glorify Me: for He shall receive of Mine, and shall show it unto you."

This means that when we hear ministry that exalts the Lord Jesus Christ, we can be sure that it is Spirit-inspired. On the other hand, when we hear messages that glorify the speaker rather than the Lord, we can be sure that the Spirit is grieved. He cannot witness to the greatness of Jesus and the greatness of the speaker at the same time.

"The most spiritual teaching will ever be characterized by a full and constant presentation of Christ. He will ever form the burden of such teaching. The Spirit cannot dwell on aught but Jesus. Of Him He delights to speak. He delights in setting forth His attractions and excellencies. Hence, when a man is ministering by the power of the Spirit of God, there will always be more of Christ than anything else in his ministry. There will be little room in such ministry for human logic and reasoning…The Spirit's sole object…will ever be to set forth Christ" (C. H. MACKINTOSH).

In that connection, the evangelical world should reconsider the practice of introducing speakers by extravagant recitals of academic achievements and theological honors. It is unrealistic to praise a man to the skies and then expect him to preach in the power of the Holy Spirit.

One great test of written ministry is whether it glorifies the Lord Jesus. I remember reading a book on the Person and work of the Holy Spirit. At first I thought it strange that the author seemed to spend more time on the moral excellencies of Christ than on the Holy Spirit. Then I realized that this presented a true view of the Person and work of the Spirit.

Jim Elliot wrote in his journal, "If men were filled with the Spirit, they would not write books on that subject, but on the Person whom the Spirit has come to reveal. Occupation with Christ is God's object, not fullness of the Spirit."

October 24

And anyone not found written in the Book of Life was cast into the lake of fire.
REVELATION 20:15

T he subject of hell generates enormous resistance in the human heart. This resistance is most often expressed in the question, "How could a God of love sustain an everlasting hell?"

If Paul were answering the question, he would probably say at the outset, "Who are you to reply against God?" or "Let God be true and every man a liar." *Translation:* the creature really has no right to question the Creator. If God sustains an everlasting hell, He has valid reasons for doing so. We have no right to question His love or His justice. Yet we are given sufficient information in the Bible to vindicate God in this matter.

First of all, we know that God did not make hell for man, but for the devil and his angels (Mt. 25:41).

We also know that it is not God's desire that any should perish, but that all should come to repentance (2 Pet. 3:9). If any man goes to hell, it is a great sorrow to the heart of the Lord.

It is man's sin that causes the problem. The holiness, righteousness, and justice of God demand that sin be punished. The divine decree is, "The soul who sins shall die" (Ezek. 18:4). This is not arbitrary on God's part. It is the only attitude that a Holy Being can take toward sin.

God could have let the matter rest there. Man sinned, therefore he must die.

But God's love intervened. In order that man might not perish eternally, He went to the ultimate extreme to provide a way of salvation. He sent His unique Son to die as a Substitute for sinful men, paying the penalty for them. It was wonderful grace on the Savior's part to bear man's sins in His body on the cross.

Now God offers eternal life as a free gift to all who repent of their sins and believe on the Lord Jesus Christ. He will not save men against their will. They must choose the way of life.

Frankly there is nothing else that God could have done. He has already done more than could be expected. If men refuse His free offer of mercy, there is no alternative. Hell is the deliberate choice of those who refuse heaven.

To charge God with blame for sustaining an everlasting hell is completely unjust. It overlooks the fact that He emptied heaven of its Best so that earth's worst might never know the agonies of the lake of fire.

October 25

...There is a friend who sticks closer than a brother.
PROVERBS 18:24B

T he friendship of Jesus is a theme that evokes a warm response in the hearts of His people everywhere. When He was on earth, He was derided as "a friend of tax collectors and sinners (Mt. 11:19), but Christians have taken the taunt and converted it to a title of honor.

Before going to the cross, our Lord called His disciples "friends." "You are My friends if you do whatever I command you. No longer do I call you servants, for a servant does not know what his master is doing; but I have called you friends, for all things that I heard from My Father I have made known to you" (Jn. 15:14-15).

Some of our best-loved hymns take up this theme; for example, "What a friend we have in Jesus"; "There's not a friend like the lowly Jesus"; and "I've found a friend, oh, such a friend."

Why does the friendship of Jesus strike such a responsive chord? I think the primary reason is that many people are lonely. They may be surrounded by other people, yet not surrounded by friends. Or they may be largely cut off from meaningful communication with others. This is often the case with older people who have outlived their contemporaries.

Loneliness is cruel. It is bad for a person's physical, mental, and emotional health. It gnaws away at his morale, sets his nerves on edge, and makes him weary of life. Often it drives people to desperation so that they are willing to compromise with sin or take other insane plunges. To such people the friendship of Jesus comes with the healing properties of the balm of Gilead.

Another reason why His friendship is so appreciated is that it never fails. Human friends often let us down or drift out of our lives, but this Friend proves true and steadfast.

> *Earthly friends may fail and leave us,*
> *One day soothe, the next day grieve us;*
> *But this Friend will ne'er deceive us.*
> *Oh, how He loves!*

Jesus is the Friend who sticks closer than a brother. He is the Friend who loves at all times (Prov. 17:17).

The fact that the Lord Jesus is not bodily present with us does not set a limit on the reality of His friendship. Through the Word He speaks to us, and in prayer we speak to Him. It is in this way that He makes Himself real to us as the Friend we need. It is in this way that He answers the prayer,

> *Lord Jesus, make Thyself to me a living, bright reality;*
> *More present to faith's vision keen than any earthly object seen;*
> *More dear, more intimately nigh than e'en the closest earthly tie.*

October 26

Beloved, I beg you as sojourners and pilgrims, abstain from fleshly lusts which war against the soul.
1 PETER 2:11

Peter reminds his readers that they are strangers and pilgrims, a reminder that was never more needed than today. Pilgrims are people who are travelling from one country to another. The country they are passing through is not their own; they are aliens in it. It is the country to which they are going that is their homeland.

The hallmark of a pilgrim is a tent. Thus, when we read that Abraham dwelt in tents with Isaac and Jacob, we are to understand that he considered Canaan an alien land (even though it had been promised to him). He lived in a temporary dwelling because he "looked for the city which hath the foundations, whose builder and maker is God" (Heb. 11:10, RV). So the pilgrim is not a settler. He is a man on the move.

Because he is going on a long journey, he travels light. He does not allow himself to be weighed down with a lot of material possessions. He cannot afford to be burdened with unnecessary baggage. He must jettison anything that hinders his mobility.

Another feature of the pilgrim is that he is different from the people around him who are at home. He does not conform to their lifestyle, their habits, or even their form of worship. In the case of the Christian pilgrim, this means that he heeds Peter's admonition to abstain from "fleshly lusts, which war against the soul." He does not allow his character to be molded by his environment. He is in the world, but not of it. He passes through an alien country without adopting its mores and value judgments.

If the pilgrim is passing through hostile territory, he is careful not to fraternize with the enemy. That would constitute disloyalty to his leader. He would be a traitor to the cause.

The Christian pilgrim is passing through enemy territory. This world gave our Leader nothing but a cross and a grave. To befriend such a world is to betray the Lord Jesus. The cross of Christ has severed any ties which ever bound us to the world. We do not covet the world's praise or fear its condemnation.

The pilgrim is sustained on his journey by the knowledge that every day's march brings him that much closer to home. He knows that once he reaches his destination, he will quickly forget all the hardships and dangers of the way.

October 27

*There is neither Jew nor Greek, there is neither slave nor free,
there is neither male nor female; for you are all one in Christ Jesus.*
GALATIANS 3:28

1 n reading a verse like this, it is tremendously important to know what it means and what it does not mean. Otherwise we might find ourselves adopting grotesque positions that do violence to the rest of Scripture and to the facts of life.

The key to the verse is found in the words, "in Christ Jesus." Those words describe our position, that is, what we are in the sight of God. They do not refer to our everyday practice, that is, what we are in ourselves or in the society in which we live.

What the verse is saying, then, is that there is neither Jew nor Greek as far as standing before God is concerned. Both the believing Jew and the believing Gentile are in Christ Jesus and therefore both stand before God in a position of absolute favor. Neither has any advantage over the other. It does not mean that physical differences or temperamental distinctions are abolished.

In Christ Jesus, there is neither bond nor free. The slave finds the same acceptance through the Person and work of Christ that the free man does. And yet, in everyday life, the social distinctions persist.

There is neither male nor female in Christ Jesus. A believing woman is complete in Christ, accepted in the Beloved, justified freely—just the same as a believing man. She has the same freedom of access into the presence of God.

But the verse must not be pressed to refer to everyday life. The sexual distinction remains—male and female. The resultant roles remain—father and mother. The divinely appointed positions of authority and subjection to that authority remain—the man is given the place of headship and the woman that of subjection to the authority of the man. The New Testament even specifies difference in the ministries of the man and the woman in the church (1 Tim. 2:8, 12; 1 Cor. 14:34-35). Those who argue that there should be neither male nor female in the church are forced to twist these Scriptures, assign unworthy motives to the Apostle Paul, or even question the inspiration of his words in these passages.

What they must understand is that whereas racial, social, and sexual differences are abolished as far as standing before God is concerned, they are not abolished in everyday life. They should also realize that these differences have nothing to do with inferiority. The Gentile, the slave, the woman are not inferior to the Jew, the free man, or the male. In many ways they may be superior. Instead of trying to rewrite God's order in creation and in providence, they should accept it and rejoice in it.

October 28

There is one who scatters, yet increases more;
and there is one who withholds more than is right, but it leads to poverty.
PROVERBS 11:24

T he Holy Spirit here lets us in on a delightful secret. It is contrary to all that we would expect, and yet is invariably true. The secret is this: the more you give, the more you have. The more you hoard, the less you have. Generosity multiplies itself. Stinginess breeds poverty. "What I gave, I have; what I spent, I had; what I kept, I lost."

It doesn't mean that you will reap the same coinage that you sow, that the faithful steward will become financially rich. He may sow dollars and reap souls. He may sow kindness and reap friends. He may sow compassion and reap love.

It means that a generous person reaps rewards that others cannot know. He opens his mail and learns that the gift of money he sent met a critical need at just the right time and in exactly the right amount. He learns that a book he bought for a young believer was used by God to change the whole direction of a life. He hears that a kindness he showed in the Name of Jesus was a link in the chain of that person's salvation. He is deliriously happy. His joy knows no bounds. He would never trade places with others who seem to have more than he.

The other side of the truth is that hoarding leads to poverty. We really don't get pleasure out of money that is lying in the bank. It may delude us with a false sense of security, but it cannot provide true and lasting enjoyment. Any meager interest that the money may earn is peanuts compared with the thrill of seeing money used for the glory of Christ and the blessing of our fellow-men. The man who withholds more than is meet may have a large bank balance but he has a small joy balance in this life and a small credit balance in the bank of heaven.

Today's verse is intended not only to set forth a divine principle but also to issue a divine challenge. The Lord is saying to us, "Prove it for yourself. Make your loaves and fishes available to Me. I know you intended to have them for your own lunch. But if you turn them over to Me, there will be plenty for your own lunch and for thousands of others. You would feel awkward to eat your lunch while those around you were just sitting, watching you eat. But think of the satisfaction of knowing that I used your lunch to feed the multitude."

> *We lose what on ourselves we spend*
> *We have as treasure without end*
> *Whatever, Lord, to Thee we lend,*
> *Who givest all.*
> —CHARLES WORDSWORTH

October 29

But whoso hath the world's goods, and beholdeth his brother in need, and shutteth up his compassion from him, how doth the love of God abide in him?
1 JOHN 3:17, RV

1n medical circles, it would be unthinkable to have a cure for cancer and not share it with cancer patients throughout the world. To withhold the cure would betray a callous and inhumane lack of compassion.

The Apostle John paints a parallel picture in the spiritual realm. Here is a man, a professing believer, who has accumulated a fair amount of wealth. He lives in luxury, comfort, and ease. All around him is a world of enormous spiritual and physical need. Millions throughout the world have never heard the gospel. They live in darkness, superstition, and hopelessness. Many of them are suffering the ravages of famine, war, and natural disaster. The man of wealth is oblivious to all this need. He is able to block out the moans of a sobbing, suffering humanity. He could help if he wanted to, but he prefers to hold on to his money.

It is at this point that John drops his bomb. He asks, "How does the love of God abide in him?" The question implies, of course, that the love of God does not dwell in him. And if the love of God does not dwell in him, there is valid reason for doubting that he is a true believer.

This is very serious. The church today exalts the man of wealth, appoints him to the board of elders, and points him out to visitors. The sentiment prevails, "It's nice to see rich Christians." But John asks, "If he is a real Christian, how can he hold on to all that surplus wealth when so many are starving for bread?"

It seems to me that this verse forces us to one of two courses of action. On the one hand we can reject the plain meaning of John's words, stifle the voice of conscience, and condemn the man who dares preach the message. Or we can receive the word with meekness, use our wealth to meet our brother's need, and have a conscience void of offense toward God and man. The believer who is satisfied with a modest standard of living so that everything above that can go into the work of the Lord, can live at peace with God and with his needy brother.

October 30

I have no greater joy than to hear that my children walk in truth.
3 JOHN 4

T he Apostle John was certainly not unaware of the joy of personal soul-winning. It brings tremendous spiritual exhilaration to lead a sinner to the Lord Jesus. But for John, a greater joy—in fact, the greatest joy, was to see his children in the faith going on steadfastly for the Lord.

Dr. M. R. DeHaan wrote, "There was a time in my ministry that I often said, 'The greatest joy of a Christian is to lead a soul to Christ.' As the years passed, I changed my mind…So many, over whom we rejoiced when they made their professions, soon fell by the wayside, and our joy came to ultimate grief and sorrow. But to come back to a place years afterward and find 'converts' growing in grace, walking in the truth—this is the greatest joy."

When asked for the thing that brings more joy than anything else in life, LeRoy Eims said, "When the person you have led to Christ grows and develops into a dedicated, fruitful, mature disciple who then goes on to lead others to Christ and help them in turn as well."

It is not surprising that this should provide the greatest joy. The spiritual has its parallel in the natural. There is great joy when a baby is born, but there is always the nagging question. "How will he turn out?" How pleased the parents are when he matures and proves to be a man of excellent character and accomplishments! So we read in Proverbs 23:15-16: "My son, if your heart is wise, My heart will rejoice—indeed, I myself; yes, my inmost being will rejoice when your lips speak right things."

One practical lesson that emerges from all this is that we should not be satisfied with superficial methods of evangelism and of discipleship. If we want spiritual children who will walk in the truth, we must be prepared to pour our lives into theirs, a costly process involving prayer, instruction, encouragement, counseling and correction.

October 31

A wise son makes a glad father, but a foolish son is the grief of his mother.
PROVERBS 10:1

W hat determines whether a son turns out to be wise or foolish? What are the factors that determine whether he becomes a John or a Judas?

Parental training is certainly one important consideration. This includes a thorough grounding in the sacred Scriptures. The sanctifying influence of the Word cannot be overemphasized.

It includes a home that is fortified by prayer. The mother of an outstanding evangelical preacher attributed his preservation from moral and doctrinal evil to the fact that she "wore out her knees in prayer for him."

It means the use of firm discipline so that the child learns to obey, and to submit to authority. We hear loud outcries today against strict discipline, but more lives have been wrecked by indulgence than by the use of the rod (Prov. 13:24; 23:13-14).

It means providing the child with the security of knowing he is loved. Discipline must be administered as an act of love and not of temper.

It means that the parents must provide a living example of what they profess. Hypocrisy in religion has proved a stumbling block to many children of Christian parents.

But then the child's will is also involved. When he leaves home, he is free to make his own decisions. Often children brought up in the same home under the same conditions turn out differently.

Two facts of life have to be faced. One is that most people have to get a taste of the world for themselves. The other is that most people prefer to learn through shame and disgrace rather than through wise counsel.

Wise parents do not pressure their children into making a profession of faith. If children want to come to the Lord, they should be encouraged. But if they are talked into a false profession, then abandon that profession in later years, they are harder to win for Christ. If Christian parents have done their best to raise a child in the fear and admonition of the Lord, only to have the child later make shipwreck, what then? For one thing, they should remember that the last chapter hasn't been written. No case is too difficult for the Lord. By continuing earnestly in prayer and by keeping channels of communication open, many have lived to see their prodigal return. In other cases, the prayers of parents have been answered after they themselves have gone home to be with the Lord.

November 1

In the morning sow your seed, and in the evening do not withhold your hand;
for you do not know which will prosper, either this or that,
or whether both alike will be good.
ECCLESIASTES 11:6

ur ignorance as to how and when God will use our service should prompt us to be tireless in buying up opportunities. The Lord often works when we least expect it, and He works in an infinite number of novel ways.

A Christian sailor, stationed at a naval air base, was standing near the corner of a hangar, witnessing to a buddy. A third sailor, out of sight around the corner, heard the gospel, became convicted of his sins, and was soundly converted. The fellow to whom the message was directly addressed did not respond.

A preacher, checking the acoustics of a new auditorium, boomed out the words of John 1:29, "Behold the Lamb of God, who takes away the sin of the world!" To all appearance there was no one listening. Again he sounded out the timeless words of John the Baptist: "Behold the Lamb of God, who takes away the sin of the world." The main floor was empty, but a workman in the first balcony was smitten by the message and turned to the Lamb of God for forgiveness and new life.

An American Bible teacher spoke to a young American tourist in a railroad station in Paris. (Both came from the same city in the United States and from the same neighborhood in that city). The young man was irritated to be confronted. He said, "Do you think you're going to save me in a Paris railroad station?" The Bible teacher replied, "No, I can't save you. But nothing happens by chance in life. It was no accident that we met here. I think that God is speaking to you and that you'd better listen." In the days that followed, a Christian gave the traveler a ride to Vienna, witnessing to him on the way. Back in the States, that same believer invited him to a Christian ranch in Colorado. On the last day of his stay at the ranch, the fellow was standing alone in the swimming pool. Soon another guest joined him in the water, spoke to him quietly about the Lord, and had the great joy of leading him to the Savior. Years later, the American Bible teacher was introduced to an earnest young disciple at the close of a meeting. The name sounded faintly familiar. Then he remembered. It was the tourist he had spoken to in a railroad station in Paris.

The moral, of course, is that we should be diligent for Christ in the morning and evening, in season and out of season. We never know which blow will break the granite or which word will be the life-giving one.

November 2

Therefore, my beloved brethren, be steadfast, immovable,
always abounding in the work of the Lord,
knowing that your labor is not in vain in the Lord.
1 CORINTHIANS 15:58

I t is not uncommon for a person to become discouraged in his service for the Lord and to quit. I suppose that most of us have faced that temptation at one time or another. Therefore, in today's reading I would like to share four passages that have been a tremendous encouragement to me and that have kept me from quitting. The first is Isaiah 49:4: "Then I said, I have labored in vain, I have spent my strength for nothing and in vain; yet surely my just reward is with the Lord, and my work with my God." There are moments, fortunately rare, when years of service for the Lord seem to evaporate into nothingness. All our work seems to have been wasted effort. It appears to be another case of "love's labor lost." But not so! Our verse assures us that God's justice will insure that we are royally rewarded. Nothing that is done for Him is ever in vain.

The second passage is Isaiah 55:10-11: "For as the rain comes down, and the snow from heaven, and do not return there, but water the earth, and make it bring forth and bud, that it may give seed to the sower and bread to the eater, so shall My word be that goes forth from My mouth; it shall not return to Me void, but it shall accomplish what I please, and it shall prosper in the thing for which I sent it." Those engaged in distributing the living Word of God are assured of success. Results are guaranteed. His Word is irresistible. Just as the armies of the world are powerless to prevent the rain and snow from falling, so all the hosts of demons and of men are unable to stop the Word from going forth and producing revolutions in human lives. We are on the winning side.

Then there is that remarkable encouragement in Matthew 10:40: "He who receives you receives Me, and he who receives Me receives Him who sent Me." Have you ever been snubbed because of your Christian testimony? Or ostracized? Or mocked? Or abused? Has someone slammed the door in your face? Well, don't take it too personally. In rejecting you, people are really rejecting the Savior. The way people treat you is the way they treat the Lord. How wonderful to be so closely linked with the Son of God!

Then, of course, there is 1 Corinthians 15:58 (quoted above). Paul has been setting forth the truth of the resurrection. If this life were all, then our labor would be in vain. However, beyond the grave lies the eternal glory. Everything done in the Lord's Name will be rewarded then. No loving service will have been fruitless or futile.

Christian service is the most glorious of all callings. There is never a valid reason for quitting. The encouragements of God's Word are enough to keep us from turning back.

November 3

Nevertheless the solid foundation of God stands, having this seal:
The Lord knows those who are His, and,
Let everyone who names the name of Christ depart from iniquity.
2 TIMOTHY 2:19

Even in the days of the apostles, there was a great deal of confusion in the religious world. Two men, for instance, were teaching the bizarre doctrine that the resurrection of believers was past. To us such an idea is crazy. But it was serious enough to overthrow the faith of some people. The question naturally arises, "Were these two men genuine Christians?"

We often face the same question today. Here is a prominent clergyman who denies the Virgin Birth. A seminary professor teaches that the Bible contains error. A college student claims to be saved by grace through faith, yet clings to Sabbath-keeping as an essential for salvation. A businessman tells of a conversion experience, yet remains in a church that venerates idols, teaching salvation through sacraments, and claims that its leader is infallible in matters of faith and morals. Are these people true Christians?

To be very frank, there are cases where we cannot know definitely whether a person's Christianity is genuine or counterfeit. Between the true and the false, the white and the black, there is a gray area. We cannot be sure in this area. Only God knows.

What is sure in a world of uncertainty is the foundation of God. Whatever He builds is firm and solid. There is a seal on His foundation and on that seal are two inscriptions. One presents the divine side, the other the human. The first is a declarative, the second an imperative.

The divine side is that the Lord knows those who are His. He knows those who genuinely belong to Him even if their actions are not always what they should be. On the other hand, He is aware of all pretense and hypocrisy, of all who have an outward show but no inward reality. We may not be able to distinguish the sheep from the goats, but He can and does.

The human side is that everyone who names the Name of Christ should depart from iniquity. This is how a man can prove the reality of his profession. Anyone who continues in sin loses credibility as far as his claim to being a Christian is concerned.

This, then, is our resource when we find it difficult to distinguish between wheat and tares. The Lord knows those who are His. All who claim to be can demonstrate it to others by separation from sin.

November 4

In this the children of God and the children of the devil are manifest:
Whoever does not practice righteousness is not of God,
nor is he who does not love his brother.
1 JOHN 3:10

Years ago, almost every home had a large family album in the living room. It had a stuffed leather cover embossed in gold. A leather strap with clasp extended from the right edge of the back cover over to the right side of the top cover where the clasp latched securely into its socket. The pages were of stiff, glossy paper-board, ornamented with floral patterns and gilt edges. On each side of a page were cut-out sections where photographs were inserted. When visitors looked through the album, they would often remark that "Josh looks just like his grandpa" or that "Sarah surely has the family likeness."

John's first epistle reminds me of that old family album because it pictures those who are members of God's family and who have the family likeness. However, here it is a matter of spiritual and moral resemblance rather than physical.

There are at least eight ways in which Christians are spiritual "look-alikes." The first is that they all say the same thing about Jesus. They confess that He is the Christ, that is, the Messiah or Anointed One (1 Jn. 4:2; 5:1). To them, Jesus and Christ are one and the same Person.

All Christians love God (5:2). Even though that love may often be weak and vacillating, there is never a time when a believer cannot look up into the face of God and say, "You know that I love You."

All Christians love the brethren (2:10; 3:10, 14; 4:7, 12). This is the hallmark of all who have passed from death to life. Because they love God, they love those who are born of God.

Those who love God characteristically keep His commandments (3:24). Their obedience is motivated, not by fear of punishment, but by love to Him who gave His all.

Christians do not practice sin (3:6, 9; 5:18). True, they commit acts of sin, but sin is not the dominating power in their lives. They are not sinless but they do sin less.

Members of God's family practice righteousness (2:29; 3:7). It is not just that they do not habitually sin—that could be negative and passive. They reach out to others with deeds of righteousness—that is positive and active.

The seventh characteristic of members of God's family is that they do not love the world (2:15). They realize that the world is a system that man has built up in opposition to God, and that to be a friend of the world is to be an enemy of God.

Finally, Christians overcome the world by faith (5:4). They see beyond the sham of passing things to those things that are eternal. They live for the things that are not seen.

November 5

Having faith and a good conscience.
1 TIMOTHY 1:19

T he conscience is a monitoring mechanism which God has given to man to approve right conduct and to protest against what is wrong. When Adam and Eve sinned, their consciences condemned them and they knew they were naked.

Like all other parts of man's nature, the conscience was affected by the entrance of sin so that it is not always completely reliable. The old maxim, "Let your conscience be your guide," is not an invariable rule. However, even in the most depraved, the conscience still flashes its red and green signals.

At the time of conversion a person's conscience is purged from dead works by the blood of Christ (Heb. 9:14). This means that he no longer depends on his own works to give him a favorable standing before God. His heart is sprinkled from an evil conscience (Heb. 10:22) because he knows that the sin question has been settled once for all by the work of Christ. Conscience does not condemn him any more as far as the guilt and condemnation of sin are concerned.

Henceforth the believer desires to have a conscience void of offense toward God and man (Acts 24:16). He desires to have a good conscience (1 Tim. 1:5, 19; Heb. 13:18; 1 Pet. 3:16). And he desires to have a pure conscience (1 Tim. 3:9).

The believer's conscience needs to be educated by the Spirit of God through the Word of God. In this way he develops an increasing sensitivity toward questionable areas of Christian conduct.

Believers who are excessively scrupulous over matters that are not right or wrong in themselves have a weak conscience. If they go ahead and do something that their conscience condemns, they sin (Rom. 14:23) and defile their conscience (1 Cor. 8:7).

The conscience is something like an elastic band. The more it is stretched, the more it loses its elasticity. Also, the conscience can be stifled. A man can so rationalize his wrong behavior that he can make the conscience say anything he wants it to say.

Unbelievers can have a seared conscience (1 Tim. 4:2), as if cauterized by a hot iron. By the continual rejection of the voice of conscience, they finally reach the stage where they are past feelings. It no longer hurts them to sin (Eph. 4:19).

God holds men responsible for what they do with their consciences. No divinely-given faculty can be abused with impunity.

November 6

So the ransomed of the Lord shall return, and come to Zion with singing,
with everlasting joy on their heads. They shall obtain joy and gladness;
sorrow and sighing shall flee away.
ISAIAH 51:11

In its setting, this prophecy of Isaiah looked forward to the joyous return of God's chosen people from their seventy-year captivity in Babylon.

It may also refer to Israel's still-future restoration when the Messiah will regather them to the land from all over the world. That, too, will be a time of great jubilation.

But in its widest sense, we are justified in applying the verse to the rapture of the Church. Awakened by the shout of the Lord, the voice of the archangel, and the trump of God, the bodies of the redeemed of all the ages will rise from the grave. Living believers, changed in a moment, will join them as they ascend to meet the Lord in the air. Then begins the grand processional to the Father's house.

It is quite possible that the entire route will be flanked by angelic hosts. At the head of the procession will be the Redeemer Himself, flushed with His glorious victory over death and the grave. Then come the ransomed throng, some from every tribe, tongue, people, and nation. Ten thousand times ten thousand and thousands of thousands, they are singing with all musical perfection, "Worthy is the Lamb that was slain to receive power, and riches, and wisdom, and strength, and honor and glory, and blessing."

Everyone in the multitude is a trophy of God's wonderful grace. Each was ransomed from sin and shame, and made a new creature in Christ Jesus. Some went through deep suffering for their faith, others laid down their lives for the Savior. But now all the scars and mutilations are gone, and the saints have their deathless, glorified bodies.

Abraham and Moses are there, with David and Solomon. There are the beloved Peter, James, John and Paul. Martin Luther, John Wesley, John Knox and John Calvin are there. But they are no more conspicuous now than God's hidden ones, unknown on earth, yet well-known in heaven.

Now the saints are marching into the King's palace. Sorrow and sighing are gone forever, and everlasting joy is on their heads. Faith has become sight and hope has received its long-awaited consummation. Loved ones greet each other with fervent embraces. Overflowing gladness prevails. Everyone is awed by the amazing grace that has brought them from the depths of sin to such heights of glory.

November 7

Go home to your friends, and tell them what great things
the Lord has done for you, and how He has had compassion on you.
MARK 5:19

When we are first saved, we think it is so simple, so wonderful that all our relatives will want to believe on the Savior when we tell them. Instead we find in some cases that they are resentful, suspicious, and hostile. They act as if we had betrayed them. Finding ourselves in such an atmosphere, we often respond in ways that actually hinder their coming to Christ. Sometimes we lash back at them, then become distant, moody, and withdrawn. Or we criticize them for their unChristian lifestyle, forgetting that they do not have the divine power necessary for meeting Christian standards. It is easy under such circumstances to give them the impression that we consider ourselves superior to them. Since they are likely to accuse us of a "holier than thou" attitude anyway, we should carefully avoid giving them just cause for doing so.

Another mistake we often make is to force the gospel down their throats. In our love for them and our zeal for their souls, we estrange them by our offensive evangelism.

One thing leads to another. We fail to show loving submission to our parents, as if our Christian faith released us from any obligation to obey them. Then we increasingly absent ourselves from home, spending the time at church services and with Christians. This, in turn, increases their resentment against church and Christians. When Jesus healed the demoniac, Legion, He told him to go home and tell his friends what great things the Lord had done for him. That is the first thing we should do—give a simple, humble, loving testimony of our conversion.

Then this should be coupled with the witness of a changed life. We should let our light so shine before them that they will see our good works, and glorify our Father in heaven (Mt. 5:16).

This will mean showing new honor, submission, love, and respect for our parents; taking their advice unless it conflicts with Scripture. We should be more helpful at home than we have ever been before—cleaning our room, washing dishes, taking out the trash—and all this without being asked.

It will mean taking criticism patiently without retaliating. They will be pleasantly stunned by our spirit of brokenness, especially if they have never seen it before. Little kindnesses help break down opposition—letters of appreciation, greeting cards, phone calls, and gifts. Instead of cutting ourselves off from our parents, we should spend time with them in an effort to strengthen relationships. Then they will be more likely to accept an invitation to attend a church meeting with us—and eventually to commit themselves to the Lord Jesus Christ.

November 8

Let each one remain in the same calling in which he was called.
1 CORINTHIANS 7:20

When a person becomes a Christian, he might think that he has to make a clean break with everything associated with his former life. To correct this thinking, the Apostle Paul lays down the general rule that a person should remain in the same calling in which he was at the time of his conversion. Let us consider this rule and suggest what it means and what it does not mean.

In its immediate context, the verse applies to a special marriage relationship. It is the case where one partner gets saved but the other does not. What should the believer do? Should he divorce his wife? No, says Paul, he should remain in that marriage relationship with the hope that his partner will be converted through his testimony.

In general, Paul's rule means that conversion does not require the violent disruption or forcible overthrow of pre-salvation relationships and associations that are not expressly forbidden by Scripture. For instance, a Jew need not resort to surgery in order to obliterate the physical mark of his Jewishness. Neither should a believing Gentile submit to some physical change like circumcision in order to distinguish him from the heathen. Physical features or marks are not what really matter. What God wants to see is obedience to His commandments.

A man who is a slave at the time of his new birth should not rebel against his servitude and thus bring trouble and punishment upon himself. He can be a good slave and a good Christian at the same time. Social position and class distinctions do not matter with God. However, if a slave can obtain his freedom by legitimate means, he should do so.

So much for what Paul's rule means. It should be obvious that there are important exceptions to the rule. For instance, it does not mean that a man in an ungodly occupation should continue in it. If a man is a bartender or operates a house of prostitution or a gambling casino, he will know by spiritual instinct that he has to make a change.

Another exception to the general rule has to do with religious associations. A new convert must not continue in any system where the great fundamentals of the Christian faith are denied. He must separate himself from any church where the Savior is dishonored. This would also apply to membership in social clubs where the Name of Christ is banned or even unwelcome. Loyalty to the Son of God requires that a believer resign from all such.

To summarize, then, the rule is that a new believer should remain in the calling in which he was called unless that calling is sinful and dishonoring to the Lord. He does not have to break with past associations unless they are clearly forbidden by the Word of God.

November 9

*What does it profit, my brethren, if someone says he has faith
but does not have works? Can faith save him?*
JAMES 2:14

James does not say that the man in today's verse has faith. The man himself says he has faith, but if he really had saving faith, he would have works also. His faith is a matter of words only, and that kind of faith cannot save anyone. Words without works are dead.

Salvation is not by works. Neither is it by faith plus works. Rather it is by the kind of faith that results in good works.

Why then does James say in verse 24 that a man is justified by works? Isn't this a flat contradiction of Paul's teaching that we are justified by faith? Actually, there is no contradiction. Both are true. The fact is that there are six different aspects of justification in the New Testament, as follows:

We are justified by God (Rom. 8:33)—He is the One who reckons us righteous.

We are justified by grace (Rom. 3:24)—God gives us justification as a free, undeserved gift.

We are justified by faith (Rom. 5:1)—we receive this gift by believing on the Lord Jesus Christ.

We are justified by blood (Rom. 5:9)—the precious blood of Christ is the price that was paid for our justification.

We are justified by power (Rom. 4:25)—the power that raised Jesus our Lord from the dead is the power that makes our justification possible.

We are justified by works (Jas. 2:24)—good works are the outward evidence to all that we have been truly justified.

It is not enough to testify to a conversion experience. We must demonstrate it by the good works that inevitably follow the new birth.

Faith is invisible. It is an unseen transaction that takes place between the soul and God. People cannot see our faith. But they can see the good works that are the fruit of saving faith. They have reason to doubt our faith until they see the works.

Abraham's good work was his willingness to slay his son as an offering to God (Jas. 2:21). Rahab's good work was betraying her country (Jas. 2:25). The reason they were "good" works is because they demonstrated faith in Jehovah. Otherwise they would have been bad works, namely, murder and treason.

The body separated from the spirit is dead. That's what death is—the separation of the spirit from the body. So faith without works is dead also. It is lifeless, powerless and inoperative.

A living body demonstrates that an invisible spirit dwells within. So good works are the sure sign that there is saving faith, invisible as it is, dwelling within the person.

November 10

Maintain the spiritual glow.
ROMANS 12:11, MOFFATT

ne of the laws that operates in the physical realm is that things tend to lose momentum or unwind or burn out. That is not a scientific statement of the law, but it gives the general idea.

We are told, for instance, that the sun is burning at a furious rate, and that although it can continue for a long time, its time-span is declining.

Bodies age, die, and return to dust. A pendulum set in motion by hand slows down and then stops. We wind a clock or watch and soon it needs to be rewound. Hot water cools off to room temperature. Metals tarnish and grow dim. Colors fade. Nothing lasts indefinitely and there is no perpetual motion. Change and decay affect everything.

The world itself grows old. Speaking of the heavens and the earth, the Scripture says, "They will perish, but You (God's Son) remain; and they will all grow old like a garment; like a cloak You will fold them up, and they will be changed" (Heb. 1:11-12).

Unfortunately, there seems to be a similar principle in the spiritual realm. It is true of individuals, churches, movements, and institutions.

Even if a person begins the Christian life brilliantly, there is always the danger of zeal abating, of power subsiding, and of vision ebbing. We grow weary, complacent, cold, and old.

The same is true of churches. Many have started on the crest of a great movement of the Holy Spirit. The fire continues to burn brightly for years. Then decline sets in. The church leaves its first love (Rev. 2:4). The honeymoon is over. Evangelistic fervor gives way to routine services. Doctrinal purity may be sacrificed for a worthless unity. At last an empty building is a silent witness that the glory has departed.

Movements and institutions are subject to decay. They may start off as mighty evangelistic outreaches, then become so engrossed in social work that the gospel is largely neglected. Or they may begin with the enthusiasm and spontaneity of the Spirit, then lapse into cold ritual and formality. We need to guard against spiritual decline. We need to experience what Norman Grubb calls continuous revival. We need to "maintain the spiritual glow."

November 11

He who answers a matter before he hears it, it is folly and shame to him.
PROVERBS 18:13

T he Living Bible paraphrases this verse, "What a shame—yes, how stupid!—to decide before knowing the facts!" This pinpoints an important lesson. You cannot make an intelligent decision until you hear all the facts. Unfortunately, many Christians do not wait to hear both sides of an issue. They form a judgment on the basis of one man's story, and often that judgment is totally wrong.

In 1979, Gary Brooks (fictitious name) was a member of the Board of Deacons of an evangelical church. He was extremely popular. He had a warm, outgoing personality. Whenever he entered a room full of people, it seemed to light up. He distinguished himself by serving the members of the church whenever they needed help. He was always attentive to the older folks in the congregation. His wife and two sons were also active in church affairs. The Brooks were looked on as a model family.

It was like an exploding bomb, therefore, when word got out that the elders had disciplined Gary by relieving him of his work as a deacon and asking him to refrain from participating in the communion service. Friends rallied to his defense and called on other church members to oppose the elders in this decision. The elders were at a disadvantage, not wishing to make a public announcement of all they knew. So they had to sit back and listen to Gary's virtues being extolled, knowing that there was another side to the story. And they had to take considerable abuse in the process.

What did the elders know? They knew that Gary's marriage was on the rocks because he had been carrying on an affair with his secretary. They knew that he had misappropriated church funds to finance his high lifestyle. They knew that he had enaged in unethical business practices, and that his testimony in the business world was negative. They also knew that he had lied to them when they confronted him with evidence of his wrongdoing.

Rather than submit to the discipline of the elders, Gary organized his friends in open defiance, even at the risk of splitting the church. Eventually, a few of his followers spoke to one of the elders and learned some of the sad facts, but then they were too ashamed to do an about face. So they continued to fight on his behalf.

Three lessons emerge from all of this for us. First, don't try to form a judgment until you know all the facts. Second, if you can't get all the facts, withhold your judgment. Finally, don't let the bonds of friendship pressure you into defending unrighteousness.

November 12

The first one to plead his cause seems right,
Until his neighbor comes and examines him.
PROVERBS 18:17

T he first part of this verse points out a failing that is common to most of us—we invariably present evidence in such a way as to put ourselves in the best possible light. It comes quite naturally to us. For instance, we withhold facts that would prove damaging to us and concentrate on our good points. We compare ourselves with others whose failings are more obvious. We pass the blame for our actions on to others. We assign pious motives to actions that are blatantly wrong. We twist and distort the facts until they have only a faint resemblance to the reality. We use emotionally colored words to paint a more favorable picture.

Adam blamed Eve, "The woman whom You gave to be with me, she gave me of the tree, and I ate" (Gen. 3:12). Eve blamed the Devil, "The serpent deceived me, and I ate" (Gen. 3:13).

Saul defended his disobedience in sparing the sheep and oxen of the Amalekites by assigning a pious motive: "the people took of the plunder...to sacrifice to the Lord your God" (1 Sam. 15:21). He also suggested, of course, that if there was blame, it was the people's, not his.

David lied to Ahimelech in order to get weapons, saying, "The king's business required haste" (1 Sam. 21:8). Actually David wasn't on the king's business; he was fleeing from King Saul.

The woman at the well withheld the truth. She said, "I have no husband" (Jn. 4:17). Actually, she had had five husbands and was now cohabiting with a man to whom she was not married.

And so it goes! Because of our fallen nature, inherited from Adam, it is difficult for us to be completely objective when presenting our own side of a matter. Our tendency is to picture ourselves in the most favorable light. We can have a kindly regard toward sins in our own life when we would vigorously condemn those same sins in someone else's.

"The first one to plead his cause seems right, until his neighbor comes and examines him." That is, when his neighbor has a chance to testify, he gives a more accurate presentation of the facts. He exposes all the subtle attempts at whitewashing and self-vindication. He tells the story without distortion.

Ultimately God is our Neighbor—the One who brings to light the hidden things of darkness and reveals the thoughts and intents of the heart. He is light, and in Him is no darkness at all. If we are to walk in unclouded communion with Him, we must be honest and aboveboard in all our testimony, even if it results in our own undoing.

330

November 13

Yet you do not have because you do not ask.
JAMES 4:2

 verse like this raises an interesting question. If we have not because we ask not, what great things are we missing in life simply because we do not pray for them?

A similar question arises from James 5:16, "The effective, fervent prayer of a righteous man avails much." If this righteous man doesn't pray, then does it not follow that little is accomplished through him?

The trouble with most of us is that we do not pray enough, or when we do pray, we ask for so little. We are what C. T. Studd called "nibblers of the possible instead of grabbers of the impossible." Our prayers are timid and unimaginative when they should be bold and daring. We should be honoring God by praying for great things. In John Newton's words,

> *Thou art coming to a King,*
> *Large petitions with thee bring;*
> *For His grace and power are such,*
> *None can ever ask too much.*

When we do this, we not only honor God; we enrich ourselves spiritually. He loves to open heaven's treasures to us, but today's verse suggests that He only does it in answer to prayer.

It seems to me that this verse answers a question that we often hear. The question is this: Does prayer actually move God to do things that He would not have done otherwise, or does it merely bring us into harmony with what He would have done anyway? The answer seems clear: God does things in answer to prayer that He would not have done otherwise.

Our imaginations can run riot in two directions as we ponder this. First, we can think of the tremendous achievements that have come as a direct result of prayer. Borrowing the words of Hebrews 11:33-34, we remember those who "subdued kingdoms, worked righteousness, obtained promises, stopped the mouths of lions, quenched the violence of fire, escaped the edge of the sword, out of weakness were made strong, became valiant in battle, turned to flight the armies of the aliens."

But we can also think of what we ourselves might have accomplished for Christ if we had only asked. We can think of the many exceedingly great and precious promises in the Word which we have failed to claim. We have been weak when we might have been powerful. We have touched a few lives for God when we might have touched thousands or even millions. We have asked for acres when we might have asked for continents. We have been spiritual paupers when we might have been plutocrats. We do not have because we do not ask.

November 14

Whoever desires to become great among you, let him be your servant.
And whoever desires to be first among you, let him be your slave
MATTHEW 20:26-27

T here are two kinds of greatness in the New Testament and it is helpful to distinguish them. There is a greatness associated with one's position and another greatness linked with one's personal character.

In speaking of John the Baptist, Jesus said that there was no greater prophet than he (Lk. 7:28). Here the Savior was speaking about the greatness of John's position. No other prophet had the privilege of being the forerunner of the Messiah. It does not mean that John had a better character than any of the Old Testament prophets, but only that his was the unique assignment of introducing the Lamb of God who takes away the sin of the world.

In John 14:28, Jesus said to the disciples, "My Father is greater than I." Did He mean that His Father was greater personally? No, because all members of the Godhead are equal. He meant that the Father was enthroned in heavenly glory whereas He Himself was being despised and rejected by men on earth. The disciples should have rejoiced to know that Jesus was going back to the Father because then He would have the same glorious position as the Father.

All believers enjoy a great position by reason of their identification with the Lord Jesus. They are sons of God, heirs of God and joint-heirs with Jesus Christ.

But then the New Testament also speaks of personal greatness. For instance, in Matthew 20:26-27, Jesus said, "Whoever desires to become great among you, let him be your servant. And whoever desires to be first among you, let him be your slave." The greatness here is a greatness of personal character, demonstrated by a life of service to others.

Most men of the world are interested only in greatness as far as their position is concerned. The Lord Jesus referred to this when he said, "The kings of the Gentiles exercise lordship over them, and those who exercise authority over them are called benefactors" (Lk. 22:25). But as far as their personal character is concerned, they may be utterly devoid of greatness. They may be adulterers, embezzlers, and alcoholics.

The Christian realizes that positional greatness without greatness of character is worthless. It's what's inside a person that counts. The fruit of the Spirit is more important than a high place on the corporate ladder. It's better to be listed among the saints than among the stars.

November 15

One thing I do, forgetting those things which are behind.
PHILIPPIANS 3:13B

Ordinarily when we read these words, we tend to think that Paul was speaking about his past sins. He knew that these sins had been forgiven, that God had put them behind His back, and that He would never remember them again. So Paul was determined to forget them too, and to "press toward the mark for the prize of the high calling of God in Christ Jesus."

I still think that is a valid application of the verse. But Paul is not thinking about his sins in this passage. Rather he is thinking about the things in which he might have boasted—his lineage, his former religion, his zeal and his legal righteousness. Now these things meant nothing to him. He was determined to forget them.

I am reminded of John Sung, the devoted Chinese evangelist, who had come to the United States for training. Now he was on his way back to China. Leslie Lyall writes that "one day, as the vessel neared the end of its voyage, John Sung went down to his cabin, took out of his trunk his diplomas, his medals, and his fraternity keys and threw them all overboard except his doctor's diploma, which he retained to satisfy his father. This was later framed and hung in his old home. The Rev. W. B. Cole saw it there about 1938. Dr. Sung noticed Mr. Cole looking at it one day and said, 'Things like that are useless. They mean nothing to me.'"

"There must be great renunciations if there are to be great Christian careers!" Dr. Denney's words might have been written with Dr. Sung in mind. It is probably the chief secret of John Sung's career that there came a day when he made just such a renunciation of all that this world holds dear.

> *Forbid it, Lord, that I should boast*
> *Save in the Cross of Christ my God;*
> *All the vain things that charm me most,*
> *I sacrifice them to His blood.*

Man's honors are transient, empty things. They are cherished for a moment, then gather dust for decades. The Cross is all our glory. We make it our ambition to be well-pleasing to Him who died for us and rose again. All that matters is to hear His "Well done!" and to be approved unto God. We are willing to renounce everything else to win that prize.

November 16

Untaught and unstable people twist to their own destruction,
as they do also the rest of the Scriptures.
2 PETER 3:16B

D r. P. J. Van Gorder used to tell about a sign over a woodworker's shop which said, "All kinds of twisting and turning done here." It is not only woodworkers that are good at that; many professing Christians twist and turn the Scriptures when it suits them. Some, as our verse says, even twist the Scriptures to their own destruction.

We are all fairly expert at rationalizing, i.e., at excusing our sinful disobedience by giving creditable explanations or assigning worthy motives to our actions. We often try to bend the Scriptures to suit our behavior. We give plausible but untrue reasons for our conduct or attitudes. Here are some examples:

A Christian businessman knows that it is wrong for him to go to law against another believer (1 Cor. 6:1-8). Yet when he is challenged about it, he says, "Yes, but he was definitely wrong, and the Lord doesn't want him to get away with it."

Jane is planning to marry John, even when she knows he is not a believer. When a Christian friend reminds her that this is forbidden by 2 Corinthians 6:14, she says, "Yes, but the Lord told me to marry him so I can lead him to Christ."

Glen and Ruth profess to be Christians, yet they are living together without being married. When a friend of Glen pointed out that this was fornication and that no fornicator will inherit the kingdom of God (1 Cor. 6:9-10), Glen replied, "That's what you say. We are deeply in love with one another, and in God's sight we are married."

Here is a Christian family living in luxury and splendor, in spite of Paul's admonition that we should live simply, being content with food and covering (1 Tim. 6:8). They justify their lifestyle with the pat answer, "There's nothing too good for the people of God."

Or here is a covetous businessman, greedily amassing all the wealth he can. His philosophy is, "There's nothing the matter with money. It's the love of money that's the root of all evil." It never occurs to him that he might be guilty of loving money.

Men try to put a better interpretation on their sins than the Scriptures allow. And when they are determined to disobey the Word, one excuse is as good (or bad) as another.

November 17

*When you offer the blind as a sacrifice, is it not evil? And when you offer the
lame and sick, is it not evil? Offer it then to your governor! Would he be pleased
with you? Would he accept you favorably? says the Lord of hosts.*

MALACHI 1:8

There was no question as to what God required in sacrificial animals.
They had to be without spot or blemish. He expected His people to
offer the choicest animals from their herds or flocks. God wants
the best.

But what were the Israelites doing? They were offering blind, lame and sick
animals. The choice animals would bring a high price in the market, or would be
desirable for breeding. So the people offered the culls, saying in effect, "Anything
is good enough for the Lord."

Before we look down on the Israelites with shock and scorn, we should ponder
whether we twentieth century Christians might also be dishonoring God by
failing to give Him the best.

We spend our lives building a fortune, trying to make a name for ourselves, living in a status home in suburbia, enjoying the finer things—then give God the
worn end of a burned-out life. Our finest talents go to business and the professions, and the Lord gets our spare evenings or weekends.

We raise our children for the world, encouraging them to make a lot of money,
marry well, and own a prestigious home with all the modern conveniences. We
never hold the work of the Lord before them as a desirable way in which they
should spend their lives. The mission field is all right for other people's children,
but not for ours.

We spend our money on expensive cars, recreational vehicles, sailing boats,
and high-class sports equipment, then give a paltry dollar or two to the work of
the Lord. We wear expensive clothes, then get a feeling of euphoria when we
donate our castoffs to the Salvation Army.

What we are saying, in effect, is that anything is good enough for the Lord, but
that we want the best for ourselves. And the Lord is saying to us, "Go, and offer
it to the President. See if he would be pleased with it." The President would be
insulted. Well, so is the Lord. Why should we treat Him in a way we would not
think of treating the President?

God wants the best. He deserves the best. Let us determine with all sincerity
that He will have our best.

November 18

Be wise as serpents and harmless as doves.
MATTHEW 10:16

O ne important element of practical wisdom is tactfulness. The Christian should learn how to be tactful. This means that he should develop a delicate sensitivity as to what to do or say, so as to avoid offense and cement good relations. The tactful person puts himself in the other fellow's shoes and asks himself, "How would I like to have that said or done to me?" He seeks to be diplomatic, considerate, gracious and discerning.

Unfortunately, the Christian faith has had its share of tactless adherents. One classic example was a Christian barber in a small midwestern town. When a luckless customer entered the shop one day and asked for a shave, the barber seated him, tied the usual white cloth around his neck and tilted back the chair. On the ceiling the customer saw the words "Where will you spend eternity?" The barber lathered his face liberally; then as he began to sharpen the razor on the strop, he began his evangelistic witness with the question, "Are you prepared to meet God?" The customer bolted out of the chair—towel, lather and all…and hasn't been heard from since.

Then there was the zealous student who went out one night to do some personal evangelism. Walking down a dark street, he saw a young lady walking ahead of him in the shadows. As he tried to catch up with her she began to run. Anxious, he ran after her. When she doubled her pace, he did the same. Finally she ran up onto the porch of a house in near shock and started fumbling in her handbag for her keys. As he ran up onto the porch, she was too paralyzed with fear to scream. Then smilingly he handed her a tract and left, happy to have reached another sinner with the gospel.

Great tact is needed in visiting the sick. It doesn't help to say, "You really do look sick," or "I knew a person with the same trouble—and he died." Who needs that kind of comfort?

And we should be tactful when we visit the bereaved. We shouldn't be like the Texan who said to the widow of a slain politician, "And just to think that it had to happen in Texas!"

God bless those choice saints who always seem to know how to speak the gracious, appropriate word. And God teach the rest of us how to be tactful diplomats instead of tactless bumblers.

November 19

I know your...tribulation, and poverty.
REVELATION 2:9

Seven times in His letters to the churches of Asia, the Lord Jesus says, "I know" and usually those words are used in a favorable sense. "I know your works...your labor...your patience...your tribulation ...your poverty...and charity...and faith." In those words "I know" there is tremendous comfort and sympathy and encouragement for God's people.

Lehman Strauss points out that when Jesus said "I know," He did not use the word *ginoske,* which frequently means to know in the sense of realizing through progress in knowledge. He used the word *oida,* which suggests fullness of knowledge, to know perfectly, not merely from observation, but from experience.

Though suffering saints are unknown and hated by the world, they are known to the Lord and loved by Him. Christ knows the persecution and poverty of His own; He knows how the world looks upon them. Many a tired, tried, and troubled saint has been strengthened and encouraged by those two monosyllables, "I know." Those two words uttered by our Saviour touch our troubles with the smile of God, and make this world's suffering "not worthy to be compared with the glory which shall be revealed in us" (Rom. 8:18).

They are words of sympathy. Our Great High Priest knows what we are going through because He has been through it Himself. He is the Man of Sorrows and is acquainted with grief. He has suffered, being tempted.

They are words of sharing. As the Head of the body, He shares the trials and persecutions of the members. "In every pang that rends the heart, the Man of Sorrows has a part." He not only knows intellectually what we are going through; He knows it as a matter of present experience. He feels it.

They are words of promised help. As our Paraclete, He comes alongside to bear our burdens and wipe away our falling tears. He is there to bind up our wounds and to drive back our foes.

Finally, they are words of assured rewards. He knows everything we do and suffer because of our identification with Him. He keeps a careful record of every act of love, obedience and patience. One day soon He will richly repay.

If you are passing through a valley of sorrow or suffering just now, hear the Savior saying to you, "I know." You are not alone. He is with you in the valley, will bring you safely through, and will lead you safely to your desired destination.

November 20

Be careful that nobody spoils your faith through intellectualism
or high-sounding nonsense. Such stuff is at best founded on men's ideas
of the nature of the world and disregards Christ!
COLOSSIANS 2:8, PHILLIPS

The word which Phillips translates "intellectualism" here is the one from which we get the word "philosophy." Basically it means the love of wisdom, but then it has acquired a further meaning, namely, the search for reality and the purpose of life.

Most human philosophies are expressed in complicated, high-sounding language. They are above the head of the common man. They appeal to those who like to use their intellectual powers in clothing human speculations with words that are difficult to understand.

Frankly, human philosophies are inadequate. Phillips speaks of them as "intellectualism and high-sounding nonsense." They are based on man's ideas of the nature of things and disregard Christ. As famous a philosopher as Bertrand Russell is quoted as saying toward the close of his life, "Philosophy has proved a washout to me."

The wise Christian is not taken in by the high-sounding nonsense of modern intellectualism. He refuses to bow at the shrine of man's wisdom. Instead, he realizes that all the treasures of wisdom and knowledge are found in Christ. He tests all human philosophies by the Word of God and rejects all that is contrary to the Scriptures.

He is not moved when philosophers hit the headlines with some new attack on the Christian faith. He has the maturity of judgment to realize that he cannot expect anything better from them.

He does not feel inferior that he cannot converse with the philosophers in words of many syllables or follow them in their involved reasonings. He is suspicious of their inability to state their message simply, and rejoices that the gospel is such that wayfaring men, though fools, can grasp it.

He detects in modem philosophies the lure of the serpent, "You will be like God" (Gen. 3:5). Man is tempted to exalt his mind above the mind of God. But the wise Christian rejects the devil's lie. He casts down human reasonings and every high thing that exalts itself against the knowledge of God (2 Cor. 10:5).

November 21

That at the name of Jesus every knee should bow, of those in heaven,
and of those on earth, and of those under the earth, and that every tongue
should confess that Jesus Christ is Lord, to the glory of God the Father
PHILIPPIANS 2:10-11

What a scene that will be! Every knee in the universe bowing to the sacred name of Jesus! Every tongue confessing that He is Lord! God has decreed it and it will surely come to pass.

This is not universal salvation. Paul is not suggesting here that all created beings will eventually embrace Christ as their living, loving Lord. Rather he is saying that those who refuse to make the great confession in this life will be compelled to make it in the next. All created beings will eventually acknowledge the truth about Jesus Christ. There will be universal submission.

In one of his messages, *Jesus is Lord,* John Stott said, "During the coronation of Her Majesty the Queen in Westminster Abbey, one of the most moving moments was when the crown was about to be placed upon her head and when the Archbishop of Canterbury, the chief citizen in the country, called four times towards each point of the compass in the Abbey, north, south, east and west, "Sirs, I present unto you the undoubted Queen of this realm. Are you willing to do her homage? And not until a great affirmative shout had thundered down the nave of Westminster Abbey four times was the crown placed upon her head."

Then John Stott added, "And I say to you tonight, Ladies and Gentlemen, 'I present unto you Jesus Christ as your undoubted King and Lord. Are you willing to do Him homage?'"

That insistent question rings down the centuries. From many, a great affirmative shout goes up, "Jesus Christ is our Lord." From others the defiant reply is, "We will not have this man to reign over us." The clenched fist will one day be forced open and the hitherto unbending knee will bow to Him whose Name is above every Name. The tragedy is that it will be too late then. The day of God's grace will have ended. The opportunity to trust the sinner's Savior will have passed. The One whose Lordship had been spurned will then become the Judge, seated upon a great white throne.

If He is not your Lord today, confess Him as such. Be willing to do Him homage!

November 22

Though I speak with the tongues of men and of angels, but have not love....
1 Corinthians 13:1

After a young soprano had made her debut on the opera stage, a critic wrote that her brilliant performance would have been even better if she had ever loved. He detected the absence of love. Apparently her singing was technically correct, but it lacked warmth.

We, too, can go through life, doing everything according to the rules. We can be honest, dependable, righteous, generous, energetic, and humble. Yet all these virtues cannot compensate for a lack of love.

Many of us have a hard time knowing how to give love and to receive it. I read recently of a celebrity "who could do everything except express what he felt for the people he loved."

In his book, *People in Prayer,* John White wrote, "For many years I was frightened of being loved. I did not mind giving love (or what I thought was love), but I grew ill at ease if anyone—man, woman or child—showed too much affection for me. In our family we had never learned how to handle love. We were not very expert at demonstrating it or receiving it. I don't mean that we did not love one another or that we did not find ways of showing it. But we were very British. When I was nineteen and leaving home to go to war, my father did something quite unprecedented. He put his hands on my shoulder and kissed me. I was stunned. I knew neither what to say nor what to do. For me it was very embarrassing while for my father it must have been very sad."

One day White had a vision of Christ standing before him, with nail-scarred hands outstretched toward him. At first he felt helpless to receive Christ's love. Then he prayed, "O Lord, I want to grasp your hands. But I can't."

"In the quietness that followed, there came to me an assurance that the defensive wall I had built around me would gradually be dismantled and that I would learn what it was to let Christ's love wrap around me and fill me."

If we have built defensive walls around ourselves, hindering the flow of love to and from us, we must let the Lord dismantle those walls, and deliver us from the fears that make us cold Christians.

November 23

...The way of transgressors is hard.
PROVERBS 13:15B, KJV

If proof were needed that the way of transgressors is hard, we would only need to pick out a daily newspaper at random and we would find plenty of illustrations. I did that just as an experiment and here are the results:

A Nazi war criminal who had escaped detection and capture in South America for 35 years committed suicide. The fear of trial and probable execution made further living unendurable.

A 74-year-old man was kidnapped at gunpoint by three men who demanded $90,000 ransom from his son. The son is a reputed drug dealer, currently fleeing from police and federal drug agents.

A member of the U.S. House of Representatives was expelled from the House for accepting a bribe in return for a promise to grant a political favor. It appears that his ouster from Congress will be permanent.

Afghan rebels continue to battle invading Russian troops. The newspaper article does not mention the fact that the government of Afghanistan had previously bulldozed the only Christian church building in the country. Could the Russian invasion be divine retribution?

A police captain falsely reported that his car had been stolen. He hoped to collect insurance on it. He had been considered an outstanding officer and was likely to be tapped for police chief one day. Now he has been dropped from the force and awaits a criminal investigation.

Sometimes we, like the Psalmist, are tempted to envy the wicked. It seems that the world is their oyster and everything works out well for them. But we forget that they reap an inevitable harvest of guilt, shame, and fear of exposure. Often they become victims of blackmail and extortion. They fear for their own lives and the lives of their family members. They have to maintain elaborate and expensive protection systems. They face the prospect of arrest, costly litigation and fines or imprisonment. Life becomes a nightmare instead of the dream for which they had hoped.

One man who had learned the lesson well said to Sam Jones, the preacher, with deep conviction, "I know one verse of Scripture, and I know that one is true: 'The way of transgressors is hard.'" He had proved that sin's built-in consequences are inescapable and extremely unpleasant.

November 24

Then he began to curse and swear.
MATTHEW 26:74

A bishop was walking alone in his garden one day, meditating on the activities of the past week. When the memory of a very embarrassing incident flashed across his mind, he let out a string of expletives that were rather salty, to say the least. One of his parishioners, walking on the other side of the high garden wall, heard the unministerial language and gasped in disbelief.

It was a case of private profanity—a heartbreaking trial in the life of many an earnest child of God. Hundreds groan under the oppression of this hideous habit, realizing how dishonoring it is to the Lord and how defiling it is in one's own life. Yet all their efforts to break the habit prove fruitless.

The unwelcome words usually pour forth when a person is alone (or thinks he is) and when he is under nervous tension. Sometimes they are the audible expression of pent-up anger. Sometimes they give vent to our feelings of frustration. In the bishop's case, they were his natural reaction to the shame of being embarrassed.

Even worse than the agony of private profanity is the fear that some day the words will slip out in public. Or when we are asleep. Or when we are under an anesthetic in the hospital.

This old habit returned to Peter on the night of the Savior's trial. When he was pointed out as a companion of Jesus of Galilee, he denied it with curses and swearing (Mt. 26:74). He never would have done it in a relaxed state, but now he was in peril and in extreme duress, and the words came forth with all the facility of his unconverted days.

In spite of our best intentions and most earnest resolutions, the words slip out before we have a chance to think. They catch us completely off guard.

Must we despair of ever conquering this Goliath in our lives? No, there is the promise of victory over this as over all other temptations (1 Cor. 10:13). First, we must confess and forsake the sin every time we fall. Then we must cry to God to put a watch before our lips. We must ask for power to respond to the unfavorable circumstances of life with poise and quietness. Sometimes the act of confessing the fault to some other believer helps to break the powerful habit. Finally, we must always remember that while others may not hear it on earth, our Father hears it in heaven. The remembrance of how offensive it is to Him should serve as a powerful deterrent for us.

November 25

And be thankful.
COLOSSIANS 3:15

 thankful heart adds sparkle to all of life. At the close of a dinner, one of the children said, "That was a good meal, Mother." That remark created a new sense of warmth in an already happy house.

Too often we fail to express our thanks. The Lord Jesus healed ten lepers, but only one returned to give thanks, and that one was a Samaritan (Lk. 17:17). Two lessons emerge. Gratitude is rare in a world of fallen men. And when it does appear, it often comes from the least-expected sources.

It is easy for us to feel grieved when we show kindness to others and they do not even have the courtesy to say "Thank you." By the same token, we should realize how others feel when we fail to express gratitude for favors received.

Even a cursory examination of the Bible reveals that it is punctuated with exhortations and examples of thanksgiving to God. We have so many things for which to be grateful to Him; we could not possibly tabulate them all. Our whole lives should be psalms of thanks to Him.

> Ten thousand, thousand precious gifts
> My daily thanks employ;
> Nor is the least a cheerful heart
> To taste those gifts with joy.

And we should cultivate the habit of expressing thanks to one another as well. A warm handshake, a phone call or a letter—what uplift they bring! An aged doctor received a note of thanks along with the payment from one of his patients. He kept that note among his prized possessions; it was the first one he had ever received.

We should be quick to express gratitude for gifts, for hospitality, for free transportation, for the loan of tools or other equipment, for help with our work projects, for every form of kindness and service that is shown to us.

The trouble is that too often we take these things for granted. Or we are too undisciplined to sit down and write a letter. In that case, we must work at the habit of thanksgiving, developing an awareness of all that we have for which to be grateful, then training ourselves to acknowledge these things promptly. The promptness of the acknowledgment doubles the thanks.

November 26

Where there is no vision, the people perish:
but he that keepeth the law, happy is he.
PROVERBS 29:18, KJV

T he first part of today's verse is: "Where there is no vision, the people perish." This is usually taken to mean that people must have goals toward which they are working. They must have a definite program in mind with a clear picture of the results desired and the steps leading to them.

But the word vision here means "a revelation from God." And the word "perish" means "cast off restraint." So the thought is that where the Word of God is not known and respected, the people run wild.

The contrast is found in the second half of the verse: "He that keepeth the law, happy is he." In other words, the path of blessedness is found in obeying the will of God as it is found in the Word.

Let us think about the first part of the verse. Where people abandon the knowledge of God, they become unrestrained in their conduct. Suppose, for instance, that a nation turns away from God and explains everything on the basis of the evolutionary process. That means that man is the result of purely natural processes and not the creation of a supernatural Being. If that is so, then there is no basis for ethical standards. All our behavior is the inevitable result of natural causes. As Lunn and Lean point out in *The New Morality,* "If the first living cell evolved by a purely natural process on the surface of a lifeless planet, if the mind of man be as much the product of natural and material forces as a volcano, it is as irrational to condemn South African politicians for apartheid as to condemn a volcano for erupting lava."

If God's Word is rejected, then there are no absolute standards of right and wrong. Ethical truths depend on the individuals or groups holding them. People become the judge of their own conduct. Their philosophy is: "If it feels good, do it." The fact that "everyone's doing it" is all the justification that is needed.

Thus the people cast off restraint. They abandon themselves to fornication, adultery, and homosexuality. Crime and violence increase to alarming proportions. Corruption spreads throughout business and government. Lying and deceit become accepted forms of behavior. The fabric of society disintegrates.

"...but he that keepeth the law, happy is he." Even when the rest of the world runs riot, the individual believer can find the good life in believing and obeying God's Word. This is the only way to go.

November 27

Surely I am coming quickly.
REVELATION 22:20

 s we approach the end of the age, it is predictable that many will abandon the hope of Christ's any-moment return. But the truth is still there,
whether men hold it or not.

The fact is that the Lord Jesus may come at any time. We do not know the day
or hour of the Bridegroom's return for His bride; this means that He could come
today. There is no prophecy that needs to be fulfilled before we hear His shout,
the voice of the archangel, and the trump of God. True, the church expects to
experience tribulation throughout its time on earth, but the horrors of the Great
Tribulation period are not part of its destiny. If the church has to go through the
Tribulation, that would mean that the Lord couldn't come for at least seven years,
because we certainly are not in the Tribulation now, and when it does come, it will
last for seven years.

There is a large body of Scripture texts that teach us to be ready at all times for
the Savior to appear. Notice the following:

"…nearer than when we first believed" (Rom. 13:11).

"The night is far spent, the day is at hand" (Rom. 13:12).

"The Lord is at hand" (Phil. 4:5).

"For yet a little while, and He who is coming will come and will not tarry"
(Heb. 10:37).

"…the coming of the Lord is at hand" (Jas. 5:8).

"…The Judge is standing at the door!" (Jas. 5:9).

"But the end of all things is at hand" (1 Pet. 4:7).

These verses seem designed to create the impression on the mind that the
Lord's coming is imminent. It is an event for which we should be watching and
waiting. We should be busy in His service, faithfully carrying out our stewardship.

R. A. Torrey once said, "The imminent return of our Lord is the great Bible
argument for a pure, unselfish, devoted, unworldly, active life of service. In much
of our preaching we urge people to live holy and work diligently because death is
swiftly coming, but this is never the Bible argument. The Bible argument always
is, Christ is coming; be ready when He comes."

Our responsibility is clear. Our loins should be girded, our lights should be
burning, and we should be like those who wait for their Lord (see Lk. 12:35-36).
Let us not succumb to those who teach that we have no right to expect Him at any
moment. Rather let us believe in His imminent return, teach it enthusiastically,
and let the truth shine out in our lives.

November 28

By the grace of God I am what I am.
1 CORINTHIANS 15:10

One of the self-inflicted agonies of life is trying to be someone you were never intended to be. Everyone is a unique creation of God. As someone has said, "When He made us, He threw away the pattern." He never intended for us to try to change it.

Maxwell Maltz wrote, "'You' as a personality are not in competition with any other personality simply because there is not another person on the face of the earth like you, or in your particular class. You are an individual. You are unique. You are not 'like' any other person and can never become 'like' any other person. You are not 'supposed' to be like any other person and no other person is 'supposed' to be like you.

"God did not create a standard person and in some way label that person by saying 'This is it.' He made every human being individual and unique—just as He made every snowflake individual and unique."

Everyone of us is the product of the wisdom and love of God. In making us as we are, He knew exactly what He was doing. Our appearance, our intelligence, and our talents represent His best for us. Anyone with infinite knowledge and infinite love would have done the same.

Now then, to wish we were someone else is an insult to God. It suggests that He has made a mistake or has withheld from us something that would have been for our good.

Lusting to be like someone else is futile. There is a finality about what God has made us, and what He has given us. Of course we can imitate the virtues of other people, but what we are thinking about here is what we are as God's creation.

If we go through life dissatisfied with God's design for our lives, we will be paralyzed with feelings of inferiority. But it is not a question of inferiority. We are not inferior—just individual and unique.

The attempt to be someone else is doomed to end in failure. It is as unthinkable as a little finger trying to do the work of the heart. That was not God's design, and it simply won't work.

The proper attitude is to say with Paul, "By the grace of God I am what I am" (1 Cor. 15:10). We should rejoice in what we are as a distinct design of God and determine to use what we are and have to the maximum for His glory. There are many things we won't be able to do, but there are other things we can do that others cannot.

November 29

I can of Myself do nothing.
JOHN 5:30

Twice in John 5 the Lord Jesus says that He can do nothing of Himself. In verse 19, He says, "Most assuredly, I say to you, the Son can do nothing of Himself." Then again in verse 30, He says, "I can of Myself do nothing."

When we first read these verses, we are apt to feel disappointed. They seem to say that Jesus was limited in His power, just like ourselves. But if He is God, as He claimed to be, He must be omnipotent. How then could He say that He could do nothing of Himself? Indeed, the enemies of the gospel have used these verses to show that Jesus was just a man with all the limitations of humanity.

But look more closely: Our Lord was not speaking of His physical power. What He was insisting was that He was so devoted to the will of His Father that He could not do anything on His own initiative. He was so morally perfect that He could not act in self-will. He wanted nothing apart from the will of God.

You and I cannot say that we can do nothing of ourselves. Too often we act independently of the Lord. We make decisions without consulting Him. We yield to temptation with full knowledge that we are sinning. We choose our own will above His. The Lord Jesus could do none of these things.

Therefore, instead of suggesting that Jesus Christ was weak and finite, the verses prove the very opposite—that He was divinely perfect. This is made clear by reading the verses in their entirety rather than stopping at midpoint. What Jesus said in verse 19 was, "The Son can do nothing of Himself, but what He sees the Father do; for whatever He does, the Son also does in like manner." In other words, the Son cannot act independently of the Father, but He can do whatever the Father does. It is a claim to equality with God.

Then again in verse 30, Jesus said, "I can of Myself do nothing. As I hear, I judge; and My judgment is righteous, because I do not seek My own will but the will of the Father who sent Me." This means that He made decisions only on the basis of instructions that He received from His Father, and that His complete submission to God's will insured that these decisions were correct.

J. Sidlow Baxter points out that this passage contains seven distinct claims by Christ to be equal with God. Equal in working (v. 19); equal in knowing (v. 20); equal in resurrecting (vv. 21, 28, 29); equal in judging (vv. 22, 27); equal in honor (v. 23); equal in regenerating (vv. 24-25); equal in self-existence (v. 26). Our Savior is not a weak, frail creature with limited power but omnipotent God manifest in the flesh.

November 30

Bear one another's burdens, and so fulfill the law of Christ...
for each one shall bear his own load.
GALATIANS 6:2, 5

 casual reading of these two verses might easily convince a person that they present a glaring contradiction. The first says we should bear one another's burdens, the second that we must bear our own burden.

The word translated "burdens" in verse 2 means anything that weighs a person down spiritually, physically and emotionally. In its immediate context it refers to the heavy weight of guilt and despondency that has come into the life of a man who has been overtaken in a fault (v. 1). We help such a brother when we throw a loving arm around him and win him back to a life of fellowship with God and with God's people. But burdens also include the sorrows, troubles, trials, and frustrations of life which come to us all. We bear one another's burdens when we comfort, encourage, share our material things, and give constructive advice. It means to involve ourselves in the problems of others, even at a great personal cost. When we do this, we fulfill the law of Christ; which is to love one another. We demonstrate our love in a practical way by spending and being spent for others.

A different word is used for "burden" in verse 5. Here it means anything that has to be carried, without any hint as to whether the load is heavy or light. What Paul is saying here is that everyone will have to bear his own load of responsibility at the judgment seat of Christ. It will not be a question then as to how we compare with others. We will be judged on the basis of our own record, and the rewards will be passed out accordingly.

The connection between the two verses seems to be this: A person who restores one who is overtaken in a fault might fall into the trap of feeling himself superior. In bearing the burdens of the fallen brother, he might somehow think of himself as being on a higher level of spirituality. He sees himself as comparing favorably with the sinning saint. Paul reminds him that when he stands before the Lord, he will have to give account for himself, for his own work and for his own character, and not for the other person. He will have to bear his own load of accountability.

So the two verses do not fight against one another. Rather they live in the closest harmony.

December 1

If you hear someone...saying...then you shall inquire,
search out, and ask diligently. And if it is indeed true and certain...
DEUTERONOMY 13:12, 14

 f a rumor circulated that the people of a city in Israel had forsaken God for idols, there had to be an intensive investigation before any punitive action could be taken.

We should be no less careful when we hear a rumor or gossip but should apply the six tests: Is it hearsay? Have I inquired? Have I made search? Have I asked diligently? Is it true? Is it certain?

In fact, it would be a good idea if we used the same thoroughness and caution before passing on sensational news items that appear in religious circles from time to time. Let me give some illustrations:

Some time ago the story circulated that stones for building a temple in Jerusalem were stored at a pier in New York, ready for shipment to Israel when the proper time arrived. The stones were reported to be of Indiana limestone. Christians circulated the news enthusiastically, only to be discredited when it was learned that there was no truth to the report.

At another time, the story broke that scientists had fed extensive data concerning the calendar of human history into a computer and that the results confirmed the scriptural narrative of Joshua's long day. Anxious for any news that confirms the Bible, believers avidly spread the story in magazines and by the spoken word. Then the bubble burst. The story proved to be without foundation.

More recently, a mathematical computation has been used to suggest that some unpopular public figure might be the Antichrist. Here is how it works: A numerical value is assigned to each letter of this personality's name. Then by following a certain series of additions, subtractions, multiplications and divisions, you come up with the number 666. Of course, it proves nothing at all. Mathematical computations could be devised to yield 666 for almost anyone's name.

I have a tract stating that Charles Darwin, in the closing days of his life, disavowed evolution and returned to his faith in the Bible. This may be true. I would like to believe that it is true. Maybe some day I'll find that it is true. But in the meantime I have no documentation for the story, and I dare not circulate it until I do have.

We will save ourselves a lot of embarrassment and save the Christian faith from being discredited if we apply the six tests in today's verses: Is it hearsay? Have I inquired? Have I made search? Have I asked diligently? Is it true? Is it certain?

December 2

Speaking to one another in psalms and hymns and spiritual songs,
singing and making melody in your heart to the Lord.
EPHESIANS 5:19

Singing here is linked to the filling of the Spirit, as if song is one of the sure results of the filling. Perhaps this is why almost all the great revivals of history have been accompanied by singing. The Welsh revival is a notable example.

No people have as much to sing about as Christians, and no people have such a rich heritage of psalms, hymns, and spiritual songs. Our hymns express in majestic language what we so often feel but cannot express. Some hymns express thoughts that may be beyond our own experience—hymns of total commitment such as "All to Jesus I Surrender." In such cases, we can sing them as the aspiration of our hearts.

In spiritual singing, it is not the rhythm or the melody or the harmony that counts. The important thing is that the message comes from the heart and rises to God in the power of the Holy Spirit. Mary Bowley expressed this truth well in the lines:

> *O Lord, we know it matters not*
> *How sweet the song may be;*
> *No heart but of the Spirit taught*
> *Makes melody to Thee.*

The Spirit of God can use singing just as He can use the reading of the Word. The mother of Grattan Guinness heard a farmer singing as he plowed his field, and she decided not to commit suicide by drowning in the river. Dr. Guinness said later, "All that I am for God, I owe to a humble Christian plowman singing the praises of the Lord as he did his lowly task."

Those who engage in the ministry of Christian music have to guard against two perils. One is the danger of self creeping in. As with other forms of public ministry, it is easy to embark on a giant ego trip. There is always the temptation to try to impress people with one's talent rather than singing to the glory of God and for the blessing of His people.

The other is the danger of entertaining rather than edifying. It is all too possible to sing words with great musical skill and yet not convey the message to the hearts of the listeners. And it is possible to excite people emotionally with songs that are frothy, frivolous, and quite unworthy of the Lord we love.

Different cultures have different tastes in music, but in all cultures the songs should be doctrinally sound, uniformly reverent, and spiritually edifying.

December 3

He...now preaches the faith which he once tried to destroy.
GALATIANS 1:23

After Saul of Tarsus was converted, the churches of Judea heard that this arch-persecutor of the Christian faith had become an ardent preacher and defender of the faith. It was a remarkable reversal.

In more recent times, there have been spectacular incidents where men have done a similar about-face.

Lord Littleton and Gilbert West decided jointly that they would overthrow the faith of those who defended the Bible. Littleton would disprove the records of the conversion of Saul, while West would prove conclusively that the resurrection of Christ was a myth. "They both had to acknowledge that they were rusty about the Bible records, but they decided, 'If we are to be honest, we ought at least to study the evidence. They conferred often during their work on the subjects in hand. In one of these conferences Littleton opened his heart to his friend and confessed that he was beginning to feel that there was something in it. The other man replied that he himself had been a bit shaken by the results of his study. Finally, when the books were finished, the two authors met and found that each of them, instead of writing against, had produced books in favor of the subjects they had set out to ridicule. They agreed that after going into all the evidence as legal experts, they could honestly do nothing else but accept what the Bible records state as true regarding both subjects" (FREDERICK P. WOOD). Lord Littleton's book was, *The Conversion of St. Paul.* West's book was titled, *The Resurrection of Jesus Christ.*

The infidel, Robert C. Ingersoll challenged an agnostic, Lew Wallace, to write a book showing the falsity of the record concerning Jesus Christ. Wallace spent years in researching the subject, much to the sorrow of his Methodist wife. Then he began to write. When he had finished nearly four chapters, he realized that the records concerning Christ were true. He fell on his knees in repentance and trusted Christ as Lord and Savior. Then he wrote the book *Ben Hur,* presenting Christ as the divine Son of God.

Frank Morison wanted to write a story concerning Christ, but since he didn't believe in the miraculous, he decided to limit himself to the seven days leading up to the crucifixion. However, as he studied the biblical records, he extended the subject to the resurrection. Convinced now that Christ had truly risen, he received Him as his Savior and wrote the book, *Who Moved the Stone?* The first chapter is titled "The Book that Refused to be Written."

The Bible is living and powerful and sharper than any two-edged sword. It is its own best proof. Those who attack and ridicule it should face the possibility of one day believing it and becoming its devoted champions.

December 4

I have filled him with the Spirit of God...in all manner of workmanship.
EXODUS 31:3

Today's text refers to Bezaleel, who was equipped by the Holy Spirit to superintend the building of the Tabernacle. He was skilled to work in gold, silver, and bronze, to cut and set stones and to carve timber. The Spirit of God made him a craftsman to do these practical types of work.

The *Choice Gleanings* calendar quotes E. Tramp as saying, "We generally overlook this phase of the Spirit's ministry. Whether in the field or the factory, the office or the home, the believer can claim the Spirit's assistance in daily labor. A man I know has made an altar out of his factory bench. A Martha in our midst has made her kitchen table into a communion table. Another still has changed his office desk into a pulpit, from which to speak and write, transforming commonplace affairs into the business of the King."

In Nazareth, Israel, there is a Christian hospital that ministers primarily to Arabs. On the grounds of the hospital is a chapel. But when a preacher gets up to speak, he does not stand behind a pulpit. Instead he stands behind a polished carpenter's bench with a wooden vise at one end. This is a beautiful and needed reminder that our Lord worked as a carpenter in Nazareth, and that a workbench was His pulpit.

A doctor in the Midwest sought to treat men's souls as well as their bodies. Sometimes after he had talked with a person in the clinic and given a thorough examination, he would suspect that the problem was spiritual rather than physical. That night he would go to the patient's house and ring the bell. At first the patient would be startled to see the doctor. But then the kindly physician would say something like this: "I am not coming to see you as a doctor, but to visit you as a friend. There's something I'd like to talk to you about. Do you mind if I come in?" Of course, the person didn't mind, so the doctor would go in and talk to him about his spiritual need. Then he would explain how the Lord Jesus was the answer to that need. Many of the patients committed their lives to the Lord and went on to serve Him well. Many will be forever thankful for the ministry of the beloved doctor who cared for their souls as well as their bodies.

The Lord has many unconventional pulpits in the world today. As Tramp said, many have learned how to transform ordinary affairs into the business of the King.

December 5

When the enemy comes in like a flood,
the Spirit of the Lord will lift up a standard against him.
ISAIAH 59:19B

There are desperate crisis times in life when Satan launches all his heaviest artillery against the Lord's people. The sky is dark, the earth trembles and there does not seem to be a single ray of hope. But God has promised to send reinforcements to His people in the moment of extremity. The Spirit of the Lord lifts up a standard against the Devil in the nick of time.

Enslaved by the Egyptian tyrant, the outlook for the people of Israel was bleak. They were cringing under the lashes of the taskmaster. But God was not indifferent to their groans. He raised up Moses to confront the Pharaoh and finally to lead His people out to freedom.

In the time of the Judges, foreign invaders held the tribes of Israel in servitude. Yet in the darkest hour, the Lord raised up military deliverers to drive back the enemy and usher in a period of tranquility.

When Sennacherib led the Assyrian army against Jerusalem, the captivity of Judah seemed certain. Humanly speaking, there was no way of stopping the invading juggernaut. However, the angel of the Lord went throughout the camp of the Assyrians at night and slew 185,000 men.

When Esther was queen in Persia, the enemy came in like a flood, passing an unchangeable decree that all the Jews in the kingdom should be executed. Was God checkmated by this decree of the Medes and the Persians? No, He so arranged matters that another decree was passed, permitting the Jews to defend themselves on the fateful day. The Jews, of course, were overwhelmingly victorious.

When Savonarola saw poverty, oppression, and injustice in Florence, he became a standard in the hands of the Spirit to bring reform.

When Martin Luther began to thunder out against the sale of indulgences and other sins of the church, it was as if a light went on in an age of darkness.

Queen Mary was making havoc of the true Christian faith in England and Scotland. But God raised up a man named John Knox in that time of desperate need. "Throwing himself on his face in the dust before God, Knox pled with God through the night to avenge His elect and give him Scotland or he would die. The Lord gave him Scotland and removed the Queen from her throne."

It may be that you are facing one of the gravest crises of your life at the present time. Never fear. The Spirit of the Lord will send timely reinforcements and lead you out into a broad place. Only trust Him.

December 6

There is tremendous forcefulness and authority in the words of a righteous man. When he speaks, he has impact on the lives of others. His words carry weight. Men look up to him as one who deserves respect and obedience.

But if that same man falls into sin, he loses all that positive influence on others. The authoritative tone with which he spoke is dissipated. People no longer look to him for counsel. If he attempts to give it, they are apt to look at him with a jaundiced eye and say, "Physician, heal yourself" or "First take the beam out of your own eye; then you'll be able to remove the mote from mine." His lips are sealed.

This emphasizes the importance of maintaining a consistent testimony right to the end. It is important to begin well, but that is not enough. If we let down our guards in the closing stretch, the glory of earlier days will be obscured in the mists of dishonor.

"When Ephraim spoke, men trembled." Williams comments, "When Ephraim walked with God, as in the days of Joshua, he spoke with authority and people trembled, and so he had a position of dignity and power. But he turned to idolatry and died spiritually...The Christian has moral power and dignity so long as his heart is wholly governed by Christ and free from idolatry."

Gideon is another case in point. The Lord was with this mighty man of valor. With an army of 300 men he defeated the Midianites, 135,000 strong. When the men of Israel wanted to make him king, he wisely refused, because he realized that Jehovah was the rightful King.

But having gained illustrious victories and having successfully resisted great temptations, he caved in on what we might think was a minor matter. He asked his soldiers to give him the gold earrings they had taken as prey from the Ishmaelites. With these earrings, he made an ephod, which became an idol to the people of Israel, and a snare to Gideon and his family.

Of course, we know that when we fail, we can go to God in confession and find forgiveness. We know that He can even restore the years that the locusts have eaten, that is, He can enable us to make up for wasted time. But no one will deny that it is better to avoid a fall altogether than to recover from it, better not to smash our testimony than to try to glue the pieces back together again. Andrew Bonar's father used to say to him, "Andrew, pray that we both may wear well to the end!" So let us pray that we might finish our course with joy!

December 7

The greatest of these is love.
1 CORINTHIANS 13:13

L ove is the conquering power in a world of hatred, strife, and selfishness. It can do what no other virtue can do, and, in that sense, is the queen of the graces. Love repays abuse with kindness. It prays for mercy for its executioners. It acts unselfishly when all around are clamoring for their rights. It gives until it can give no more.

An Indian was driving his elephant along the street, goading it continually to increase its speed. Suddenly the steel goad slipped from his hand, tumbling with loud clanging on the pavement. The elephant swung around, picked up the goad with its trunk, and held it out to the master. Love is like that.

In one of Aesop's fables, there was a contest between the sun and the wind over who could make a man remove his coat. The wind blew furiously, but the more it blew, the more he pulled the coat tightly around him. Then the sun shone down on him and he took off his coat. It changed him through warmth. Love is like that.

Sir Walter Scott once threw a stone at a stray dog with such power and accuracy that it broke the dog's leg. As Scott stood there remorsefully, the dog limped up to him and licked the hand that had thrown the rock. Love is like that.

Stanton hurled bitter invective at Lincoln, calling him a "low cunning clown" and "the original gorilla." He said that anyone would be foolish to go to Africa for a gorilla when there was one in Springfield. Lincoln turned the other cheek. In fact, he later appointed Stanton as War Minister, insisting he was the most qualified man for the job. When Lincoln was shot, Stanton stood by his lifeless body, wept openly and said, "There lies the greatest ruler of men the world has ever seen." Lincoln had conquered by turning the other cheek. Love is like that.

E. Stanley Jones wrote, "By turning the other cheek you disarm your enemy. He hits you on the cheek and you, by your moral audacity, hit him on the heart by turning the other cheek. His enmity is dissolved. Your enemy is gone. You get rid of your enemy by getting rid of your enmity…The world is at the feet of the Man who had power to strike back but who had power not to strike back. That is power—the ultimate power."

Sometimes it may seem that more can be accomplished by speaking the harsh word, by repaying tit for tat and by standing up for one's rights. These methods do have a certain amount of power. But the balance of power is on the side of love, because, instead of deepening hostility, love changes enemies into friends.

December 8

Because the sentence against an evil work is not executed speedily, therefore the heart of the sons of men is fully set in them to do evil.
ECCLESIASTES 8:11

s I write this, there is a great wave of public indignation over the mounting crime rate in our country. People are calling for law and order. It seems that our laws and courts favor the criminal, while the victims of crime receive little or no redress.

Court cases drag on endlessly and often a criminal lawyer can win his case through silly loopholes in the law.

Contributing to the general disorder are the pontifical utterances of liberal sociologists, psychiatrists, and other "experts." They insist that capital punishment is unreasonable and inhumane. They testify that the fear of punishment does not serve as a deterrent to criminals. They suggest that the solution lies in rehabilitating criminals, not in punishing them.

But they are wrong. The more a man is confident that he can "get away with it," the more readily he will resort to crime. Or if he feels that the sentence will be light, he will be emboldened to take the risk of being caught. Or if he thinks that the trial will have countless continuations, he will be encouraged.

And in spite of what they say, the death sentence does act as a deterrent.

In analyzing the increasing crime rate, a popular news magazine said that "one of the reasons is the lack of a strong deterrent from America's clanking criminal justice system. All authorities agree that if the threat of punishment is to be credible, it must be sure and quick. Because of the overload, the U.S. system is neither."

An expert on criminology recently declared that for every man who is virtuous because of the love of virtue, 10,000 are good because they are afraid of punishment. And Isaac Ehrlich of the University of Chicago said, "Statistics show that the news about the execution of one murderer prevents 17 other murders." Reform and rehabilitation are not the answer. They have consistently failed to change men. We know that only the new birth by the Spirit of God will transform a sinner into a saint. But unfortunately few of the authorities, relatively speaking, will agree to that, either for themselves or for their prisoners.

That being the case, the best thing they can do is take today's verse seriously. "Because sentence against an evil work is not executed speedily, therefore the heart of the sons of men is fully set in them to do evil." Not until punishment is meted out swiftly and fairly will we see a decline in the crime statistics. The solution is right there in the Bible—if men would only accept it.

December 9

But thanks be to God, who gives us the victory through our Lord Jesus Christ.
1 CORINTHIANS 15:57

No created mind can ever comprehend the dimensions of the victory which the Lord Jesus won at the Cross of Calvary. He overcame the world (Jn. 16:33). He doomed Satan, the prince of this world (Jn. 16:11). He triumphed over principalities and powers (Col. 2:15). He so conquered death that it is now swallowed up in victory (1 Cor. 15:54, 55, 57).

And His victory is ours. Just as David's victory over Goliath brought deliverance to all of Israel, so Christ's glorious triumph is passed on to all who belong to Him. Therefore, we can sing with Horatius Bonar:

> *The victory is ours!*
> *For us in might came forth the mighty One;*
> *For us He fought the fight, the triumph won:*
> *The victory is ours.*

We are more than conquerors through Him who loved us because "neither death nor life, nor angels, nor principalities, nor powers, nor things present, nor things to come, nor height, nor depth, nor any other created thing, shall be able to separate us from the love of God" (Rom. 8:38-39).

Guy King told of a young lad who was at the station when a train pulled in, bringing the local soccer team home after an important game. The boy ran up to the first person who stepped off the train and asked breathlessly, "Who won?" Then he ran along the station platform, shouting ecstatically, "We won! We won!" As Mr. King watched, he thought to himself, "Now really, how much had he done to gain the victory? What did he have to do with the struggle on the football field?" The answer, of course, is "Nothing at all." But because he belonged to the same city, he identified himself with the city's team, and claimed their victory as his own.

I heard once of a Frenchman who passed from a position of defeat to one of victory by changing his citizenship. It was when Wellington, the so-called Iron Duke of England, won his illustrious victory over Napoleon at Waterloo. At first the Frenchman was associated with the defeat, but the day he became a British citizen, he could claim Wellington's victory as his own.

By birth we are all subjects of Satan's kingdom, and therefore we are on the losing side. But the moment we choose Christ as Lord and Savior, we pass from defeat to victory.

December 10

They...explained to him the way of God more accurately.
ACTS 18:26

In explaining the way of salvation to others, it is tremendously important to "make the message clear and plain," avoiding anything that might confuse them. They are usually confused enough already "whose minds the god of this age (Satan) has blinded" (2 Cor. 4:4).

Let me give an example of how we can say things that are real earstoppers to the unconverted. We begin witnessing to a young man whom we have just met for the first time. Before we get very far, he interrupts us, saying, "I don't believe in religion. I tried religion and it didn't do anything for me." To which we are apt to reply, "I don't believe in religion either, and I don't preach religion."

Just stop there! Can you imagine how confusing this is to our prospect? Here we are, talking to him about matters that are obviously religious, and yet we are telling him that we don't believe in religion. It's enough to blow his mind!

Of course I know what we mean. We mean that we are not asking him to join a church or denomination but to enter into a relationship with the Lord Jesus. We are not pushing a creed but a Person. We are not advocating reformation but regeneration, not a new suit on the man but a new man in the suit.

But when he thinks about religion, he thinks of anything that deals with the worship and service of God. The word "religion" to most people signifies a system of beliefs and a distinctive lifestyle that are connected with man's relationship to Deity.

So when we tell him that we don't believe in religion, the thought immediately races through his mind that we must be pagans or atheists. Before we have a chance to explain what we mean, he has already tagged us as irreligious.

Actually, it isn't true to say that we don't believe in religion. We do believe in the fundamental doctrines of the Christian faith. We do believe that those who profess faith in Christ should show it by their lives. We believe that pure and undefiled religion is found in caring for orphans and widows and keeping ourselves unspotted from the world (Jas. 1:27).

What we don't believe is that religion is the savior. Only the living Christ can save. We don't believe in the watered-down versions of Christianity that are abroad today. We don't believe in any system that encourages people to think that they can get to heaven by their own works or merit. But we ought to be able to explain this to people without stunning them with such bombshells as "I don't believe in religion, either." Let us not play games with words when souls are at stake.

December 11

Therefore you shall lay up these words of Mine in your heart and in your soul,
and bind them as a sign on your hand,
and they shall be as frontlets between your eyes.

DEUTERONOMY 11:18

Today's verse is incomplete without the three verses that follow, and so we quote them here: "You shall teach them to your children, speaking of them when you sit in your house, when you walk by the way, when you lie down, and when you rise up. And you shall write them on the doorposts of your house and on your gates, that your days and the days of your children may be multiplied in the land of which the Lord swore to your fathers to give them, like the days of the heavens above the earth" (Deut. 11:19-21).

Here we have a no-nonsense account of the important place that the Word of God should have in the lives of His people. When these conditions are met, believers will experience days of heaven upon earth.

First we should memorize the Word, or as the text says, lay it up in our hearts and souls. The man who learns vast portions of the Scriptures by heart enriches his own life and increases his potential for blessing others.

Next, the Word should be bound to our hands and to our foreheads. This does not mean using phylacteries, as some think, but rather that our actions (hands) and desires (eyes) should be under the Lordship of Christ.

God's Word should be the central topic of conversation in the home. In addition, every home should have the family altar, when the Scriptures are read daily and the household prays together. No one can gauge the sanctifying influence of the Bible on such a home.

This same Word should occupy us when we walk by the way, when we lie down, and when we get up. In other words, the Scriptures should become so much a part of our lives that they mold our conversation wherever we are and whatever we are doing. We should talk in the language of the Bible.

Should we write verses on our doorposts and gates? A very good idea! Many Christian homes have Joshua 24:15 on the front door: "As for me and my house, we will serve the Lord." And many more homes have Scripture texts hanging on the walls inside.

When we give the Holy Scriptures their proper place in our lives, we not only save ourselves from wasted hours of small talk, but we occupy ourselves with the subjects that really matter, the subjects that are of eternal consequence, and we maintain a Christian atmosphere in our homes.

December 12

You shall not tempt the Lord your God
MATTHEW 4:7

W hat does it mean to tempt the Lord? Is it something of which we can be guilty?

The children of Israel tempted the Lord when they complained about the lack of water in the wilderness (Ex. 17:7). In saying, "Is the Lord among us, or not?" they doubted not only His divine presence but His providential care for them as well.

Satan tempted the Lord when he challenged Him to jump down from the peak of the Temple (Lk. 4:9-12). Jesus would have tempted God the Father if He had done so, because He would have been performing a stunt, something that was outside the Father's will.

The Pharisees tempted the Lord when they asked Him if it was lawful to pay tribute to Caesar (Mt. 22:15-18). They thought that no matter how He answered, He would alienate either the Romans or those Jews who were violently anti-Roman.

Sapphira tempted the Spirit of the Lord by pretending to give the total proceeds from a sale of property to the Lord, when actually she held back some for herself (Acts 5:9).

Peter told the council at Jerusalem that it would be tempting God to put Gentile believers under the law, a yoke that the Jewish people themselves had not been able to bear (Acts 15:10).

To tempt God is "to see how much one can get away with before He judges; it means to presume on Him, to see if He will perform His Word, or to stretch Him to the limits of judgment (cf. Deut. 6:16; Mt. 4:7)" (TOUSSAINT). We tempt God when we murmur or complain, because we are, in effect, doubting His presence, power, or goodness. We are saying that He doesn't know our circumstances, He doesn't care, or He isn't able to deliver us.

We tempt God when we needlessly expose ourselves to danger and expect Him to rescue us. Every so often we read of misguided believers who handle poisonous snakes and die as a result. Their reasoning was that God had promised safety in Mark 16:18; "They will take up serpents." But this was intended to justify our performing miracles only when they are necessary in carrying out His will.

We tempt God when we lie to Him, and we do this when we profess greater dedication, sacrifice and commitment than we actually intend to deliver. Just as the Pharisees tempted Christ by their hypocrisy, so we tempt Him by ours.

Finally, we tempt the Lord whenever we remove ourselves from the sphere of His will for us and act in self-will.

It is an astounding thing that a creature should ever desire or dare to tempt his Creator, or that a sinner should thus insult his Savior!

December 13

Then those who feared the Lord spoke to one another, and the Lord listened and heard them; so a book of remembrance was written before Him for those who fear the Lord and who meditate on His name.

MALACHI 3:16

I t is possible to be so busy that our souls become barren. Too much activity causes us to be occupied too much with our work and too little with our God. Preachers who do not spend much time alone in meditation and communion with the Lord soon give out second-hand messages that have little or no spiritual power. We should all pray, "Lord, deliver me from the barrenness of a busy life." Many believers are afraid to be alone. They must be with others, talking, working, or traveling. No time is spent in quiet contemplation. The pressures of modern life encourage us to be hyperactive, to be overachievers. We build up a momentum of activity and it is difficult to slow down. Life seems to be a continual push, push, push, go, go, go. The result is that we do not develop deep spiritual roots. We still spout the same pious truisms that we shared with people twenty years ago. No progress in twenty years!

And yet there are those who discipline themselves to break away from the rat race, who refuse invitations, who put aside secondary activities so that they can spend time alone with the Lord. They resolutely make time for prayerful meditation. They have a hideaway where they can tune out the noise of the world in order to be alone with the Lord Jesus.

These people have an inside track with the Lord. "The secret of the Lord is with those who fear Him" (Ps. 25:14). God reveals secrets to them that we, in our frenzied lives, know nothing about. There is a communication of divine intelligence concerning guidance, concerning events transpiring in the spiritual realm, concerning the future. Those who dwell in the sanctuary often have visions of God that those who live in the suburbs know nothing about. It was the one who leaned on the Savior's bosom who was given the Revelation of Jesus Christ.

I often think of these words of Cecil: "I say everywhere and to all, you must hold intercourse with God or your soul will die. You must walk with God or Satan will walk with you. You must grow in grace or you will lose it; and you cannot do this but by appropriating to this object a due portion of your time, and diligently employing suitable means. I know not how it is that some Christians can make so little of recollection and retirement. I find the spirit of the age a strong assimilating principle. I find it hurrying my mind away in its vortex, and sinking me among the dregs and filth of a carnal nature...I am obliged to withdraw myself regularly and to say to my heart, 'What are you doing? Where are you now?'"

December 14

Whom I have created for My glory; I have formed him, yes, I have made him.
ISAIAH 43:7

One of the great tragedies of our existence is to see men and women living wasted lives. Man, after all, was made in the image and likeness of God. He was destined for a throne, not for a bar stool. He was created to be a representative of God, not a slave of sin. In answer to the question, "What is the chief end of man?" the Shorter Catechism reminds us that "The chief end of man is to glorify God and to enjoy Him forever." If we miss that, we miss everything.

J. H. Jowett weeps as he realizes that the course of many people through the years is "not so much the transit of a man as the passage of an amoeba." He grieves to see men who have drivelled down to be nothing more than "minor officials in transient enterprises." He notes with pathos the epitaph of one who was "born a man and died a grocer."

F. W. H. Myers gazes out over humanity and writes:

> *Only like souls I see the folk thereunder,*
> *Bound who should conquer, slaves who should be kings,*
> *Hearing their one hope with an empty wonder,*
> *Sadly contented in a show of things.*

When Watchman Nee was a young man, he was moved to see "human creative gift squandered for an avaricious employer...In one of the shops of the old city's lacquer street an anonymous craftsman had already spent six years on three hardwood leaves of a four-leaf screen, carving reliefs of flowers in the natural wood, white against the black lacquered surface. For this he was paid eighty cents a day, 'rain, shine, holidays, or revolution,' as the shop owner put it, plus his rice and vegetables and a plank to sleep on. Having once acquired skill for this work, he might make only two such screens before eyes and nerves failed and he was flung out with the beggars."

The tragedy of life today is that men fail to appreciate their high calling. They go through life hugging the subordinate. They creep instead of fly. As someone has said, they rake around in a muck heap, not noticing the angel above them who is offering them a crown. Their time is spent making a living instead of making a life.

Many today are concerned over the spoiling of natural resources but they never think of the greater loss of human resources. Many campaign to save endangered species of birds, animals and fishes, but they can look on people wasting their lives and not be moved. One human life is worth more than the whole world. To fritter away that life is the unutterable tragedy. One woman said, "I am seventy, and I have done nothing with my life." What could be more tragic?

December 15

Those who sow in tears shall reap in joy. He who continually goes forth weeping, bearing seed for sowing, shall doubtless come again with rejoicing, bringing his sheaves with him.
PSALM 126:5-6

I n Psalm 126 the children of Israel are reminiscing about their return to the land after their captivity in Babylon. It had been as if they were in a dream world, filled with laughter and singing. Even their pagan neighbors had commented on the great things the Lord had done for His people.

Now that they were back in their own land, they had to start planting crops. But this posed a problem. They had brought back only a limited amount of grain with them. They could use it as food now; after all, there were no crops in the field for them to harvest. Or they could use it as seed, sowing it in the ground with the hope of an abundant harvest in days to come. If they decided to use most of it as seed, that meant that they would have to live frugally and sacrificially until harvest time. They decided on the latter course.

As the farmer went out into his fields, dipped his hand into the seed, and scattered it broadcast on the plowed land, he would shed tears at the thought of the privations he and his family would have to endure until the time of harvest.

But later when the fields teemed with golden grain, his tears would be turned to joy as he brought the ripened sheaves back to the barn. All the sacrifices his household had made would be richly rewarded.

We can think of this in connection with our own stewardship of material things. The Lord entrusts each of us with a limited amount of money. We can spend it in self-indulgence, buying up whatever our hearts desire. Or by living sacrificially, we can invest it in the work of the Lord—in foreign missions, in Christian literature, in gospel radio broadcasts, in the local church and in many other forms of evangelistic activity. In that case, it will mean choosing a modest standard of living so that everything above essentials will go into the work of the Lord. It will mean living on a restricted budget so that souls will not perish for want of the gospel.

But any such sacrifices will not be worth mentioning when the time of harvest comes, when we will see men and women in heaven as a result of our sacrificial living. One person saved from hell to become a worshipper of the Lamb of God for all eternity is worth any sacrifice we can make now.

December 16

Bless the Lord, O my soul, and forget not all His benefits:
...who heals all your diseases.
PSALM 103:2-3

One of the compound names of God is Jehovah-Rapha, meaning, "I am the Lord who heals you" (Ex. 15:26). It is God who heals us. He heals us of all kinds of diseases, and will ultimately deliver us permanently from every form of sickness.

Sometimes He heals us through the tremendous recuperative powers which He has placed in our bodies. This is why doctors often say, "Most things are better by morning." Sometimes He heals through medicines and surgery. Dubois, the famous French physician, said, "The surgeon dresses the wound; God heals it." Sometimes He heals miraculously. We know this from the Gospels and from personal experience.

However, it is not always God's will to heal. If it were, some would never grow old and die. But everyone dies sooner or later, until the Lord comes. God did not remove Paul's physical affliction but gave him grace to bear it (2 Cor. 12:7-10).

In a general sense, all sickness is a result of sin. In other words, if there never had been any sin, there wouldn't be any sickness. Sometimes illness is a direct result of sin in a person's ife. For example, alcoholism sometimes causes liver disease, smoking sometimes causes cancer, sexual immorality sometimes causes venereal disease, and worry sometimes causes ulcers. But not all sickness is a direct result of a person's own sin. Satan used Job's serious illness (Job 2:7), and yet Job was the most righteous man on earth (Job 1:8; 2:3). He caused an unknown woman to be afflicted with curvature of the spine (Lk. 13:11-17). And he caused Paul's thorn in the flesh (2 Cor. 12:7). In John 9:2-3, it could not have been the man's own sin that caused him to be born blind. Epaphroditus was critically ill, not because of sin, but because of his untiring service for the Lord (Phil. 2:30). Gaius was spiritually healthy but physically unwell (3 John 2).

Finally, failure to be healed does not necessarily indicate a lack of faith. Only when God has given a specific promise that He will heal can faith claim healing. Otherwise we commit ourselves to our living, loving Lord and pray that His will be done.

December 17

Where there is no wood, the fire goes out.
PROVERBS 26:20

T wo men are quarreling. One delivers an angry blast and the other answers with a sharp retort. One charges heatedly and the other countercharges with equal vehemence. Neither is willing to stop lest his silence be counted as weakness or defeat. And so the fire increases in intensity and billows of hate back and forth.

But change the picture. One man levels a verbal barrage at his opponent, but receives no fire in return. He tries to aggravate, to irritate, to slander, and to shame. But the other man refuses to join the fray. Finally, the antagonist realizes he is wasting his time so he slinks off, mumbling and cursing. The fire went out because the defendant refused to add fuel to it.

Dr. H. A. Ironside often encountered people at the end of a meeting who wanted to argue with him over something he had said. Usually they were picking nits, not discussing some fundamental doctrine. Dr. Ironside would listen patiently, then when the contentious one came up for air, he would say, "Well, brother, when we get to heaven, one of us will be wrong, and perhaps it will be me." That answer invariably freed the good Doctor to speak to somebody else.

How do we take criticism? Do we defend ourselves, return tit for tat, release all the critical thoughts we have ever entertained about the other person? Or do we say calmly, "Brother, I'm glad you don't know me better, because if you did, you'd have a lot more to criticize." A reply like this has put out many a fire.

I suppose that most of us have received a letter at some time fairly blasting us off the face of the earth. The natural reaction for us at such a time is to dip our pen in acid and deliver a stinging reply. This fuels the fire and pretty soon poison-pen letters are racing back and forth. How much better to write back one simple reply, "Dear brother, if you want to fight someone, please fight the devil."

Life is too short to be spent in self-defense, in quarreling, or in heated words. These things divert us from what is of first importance, they lower our spiritual tone, and they impair our testimony. Others may carry the torch with which to deliberately start a fire, but we control the fuel. When we refuse to add fuel to the fire, the fire goes out.

December 18

Woe to those who call evil good, and good evil; who put darkness for light, and light for darkness; who put bitter for sweet, and sweet for bitter!
ISAIAH 5:20

God pronounces a woe on those who reverse moral standards, making sin respectable and suggesting that purity is something less than desirable. Herbert Vander Lugt cited three contemporary illustrations of how men tamper with moral distinctions. "First, I read an article which treated lightly the bad results of pornography, but deplored the 'puritanical attitude of religionists.' Second, I came across a newspaper account about a group of concerned parents who were trying to get an unmarried pregnant teacher removed from her job. The writer portrayed her as a beautiful person, while the moms and dads were made out to be villains. And third, I watched as a guest on a television program defended the hard rock, the drunkenness, and the use of drugs connected with a concert in which several young people were killed. He blamed our social problems on individuals who don't like these kinds of gatherings."

I would suggest two reasons why we are witnessing an increasing wave of moral reversals. First of all, people have abandoned the standards of absolutes that are found in the Bible. Now morality is a matter of one's own interpretation. Secondly, the more that people indulge in sin, the more they feel that they must rationalize the sin as justifiable behavior, and thus vindicate themselves.

Some who find it hard to justify sin resort instead to *ad hominem* arguments, that is, they attack the opponent's character rather than answer his contentions. Thus, in the illustrations cited above, the libertarians attacked the "puritanical attitude of religionists"; they made moms and dads out as villains; and they blamed social problems on people who speak out against drunkenness, drugs, and a rock concert in which several young people were killed.

In addition to those who reverse moral distinctions, there are those who satisfy themselves with blurring them. Unfortunately, a large number of these are religious leaders. Instead of coming out squarely on the side of the Bible and calling sins by their right names, they pussyfoot around, implying that they're really not that bad after all. Drunkenness is a sickness. Perversion is an alternate lifestyle. Sex outside of marriage is allowable if it is culturally acceptable. Abortions, public nudity, and prostitution are personal rights that should not be abridged.

Such confused thinking betrays a serious lack of moral intelligence. These perverse arguments are lies of the devil that eventually drown men in perdition.

December 19

Heaven and earth will pass away, but My words will by no means pass away.
LUKE 21:33

T he Word of God is not only eternal; it is absolutely sure of fulfillment. In Matthew 5:18 Jesus said that not one jot or tittle will pass from the law until all be fulfilled. A jot is a letter of the Hebrew alphabet that resembles a comma or an apostrophe. A tittle is a stroke of a Hebrew letter, we might compare it to the bottom stroke of a capital E that distinguishes the E from the F. In other words, Jesus was saying that God's Word will be fulfilled down to the minutest details.

Julian the Apostate, a Roman emperor who lived AD 331-36, decided that he would disprove the Bible and discredit Christianity. The particular passage he chose to disprove was Luke 21:24: "And they will fall by the edge of the sword, and be led away captive into all nations. And Jerusalem will be trampled by Gentiles until the times of the Gentiles are fulfilled." He began by encouraging the Jews to rebuild the temple. According to Gibbon in *The Decline and Fall of the Roman Empire,* they went to work eagerly, using even silver shovels in their extravagance, and carrying the dirt in purple veils. But while they were working, they were interrupted by an earthquake and by balls of fire coming from the ground. They had to abandon the project.

Almost 600 years before Christ, Ezekiel predicted that the Eastern Gate of Jerusalem would be shut, and that it would remain shut until "the prince" would come (Ezek. 44:3). Many Bible students understand "the prince" to be the Messiah. The gate, subsequently called the Golden Gate, was closed up by Sultan Seuleman in AD 1543. In Kaiser Wilhelm's plan to capture Jerusalem, he hoped to enter by this gate, but his hope was dashed. The gate remains closed.

Voltaire boasted that the Bible would be a dead book in 100 years. When the hundred years had passed, Voltaire was dead and his house had become head-quarters for the Geneva Bible Society. Ingersoll made a similar boast. He said that he would have the Bible in the morgue in 15 years. It was he, not the Bible, who went to the morgue. The Bible outlives all its critics.

You would think that men would wake up to the fact that the Bible is God's eternal Word and that it will never pass away. But then, as Jonathan Swift said, "There are none so blind as they that will not see."

December 20

I have learned in whatever state I am, to be content.
Philippians 4:11

W e are often told that it isn't the circumstances of life that are important; it's how we react to those circumstances that really matters. This
is true. Rather than always trying to change our circumstances, we
should think more about changing ourselves.

There are several ways in which people respond to adverse happenings. The
first is *stoically*. This means that they are completely impassive, gritting their
teeth, and showing no emotion. Their policy is to "cooperate with the inevitable."

Others respond *hysterically*. They go to pieces emotionally with loud crying,
tears and spectacular physical displays.

Some react *defeatedly*. They give up in abject despondency. In extreme cases,
this can end in suicide.

The normal Christian way is to respond *submissively*. The believer reasons,
"This did not happen by accident. God controls everything that comes into my
life. He has not made a mistake. He has allowed this in order to bring glory to
Himself, blessing to others, and good to me. I can't see the full outworking of His
program, but I will trust Him nevertheless. So I bow to His will, and pray that He
will glorify Himself and teach me whatever He wants me to learn."

There is another way that some choice saints react, that is, *super-triumphantly*.
I dare not count myself among the number, even though I aspire to their company. These are the ones who use adversity as a stepping stone to victory. They trans-
mute the bitter into the sweet and ashes into beauty. They do not let circumstances
rule them, rather they make the circumstances serve them. In this sense, they are
"more than conquerors." Let me give a few illustrations.

There was a Christian woman whose life seemed to be filled with disappointment and frustration. Yet her biographer wrote, "She made magnificent bouquets
out of the refusals of God."

Believers in an oriental country had been attacked with stones by an angry
mob. When these same believers returned, they built a chapel with the stones that
had been hurled at them.

After buying a home, a man found a huge boulder in the middle of the garden.
He decided to make a rock garden.

E. Stanley Jones said, "Use your denials and turn them into doors." Or, as
someone else said, "When life gives you lemons, make lemonade."

I especially like the story of the man who was told by his doctor that he would
lose an eye and would have to have a glass eye. His immediate response was, "Be
sure to put in one with a twinkle." That's what I call living above the circumstances.

December 21

Christ also loved the church and gave Himself for her.
Ephesians 5:25

T he church occupies a place of tremendous importance in the mind of Christ, and it should be extremely important in our estimation as well. We sense its importance by the prominent space it occupies in the New Testament. Also it claimed a significant place in the ministry of the apostles. Paul, for instance, spoke of his two-fold ministry—to preach the gospel and to declare the truth of the church (Eph. 3:8-9). The apostles spoke of the church with an enthusiasm that is strangely missing today. Everywhere they went they planted churches, whereas the tendency today is to start Christian organizations.

The truth of the church formed the capstone of scriptural revelation (Col. 1:25-26). It was the last major doctrine to be revealed.

The church is an object lesson to angelic beings (Eph. 3:10). They learn lessons from it about the multi-faceted wisdom of God.

The church is the unit on earth through which God has chosen to propagate and defend the faith (1 Tim. 3:15). He speaks of it as the pillar and ground of the truth. We are thankful for para-church organizations that are devoted to the spread of the gospel and the instruction of believers, but it is a mistake when they take the place of the local church in their members' lives. God promised that the gates of Hades would not prevail against the church (Mt. 16:18), but He never gave that promise to Christian organizations.

Paul speaks of the church as the fullness of Him who fills all in all (Eph. 1:20-23). In marvelous grace, the Head does not consider Himself complete without His members.

The church is not only the body of Christ (1 Cor. 12:12-13); it is His bride as well (Eph. 5:25-27, 31-32). As the body, it is the vehicle through which He chooses to express Himself to the world in this era. As the bride, it is the special object of His affection which He is preparing to share His reign and His glory.

From all the above, we are forced to conclude that the weakest assembly of believers means more to Christ than the greatest empire in the world. He speaks of the church in terms of tender endearment and unique dignity. We also conclude that an elder in a local assembly means more to God than a president or a king. Few instructions are found in the New Testament on how to be a good ruler, but considerable space is devoted to the work of an elder.

If we once see the church as the Lord sees it, it will revolutionize our life and ministry.

December 22

For if we sin willfully after we have received the knowledge of the truth,
there no longer remains a sacrifice for sins, but a certain fearful expectation
of judgment, and fiery indignation which will devour the adversaries.
HEBREWS 10:26-27

T his is one of several verses in the New Testament which is extremely unsettling to many earnest, conscientious Christians. They reason this way: I am faced with a temptation; I know it is wrong. I know I shouldn't do it, and yet I go ahead and do it anyway. I deliberately disobey. It seems to me that I am sinning willfully. Therefore, it sounds from this verse as though I have lost my salvation.

The problem arises because they take the verse out of its context and make it say something it was never intended to say. The context has to do with the sin of apostasy—the sin of one who professes to be a believer for a while, but who subsequently repudiates the Christian faith and usually identifies himself with some system that opposes Christ. The apostate is described in verse 29: he has trodden under foot the Son of God, and has counted the blood of the covenant wherewith he was sanctified an unholy thing, and has done despite to the Spirit of grace. He shows by his bitter turning against Christ that he was never born again.

Suppose that a man hears the gospel and develops warm feelings toward the Christian faith. He leaves his ancestral religion and adopts the Christian label without being genuinely converted. But then persecution begins, and he has second thoughts about being known as a Christian. Finally he decides to go back to his old religion. But it isn't that easy. Suppose that before the leaders are willing to take the turncoat back, they have a little ceremony that he must go through. They take the blood of a pig and sprinkle it on the floor. Then they say, "That blood represents the blood of Christ. If you want to return to your parents' religion, you must walk over it." And so he does.

In effect, he is trampling under foot the Son of God and counting His blood as an unholy thing. That man is an apostate. He has committed the willful sin.

A true believer cannot commit this willful sin. He may commit other acts of sin when he knows it is wrong. He may deliberately violate his conscience. This is serious in God's eyes, and we must not say anything that would excuse it. But still he can find forgiveness by confessing and forsaking his sin. Not so with the apostate. For him the verdict is that there remains no more sacrifice for sins (v. 26b), and it is impossible to renew him again to repentance (Heb. 6:6).

December 23

Whoever abides in Him does not sin.
Whoever sins has neither seen Him nor known Him.
1 JOHN 3:6

Yesterday we considered a passage that often proves distressing to sincere Christians. Today we will look at three verses in John's first epistle that also disturb believers who are all too aware of their sinfulness. There is the verse already quoted at the top of the page. Then there is 1 John 3:9: "Whoever has been born of God does not sin, for His seed remains in him; and he cannot sin, because he has been born of God." And 1 John 5:18: "We know that whoever is born of God does not sin; but he who has been born of God keeps himself, and the wicked one does not touch him." Taken as is, these verses might very well make any one of us question whether he is a true believer.

And yet other verses in this same letter recognize that the believer does sin, for example 1:8-10; 2:1b.

The problem is largely one of translation. In the original language of the New Testament, there is a difference between committing occasional acts of sin and practicing sin as a way of life. The Christian does commit acts of sin, but sin is not what characterizes his life. He has been freed from sin as his master.

The New International Version shows that the verbs in these verses are in what we might call the present continuous tense, as follows: "No one who lives in Him keeps on sinning. No one who continues to sin has either seen Him or known him" (3:6). "No one who is born of God will continue to sin, because God's seed remains in him; he cannot go on sinning, because he has been born of God" (vv. 3-9). "We know that anyone born of God does not continue to sin; the one who was born of God keeps him safe, and the evil one does not touch him" (5:18).

Any Christian who says he does not sin has imperfect views of what sin is. He apparently doesn't realize that anything that falls short of God's perfect standard is sin. The fact is that we do commit acts of sin every day in thought, word, and deed.

But John makes a distinction between what is exceptional and what is habitual. With the true saint, sin is alien and righteousness is characteristic.

When we see this, there is no need to torture ourselves with these verses that make us doubt our salvation. The simple facts are these: God's will is that we should not sin. Unfortunately we do sin. But sin is no longer the dominating power in our lives. We no longer practice sin as we did before we were saved. If we do sin, we find forgiveness through confessing and forsaking our sin.

December 24

The rich man thinks of his wealth as an impregnable defense,
a high wall of safety. What a dreamer!
PROVERBS 18:11, LIVING BIBLE

T he rich fool in Luke's Gospel had so much wealth he didn't know what to do with it. So he decided to tear down his barns and silos and build bigger ones. Then he thought he would feel satisfied, not knowing that he would die as soon as his building project was completed. His wealth wouldn't save him from death and the grave.

Sider says, "The rich fool is the epitome of the covetous person. He has a greedy compulsion to acquire more and more possessions, even though he does not need them. And his phenomenal success at piling up more and more property leads to the blasphemous conclusion that material possessions can satisfy all his needs. From the divine perspective, however, this attitude is sheer madness. He is a raving fool."

There is a legend about a man who wanted to become rich in the stock market. When someone told him he could have anything he wanted, he said he would like to see the newspaper one year from that day. His idea, of course, was that he could make a fortune by buying the stocks that would rise the most during the ensuing year. When he got the paper, he gloated about how rich he would become. But then he looked at the death notices and his name was there.

The psalmist pours scorn on the rich people whose "inner thought is, that their houses are forever, and their dwelling places to all generations; they have called their lands after their own names" (Ps. 49:11, NASB). But they die and leave their wealth to others. "Man in his pomp will not endure; he is like the beasts that perish" (Ps. 49:12, NASB).

It is a true saying that money is the universal passport for everywhere except heaven, and the universal provider for everything but happiness.

No rich person ever has a dollar sign inscribed on his tombstone, even though money has been the obsession of his life. If he used the symbol of what has been paramount to him, it would be the $. But in death he chooses a religious symbol, such as a cross. It is a final gesture of hypocrisy. The righteous look on and say, "Here is the man who did not make God his strength, but trusted in the abundance of his riches, and strengthened himself in his wickedness" (Ps. 52:7). And God writes his epitaph, "So is he who lays up treasure for himself, and is not rich toward God" (Lk. 12:21).

December 25

And without controversy great is the mystery of godliness:
God was manifested in the flesh.
1 TIMOTHY 3:16

T he mystery is great—not because it is very mysterious but because it is so astounding. The mystery is the amazing truth that God was manifest in the flesh.

It means, for instance, that the Eternal One was born into a world of time. He, the Timeless One, lived in a sphere of calendars and timepieces.

The One who is omnipresent, existing in all places at one and the same time, confined Himself to a single place—like Bethlehem, or Nazareth, Capernaum, or Jerusalem.

It is wonderful to think that the Great God, who fills heaven and earth, should compress Himself into a human body. As men looked at Him, they could say accurately, "In Him dwells all the fullness of the Godhead bodily."

The mystery reminds us that the Creator visited this insignificant planet called Earth. It is only a speck of cosmic dust, relative to the rest of the universe, yet He by-passed all the rest to come here. From the palace of heaven to a cattle shed, a stable, a manger!

The omnipotent One became a helpless Baby. It is no exaggeration to say that He whom Mary held in her arms held Mary, for He is the Sustainer as well as the Maker.

The omniscient One is the fountain of all wisdom and knowledge, and yet we read of Him that, as a Child, He increased in wisdom and knowledge. It is almost incredible to think of the Owner of all arriving unwelcome on His own premises. There was no room for Him in the inn. The world knew Him not. His own received Him not.

The Master came into the world as a Servant. The Lord of glory veiled that glory in a body of flesh. The Lord of life came into the world to die. The Holy One came to a jungle of sin. The One who is infinitely high became intimately nigh. The Object of the Father's delight and of angelic worship hungered and thirsted, was weary at Jacob's well, slept in a boat on Galilee, wandered "as a homeless stranger in the world His hands had made." He came from luxury to poverty, with no place to lay His head. He worked as a carpenter. Never slept on a mattress. Never had hot and cold running water, or the other conveniences that we take for granted.

And it was all for you and for me!
O, come, let us adore Him!

December 26

*Now the king of Sodom said to Abram, Give me the persons,
and take the goods for yourself.*
GENESIS 14:21

1nvading armies had come to Sodom and had captured Lot, his family and great quantities of soil. As soon as Abram heard about it, he armed his servants and pursued the invaders, finally catching up with them near Damascus and rescuing the captives and their belongings. The king of Sodom went out to meet Abram as he returned and said, "Give me the persons, and take the goods for yourself." Abram answered that he wouldn't take even a shoelace from the king lest the latter would say he had made Abram rich.

There is a sense in which the king of Sodom represents Satan, trying to get believers to be occupied with material things and to neglect the people around them. Abram resisted the temptation, but many since that time have not been so successful. They have given priority to the accumulation of possessions and have paid little attention to neighbors and friends who are facing eternity without God, without Christ, and without hope.

People are important; things are not. A young Christian walked into the living room where his mother was sewing and said, "Mother, I'm glad that God has given me a greater love for people than for things." That particular mother was glad, too.

It seems incongruous to weep when someone breaks your English bone china teacup, but never to shed a tear over perishing millions. It says something when we have a phenomenal memory for baseball scores, yet whine that we have an awful time remembering people's names. I betray my distorted sense of values when I am more upset over the damage done to my car than the injured person in the other car. It is easy to resent interruptions when we are working on some pet project, and yet the interruption may be far more important than the project.

We are often more interested in gold and silver than in men and women. A. T. Pierson said, "There is buried in gold and silver and useless ornaments in Christian homes enough to build a fleet of 50,000 vessels, ballast them with Bibles and crowd them with missionaries: build a church in every destitute hamlet and supply every living soul with the gospel within a score of years. Another prophet of God, J. A. Stewart, wrote, "We have used our wealth to indulge in luxuries that we do not need. We have 'caviar tastes' while millions in other parts of our world are dying in the starvation of sin. We have sold our spiritual birthright-heritage for a mess of pottage."

My heart often wonders when we Christians will abandon the mad scramble for material possessions and concentrate on the spiritual welfare of people. One human soul is worth more than all the wealth in the world. Things don't matter. People do.

December 27

My body, which is broken for you.
1 CORINTHIANS 11:24

my Carmichael lists four broken things in the Bible and the results achieved by them.

Broken pitchers (Jud. 7:18, 19)—and the light shone out.

A broken flask (Mk. 14:3)—and the ointment was poured forth.

Broken bread (Mt. 14:19)—and the hungry were fed.

A broken Body (1 Cor. 11:24)—and the world was redeemed.

Now it is our privilege to add a fifth to the list—a broken will, and the result will be a life flooded with peace and fulfillment.

Many who have been to the Cross for salvation have never been there for the breaking of their will. They may have a gentle, mild disposition; they may never speak above a whisper; they may have an outward appearance of spirituality; yet they may have a will of iron that keeps them from God's best in life.

It sometimes happens with young people who are in love and are contemplating marriage. Parents and friends with mature, wise judgment can see that it will never work. Yet the headstrong couple rejects any counsel that they do not want to hear. The same intractable wills that led them to the marriage altar soon lead them to the divorce court.

We've seen it with Christians who are determined to go into a certain business when they clearly have no experience or the necessary know-how. Against the advice of knowledgeable associates, they sink their own money and often money borrowed from loving friends. The inevitable happens. The business fails, and the creditors move in to pick up the pieces.

It is not uncommon to see the shattering effects of an unbroken will in Christian service. It takes a man and his family to the mission field, only to be repatriated within a year at great cost to the sending church. It drains funds from gullible Christians to finance a project that was man's idea, not God's—a project that proves to be counter-productive. It creates strife and unhappiness because one person refuses to work cooperatively with others; he must have his own way.

We all need to be broken, to take all our obstinacy, all our stubbornness, all our self-will and leave them at the foot of the Cross. That will of iron must be laid upon the altar of sacrifice. We must all say with Amy Carmichael:

Thou wast broken, O my Lord, for me,
Let me be broken, Lord, for love of Thee.

December 28

Like one who takes a dog by the ears is he who passes by
and meddles with strife not belonging to him.
PROVERBS 26:17, NASB

We should realize first of all that the dog mentioned in this verse is not the friendly, gentle, Irish setter that probably wouldn't mind at all if you held him by his ears. This is the wild, snarling, alley dog with a mean disposition and bared fangs. It would be improbable that you could get close enough to him to grab him by the ears in the first place. But if you could, you'd face a desperate dilemma; you'd be afraid to hold on and afraid to let go.

Well, it's a graphic illustration of the person who gets involved in a fight that doesn't concern him. Soon he has incurred the anger of both the adversaries.

Each one feels that the meddler is interfering with any chance of victory, so they forget their own differences and unite in fighting him.

We smile at the Irishman who went up to two men engaged in a fist fight and asked, "Is this a private fight or can anyone get in?" Yet there is a meddlesome streak in every one of us that tempts us to interfere in squabbles that are none of our business.

Police officers have to be extra careful when they are called to a scene where a husband and wife are quarreling. If that is so, how much more cautious should the average citizen be in intruding in the domestic strife of others!

Perhaps one of the best illustrations of today's proverb is trouble in the church. It usually starts between two persons. Then others take sides. What started as a spark soon becomes a conflagration. People who have no connection with the problem insist on adding their own wise pronouncements, as if they were the oracle of Delphi. Tempers flare, friendships are shattered, and hearts are broken. As the battle increases in intensity the congregation hears announcements of coronaries, strokes, ulcers, and other physical problems. What started as a root of bitterness has spread until many are defiled.

The warning not to meddle in strife belonging to others might seem to conflict with the Savior's words, "Blessed are the peacemakers, For they shall be called sons of God" (Mt. 5:9). But there is no contradiction. There is a place for a peacemaker when contending parties are willing to have their dispute arbitrated. Otherwise, the one who interferes succeeds only in getting himself into a situation from which there is no easy, painless escape.

December 29

We are yours, O David; we are on your side, O son of Jesse!
Peace, peace to you, and peace to your helpers! For your God helps you.
1 CHRONICLES 12:18

This noble expression of loyalty to David should be borrowed by all believers as an expression of their devotion to the Lord Jesus Christ. There is no room for halfhearted loyalty or divided allegiance to the King of kings. He must have all our hearts.

I have always been impressed with the story of a French soldier who was seriously wounded in one of the Napoleonic wars. The doctors decided that surgery was necessary to save his life. It was in the days before anaesthesia. As the surgeon was probing in the soldier's chest, the patient said, "Probe a little deeper, Doctor, and you will find the Emperor." There was a sense in which the Emperor was enthroned in his heart.

When Elizabeth was crowned as Queen while she was still quite young, her grandmother, Queen Mary, wrote her a letter of loyalty and signed it, "Your loving grandmother and devoted subject." She thus expressed her allegiance to the Crown and to the one who wore it.

But what about us? How does all this apply in our case? Matthew Henry reminds us that "From these expressions of Amasai, we may take instruction how to testify our affection and allegiance to the Lord Jesus: his we may be without reservation or power of revocation; on his side we must be forward to appear and act; to his interest we must be hearty well-wishers; Hosanna, prosperity to his gospel and kingdom; for his God helpeth him, and will, till he have put down all rule, principality, and power."

In the words of Spurgeon, our lives should say, "Thine are we, Jesus. Neither count we anything that we possess to be our own; but all is dedicated to Thy royal use. And on Thy side, Thou Son of God. For, if we belong to Christ, of course we are on Christ's side, whatever that side may be, in religion, morals, and politics. Peace be unto Thee. Our heart salutes Him and invokes peace upon Him. And peace be to Thy helpers. We desire all good for all good men. We pray for the peace of the peaceful. For Thy God helpeth Thee. All the powers of the God of nature are working to aid the Lord of grace. Risen Christ, we look upward as the heavens receive Thee, and we adore. Ascended Christ, we fall at Thy dear feet, and say, 'Thine are we, O Son of David, anointed to be a Prince and a Savior.' Coming Christ, we wait and watch for Thine appearing. Come quickly to Thine own! Amen and Amen."

December 30

Now David said, Is there still anyone who is left of the house of Saul,
that I may show him kindness for Jonathan's sake?
2 SAMUEL 9:1

Mephibosheth was a grandson of King Saul, who had repeatedly tried to take David's life. He therefore came from a rebel family that might have expected to be wiped out when David came to the throne. In addition to that, Mephibosheth was a helpless cripple, having been dropped by his nurse when he was young. The fact that he lived in someone else's home in Lo-debar, meaning "no pasture" suggests that he was impoverished. Lo-debar was on the east side of the Jordan and therefore "afar off" from Jerusalem, God's dwelling. There was no merit in Mephibosheth as far as David's favor was concerned.

In spite of all that, David inquired concerning him, sent messengers after him, brought him to the royal palace, assured him that there was nothing to fear, enriched him with all Saul's land, provided him with a retinue of servants to wait on him, and honored him with a permanent place at the king's table as one of the king's sons.

Why did David show such mercy, grace, and compassion to one who was so unworthy? The answer is "for Jonathan's sake." David had made a covenant with Jonathan, the father of Mephibosheth, that he would never cease to show kindness to Jonathan's family. It was an unconditional covenant of grace (1 Sam. 20:14-17).

Mephibosheth realized this, for when he was first ushered into the king's presence, he prostrated himself and said that "a dead dog" like he did not deserve such kindness.

It should not be difficult for us to find ourselves in this picture. We were born of a rebel, sinful race under the condemnation of death. We were morally deformed and paralyzed by sin. We, too, dwelt in a land of "no pasture," spiritually starved. Not only were we doomed, helpless, and impoverished, we were "afar off" from God, without Christ and without hope. There was nothing in us to draw forth God's love and kindness.

Yet God sought us, found us, delivered us from the fear of death, blessed us with all spiritual blessings in the heavenlies, brought us to His banqueting table, and raised the banner of His love over us.

Why did He do it? It was for Jesus' sake. And it was because of His covenant of grace under which He chose us in Christ before the foundation of the world.

The fitting response for us is to prostrate ourselves in His presence and say, "What is Thy servant, that Thou shouldest look upon such a dead dog as I am?"

December 31

*Behold, I stand at the door and knock. If anyone hears My voice
and opens the door, I will come in to him and dine with him, and he with Me.*
REVELATION 3:20

H ere we are at the close of another year, and still the patient Savior stands at man's door, seeking admission. He has been kept outside a long time. Anyone else would have given up long ago and gone home. But not the Savior. He is longsuffering, not willing that any should perish. He waits with the hope that one day the door will be flung open and He will be welcomed inside.

It is amazing that anyone would fail to answer the knock of the Lord Jesus. If it were a neighbor, the door would be opened promptly. If it were a salesman, someone would at least give him the courtesy of opening the door and saying, "We don't need any!" Certainly if it were the President or the Governor, the family would compete for the privilege of welcoming him. Strange, then, that when the Creator, Sustainer, and Redeemer stands at the door, He is given the cold, silent treatment.

Man's refusal is all the more irrational when we realize that the Lord Jesus does not come to rob but rather to give. He comes to give life more abundant.

A Christian radio preacher once got a late night call from a listener who wanted to stop by for a brief visit. The preacher tried every excuse to dissuade him from coming, but finally relented. As it turned out, the visitor came with a large gift of money to help with the radio expenses. After he left, the preacher said, "I'm so glad I let him in."

Joe Blinco used to describe a scene where an animated conversation was going on in the living room of a home. Suddenly there was a knock at the front door. One of the family said, "There's someone at the door."

Another jumped up, went to the door and opened it. Then someone in the living room asked, "Who is it?" Back from the door came the answer. Finally the head of the house shouted, "Tell him to come in."

That is the gospel in brief. Listen! There's Someone at the door. Who is it? It's none other than the Lord of life and glory, the One who died as a Substitute for us and rose again the third day—the One who is now enthroned in glory and coming soon to take His people home to be with Himself. Tell Him to come in!

Scripture Index

9:50	Feb. 9	12:21	Sept. 28
9:57	Sept. 2	13:8	Feb. 13
10:41, 42	July 2	14:5	July 24
12:15	Aug. 15	16:27	June 8
15:21	Mar. 20		
16:11	Apr. 12	1 CORINTHIANS	
17:17	Sept. 18	1:21	May 12
19:8	July 22	1:27	Feb. 27
19:26	Mar. 16	2:14	May 31
21:33	Dec. 19	3:17	Apr. 24
		3:21-23	Jan. 14
JOHN		4:7	Jan. 12
1 :10-12	Sept. 5	7:20	Nov. 8
1 :41-42	Sept. 30	10:10	May 15
3 :8	Mar. 27	10:31	Apr. 13
4 :21	Feb. 12	11:24	Dec. 27
5 :24	June 29	13:1	Nov. 22
5 :30	Nov. 29	13:12	Apr. 18
5 :44	Feb. 26	13:12	July 1
7 :17	Apr. 6	13:13	Dec. 7
7 :24	Jan. 3	14:16	Sept. 22
8 :32	Oct. 14	14:19	Aug. 21
11:9	Mar. 1	15:10	Nov. 28
12:24	May 21	15:57	Dec. 9
12:29	Aug. 10	15:58	Nov. 2
13:8	Apr. 26		
13:17	July 10	2 CORINTHIANS	
14:14	May 1	1:9	Aug. 25
14:15	Apr. 30	2:11	May 10
16:13b, 14	Oct. 23	2:14	Apr. 25
17:21	May 23	3:18	May 28
18:36	Jan. 18	4:2	July 14
20:17	Aug. 22	4:4	Feb. 1
21:22	Mar. 26	4:6	Feb. 2
		5:7	Jan. 7
ACTS		5:10	Apr. 2
4:29	Feb. 14	5:13	Aug. 11
5:15	July 23	6:9	Apr. 16
10:36	Feb. 29	6:17, 18	Sept. 7
11:23	Apr. 27		
18:26b	Dec. 10	GALATIANS	
24:16	June 3	1:23	Dec. 3
		2:20	Feb. 7
ROMANS		3:28	Oct. 27
1:18	June 14	4:16	Sept. 25
1:18	Oct. 16	5:13	Jan. 15
2:2	May 19	5:13	Apr. 15
5:5	Sept. 15	5:16	Feb10
5:6	Sept. 19	5:22	Mar. 2
5:15	Sept. 3	5:22	Mar. 3
7:18	Jan. 6	5:22	Mar. 4
8:18	July 7	5:22	Mar. 5
8:28	Mar. 30	5:22	Mar. 6
10:9	Apr. 22	5:22	Mar. 7
10:13	July 9	5:22	Mar. 8
11:4	Sept. 26	5:23	Mar. 9
11:6	Apr. 20	5:23	Mar. 10
12:11	Nov. 10	6:2, 5	Nov. 30
12:16	Sept. 20	6:8	May 3

SCRIPTURE INDEX

EPHESIANS
2:4 — June 13
4:7 — Mar. 24
4:12 — Feb. 22
4:30 — July 6
4:31 — Oct. 10
4:32 — Apr. 5
5:4 — May 14
5:16 — Jan. 27
5:19 — Dec. 2
5:25 — June 21
5:25 — Dec. 21
6:7 — Jan. 17

PHILIPPIANS
1:18 — May 17
2:3b — Jan. 2
2:4 — Mar. 18
2:10, 11 — Nov. 21
3:7, 8 — Aug. 31
3:12 — July 11
3:13 — Oct. 7
3:13b — Nov. 15
4:6 — Jan. 24
4:11 — May 29
4:11 — Dec. 20
4:13 — Jan. 13
4:18 — Apr. 7

COLOSSIANS
2:8 — Nov. 20
2:10 — Apr. 1
3:11 — Aug. 29
3:15 — Nov. 25

1 THESSALONIANS
4:14 — June 23
5:19-20 — July 5
5:21 — June 22

1 TIMOTHY
1:19 — Nov. 5
2:15 — June 27
3:6 — Mar. 31
3:16 — Dec. 25
4:16 — Aug. 30
5:4 — Jan. 9
6:8 — Aug. 16

2 TIMOTHY
2:4 — Mar. 29
2:19 — Nov. 3
4:8 — Sept. 21

TITUS
3:10, 11 — Aug. 12

HEBREWS
4:12a — Apr. 8

4:12 — Feb. 11
10:17 — Jan. 20
10:26, 27 — Dec. 22
11:1 — Apr. 29
11:3 — Apr. 4
12:1 — Jan. 10
12:7 — Aug. 20
12:16 — May 5
13:2 — July 3
13:13 — Apr. 23

JAMES
1:20 — Aug. 5
1:22 — Feb. 6
1:27 — June 18
2:14 — Nov. 9
4:2 — Nov. 13
4:11 — Oct. 8
4:14 — Oct. 1

1 PETER
2:11 — Oct. 26
5:7 — May 7
5:7 — July 21
5:10 — June 12

2 PETER
3:16b — Nov. 16

1 JOHN
1:9 — Jan. 19
2:15 — May 16
2:27 — Apr. 10
3:6 — Dec. 23
3:10 — Nov. 4
3:17 — Oct. 29
3:20 — June 5
4:1 — July 13
4:8 — Jan. 25
4:10 — June 11
4:11 — Jan. 26
4:17b — July 19
5:13 — Apr. 19

3 JOHN
4 — Oct. 30

REVELATION
2:9 — Nov. 19
3:20 — Dec. 31
4:8 — June 9
8:3 — Feb. 3
13:16, 17 — Sept. 17
19:6 — June 7
20:15 — Oct. 24
21:8 — Sept. 27
22:20 — Nov. 27